Gender in Twentie
Eastern Europe an

C000156532

Gender and History

Series editors: Amanda Capern and Louella McCarthy

Gender in Twentieth-Century Eastern Europe and the USSR

Edited by

CATHERINE BAKER

First published 2017 by
PALGRAVE

Palgrave in the UK is an imprint of Macmillan Publishers Limited,
registered in England, company number 785998, of 4 Crinan Street,
London, N1 9XW.

Palgrave Macmillan in the US is a division of St Martin's Press LLC,
175 Fifth Avenue, New York, NY 10010.

Palgrave is the global imprint of the above companies and is represented
throughout the world.

Palgrave® and Macmillan® are registered trademarks in the United States,
the United Kingdom, Europe and other countries.

ISBN 978–1–137–52803–2 hardback
ISBN 978–1–137–52802–5 paperback

A catalogue record for this book is available from the British Library.

A catalog record for this book is available from the Library of Congress.

Contents

Notes on Contributors

Maria Adamson is Lecturer in Organisation Studies and Human Resource Management at Middlesex University Business School. Her research interests centre on understanding gender inequality in professional work, gendered workplace identities and the application of feminist theories within the field of organization studies. Her current project explores constructions of femininity in popular business celebrity autobiographies and business self-help. She is a Principal Investigator on the ESRC-funded seminar series Gendered Inclusion in Contemporary Organisations. Her research has been published in journals such as *Sociology; Gender, Work and Organization; Equality; Diversity and Inclusion*, and *Human Relations*.

Catherine Baker is Lecturer in 20th-Century History at the University of Hull. She is the author of *Sounds of the Borderland: Popular Music, War and Nationalism in Croatia since 1991* (Ashgate, 2010), *Interpreting the Peace: Peace Operations, Conflict and Language in Bosnia-Herzegovina* (Palgrave Macmillan, 2013, with Michael Kelly) and *The Yugoslav Wars of the 1990s* (Palgrave Macmillan, 2015). Her articles have been published in *Slavic Review*, *International Feminist Journal of Politics*, *History Workshop Journal* and elsewhere. She is developing a new research project on transnational imaginaries of conflict in popular culture since the end of the Cold War.

Kerstin Bischl is a PhD student and research fellow in the Department of History at Humboldt University Berlin. She is currently finishing her thesis on 'Gender Relationships and Dynamics of Violence in the Great Patriotic War', which is financed by the Hamburg Institute for Social Research. She has studied history, political science and philosophy in Berlin and Voronezh, Russia. Her thesis is based on sources from Russian, German and Polish archives, as well as the Hoover Institution Archive. She has published several articles on its subject matter in German, English and Russian.

Maria Bucur is the John V. Hill Chair in East European History at Indiana University, Bloomington. Her publications include *Heroes and Victims: Remembering War in Twentieth-Century Romania* (Indiana University Press, 2009); *Gender and War in Twentieth Century Eastern Europe* (Indiana University Press, 2006); *Eugenics and Modernization in Interwar Romania* (University of Pittsburgh Press, 2002); *Patriarhat şi emancipare în istoria gîndirii politice româneşti* (Polirom, 2002); and *Staging the Past: the Politics of Commemoration in Habsburg Central Europe, 1848 to the Present* (Purdue University Press, 2001). She is currently completing a book entitled *The Century of Women: How Women Changed the World in the Twentieth Century*.

Olga Dimitrijević, born in 1984, is (still) a Yugoslavian playwright, theatre critic and dramaturge. She co-edited the book *Među nama: neispričane priče gej i lezbejskih života* (*Between Us: Untold Stories of Gay and Lesbian Lives*) (Heartefact, 2014), a study of the history of homosexuality in Serbia. She has also directed a theatre performance based on Alexandra Kollontai's novel *Red Love*. She is an occasional lecturer at the alternative academic programme in Women's Studies at the Faculty of Political Science in Belgrade. She is a winner of the Sterijino Pozorje prize for the plays *Radnici umiru pjevajući* (*Workers Die Singing*) and *Kako je dobro videti te opet* (*It's So Good to See You Again*) and of the Borislav Mihailovič Mihiz award for playwriting.

Erica L. Fraser is an adjunct professor in the Institute of European, Russian and Eurasian Studies at Carleton University in Ottawa, Canada. Her research focuses on Soviet masculinities during the early Cold War period, and she is particularly interested in gender analysis for understudied areas such as political, diplomatic and military history. She is currently completing a book on the ways in which Soviet authorities tried to rebuild military service as a masculine endeavour after 1945, in the wake of unprecedented service by Soviet women in World War II.

Jeremy Johnson is a doctoral candidate in Anthropology and History at the University of Michigan in Ann Arbor. His research focuses on the intersection of language, nation-building and gender in the USSR with a particular focus on the South Caucasus in the interwar period. He is the recipient of fellowships from the Mellon Foundation, American Councils and the Dolores Zohrab Liebmann Fund and has conducted research in Armenia, Georgia and Russia. His dissertation is entitled 'Literacy Unveiled: Citizenship, Nationality, Gender and the Campaigns to Eradicate Illiteracy in the Soviet South Caucasus (Armenia, Georgia and Azerbaijan) 1922–1936'.

Katherine R. Jolluck is Senior Lecturer in the Department of History at Stanford University. She is also a Faculty Fellow both at the Handa Center for Human Rights and International Justice and the Haas Center for Public Service. A specialist on the history of 20th-century eastern Europe and Russia, she focuses on the topics of women and war, women in communist societies, nationalism and human trafficking. Her books include *Exile and Identity: Polish Women in the Soviet Union during WWII* (University of Pittsburgh Press, 2002), and (with Jehanne M. Gheith) *Gulag Voices: Oral Histories of Soviet Incarceration and Exile* (Palgrave Macmillan, 2011).

Jenny Kaminer is Associate Professor of Russian at the University of California-Davis. She is the author of *Women with a Thirst for Destruction: The Bad Mother in Russian Culture* (Northwestern University Press, 2014), which received the Heldt Prize for Best Book in Slavic/East European/Eurasian Gender Studies in 2014. Her current research interests include cultural representations of adolescence and post-Soviet theatre and literature.

Erika Kispeter is a Research Fellow at the Institute for Employment Research at the University of Warwick. She has a background in Gender Studies and her main research interest is in how women's working lives are shaped by work organizations, the family and the welfare state, especially work–family policies. She has published on the labour market effects of extended parental leave on women's careers in Hungary and on the impact of local welfare systems on women's inclusion in the workforce in post-state socialist cities.

Jo Laycock is Senior Lecturer in History at Sheffield Hallam University. She is the author of *Imagining Armenia: Orientalism, Ambiguity and Intervention* (Manchester University Press, 2009) and a number of articles addressing homeland–diaspora relations and repatriation to the Soviet Republic of Armenia in the aftermath of World War II. Her current research concerns the aftermaths of crisis and conflict in Armenia and the South Caucasus region, and she is working on a second book project examining Soviet and international responses to population displacement in the region following World War I and the Armenian Genocide from a transnational perspective.

Anna Muller holds a PhD from Indiana University. She works as an assistant professor at University of Michigan, Dearborn and previously worked at the Centre for European Studies, University of Florida in Gainesville. Her most recent publication is 'Polish Solidarity's Heroine: Anna Walentynowicz: an Exercise in Memory Studies' (*Rocznik Antropologii Historii*, 2015) and her book *If the Walls Could Talk: Women Political Prisoners in Stalinist Poland, 1945–1956* is under contract with Oxford University Press. She has also curated exhibitions in Poland and the USA on concentration camps and the Holocaust, contemporary femininity and masculinity in eastern Europe, and the diverse population of a small town in Michigan.

Cynthia Paces is Professor of History and Department Chair at The College of New Jersey, where she teaches courses on Modern Europe, Holocaust and Genocide Studies, and Women's History. She earned her PhD in History from Columbia University in 1998. Her publications include *Prague Panoramas: National Memory and Sacred Space in the Twentieth Century*, *1989: the End of the Twentieth Century*, and numerous articles and book chapters on nationalism, religion, gender and public space. Currently she is researching the relationship between motherhood and nationalism in Bohemia and central Europe.

Ivan Simić is a PhD candidate at University College London where he is completing a dissertation about Soviet influence on Yugoslav gender policies. He examines how and which Soviet models were transferred, adapted and applied to Yugoslav practices. By looking at the main agents and channels of cultural transfer, he aims to place Yugoslav cultural history into global perspective and shed a new light on transnational circulation of Stalinist gender policies. He has published one article on 'The Soviet Model for Yugoslav Post-War Legal Transformation: Divorce Panic and Specialist Debate' and is preparing another on the impacts of collectivization on Yugoslav gender relations.

Judit Takács is a Research Chair at the Institute of Sociology, Centre for Social Sciences, Hungarian Academy of Sciences, leading research on the social history of homosexuality, social exclusion/inclusion of LGBTQ+ people, HIV/AIDS prevention, family practices, work–life balance and childlessness. She graduated in History, Hungarian Language and Literature and Cultural Anthropology (ELTE, Budapest), completed an MA in Social Sciences at the University of Amsterdam and holds a PhD in Sociology (Corvinus University of Budapest). Her most recent publications include *Homophobia and Genderphobia in the European Union* (Swedish Institute for European Policy Studies, 2015) and 'Disciplining Gender and (Homo)Sexuality in State Socialist Hungary in the 1970s' (*European Review of History*, 2015). A list of her publications can be found at www.policy.hu/takacs/publications.php.

Adriana Zaharijević is an associate researcher at the Institute for Philosophy and Social Theory, University of Belgrade. She is the author of two books (*Who is an Individual?: A Genealogical Inquiry into the Idea of the Citizen* (2014) and *Becoming a Woman* (2010), both published in Serbian) and more than 40 articles and book chapters. She has also edited several books, the most important being *Somebody Said Feminism?: How Feminism Affected Women in the 21st Century* (4 eds, in Serbian). She is part of the vibrant post-Yugoslav feminist activist scene.

Introduction: Gender in Twentieth-Century Eastern Europe and the USSR

Catherine Baker

In 2013 a blog called *Cosmarxpolitan*, reimagining *Cosmopolitan* magazine covers with photographs and headlines evoking Communist ideology, briefly amused social media users.[1] Its imaginary contents, from '293 fun, sexy ways to urge capitalism towards a classless utopia' to 'Stalin strips down: we bet you've never seen him like *THIS!*' (with the young Stalin's head superimposed on a topless male model's body),[2] invited the reader to laugh at a contradiction: why would tropes of 20th-century state socialist political discourse be presented in the style of as capitalist a medium as the women's lifestyle magazine? Yet gender historians of eastern Europe and the USSR had explored this apparent oxymoron for some time, demonstrating – for the USSR, Hungary, Yugoslavia and elsewhere – that Communist women's magazines were integral to state socialist projects of reordering gender relations, in what amounted to creating, in the Soviet example, a New Soviet Woman and a New Soviet Man.[3] These very magazines would indeed become rich sources for historians studying how official discourses and images of gender changed over time, how Communist Party women's sections and activists negotiated Party structures, and even – through the prism of readers' letters – some public responses to changing gender policies.[4] With allowances for vernacular, a few stories invented by *Cosmarxpolitan*'s anonymous authors ('15 wedding traditions that are sooooo reactionary!'; '"My boyfriend was a counter-revolutionary": could it happen to you?') could almost have appeared in a *Rabotnitsa* (*Woman Worker*, the main Soviet women's magazine), a *Nők lapja* (*Women's Journal*, the Hungarian weekly founded in 1949) or a *Tina* (the 1971–6 Yugoslav franchise of the British teenage magazine).

Yet what would the New Socialist Woman and the New Socialist Man actually be, and how was the power to intervene in the structure of gender relations contested under state socialism? How successful were these interventions even in their own terms, and how far did they alter structures of inequality between genders that had existed before Communist parties came to power? These questions preoccupy gender historians of 20th-century eastern Europe and the USSR.[5] Yet state socialism alone did not define the region's century. This was also a century when national self-determination became enshrined as the organizing ideological principle for the region's territory, and when, after

1

socialism collapsed, gender relations were yet again restructured as societies adapted to free-market ideologies.[6] Themes running through the whole century – such as the politics of women's movements, gendered divisions of labour, intersections of gender and ethno-national belonging, or the micropolitics of intimacy and sexuality – have all demanded historians' attention; but so has the problem of what, if anything, conceptually holds together the region that historians construct.

Themes in Gender Histories of Eastern Europe and the Former USSR

The study of women's movements has been foundational for gender historians of eastern Europe, as elsewhere.[7] Research has shown how gender politics have been deeply embedded in contemporaneous notions of citizenship, democracy, national belonging and modernity.[8]

Under state socialism, however, the so-called 'woman question' was institutionalized in ways that – potentially – make the region distinct: state socialism professed commitments to gender equality on one hand but fettered all its subjects' autonomy on the other.[9] Historians have debated (first for the USSR, then also for eastern Europe) whether Communist women activists or women's sections could, or should, be said to represent forms of 'Communist feminism'; whether state socialist policies in areas like welfare had any positive effects on gender equality; or whether women operating within state socialist structures could exert any political and social agency.[10] This is far from just an eastern European question – indeed, it opened up in the 2000s after Wang Zheng's study of 'state feminism' in Communist China[11] – but it is particularly important in the region's gender historiography.

An inaugural forum in *Aspasia: the International Yearbook of Central, Eastern and Southeastern Women's and Gender History* presented opposing views on this question. Mihaela Miroiu argued that feminism should be about 'women's personal autonomy' and, since Communism had repressed this, historians should consider it 'state patriarchy' not 'state feminism'.[12] Krassimira Daskalova, meanwhile, warned against pitting state socialism against idealized concepts of women's autonomy in democratic states, especially given how unequal gender relations had been before state socialism. Daskalova even suggested – provocative as this would continue to be – that comparing women's economic, social and cultural situations in ex-state socialist countries with Western societies might (despite Cold War stereotypes) favour the former.[13] She added that only a wide comparative study of women's 'real life […] in the former socialist states', using sources including archives, periodicals and oral history, would resolve the question,[14] which remains a live one for gender historians.

Other periods, too, bring research agendas on women's activism and agency. As state socialism collapsed, feminists inside and outside eastern Europe almost immediately began documenting how movements would organize in the new political–economic systems and what they would be fighting against: nationalist 'retraditionalization' or 'repatriarchalization' combined with the economic damage of post-socialist privatization.[15] The work of Barbara Einhorn and the contributors to Jasmina Lukić, Joanna Regulska and Darja Zaviršek's volume *Women and Citizenship in Central and Eastern Europe* made 'citizenship' an important analytic for this period, inviting comparisons with pre-state socialist regimes that historians such as Melissa Feinberg would take up.[16] A new organizational form, the women's non-governmental organization (NGO), had to be situated within post-Cold War global inequalities in movement of ideas, policies and capital.[17] Meanwhile, historians of Fascist occupation and collaboration, as well as those studying state socialism, have tried to ask often uncomfortable questions about gender and agency under authoritarian rule. This aim has inspired studies of gender and resistance while permitting historians to understand the gender relations of persecution, victimhood and even perpetration of mass violence and genocide.[18] As Nancy Wingfield and Maria Bucur reminded historians (with implications for thinking about state socialism as well as their own volume's topic, war), 'female agency does not necessarily represent a positive force'.[19]

Another key theme for gender historians is how access to and remuneration for labour have been structured by perceived differences between men and women. The workplace, like any other social institution, exemplifies what Raewyn Connell called a 'gender regime' – the ideologies and practices that construct social understandings of gender – and evidence about work provides rich material for making 'gender' an 'analytic category' in history as Joan Scott urged historians to do.[20] Following Scott, understanding power through the category of gender requires attention to 'symbolic representations', 'normative statements' about the meanings of gender, the workings of 'social institutions and organizations' and the construction of subjective identities.[21] All can be traced through studies of socialist industrialization; the gendered division of labour outside and inside the home; women's so-called 'double burden' (of paid work and unpaid domestic work) under state socialism, even expanded to a 'triple' or 'quadruple' burden by some scholars; and late-20th-century free-market reforms.

Gender histories of work strikingly illustrate the point that gender is a *relational* concept – one that contains ideas about what it means to be a woman and ideas about what it means to be a man, and sets them against each other in a binary hierarchy.[22] Scholars can ask how and why jobs were 'regendered' at different times, how discourses justifying new divisions of labour were disseminated and how far images matched experience.[23] The smiling female tractor driver of Stalinist agricultural propaganda, for instance, was neither as common as official representations suggested nor, often, quite so happy to be assigned the work.[24] Historians have also shown that state socialism aimed to reconfigure masculinities as well as femininities: consider what place certain state socialist gender orders at certain times would have given the masculinities of, for instance, the revolutionary, the secret policeman, the nuclear scientist or the target-busting shock worker.[25] (Or consider, indeed, the masculinities of US defence intellectuals on the other side of the Cold War.[26]) Finally, studying labour emphasizes gender's interrelationship with another axis of inequality, class. Ethnographies of post-socialism illustrate this vividly, showing that people's life courses in post-socialist class and gender orders depended on what social and cultural resources they had been able to acquire under state socialism.[27]

Studying gender and the nation, meanwhile, reveals that gender and nationalism are both ways of using power to categorize people. If narratives of national and ethnic identity determine *who* belongs to the nation, gender regimes intersect with these to determine *how* a person categorized as male or female is supposed to belong. This insight was confirmed again and again in the post-socialist 1990s through studies of the stigmatization of ethnic 'Others' (in settings including, but not limited to, the Yugoslav wars) and of nationalist/ religious opposition to reproductive rights;[28] an important theoretical basis for some of these studies was Nira Yuval-Davis' *Gender and Nation*. For a generation of international feminists, wartime sexualized violence in Croatia, Bosnia-Herzegovina and later Kosovo during the Yugoslav wars would come to stand as the extreme example of nationalism and patriarchy in action.[29] Less often discussed, but just as important for understanding gender, violence and power during the Yugoslav wars, were the matters of sexualized violence against men and of wartime/post-war increases in domestic violence.[30]

Yet gender and nationalism were not just 1990s questions; the whole century testified to the gendering of ethnicity and nationhood, especially in wartime. Indeed, which wartime experiences were publicly remembered, and how, depended heavily on how well they matched gendered 'scripts' of national memory.[31] Wingfield and Bucur's *Gender and War in Twentieth-Century Eastern Europe* argued against simple binaries of masculine fighting fronts and feminine home fronts during the world wars and suggested that gender historians would not be able to make full conclusions about the transformations those wars caused without evidence from eastern Europe.[32] Yet nationalism also operates outside war. Historians of any 20th-century place and moment can ask how nationalist movements and governments combined constructions of gender and ethnicity in their discourses of belonging, their practices of public mobilization, their differential treatment of ethno-national majorities and minorities (especially Jews, Roma and Sinti), and their political struggles over domains such as language and education.[33]

Likewise, gender historians can expose any place or period's articulations between state power and intimate, everyday experience by investigating politics of sexuality and reproduction. Governments before, during and after state socialism could all equate national strength with population growth and pursue pro-natalist policies such as state-provided childcare, paid benefits, contraception and access to abortion; they might simultaneously seek to restrain birth rates of ethnic and religious minorities, especially Roma.[34] State socialism was not necessarily incompatible with nationalist discourses of demographic panic (as in the USSR under Stalin or many eastern European states in the 1960s).[35] Abortion, as Susan Gal and Gail Kligman's landmark volume *Reproducing Gender* showed, would become the most contested topic in 1990s gender politics: many countries' religious and ethno-nationalist interest groups sought to use their new access to political power to restrict abortion, while post-socialist Romanian gender politics were still marked by the legacies of Nicolae Ceauşescu's extreme pro-natalism.[36] Throughout the century, changing gender regimes shaped all areas of intimate and domestic life. State interventions in housing, leisure, consumer production and food supply all depended on gendered understandings of family and household.[37] There is usually more research on ideologies of motherhood than fatherhood,[38] though in Soviet gender history this is changing as interest in Soviet masculinities expands.[39] Other studies look relationally at ideologies of marriage,[40] or sex.[41] Meanwhile, scholars of sexual and gender variance – where major topics include homosexuality in 20th-century Russia, and the region-wide politics of 'LGBT' activism under post-socialism – both seek to historicize how specific sexual and gender-non-conforming identities emerged and to use historical evidence to challenge public silences about them in the present.[42]

Historians of gender confront historiographical tensions between 'discourse' and 'experience', and between 'women's history' and 'gender history'. Another, for this region, is between 'agency' and 'disempowerment', especially under state socialism. Studies of everyday life under state socialism and of public views about party-states' gendered policies and practices have positioned themselves as depicting agency with more nuance than earlier studies of Communist state power: the overall argument of Jill Massino and Shana Penn's volume on state socialist gender politics and everyday life, for instance, was that 'agency, while limited, did exist for women and men under state socialism'.[43] Małgorzata Fidelis's study of gender and industrialization in Poland similarly sought 'to restore agency to women, who have often been depicted in popular and scholarly literature as passive objects of party-state policies'.[44] Searches for where and how agency might have been located in these structures, as well as awareness that in the early 21st century time to conduct first-hand research with former Communists was running short, helped official state socialist women's organizations emerge as a research topic.

Scholars tackling these subjects agree there are risks in oversimplifying the past but differ deeply over how, where and why oversimplification has been taking place. Again, an argument about the history of women's movements can exemplify what is at stake, this time a 2014–15 debate between Nanette Funk and Kristen Ghodsee in *European Journal of Women's Studies*. This began when Funk called recent historians of women's movements too keen to find agency in systems which had 'in fact [been] built on denying many women chances to act'.[45] Ghodsee responded that women who had believed in Marxist–Leninist ideals or working for material improvements for women would still have been exercising proactive agency although they had not been struggling for liberal political ideals.[46] Elsewhere, Ghodsee drew on work by Saba Mahmood (about women's religious activism in Egypt) to argue that viewing 'creating individual, autonomous political subjects' as feminism's only possible aim 'reifies a particularly Anglo-American conception of the feminist project'.[47]

The women's movements and agency debate turns on histories and legacies of state socialism, but also on how one might conceive of social action within and against structures of power, giving it implications beyond the years of 1917–91 or 1945–91. These questions are, again, not unique to the region; compare Lynn Abrams' search for women's 'potential for power' inside the patriarchal family structures of 19th-century Germany.[48] What distinguishes eastern Europe and the ex-USSR as a site of gender history might – perhaps – be the nationalism/state socialism interrelationship combined with the political charge of studying historical gender relations in a present when post-socialist gender relations were being reconfigured. Pathways for establishing women's and gender studies as fields of knowledge in eastern Europe and the ex-USSR have been diverse yet, almost always, precarious.[49] Maria Bucur, in 2008, compared eastern European gender history to 'an archipelago of individual efforts', 'erupting periodically' with only tenuous connections to 'institutional seats of power', and the links between its islands often being forged outside the region.[50] Working together, scholars have nevertheless been able to constitute a gender history of the region – most commonly through edited volumes (the same format as this book), given the diversity of linguistic, cultural and historical knowledge necessary to draw conclusions that recognize the complexity of the entire space.

'Region' in Eastern European and Soviet Gender History

All edited volumes on gender in eastern Europe and/or the ex-USSR need to define their geographical limits, identify a historical period with a beginning and end, and establish a purpose for the whole collection. They may, for instance, capture pan-regional moments of rupture, such as Funk and Mueller's *Gender Politics and Post-Communism*, recording the state of gender politics and women's activism in the first few years after 1989.[51] They may test a certain interpretive lens, such as Penn and Massino's *Gender Politics and Everyday Life in State Socialist Eastern and Central Europe*, which emphasized cultural/social history approaches, the history of everyday life and individuals' (limited) agency in negotiating state socialist structures.[52] They may seek to reshape another field using evidence from gender history, such as Wingfield and Bucur's *Gender and War in Twentieth-Century Eastern Europe*, which sought to intervene in the wider social history of war in Europe. Other volumes do the same for subsidiary regions such as Russia or south-east Europe,[53] while the important recent collection edited by Joanna Regulska and Bonnie Smith, *Women and Gender in Postwar Europe*, drew both on eastern European and western European microhistories in tracing a gender history of the Cold War that would encompass the whole continent, not one half.[54]

The problem of how far eastern European/Soviet gender relations can be understood through analytical frameworks developed elsewhere, and why feminist insights from the region have not been widely taken up outside, has troubled gender scholars since research on gender in this area began. Eastern European theorists consistently stress the risks of uncritically importing Western analytical moves – from Hana Havelková's warning that early-1990s Western feminists were missing 'the specific historical experience of women in Eastern Europe' when talking about the region,[55] to Robert Kulpa and Joanna Mizielińska's refutation of the idea that post-socialist eastern Europe needed to learn about LGBT equality from the West.[56] Postcolonial critiques of 'area studies' thus also resonate in and for this region,[57] and indeed some eastern European feminists who heard their criticisms of Western feminism's universalizing and patronizing currents echoed by feminists of colour around the world use postcolonial and decolonial thought to theorize their own positions globally.[58]

Contextualizing eastern Europe as a region also requires care not to assume one undifferentiated category of 'women' (or 'men', or 'gender').[59] Despite the transnational commonalities that mean it can be thought about as a 'region' in the first place, every country had a specific history as an independent state and as part(s) of other states; moreover, one country over time could go through multiple shifts in gender regimes even as the political system stayed broadly the same. Lynne Haney, for instance, suggested that changing welfare policy in socialist Hungary revealed very different concepts of gender and need between 1948 to 1968, 1968 to 1985 and 1985 to 1996 – and her last period (before another, more neoliberal welfare reform) bridged late socialism and early post-socialism.[60] Haney, and many others, argued against the homogenizing idea of 'transitology' (common in mainstream sociology and political science during the 1990s) that considered that all state socialist countries had had the same experiences and would follow the same path into the free market and liberal democracy. (Indeed, the dislocations 'transitology' helped cause are themselves now topics for post-Cold War gender history.) The region, however one conceived of it, also needed to be connected with broader transnational and global processes, and with other regions to which a place of study might concurrently belong (the wider post-Ottoman space, for instance, was just as much a 'region' as 'eastern Europe'). Comparative projects rarely straddled the region's 'inside' and 'outside', with some exceptions such as Regulska and Smith's volume, Silke Roth's collection on European Union gender policies after the 2004 EU enlargement,[61] or Éva Fodor's study of women's employment in 1945–95 Hungary and Austria.[62] Fodor's research design also illustrated how boundaries of region shifted: Austria and Hungary, part of the 'West' and 'East' respectively after 1945, would have been on the *same* side of most analytical categorizations for earlier periods, representing the two political power centres of the late Habsburg Empire.

The spatial category of 'eastern Europe and the (former) USSR' nevertheless presents enough commonalities (albeit different ones at different times, and rarely universal) to function as the kind of 'temporary fixity' Ann Stoler describes in her studies of colonial power and sexuality.[63] Stoler calls on historians to view designations deriving from categories such as race, class, gender or in this volume's case region as *contingent* ideas that can represent 'working concepts' as long as one recognizes their limitations. These are concepts 'that we *work with* to track variation in their use and usefulness' (and many scholars of this region reflect on this); 'concepts that *do work* to destabilize received historical narratives' (though in our case the very narrative of eastern Europe as a coherent region is one that needs destabilizing); and 'concepts that are "working" in the sense that they are [...] subject to review and revision rather than being fully formed'.[64] As long as one is transparent about how concepts of 'region' order knowledge, they can still serve as working bases for comparison. This volume has approached its task accordingly.

Gender in Eastern Europe and the (Former) USSR Across the Century

This volume, simply by being conceived, does perpetuate the intellectual construction of 'eastern Europe and the (former) USSR' as a meaningful space; moreover, by combining the ex-USSR and eastern Europe, it centres state socialism as the defining feature of its 'region-ness'. Yet it also aims to show how politics and negotiations of gender have transcended the region and formed part of currents that also matter to gender historians elsewhere. Weighing up changes, continuities and even reversals in the region's gender regimes across the 20th century and into the early 21st, it seeks to resolve the tension that gender historians and specialists in Women's and Gender Studies whose expertise centres on other regions face in integrating these areas into understandings of global gender history in the 20th century: the account would not be complete unless it did incorporate this area, but neither can it view the region (in the state socialist period or at any other time) as monolithic, or as detached from the gender histories of the rest of the globe. Nor, this volume demonstrates, should such an account view the region as a space where the state of gender relations moved inexorably from patriarchal oppression towards equality over the course of the 20th century, or even just since the end of state socialism.

A decade after the collapse of state socialism in eastern Europe, the sociologist Peggy Watson was among many gender scholars who observed that even then, 'whatever the gains, democratization ha[d] not been experienced as an unequivocal improvement' on what had gone before.[65] Neither was the impact the same for all women, or all men. Instead, as Kirsten Ghodsee and other ethnographers of post-socialism showed, individuals' prospects after the Cold War were stratified by intersections of gender/class/ethnicity and what these had given people access to under state socialism.[66] In this vein, Susan Gal and Gail Kligman's book *The Politics of Gender after Socialism* – still a foundational text for any study of gender in post-Cold War Europe – both exemplified the pushback against teleologies of 'transition' and insisted that gender was an essential 'analytic category' in revealing why these were so flawed.[67] They observed, moreover, that '[s]ome of the most interesting questions about social process are lost' in studying gender if scholars neglect 'continuities between pre- and post-1989' or those between 'capitalist and socialist societies'.[68]

This volume affirms and deepens Gal and Kligman's observation through fourteen specially commissioned chapters of new historical research, in settings ranging from central Europe before World War I to struggles over LGBT rights that continued to unfold even as the volume was being written. In the process, it offers further dimensions: the perspective of an extra fifteen years for assessing the legacies of state socialism and its collapse; an even finer-grained attention to the intimate politics of gender regimes, drawing on new perspectives on the history of the everyday and on the history of sexuality and gender non-conformity; and recognition of the continued efforts of east European gender scholars in the 2000s and 2010s to push the problem of defining this region as a category of analysis far beyond simplistic differentiations of one 'West' and one 'East'.

The first section of the volume, 'Between the *Fin de Siècle* and the Interwar Period', shows that parallels between pre-socialism and post-socialism, as well as just pre- and post-1989, can offer important insights into 20th-century gender history. Some kinds of parallel are well established: the topic of maternity, explored in Cynthia Paces' study of constructions of health and nation in the visual culture of Czech motherhood before 1918, has been central to women's history from the beginning. Others can only emerge as new fields of scholarship develop: Olga Dimitrijević's research as she seeks to develop lesbian history in Serbia has also revealed networks of Anglo-Yugoslav romance and friendship during and after World War I that permit historians to revisit the topic of 'sapphic modernities'. Both the nexus between reproductive politics and nationalism and the question of historicizing the emergence of sexual identities are simultaneously key topics after 1989–91. At the very same time Czech nationalists were founding their nation and British and Yugoslav sapphists were participating in a transnational avant-garde, state socialism was already being established in part of this volume's region, what would become known as the (former) USSR. Joanne Laycock and Jeremy Johnson's chapter on creating 'New Soviet Women' in 1920s Armenia draws direct comparisons between the interwar period and the present as it traces gendered ideas of modernity and tradition, showing that Soviet gender policies were not uniform across the federation but depended on how gender and ethnicity intersected in Communists' eyes.

State socialism provides the focus for the next two sections of the volume. The gender politics of Stalinism in the USSR and the effects of genocide, occupation and total war in eastern Europe, discussed in the section on 'Gender Regimes of Revolution and War', were preconditions for how post-war Communist parties in eastern Europe tried to reshape their own countries' gender order. Ideologies of maternity and the family, first introduced in this volume in the context of pre-World War I nationalism, recur in Jenny Kaminer's chapter on changing representations of Soviet motherhood between the Russian Revolution and the 1980s, which questions how far Soviet Communists either imagined or achieved a revolutionary transformation of maternity and domestic work. The intersection of ethnicity and gender, already observed in 1920s Armenia, is seen in Katherine Jolluck's chapter on Poland under Nazi and Soviet occupation to be a necessary analytic for understanding how each occupying force exerted power over conquered civilians and sought to destroy or subjugate its racial, ethnic and class enemies – and also for understanding how Poles, Jews and other victims reacted to the unparalleled violence of World War II and the Holocaust. Kerstin Bischl's chapter on female soldiers in the wartime Red Army both discusses how women negotiated patriarchal structures during their service and shows how women narrated their experiences in different ways according to shifts in later Soviet and post-Soviet gender politics. The last chapter, by Erica Fraser, uses a similar time frame to the section's first chapter on motherhood and represents a study of so-called 'revolutionary masculinities' in Bolshevik and Soviet ideology. By drawing on scholarship in French Revolutionary and Latin American gender history, Fraser indicates one way in which this region's gender history and the gender history of other regions can enrich each other.

At war's end, eastern European populations and the Communist parties that took power across the region in 1945–8 contended with the legacies of revolution, occupation, violence and genocide seen in the previous section. These were the contexts in which the new state socialist authorities in eastern Europe made their gender policies, the subject of the volume's third section ('Gender Politics and State Socialist Power'). These were informed by, and had parallels with, the Soviet gender regimes seen earlier in the volume. Yet they were neither identical impositions of Soviet policy on to distinct local realities (as Ivan Simić demonstrates in his chapter on the youth work actions of newly Communist Yugoslavia) nor always a complete rupture from the practices of the regimes they had replaced (as Judit Takács found when, during the research her chapter is based on, she discovered state socialist police in Hungary had continued previous regimes' 'listing' of gay men for blackmail and manipulation). The multiple forms of state socialism combined a rhetoric of gender equality that supposedly set them above the West with a dependence on scarcity and an intrusion into – as Maria Bucur illustrates in a chapter contextualizing her own experiences in state socialist Romania and as a historian researching post-socialist gender relations – the most intimate spheres of everyday life that nevertheless created a recognizably distinct set of gender regimes within 20th-century gender history. This set was not a monolith: gender policies could vary widely within the same country over time, let alone between countries, and (as Kaminer, Bischl, Simić and Takács all help to suggest) it retained much of the patriarchal gender order that preceded it. It nevertheless helps explain what holds eastern Europe together as a region of analysis for gender historians.

The final section, 'Gender During and After the Collapse of Communism', offers several ways to question whether the collapse of state socialism in 1989–91 was as complete a break with the past as it has sometimes been popularly portrayed. Anna Muller's study of the imaginative strategies through which imprisoned political prisoners redefined their masculinities, yet continued to essentialize femininity, in 1980s Poland suggests that the origins of 'retraditionalized' post-socialist gender orders need to be sought before as well as after the fall of state socialism itself. Adriana Zaharijević, assessing the priorities of feminist activism after the break-up of Yugoslavia and the wars that ensued, demonstrates that the post-Cold War period has been more complex than simply representing one unchanging post-socialist context within which activists worked. Maria Adamson and Erika Kispeter, taking women's access to professional work in Hungary and Russia as their example, demonstrate a twofold comparative analytic which balances continuity and change on either side of the temporal rupture of 1989–91 as well as across national borders. My overview of LGBT politics since the end of the Cold War, meanwhile, shows that new possibilities for social action and identity formation (not only concerning sexuality but also understandings of the embodiment of gender itself), themselves unfolding in transnational contexts that transcend the region, have encountered such varying outcomes and, most recently, such sustained backlash by some religious movements and governments that simple 'progress narratives' of movement towards equality are empirically as well as conceptually problematic. The 'retraditionalization' argument advanced by Verdery, Gal, Kligman and others already suggested, in the 1990s, that post-socialism reversed, rather than improved, gender equality. By the mid-2010s the temporalities of post-socialism seemed even more complex, with some gay, lesbian and queer people in the region first experiencing new freedoms then seeing them withdrawn; and with the memory or reinterpretation of gender relations under state socialism continuing to be a resource in contestations of gender politics more than two decades after the end of state socialist rule. Laycock and Johnson's observation about the gap between rhetoric and experience in the Soviet transformation of Armenia is relevant for the entire region and century covered in this volume: that often 'the *representation* of transformation [...] may in fact be more powerful than transformation itself'.

While some chapters in this volume have broader geographical scope than others, all can be used to pose questions about chronology and temporality in modern gender history which are important for historians seeking to draw transnational conclusions. When Zaharijević, for instance, suggests the post-Cold War Yugoslav region has experienced a distinct 'neoliberal' period as well as an immediately 'post-socialist' period and that questions of activism and citizenship might need to be posed differently for each one, her rationale is grounded in those societies' specific experiences; but what would asking the same questions about another society reveal? If Fraser's discussion of Soviet, French and Latin American 'revolutionary masculinities' is already striving to span political systems in understanding that aspect of gender history, what might become possible through turning such a lens on the gender orders produced through, say, Irish as well as Polish experiences of political imprisonment during the late Cold War, or on how the types of narratives that Australian as well as Soviet veterans felt able to express in public were shaped by systemic social and political shifts? Or, indeed, on any other topic?

The chapters also seek to highlight the ways in which scholars' ideas of region influence the conclusions they draw. Laycock and Johnson, for instance, contend that many conclusions about 'Soviet' gender history rely solely on evidence from metropolitan Russia whereas studies of Transcaucasia – or indeed, as others have argued, Central Asia – show even more complex and contradictory pictures of Soviet gender ideology. Jolluck demonstrates that appreciating the background behind Soviet gender relations is essential context for understanding gendered experiences of Soviet occupation during World War II or, as Simić continues to show, Soviet influences (and their limits) on state socialist gender policies in eastern Europe. Together, the chapters provide evidence and conclusions which would enable students to ask: how coherent is 'eastern Europe and the former USSR' as a region, or indeed as two regions? Where and how does the notion of subsidiary regions such as 'central Europe', 'former Yugoslavia' or 'Transcaucasia' help scholars form research questions and weigh up similarity against specificity? Are there other regions, such as a 'post-Ottoman space' that would include south-east Europe and Transcaucasia but also much of the Middle East, which should cross-cut the boundaries of an area defined by its experience of state socialism? And to what extent should the region(s) in this volume be studied through comparison with gender histories elsewhere? These matters are important to decide in the course of framing globally aware, yet locally rooted, gender histories.

Eastern Europe and the USSR in Global Gender Histories

The project of 'gendering the Cold War', as Małgorzata Fidelis, Renata Jambrešić Kirin, Jill Massino and Libora Oates-Indruchová termed one current approach to transnationalizing 20th-century gender history,[69] simultaneously requires (as Fidelis and colleagues argued) more attention to be paid to smaller states as well as superpowers and, with Cold War history itself experiencing a global turn, suggests new directions in which east European and Soviet gender history might expand. In 2009, for instance, Katherine Verdery joined Sharad Chari in calling for scholars to think 'between the posts' of post-socialism and postcolonialism and synthesize a research agenda from studies of both phenomena, rather than assigning different research questions to ex-state socialist and postcolonial societies.[70] Today, emerging research agendas on so-called Second World–Third World connections or state socialist policy towards the 'developing world' seek to decentre the West as a model for understanding global activism and mobilities (as in Kristen Ghodsee's research linking women's movements in Bulgaria and Zambia, or Anne Gorsuch's work on Soviet–Cuban encounters in the 1960s).[71] Both in these projects, and in another recent set of studies historicizing gender, migration and sex work,[72] east European gender history becomes part of a deeply global history of gender relations. Contributions both in this volume and elsewhere – Paces' references to Beth Baron's study of Egypt, or Baker's to Rahul Rao's work on India; the impact in the 'socialist feminism' debates of Saba Mahmood's work on Muslim feminism or Wang Zheng's on China – offer many ways in which historians are already laying its groundwork.

Indeed, precedents like these even open space for tracing east European involvement in the gendered projects of European colonialism – a history still hardly addressed. Stoler's history of the Dutch East Indies, for instance, tells briefly of the Dutch colonial novelist Madelon Székely-Lolofs who happened to be married to a Hungarian estate manager in 1920s Deli;[73] but historians could still study more systematically how eastern European individuals, states, organizations, capital and cultural representations were positioned within frameworks of gender and empire in this global sense, or how this interacted with gender within the east European empires. While recognizing the region's structural marginalization in relation to western Europe, historians can simultaneously ask what investments in gendering whiteness east Europeans had (and have today)[74] – and attempts to situate eastern Europe in a postcolonial or decolonial framework will need to answer this question in global dialogues of gender history.

Yet for these dialogues to be true dialogues, surveys of European or global women's history and gender history should also draw more extensively on scholarship about and from eastern Europe and the ex-USSR.[75] Russia does slightly better than eastern Europe or other Soviet republics in such surveys;[76] yet *all* these areas offer rich gender histories, with important commonalities but also complex layers of differences between (and within) countries. Too often, Jitka Malečková argued in 2010, 'encounter[s] between gender and history' in Europe produce a 'small Europe' by centring their research questions on the West; while Josie McLellan, for instance, urged 20th-century European women's history in general to push out into opening up broader questions of 'similarities and differences between societies with different economic regimes', capitalist or not.[77]

27. Elizabeth C. Dunn, *Privatizing Poland: Baby Food, Big Business, and the Remaking of Labor* (Ithaca, NY: Cornell University Press, 2004); David A. Kideckel, 'Miners and Wives in Romania's Jiu Valley: Perspectives on Postsocialist Class, Gender, and Social Change', *Identities* vol. 11, no. 1 (2004): 39–63; Kristen Ghodsee, *The Red Riviera: Gender, Tourism, and Postsocialism on the Black Sea* (Durham, NC: Duke University Press, 2005); Alison Stenning and Jane Hardy, 'Public Sector Reform and Women's Work in Poland: "Working for Juice, Coffee and Cheap Cosmetics!"', *Gender, Work and Organization* vol. 12, no. 6 (2005): 503–26; Leyla J. Keough, 'Globalizing "Post-socialism": Mobile Mothers and Neoliberalism on the Margins of Europe', *Anthropological Quarterly* vol. 79, no. 3 (2006): 431–61; Elaine Weiner, *Market Dreams: Gender, Class, and Capitalism in the Czech Republic* (Ann Arbor: University of Michigan Press, 2007); Renata Jambrešić Kirin and Marina Blagajić, 'The Ambivalence of Socialist Working Women's Heritage: a Case Study of the Jugoplastika Factory', *Narodna umjetnost* vol. 50, no. 1 (2013): 40–72; Chiara Bonfiglioli, 'Gendered Citizenship in the Global European Periphery: Textile Workers in Post-Yugoslav States', *Women's Studies International Forum* vol. 49 (2015): 57–65; Rozita Dimova, 'Between Borderlines, Betwixt Citizenship: Gender, Agency and the Crisis in the Macedonia/Greece Border Region', *Women's Studies International Forum* vol. 49 (2015): 66–72.
28. Andjelka Milić, 'Women and Nationalism in the Former Yugoslavia', in Funk and Mueller (eds), *Gender Politics*, 109–22; Žarana Papić, 'From State Socialism to State Nationalism: the Case of Serbia in Gender Perspective', *Refuge* vol. 14, no. 3 (1994): 10–14; Ana Dević, 'Redefining the Public-Private Boundary: Nationalism and Women's Activism in Former Yugoslavia', *Anthropology of East Europe Review* vol. 15, no. 2 (1997): 45–61; Maja Korac, 'Ethnic Nationalism, Wars and the Patterns of Social, Political and Sexual Violence Against Women: the Case of Post Yugoslav Countries', *Identities* vol. 5, no. 2 (1998): 153–81; Sabrina P. Ramet (ed.), *Gender Politics in the Western Balkans: Women and Society in Yugoslavia and the Yugoslav Successor States* (University Park: Pennsylvania State University Press, 1999); Jasmina Lukić, 'Media Representations of Men and Women in Times of War and Crisis: the Case of Serbia', in Gal and Kligman (eds), *Reproducing Gender*, 393–422; Julie Mostov, 'Sexing the Nation/Desexing the Body: Politics of National Identity in the Former Yugoslavia', in Tamar Mayer (ed.), *Gender Ironies of Nationalism: Sexing the Nation* (London: Routledge, 2000), 88–110; Carol S. Lilly and Jill A. Irvine, 'Negotiating Interests: Women and Nationalism in Serbia and Croatia, 1990–1997', *East European Politics and Societies* vol. 16, no. 1 (2002): 109–44; Aleksandra Sasha Milićević, 'Joining the War: Masculinity, Nationalism and War Participation in the Balkans War of Secession, 1991–1995', *Nationalities Papers* vol. 34, no. 3 (2006): 265–87; Dubravka Žarkov, *The Body of War: Media, Ethnicity, and Gender in the Break-Up of Yugoslavia* (Durham, NC: Duke University Press, 2007); Vjollca Krasniqi, 'Imagery, Gender and Power: the Politics of Representation in Post-War Kosova', *Feminist Review* no. 86 (2007): 1–23. See also Nira Yuval-Davis, *Gender and Nation* (London: Sage, 1997).
29. See Rose Lindsey, 'From Atrocity to Data: Historiographies of Rape in Former Yugoslavia and the Gendering of Genocide', *Patterns of Prejudice* vol. 36, no. 4 (2002): 59–78; Azra Hromadžić, 'Challenging the Discourse of Bosnian War Rapes', in Janet Elise Johnson and Jean C. Robinson (eds), *Living Gender after Communism* (Bloomington: Indiana University Press, 2007), 169–84; Helms, *Innocence and Victimhood*.
30. Žarkov, *Body of War*, 155–69; Zorica Mršević, 'Belgrade's SOS Hotline for Women and Children Victims of Violence: a Report', in Gal and Kligman (eds), *Reproducing Gender*, 370–92.

31. See, e.g., Andrea Pető, 'Memory and the Narrative of Rape in Budapest and Vienna in 1945', in Richard Bessel and Dirk Schumann (eds), *Life after Death: Approaches to a Cultural and Social History of Europe During the 1940s and 1950s* (Cambridge: Cambridge University Press, 2003), 129–48; James Mark, 'Remembering Rape: Divided Social Memory and the Red Army in Hungary 1944–1945', *Past and Present* vol. 188, no. 1 (2005): 133–61; Maria Bucur, *Heroes and Victims: Remembering War in Twentieth-Century Romania* (Bloomington: Indiana University Press, 2009); Lisa A. Kirschenbaum and Nancy M. Wingfield, 'Gender and the Construction of Wartime Heroism in Czechoslovakia and the Soviet Union', *European History Quarterly* vol. 39, no. 3 (2009): 465–89; Renata Jambrešić Kirin and Reana Senjković, 'Legacies of the Second World War in Croatian Cultural Memory: Women as Seen through the Media', *Aspasia* no. 4 (2010): 71–96; Irina Novikova, 'Renaming Men: the Politics of Memory and the Commemoration of War at the Baltic–Russian Crossroads', *Women's History Review* vol. 20, no. 4 (2011): 589–97.

32. Wingfield and Bucur (eds), *Gender and War*. See also Melissa K. Stockdale, '"My Death for the Motherland Is Happiness": Women, Patriotism, and Soldiering in Russia's Great War, 1914–1917', *American Historical Review* vol. 109, no. 1 (2004): 78–116; Laurie S. Stoff, *They Fought for the Motherland: Russia's Women Soldiers in World War I and the Revolution* (Lawrence: University Press of Kansas, 2006); Jovana Knežević, 'Prostitutes as a Threat to National Honor in Habsburg-Occupied Serbia During the Great War', *Journal of the History of Sexuality* vol. 20, no. 2 (2011): 312–35; Tara Zahra, *The Lost Children: Reconstructing Europe's Families after World War II* (Cambridge, MA: Harvard University Press, 2011).

33. As indicative examples, see Nayereh Tohidi, 'Soviet in Public, Azeri in Private: Gender, Islam and Nationality in Soviet and Post-Soviet Azerbaijan', *Women's Studies International Forum* vol. 19, no. 1–2 (1996): 111–23; Mary Neuburger, 'Difference Unveiled: Bulgarian National Imperatives and the Re-Dressing of Muslim Women, 1878–1989', *Nationalities Papers* vol. 25, no. 1 (1997): 169–83; Gal and Kligman (eds), *Reproducing Gender*; Feinberg, *Elusive Equality*; Maria Bucur, 'Between Liberal and Republican Citizenship: Feminism and Nationalism in Romania, 1880–1918', *Aspasia* no. 1 (2007): 84–102; Gergana Mircheva, 'Physical Education in Bulgarian Schools, 1918–1944: the (Re)Production of Masculinity and the Re-Creation of the National Body', *Women's History Review* vol. 20, no. 4 (2011): 555–67; Mark Cornwall, *The Devil's Wall: the Nationalist Youth Mission of Heinz Rutha* (Cambridge, MA: Harvard University Press, 2012); Elena Shulman, *Stalinism on the Frontier of Empire: Women and State Formation in the Soviet Far East* (Cambridge: Cambridge University Press, 2012); Tara Zahra, *Kidnapped Souls: National Indifference and the Battle for Children in the Bohemian Lands, 1900–1948* (Ithaca, NY: Cornell University Press, 2008); Rosalind Marsh, 'The Concepts of Gender, Citizenship, and Empire and Their Reflection in Post-Soviet Culture', *Russian Review* vol. 72, no. 2 (2013): 187–211; Sarah D. Phillips, 'The Women's Squad in Ukraine's Protests: Feminism, Nationalism, and Militarism on the Maidan', *American Ethnologist* vol. 41, no. 3 (2014): 414–26; Enikő Vincze, 'The Racialization of Roma in the "New" Europe and the Political Potential of Romani Women', *European Journal of Women's Studies* vol. 21, no. 4 (2014): 435–42; Alexander Maxwell, '"The Handsome Man with Hungarian Moustache and Beard": National Moustaches in Habsburg Hungary', *Cultural and Social History* vol. 12, no. 1 (2015): 51–76.

34. See, e.g., Maria Bucur, *Eugenics and Modernization in Interwar Romania* (Pittsburgh, PA: University of Pittsburgh Press, 2002); Claude Cahn, *Human Rights, State Sovereignty and Medical Ethics: Examining Struggles around Coercive Sterilisation of Romani Women* (Leiden: Brill, 2015).

35. See, e.g., Gail Kligman, *The Politics of Duplicity: Controlling Reproduction in Ceausescu's Romania* (Berkeley: University of California Press, 1998); David L. Hoffmann, 'Mothers in the Motherland: Stalinist Pronatalism in its Pan-European Context', *Journal of Social History* vol. 34, no. 1 (2000): 35–54; Ulf Brunnbauer and Karin Taylor, 'Creating a "Socialist Way of Life": Family and Reproduction Policies in Bulgaria, 1944–1989', *Continuity and Change* vol. 19, no. 2 (2004): 283–312. On efforts to reduce Roma birth rates, see, e.g., Sharon L. Wolchik, 'Reproductive Policies in the Czech and Slovak Republics', in Gal and Kligman (eds), *Reproducing Gender*, 58–91.

36. See, e.g., Małgorzata Fuszara, 'Abortion and the Formation of the Public Sphere in Poland', in Funk and Mueller (eds), *Gender Politics*, 241–52; Susan Gal, 'Gender in the Post-Socialist Transition: the Abortion Debate in Hungary', *East European Politics and Societies* vol. 8, no. 2 (1994): 256–86; Gal and Kligman (eds), *Reproducing Gender*; Rachel Alsop and Jenny Hockey, 'Women's Reproductive Lives as a Symbolic Resource in Central and Eastern Europe', *European Journal of Women's Studies* vol. 8, no. 4 (2001): 454–71; Michele Rivkin-Fish, 'Conceptualizing Feminist Strategies for Russian Reproductive Politics: Abortion, Surrogate Motherhood, and Family Support after Socialism', *Signs* vol. 38, no. 3 (2013): 569–93.

37. Wendy Z. Goldman, *Women, the State and Revolution: Soviet Family Policy and Social Life, 1917–1936* (Cambridge: Cambridge University Press, 1993); Ilic (ed.), *Women in the Stalin Era*; Mary Neuberger, 'Veils, Shalvari, and Matters of Dress: Unravelling the Fabric of Women's Lives in Communist Bulgaria', in Susan E. Reid and David Crowley (eds), *Style and Socialism: Modernity and Material Culture in Post-War Eastern Europe* (Oxford: Berg, 2000), 169–88; Susan E. Reid, 'Cold War in the Kitchen: Gender and the De-Stalinization of Consumer Taste in the Soviet Union under Khrushchev', *Slavic Review* vol. 61, no. 2 (2002): 211–52; Melanie Ilic, Susan E. Reid and Lynne Attwood (eds), *Women in the Khrushchev Era* (Basingstoke: Palgrave Macmillan, 2004); Penn and Massino (eds), *Gender Politics*; Lynne Attwood, *Gender and Housing in Soviet Russia* (Manchester: Manchester University Press, 2010); Paulina Bren, 'Women on the Verge of Desire: Women, Work, and Consumption in Socialist Czechoslovakia', in Susan E. Reid and David Crowley (eds), *Pleasures in Socialism: Leisure and Luxury in the Eastern Bloc* (Evanston, IL: Northwestern University Press, 2010), 177–96; Anikó Imre, 'Television for Socialist Women', *Screen* vol. 54, no. 2 (2013): 249–55; Philippa Hetherington, 'Dressing the Shop Window of Socialism: Gender and Consumption in the Soviet Union in the Era of "Cultured Trade", 1934–53', *Gender and History* vol. 27, no. 2 (2015): 417–45.

38. See, e.g., Wendy Bracewell, 'Women, Motherhood, and Contemporary Serbian Nationalism', *Women's Studies International Forum* vol. 19, no. 1–2 (1996): 25–33; Olga Issoupova, 'From Duty to Pleasure?: Motherhood in Soviet and Post-Soviet Russia', in Ashwin (ed.), *Gender, State and Society*, 30–54; Lynne Haney, *Inventing the Needy: Gender and the Politics of Welfare in Hungary* (Berkeley: University of California Press, 2002); Jenny Kaminer, *Women with a Thirst for Destruction: the Bad Mother in Russian Culture* (Evanston, IL: Northwestern University Press, 2014).

39. Ashwin (ed.), *Gender, State and Society*; Zhanna Chernova, 'The Model of "Soviet" Fatherhood: Discursive Prescriptions', *Russian Studies in History* vol. 51, no. 2 (2012): 35–62; Claire E. McCallum, 'The Return: Postwar Masculinity and the Domestic Space in Stalinist Visual Culture, 1945–53', *Russian Review* vol. 74, no. 1 (2015): 117–43. See also Amy E. Randall, 'Soviet Masculinities', *Russian Studies in History* vol. 51, no. 2 (2012): 3–12.

40. See, e.g., Goldman, *Women, the State and Revolution*; Jill Massino, 'Something Old, Something New: Marital Roles and Relations in State Socialist Romania', *Journal of Women's History* vol. 22, no. 1 (2010): 34–60.

41. Eric Naiman, *Sex in Public: the Incarnation of Early Soviet Ideology* (Princeton, NJ: Princeton University Press, 1997); Alexander Maxwell, 'Nationalizing Sexuality: Sexual Stereotypes in the Habsburg Empire', *Journal of the History of Sexuality* vol. 14, no. 3 (2005): 266–90; Frances Lee Bernstein, *The Dictatorship of Sex: Lifestyle Advice for the Soviet Masses* (DeKalb: Northern Illinois University Press, 2007); Keely Stauter-Halsted and Nancy M. Wingfield, 'Introduction: the Construction of Sexual Deviance in Late Imperial Eastern Europe', *Journal of the History of Sexuality* vol. 21, no. 2 (2011): 215–24, and issue contents; Zsófia Lóránd, '"A Politically Non-Dangerous Revolution is Not a Revolution": Critical Readings of the Concept of Sexual Revolution by Yugoslav Feminists in the 1970s', *European Review of History* vol. 22, no. 1 (2015): 120–37; Keely Stauter-Halsted, *The Devil's Chain: Prostitution and Social Control in Partitioned Poland* (Ithaca, NY: Cornell University Press, 2015); Hadley Z. Renkin and Agnieszka Kościańska, 'The Science of Sex in a Space of Uncertainty: Naturalizing and Modernizing Europe's East, Past and Present', *Sexualities* vol. 19, no. 1–2 (2016): 159–67.

42. Laurie Essig, *Queer in Russia: a Story of Sex, Self, and the Other* (Durham, NC: Duke University Press, 1999); Dan Healey, *Homosexual Desire in Revolutionary Russia: the Regulation of Sexual and Gender Dissent* (Chicago, IL: University of Chicago Press, 2001); Brian James Baer, *Other Russias: Homosexuality and the Crisis of Post-Soviet Identity* (Basingstoke: Palgrave Macmillan, 2009); Lisa Downing and Robert Gillett (eds), *Queer in Europe* (Farnham: Ashgate, 2011); Robert Kulpa and Joanna Mizielińska (eds), *De-Centring Western Sexualities: Central and East European Perspectives* (Farnham: Ashgate, 2011); Nárcisz Fejes and Andrea P. Balogh (eds), *Queer Visibility in Post-Socialist Cultures* (Bristol: Intellect, 2013); Francesca Stella, *Lesbian Lives in Post-Soviet Russia: Post/Socialism and Gendered Sexualities* (Basingstoke: Palgrave Macmillan, 2015); Tatjana Rosić Ilić, Jasna Koteska and Janko Ljumović (eds), *Representation of Gender Minority Groups in Media: Serbia, Montenegro and Macedonia* (Belgrade: Center for Media and Communications, 2015); Bojan Bilić (ed.), *LGBT Activism and Europeanisation in the (Post-)Yugoslav Space: On the Rainbow Way to Europe* (London: Palgrave Macmillan, 2016); Bojan Bilić and Sanja Kajinić (eds), *Intersectionality and LGBT Activist Politics: Multiple Others in Serbia and Croatia* (London: Palgrave Macmillan, 2016).

43. Jill Massino and Shana Penn, 'Introduction: Gender Politics and Everyday Life in State Socialist Eastern and Central Europe', in Penn and Massino (eds), *Gender Politics*, 5. See also Bucur et al., 'Six Historians'.

44. Fidelis, *Women, Communism, and Industrialization*, 4.

45. Nanette Funk, 'A Very Tangled Knot: Official State Socialist Women's Organizations, Women's Agency and Feminism in Eastern European State Socialism', *European Journal of Women's Studies* vol. 21, no. 4 (2014): 346.

46. Kristen Ghodsee, 'Untangling the Knot: a Response to Nanette Funk', *European Journal of Women's Studies* vol. 22, no. 2 (2015): 250.

47. Kristen Ghodsee, 'Pressuring the Politburo: the Committee of the Bulgarian Women's Movement and State Socialist Feminism', *Slavic Review* vol. 73, no. 3 (2014): 540.

48. Lynn Abrams, 'Martyrs or Matriarchs?: Working-Class Women's Experience of Marriage in Germany before the First World War', *Women's History Review* vol. 1, no. 3 (1993): 57–76.

49. See Lydia Sklevicky, 'More Horses Than Women: On the Difficulties of Founding Women's History in Yugoslavia', *Gender and History* vol. 1, no. 1 (1989): 68–73;

increasing centralization over the next three centuries destroyed the autonomy of the Czech estates. The predominantly Protestant Czech nobility was exiled during the Counter-Reformation, and German became the lingua franca. The 19th-century national revival, inspired by the French Revolution and European romanticism, resurrected Czech language and culture. Women such as Božena Němcová and Eliška Krásnohorská contributed by collecting rural folk stories and creating librettos for Czech-language operas.

After the 1848 failed uprisings and the 1867 division of the Empire between the Kingdom of Hungary and the Austrian Empire, Czechs felt even more insecure in their role as a small nation within a multinational Empire. Prague was nonetheless rapidly transforming from a German-dominated to a Czech city, whose municipal government, economy and culture increasingly reflected the shifting demographic. In this era Czechs founded voluntary organizations, political parties and educational institutions that instilled patriotism into Bohemia's Slavic majority and challenged the region's German cultural domination. An influx of Czech-speaking peasants changed Prague's predominant language, and by 1880 Czech speakers had successfully overtaken the Prague city government. In 1897 Czechs won the right to use their language in the Austrian civil service, displacing German speakers in many key positions. With linguistic rights at the heart of the nationalist movements, women's maternal roles had deep political resonance.

German and Czech Bohemians established separate cultural institutions and organizations, in effect creating parallel civil societies in Bohemia. Both Bohemian German and Czech national organizations asserted that their mother tongue, 'the most holiest legacy of our ancestors', was endangered and must be safeguarded.[4] As children became pawns within competing national movements, both Czech- and German-speaking Bohemians linked parental love to patriotic education. The historian Tara Zahra quoted a 1909 brochure aimed at Czech parents proclaiming, 'If you really love your children, allow them to be educated only in their mother tongue!'.[5] As in many European languages, the Czech terms for family, birth and nation (*rodina*, *porod*, *národ*) shared a common root. Consequently, as women demonstrated their value to the nuclear family, they also proved their indispensability to the nation.

Another complexity of the *fin-de-siècle* maternal image was its links to public health and the dynamics of social class. Europeans were heavily invested in increasing and protecting their populations, and breakthroughs in germ theory and sanitation gave them new tools for their efforts. Michel Foucault named the 'hysterization of women' as a hallmark of the Victorian era. In Bohemia, as elsewhere, female bodies were analysed and medicalized, and women (in Foucault's words) owed a 'responsibility [...] to the health of their children [...] and the safeguarding of society'.[6] In the heightened anxiety over which national group was to dominate Bohemia, this medicalized view of motherhood became crucial to concerns about the birth rate and population health. The symbolic mother transmitted gender norms and expectations for real women's behaviours. The era's visual and written texts encouraged women to connect biological functions to national and social duties. Through hygiene, clothing, exercise and comportment, mothers could display themselves as living embodiments of idealized artistic representations. However, these expectations were unrealistic for working-class women, who endured crowded living conditions, low wages and limited leisure time. Nonetheless, the idealized maternal depictions normalized bourgeois women's behaviours and became iconic, tacitly warning women of the consequences to the nation and the family if their duties were not fulfilled.

However, Bohemian women did not merely succumb to the symbolic forms of power created through nationalized and medicalized representations. Maternalism also offered women an entry point into public political discourse. The historian Ann Taylor Allen has argued that we need to complicate our understanding of European feminism's relationship to motherhood given that maternalist feminists created new forms of feminine power in both domestic and public realms.[7] Czechs and other minority nationalist movements within the Empire, such as Poles and Hungarians, often supported women's emancipation to distinguish their movements' progressive ideals from the conservative Habsburg Monarchy. Further, in this era, the New Woman was becoming a powerful European icon, signifying society's modernity and progress. This New Woman might be well educated, have a career, play sports, socialize in public or even run for political office. Czech women founded the Empire's first girls' gymnasium in 1890 without support or funding from Vienna.[8] In 1902 a Czech woman became the first Austrian woman of any nationality to earn a medical degree 'based exclusively on study in an Austrian University: the Charles-Ferdinand University in Prague'.[9]

These modern accomplishments did not necessarily exclude the New Woman from motherhood. However, the power gained in this realm was predominantly for middle-class women, whose lifestyles were thought conducive to a healthy society. Poorer women were less able to achieve the strict rules on hygiene and childcare, and thus appeared not to fulfil their maternal duties. Further, they were less likely to benefit from the educational and professional gains women made through maternalist arguments. Still, even they found voices in the growing socialist movements, whose leaders reminded the public that the working class needed social support if it was to uphold the era's expectations for mothering.

Examining the interplay of gender and nationalism in *fin-de-siècle* visual culture enables us to understand how national movements created models for future citizens of the east European nation states. As Catherine Baker explains in the introduction to this volume, 'If narratives of national and ethnic identity determine *who* belongs to the nation, gender regimes intersect with these to determine *how* a person categorized as male or female is supposed to belong.' The Czech national movement was often seen as a model for feminist leadership, and after the foundation of Czechoslovakia as a state after World War I, Czechoslovakia's first president Tomáš Garrigue Masaryk would espouse women's rights and equality. Yet, as the historian Melissa Feinberg reminds us, 'Most Czechs [...] did not see democracy as a barrier to laws that distinguished between citizens on the basis of their gender.'[10] The dichotomy between Czech women's public rights and private duties would continue through the 20th century's political regimes – democratic and Communist – that nonetheless advocated women's equality as a political platform.

Figure 1.3   Illustrations of proper and improper breastfeeding postures.
Anna Fischer-Dückelmann, Žena lékařkou: lékařská kniha, věnovaná péči o zdraví a léčbě nemocí se zvláštním ohledem na ženské a dětské nemoci, pomoc ku porodu a ošetřování dítek *(Prague: Nakl. Jos. R. Vilímek, 1907), 497–8.*

photographs, which gave his guidebook a modern, progressive feel. One set of photographs depicted a woman properly and improperly testing the temperature of an infant's bottle. The first subject's posture and demeanour suggested a scientist seriously examining the specimen of warm milk on her hand, while in the second photo the same woman swigged directly from the baby bottle, eyes closed and head thrown back as though drinking alcohol (Figure 1.4). Such images reinforced the medical profession's condescension towards rural and urban working-class mothers; bourgeois readers would have certainly seen in the second photograph the lack of sophistication, carelessness and alcohol consumption associated with working-class misbehaviour.

Another theme in mothering guides was how women's clothing affected their health. The dress reform movement, which originated in Germany, had echoes in Bohemia as well. Embracing the classical style, dress reformers decried corsets in favour of loose, comfortable undergarments and clothing (Figure 1.5). The historian Michael Hau has explained that this movement had both feminist and antifeminist advocates:

> Anna Fischer-Dückelmann [...] contended that health and feminine beauty were expressions of a fully developed female personality that had overcome the social obstacles of women's fulfilment and asserted its social and economic independence. Yet she and her adversaries were drawing on the same symbolic, neo humanistic universe: the aesthetic ideal of physical beauty from antiquity.[48]

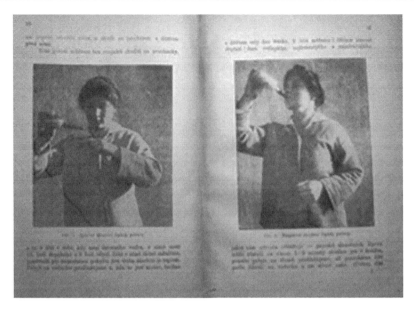

Figure 1.4 Woman demonstrates proper and improper methods of testing a bottle's temperature.
Jiří Brdlík, Ditě Kojenec *(Prague: Česká zemská komise, 1917), 32–3.*

Figure 1.5 Dress reform styles.
Anna Fischer-Dückelmann, Die Frau als Hausärztin: ein ärztliches Nachschlagebuch der Gesundheitspflege und Heilkunde in der Familie (Stuttgart: Süddeutsches Verlags-Institut, 1901), Fig. 106.

While Czech dress reformers looked to German and Austrian examples, they added a nationalist claim that women's health and modernity reflected Czech progress.[49] Czech journalists and public figures vigorously participated in the 'war against the corset' and supported purposeful clothing that allowed women to breathe easily, participate in sports and maintain their general health. The Czech physician Jaroslav Květ published a series of articles in *Národní listy*, the patriotic daily, extolling the virtues of looser corsets, hats and shoes and decrying the unhealthy styles advertised by fashion magazines. The Czech patriotic writer Jan Neruda poked fun at corsets and crinolines that made women look like centaurs and praised a Vienna shopkeeper who fitted women for undergarments designed for their special needs, such as pregnancy, singing or sports. Dr Jan Brdlík, however, wanted to make sure the movement for loose clothing did not go too far, explaining that breastfeeding mothers needed supportive undergarments, particularly bras 'that maintain the breasts in a horizontal position'.[50]

Guidebooks encouraged mothers to strengthen their bodies and obtain optimal health through appropriate 'feminine sports', including swimming, ice skating and hiking.[51] The most progressive books held that women could perform the same exercises as men; they blamed social biases, not physical limitations, for some women's lack of athletic talent. Organized sport was an essential part of central European nationalist movements.[52] Patriotic gymnastic organizations promoted healthy bodies and provided physical, moral and intellectual training. Armed with medical advice that promoted fitness, Czech women demanded membership in Sokol, the most prestigious Czech gymnastics society. Once admitted, women insisted on more opportunities to participate in festivals, competitions and sport demonstrations.[53]

Suggestions for exercise were sometimes linked to childcare practices, especially breastfeeding. Fischer-Dückelmann's book, for example, included photographs of 'gymnastics exercises' that would aid lactating women (Figure 1.6).[54]

Women could massage their breasts to stimulate milk production and prevent clogged milk ducts. Proper posture and stretching techniques would help alleviate neck and shoulder pain, associated with holding and nursing an infant. Women were told they alone could control their body's proper functioning, and they were frankly encouraged to know and touch their own bodies. While

Figure 1.6   Gymnastic exercises for breastfeeding women.
Fischer-Dückelmann, Žena lékařkou, Tafel 27.

progressive, many suggestions for exercise presupposed the availability of leisure time, childcare and funds for equipment. The advice guides purported to address all women, but clearly presumed middle-class attitudes and resources and downplayed working-class women's unique challenges.

Public Health Campaigns and the Healthy Mother

The *fin-de-siècle* impetus to safeguard the larger community's health targeted individual mothering practices. Tuberculosis and diarrhoea were the leading causes of children's deaths, and medical studies demonstrated that breastfed infants had lower mortality rates. Medical and population data were collected, sorted by region and national origin, and published in various sources. Though scientists differed in their causal explanations – citing diseased water supplies, spoiled milk, bacterial growth or lack of refrigeration – most agreed that breast-feeding offered some protection against the two most fatal childhood diseases. As the historian Anthony Wohl explained, 'From the 1860s onwards medical men thought that too many women who could nurse were turning to bottle-feeding and that bottle-feeding killed babies.'[55] Throughout Europe, public health posters frequently addressed mothers; a French anti-tuberculosis poster depicted a mother near a cradle, warning: 'Death lies in wait. By your intelligence and care you can stave off his hands.'[56]

Czech-speaking medical professionals, who were similarly engaged in public health campaigns, were committed to issuing public health information in the Slavic language. Most medical information and research in Bohemia was still in German, and Czech publications would reach another audience and would demonstrate Czech progress in the sciences. Soon after the first international tuberculosis conference, held in Berlin in 1902, the Czech Auxiliary Society for Lung Diseases in the Kingdom of Bohemia commissioned the renowned painter František Urban to create a poster for a public health campaign. Urban was known for his complex allegorical paintings and romanticized female subjects, such as the Virgin Mary and classical muses and goddesses that adorned Czech national theatres and churches.

Urban's 1904 anti-tuberculosis poster evoked strong emotion through maternal imagery. Entitled 'Ten Health Commandments Against Tuberculosis', the text warned Czechs about tuberculosis in didactic language regarding individuals' habits, practices and behaviours. The commandments echoed speeches and guidebooks for housewives and mothers:

> Do not raise dust. Do not linger in dust. Live in temperance. Do not drink alcohol. Air apartments. Do not live in dark, damp apartments. Wash in cold water and maintain cleanliness. Treat yourself to a strong and good diet. Move around often in open healthy air![57]

Urban's illustration of two women and an infant posited an intrinsic connection among health, beauty and motherhood. The first woman, dressed in rich red and gold, held an Asclepius staff entwined with snakes. Representing health and medicine, but also reminiscent of National Mother imagery, this beautiful establishment, Dr Jiří Brdlík dedicated his book *The Healthy Child* to 'all Czechoslovak mothers', who by caring for children 'care for the entire nation, both in body and in spirit'.[66] National independence had not, therefore, diminished the importance of motherhood within what was now the gender regime of a newly formed, democratic nation state. While Czechoslovak women gained political rights and made up about one-third of the interwar workforce, the national culture promoted motherhood. Public health became a mission of the new state, which established a Ministry for Information and Public Health and the National Council for Social Hygiene, uniting numerous pre-war associations. The President's daughter, Alice Masaryková, led the Czechoslovak Red Cross and brought public attention to maternal and child welfare. These organizations decried World War I's detrimental effect on the family: a dramatically decreased birth rate coupled with a staggering rise in infant mortality. The new Czechoslovak state set up clinics throughout the country to improve infant health and to advise mothers on childcare. Pro-natalist eugenics became more popular during the 1920s and medical professionals recommended premarital counselling to strengthen the population. Despite these efforts, and an immediate post-war recovery, the birth rate in Czechoslovakia decreased from the mid-1920s onwards.[67]

Women's early 20th-century struggles for access to education, careers and paid labour portended a central paradox of state socialism: how do regimes reconcile the promise of women's emancipation with the real need for societies to reproduce themselves? How does an ideology that requires full participation in the workforce also support the needs of mothers and infants? The national movements and new interwar nation states of early 20th-century eastern Europe, just as much as the nation states at the end of the century after the fall of state socialism, therefore offer historians important insights into how ideas of gender and nation have intersected to shape attitudes about, and the performance of, such intimate and everyday activities as childcare. Yet the period during and after World War I was not just a time of geopolitical transformation; it also, as the next chapter argues, established new contexts for at least some individuals to pursue their understandings of gender, sexuality and identity.

Notes

1. See, e.g., Beth Baron, 'The Construction of National Honour in Egypt', *Gender and History* vol. 5, no. 2 (1993): 244–55.
2. Joan Scott, *Gender and the Politics of History* (New York: Columbia University Press, 1999), 43; Rosemary Betterton, *An Intimate Distance: Women, Artists and the Body* (New York: Routledge, Chapman and Hall, 1996), 20.
3. Baron, 'National Honour', 245.
4. Pieter M. Judson, 'The Gendered Politics of German Nationalism in Austria, 1880–1900', in David Good, Margarete Grandner, and Mary Jo Maynes (eds), *Austrian Women in the Nineteenth and Twentieth Centuries* (Providence, RI: Berghahn), 6.
5. Tara Zahra, *Kidnapped Souls: National Indifference and the Battle for Children in the Bohemian Lands, 1900–1948* (Ithaca, NY: Cornell University Press, 2008), 23.
6. Michel Foucault, *The History of Sexuality: an Introduction*, vol. 1, trans. Robert Hurley (New York: Vintage, 1990), 146–7.

7. Ann Taylor Allen, *Feminism and Motherhood in Western Europe 1890–1970: The Maternal Dilemma* (New York: Palgrave Macmillan, 2005), 2.

8. Katherine David, 'Czech Feminists and Nationalism in the Late Habsburg Monarchy: "The First in Austria"', *Journal of Women's History* vol. 3, no. 2 (1991): 26–45.

9. Karen Johnson Freeze, 'Medical Education for Women in Austria: a Study in the Politics of the Czech Women's Movement in the 1890s', in Sharon L. Wolchik and Alfred G. Meyer (eds), *Women, State, and Party in Eastern Europe* (Durham, NC: Duke University Press, 1985), 61.

10. Melissa Feinberg, *Elusive Equality: Gender, Citizenship, and the Limits of Democracy in Czechoslovakia, 1918–1950* (Pittsburgh, PA: University of Pittsburgh Press, 2006), 4.

11. Věnceslava Lužická, *Krásno českých domácností: přednášky spolku Domácnost* (Prague: Tiskem F. Šimáčka, 1888), 1.

12. Lužická, *Krásno českých domácností*, n. p.

13. Sofie Podlipská, *Studie o práci Přednáška čtená 18. ledna 1889 ve spolku Domácnost* (Prague: Tiskem F. Šimáčka, 1889), 6.

14. Podlipská, *Studie*, 7.

15. Podlipská, *Studie*, 18.

16. Podlipská, *Studie*, 18.

17. Silke Wenk, 'Gendered Representations of the Nation's Past and Future', in Ida Blom, Karen Hagemann and Catherine Hall (eds), *Gendered Nations: Nationalisms and Gender Order in the Long Nineteenth Century* (London: Bloomsbury Academic, 2000), 65.

18. Eric Hobsbawm and Terence Ranger, *The Invention of Tradition* (Cambridge: Cambridge University Press, 1992).

19. Jitka Malečková, 'Nationalizing Women and Engendering the Nation: the Czech National Movement', in Blom, Hagemann and Hall (eds), *Gendered Nations*, 301.

20. Marina Warner, *Monuments and Maidens: the Allegory of the Female Form* (New York: Atheneum, 1985), xx.

21. Warner, *Monuments and Maidens*, xx.

22. Ladislav Šaloun, *L. Šalouna Husův pomník v Hořicích* (Prague: Unie, 1914).

23. Pieter M. Judson, *Guardians of the Nation: Activists on the Language Frontier of Austria-Hungary* (Cambridge, MA: Harvard University Press, 2007), 27.

24. Božena Němcová, *Obrázky národopisné* (Prague: Jan Laichter, 1910), 3–4.

25. Stanislav Sucharda, *Pomník Františka Palackého v Praze, Jeho vznik a význam* (Prague: Jan Štenc, 1912), 11.

26. Sucharda, *Pomník Františka Palackého*, 11.

27. Božena Němcová, *The Grandmother: Scenes from Bohemian Country Life*, trans. Frances Gregor (Chicago: A. C. McClurg and Company, 1891), 200.

28. Němcová, *The Grandmother*, 200.

29. Božena Viková-Kunětická, 'O ženském mandátu do sněmu království českého', in Marie Bahenská, Libuše Heczková, and Dana Musilová (eds), *Ženy na stráž! České feministické myšlení 19. a 20. století* (Prague: Masarykův ústav a Archiv Academie věd, 2010), 202–7.

30. Iveta Jusová, 'Figuring the Other in Nineteenth-Century Czech Literature: Gabriela Preissová and Božena Viková-Kunětická', in Marcel Cornis-Pope and John Neubauer (eds), *History of the Literary Cultures of East-Central Europe: Types and Stereotypes* (Amsterdam and Philadelphia: John Benjamins, 2010), 375.

31. Irvine Loudon, 'Some International Features of Maternal Mortality, 1880–1950', in Valerie A. Fildes, Lara Marks, and Hilary Marland (eds), *Women and Children First: International Maternal and Infant Welfare, 1870–1945* (London: Routledge, 1992), 5–28.

towards the far right.[8] For queer historians working against such obstacles, research might be a matter of inventing new reading strategies or identifying with figures from the past, in desperate attempts to reconstruct a culture where historical narratives would include them – and against the grain of Laura Doan's critique of the search for 'the ancestral' in the history of sexuality[9] – but can also present the trap of rigid identity categories that would not be appropriate for the past.

Theoretical as well as evidential problems disturb investigations like this chapter's research. Emily Hamer suggests a definition of lesbian history as the aggregate of evidence about women who have loved women in her claim: 'I would argue that lesbian history can be compiled only by examining such micro-histories: in essence "lesbian history" is no more than the sum of lesbian lives.'[10] Yet, as Terry Castle notes, it remains unclear what the constitutive elements defining the figure of a 'lesbian' might even be.[11] Instead, what one might nowadays name as 'lesbian' in historical perspective was a complex overlap of love, friendships, work, intimacy and networks among women, where different ways of naming sexuality would be more accurate to the historical period's own terms,[12] and where evidence of 'cross-gender behavior and identity' has some-times been used to claim subjects for 'lesbian' history without interrogating how the historian is able to, or if they even can, determine the gender of figures from the past.[13] While historians should problematize what identifications and termi-nology they might project on to figures from the past who might have been lesbian or queer, the microhistorical dimension of Hamer's definition on the other hand deserves to be retained. Indeed, revealing the microhistorical through the papers of Rojc and Holme could disrupt ideas about sexual identi-ties and modernities in Britain as well as the post-Yugoslav region.

To write about silenced histories, therefore, does not necessarily involve a project of writing the history of lesbian identity itself. Instead, writing about invisible relationships of love and friendship enters the field of histories of alter-natives to the rigid gender order and hegemonic narratives of and approaches to national history: the alternative lifestyles led by Rojc, Holme and others in the Yugoslav region during and after the Great War disrupt the rigid patriarchal character of official historical narratives whether or not the lifestyles are named 'lesbian'. Sometimes it is obvious that women shared a bed and lived together, named themselves as women and pronounced their sexuality out loud. Sometimes they made no explicit statements about any of these things; yet continuities of iconography, lifestyle and cultural signifiers between their circles and lifestyles and those of today might still incline the historian to view them, however contingently, through the scope of lesbian, queer or sometimes transgender history.

The reconstruction of lesbian history in this chapter is therefore both contin-gent and transnational. Access to the papers of Nasta Rojc, now held in a private collection in Zagreb, not only revises the history of the interwar Yugoslav art scene,[14] but adds an extra dimension to the history of Holme, whose papers in the Women's Library in London have informed studies of the British suffragette movement, British women's participation in Great War relief work,[15] Holme's relationship with another suffragette and medical volunteer, Evelina Haverfield,[16] and Holme's own networks in Britain.[17] None of these, however, have placed at their centre the *transnational* production of the novel expressions of identity, gender and creativity in which Rojc, Holme and their friends and partners participated. Yet the Yugoslav art scene and the post-war formation of lesbian identities in Yugoslavia as well as Britain would all be influenced by the networks formed when Holme and others travelled to Serbia as medical volunteers soon after the outbreak of the Great War.

Lesbian History and Scottish Women's Hospitals in the Great War

Current scholarship presents a stark difference in the amount of information available about lesbian histories in Britain, on one hand, and the Yugoslav region, on the other, before the Great War. Today's historians of Britain are better served than Donoghue was in the early 1990s, with Emily Hamer, Rebecca Jennings, Laura Doan and others already having shown the diversity of lesbian and gender non-conforming lives and identities in Edwardian and wartime Britain.[18] The literature on the post-war period is even greater, though the greater availability of evidence about middle- and upper-class women's lives in these periods – the classes to which Holme and other Britons in this chapter belonged – still leaves it unclear whether working-class British women whom one might now call lesbians necessarily understood their lives and identities in the same way.[19] For the Yugoslav region at the beginning of the 20th century, on the other hand, comparable evidence has largely yet to be collated: the writer Jelena Dimitrijević published an openly homoerotic poem 'Obmana' ('A Deceit') in the magazine *Bosanska vila* in 1910, and gossip about Queen Natalija Obrenović of Serbia (1882–9) entered the literature,[20] but other documents are mostly hidden and undetected.

The reconstruction of early 20th-century lesbian networks has therefore been much more feasible for the British side, with historians including Elisabeth Crawford and Anna Kisby having already demonstrated the connections between many of these women's wartime activities as volunteer doctors, nurses and ambulance drivers and their participation before the war in the women's suffrage movement, which had often been pursued by radical means.[21] This movement had divided into pacifist and pro-war sides when war broke out in August 1914, with many pro-war suffragettes connecting the war effort with feminism and rushing to contribute.[22] For many more women, outside the suffrage movement, wartime 'employment [...] redefined the boundaries of class and gender' as they entered industries or jobs where women's pre-war participation had been minimal.[23] It was therefore unsurprising that many lesbians became attracted to the idea of joining the war.

This association would be tightened further in the post-war version of lesbian identity constructed by Radclyffe Hall's 1928 novel *The Well of Loneliness*, where the lead character Stephen Gordon had met many of her own 'sort of woman' as a volunteer ambulance driver in France.[24] Though Hall claimed the novel's medical unit was a fictional creation, she drew on real-life evidence in developing her narrative that participating in the war had given lesbians more freedom of movement and greater chances to develop a lesbian subculture in Britain.[25] Hall's representation of the wartime lesbian as, in Laura Doan's summary, 'an ambulance driver with tremendous physical strength, stamina, personal courage, and a willingness to perform the manly skills of motoring and maintenance' – as anachronistic an 'origins myth' for British lesbian history as Doan argues this was – could still describe the persona Holme cultivated before and during her time as a medical volunteer.[26] Jack Halberstam cautions, however, that automatically labelling all the ambulance drivers and auxiliary volunteers with 'desires for masculine identification' and 'various degrees of overt masculine presentation' as 'lesbians' would be 'to ignore the specificity of their lives', and disregard the possibility that some might have understood their gender as well as their sexuality in alternative ways.[27] This too must be kept in mind in contextualizing the milieu around SWH; yet however Holme's relationship to gender identity and expression might have been described in today's terms, Holme's travel to the Balkans and participation in SWH would indirectly provide the node that brought the network of ex-SWH volunteers and Yugoslav artists together.

Serbia, like France, was another important destination for volunteer medical units. The first British medical relief initiative organized for Serbia, the Scottish Women's Hospitals for Foreign Service, originated with Elsie Inglis, a Scottish doctor from the non-militant wing of the suffrage movement who, Hamer writes, 'had lived with Dr Flora Murray for a number of years in Edinburgh'.[28] Inglis's initiative drew both on 'her profession as a doctor and her mission as a suffragette – to collect voluntary contributions to establish a medical unit, staffed completely by women, and offer it, fully equipped, to the War Office for service with the British forces'.[29] Inglis first approached another field hospital initiative being founded by Murray and her partner Dr Louisa Anderson (who told Inglis all places were full),[30] then the Royal Army Medical Corps officer (who told her 'My good lady, go home and sit still'),[31] then pitched her idea of forming a fully equipped female hospital unit to the French and Serbian authorities, which accepted eagerly. SWH soon put themselves at the service of the Serbian Relief Fund (founded at the Serbian Embassy in London), both organizations assisting each other thereafter.[32] Inglis wrote that the first SWH units arrived in Serbia as early as December 1914.[33]

Holme's involvement with SWH and Serbia came through her relationship with Haverfield, who became SWH's administrator in May 1915 and would be based in Serbia. Holme had met Haverfield through the suffrage movement, in which Holme had notably acted as chauffeur to Emmeline and Christabel Pankhurst – 'Britain's first female chauffeur' according to Kisby – and had a masculine style of dress, taking the nickname 'Jack' or 'Jacko'.[34] Holme had previously worked as an actor, often as a male impersonator, in a touring variety company (potentially the occasion for Holme's learning to drive).[35] Haverfield shared Holme's suffragism and masculine style.[36] Before joining SWH, she had been seeking organized ways for women to participate in the war effort by forming women's emergency and reserve organizations (she had even proposed a Women's Volunteer Rifle Corps to defend Britain's coast against invasion).[37] Holme followed Haverfield into one of these, the Women's Volunteer Reserve

(WVR), in summer 1914; then, volunteering as a SWH ambulance driver, went to join Haverfield in Serbia.

The Central Powers' occupation of Serbia at the end of 1915, with Serbian forces retreating to the Adriatic, saw most SWH volunteers evacuated but a few, including Holme and Haverfield, continuing to operate in occupied territory. Between November 1915 and February 1916, Anna Kisby has revealed, they were themselves held prisoner of war.[38] SWH continued fundraising in Britain for Serbian relief and sent field hospitals to other fronts, including Dobrudja in Romania, where Holme and Haverfield 'gathered […] a small lesbian circle […] whose intimate friendships had been forged particularly as intrepid SWH drivers'.[39] It was Serbia, however, to which Holme would return after the war, working between 1919 and 1922 in Bajina Bašta at an orphanage Haverfield had established.[40] Here, Holme and Haverfield were joined by Alexandra Onslow, another SWH volunteer from the Dobrudja group who does not appear in the networks Kisby mapped but, through her relationship with the Croatian and Yugoslav painter Nasta Rojc, formed the remaining node in the correspondence network that this chapter depicts.

Negotiating 'Sapphic Modernities' Between Britain and Serbia

The practices characteristic of the Holme–Haverfield circle, including masculine dress, short hair, practising sports, consuming tobacco, automobility and enthusiasm for auxiliary service in war, correspond to the features of newly emerged sexual identities among women that Laura Doan and Jane Garrity have termed 'sapphic modernities'.[41] Heather Love, indeed, lists 'women's ambulance units in WW1' alongside 'Harlem rent parties' and 'Paris salons' among the 'spaces of sapphic modernity' which in her view 'have come to represent the sources of a recognizable modern lesbian community'.[42] These modernities depended on a particular blend of gender, sexuality and class – but if they epitomized Holme or Radclyffe Hall's fictional Stephen Gordon, they also characterized the life of Nasta Rojc.

On arriving in war-damaged, rural Serbia, Holme and Haverfield, their unconventional behaviour notwithstanding, created contacts and friendships with the local elite of doctors and military officers. Holme's letters relate that a Serbian colonel in Kragujevac, for instance, 'asked me to go to his house and be introduced to his wife and sisters in law – they were perfectly charming and all spoke French so I had a great time there'.[43] Women in Serbia meanwhile faced severe social, political and economic inequality, with extremely limited civil and political rights (inheritance, ownership and the franchise), little access to the professions, much lower pay than men for most jobs, and (a sign that the 'double burden' of paid and domestic labour existed before state socialism) having to perform all domestic labour while receiving the most arduous work. With rare exceptions, whose 'femininity' would be tolerated as an innate handicap, women were excluded from the cultural and public sphere.[44] Their average life expectancy was around 40.[45] Nevertheless, educated officers and SWH members apparently did not have problems in establishing contact or discussing important political topics: another of Holme's letters describes a visit to the

British ambassador (including 'tea and smokes' with a 'charming' Serbian captain) and to the foreign ministry, where she '[w]as also introduced to ten very nice officers who spoke French perfectly and we had a long talk about Women's Suffrage – they told me the women have just got the vote in Denmark and can sit in both houses'.[46] The Holme papers could thus serve not just for the biographical approach employed by Kisby but also for insights into the intercultural encounters between British women and progressive Serbian elites during the Great War. Their shared French language proficiency, a class marker in both Britain and Serbia, not only facilitated conversation but seems to have mitigated perceptions of 'foreignness' through a linguistic closeness that on either side could demonstrate that the other belonged to a transnationally shared cultural space.

This warm welcome and acceptance of British feminists might sound surprising at first sight. Holme's letters do not suggest that the newly established relations required giving up or hiding old habits and romantic relationships:

> Eve looks much better and we are very happy to be together. She is just the fellow for an administrator as she speaks foreign languages so well. Eve and I sleep out and I have rigged up our moskito [sic] net in quite a swell manner. It is lovely looking up at the stars and feeling the first rays of the sun and the breeze. We have met a great many Serbian officers who are too nice for words to us, and they always want to do everything to make us enjoy ourselves, and when we tell them we came out to work and not to play they always say 'let us all enjoy ourselves while we can, because we may have very hard work later' – anyway, they could not be dearer than they are.[47]

And they enjoyed it. Holme's letters and other documents, including SWH newsletters, show SWH members spending their leisure time holding concerts and recitals in which everybody took part, from British women doctors and ambulance drivers to Serbian soldiers and officers, and even Austrian prisoners of war.[48] In the extraordinary circumstances, nobody seemed to care about Holme's non-normative gender behaviour (Kisby quotes a letter where Holme has 'my hair cut short and it is awfully wavy and curly and I look like an impresario – Eve says – and she loves it', and where 'some Serbian people' she visited dressed in 'a full Serbian man's kit [...] most awfully picturesque' were 'absolutely delighted and helped me to fix it in the authdox [sic] way'[49]). Elsie Bowerman, a suffragette and *Titanic* survivor who knew Holme, left written testimony about a 'fancy dress party' held somewhere in Serbia, 'to which Vera Holme went "as a most realistic motor mechanic"'.[50]

British women were integrated into wartime Serbia's elite social circles to such an extent that part of these circles are likely to have known of Holme's and Haverfield's relationship. It is difficult to imagine a loud person like Holme refraining from showing affections altogether; but it is also hard to tell how Serbian officers and doctors perceived their intimacy. Holme's correspondence with some of them after the war reveals a certain closeness and openness to their relationships. The officer Milan Yovitchitch, in his letters to Holme, used only the male nickname Jack, while other correspondents (including the 'chief of police', Ivo Lipovšak, and one Marko Simunović) were sending their regards to

Holme's lesbian circle of friends.[51] What we know for sure is that Holme's letters talk about a shared intimacy with Haverfield, and about their openly living together.

The complex interplay between Serbian officers and British feminists resulted in deep personal connections but was also reflected in negotiations of gender, showing an instability of gender roles in relation to social, class and ethnic status. The British volunteers' alliance with Serbian soldiers also included gaining a special status for themselves in the Balkans; their ethnicity and social status meant that the assumed proper place for women in Serbian society did not apply to them.[52] Flora Sandes, one of the rare women to officially serve as a soldier during the Great War, was also part of the same milieu and seemed to hold a similar status. The diary of Sandes, who was formally enrolled in the Serbian Army and after the war achieved the rank of captain, compares the huge respect she received from Serbian soldiers to their treatment of another woman in uniform, a Serbian named Milunka Savić who was then aged 17. '[B]eing a peasant like themselves,' Sandes wrote, 'the men did not treat her at all the same way they treated me'.[53] Julie Wheelwright suggests Serbian soldiers' respect for Sandes came from her status as a representative of Entente forces (thus important for their collective spirit), who could shoot, ride and was British, so that '[c]onsiderations of sexual difference were overridden by larger questions of social position and the politics of war'.[54] Sandes was accepted as part of the male milieu, but only through denying any connection with other, local, women.[55] The British women effectively received an honorary male status; Holme's papers, indeed, said almost nothing of local *women*, who appeared only as laundry workers or members of male officers' families.[56] After the war, on the other hand, the similar identity performances already shared by Nasta Rojc, her partner Alexandra Onslow and Holme were the foundation for long-standing friendship and connection between the Britons and Rojc, beginning around the time that Holme, Haverfield and Onslow were all present in Yugoslavia as a result of Haverfield opening an orphanage in Bajina Bašta early in 1920.

Haverfield had founded the orphanage after returning to Serbia at war's end in December 1918 and launching the 'Haverfield Fund for Serbian Children'. Serbia in the meantime had unified with Montenegro and lands inhabited by South Slavs in the former Habsburg Empire to become the Kingdom of the Serbs, Croats and Slovenes (colloquially 'Yugoslavia'). During 1918–19, Kisby suggests, the Holme–Haverfield relationship had temporarily 'cooled', with Holme involved with the Scottish artist Dorothy Johnstone and spending time with a set of women artists in Kirkcudbright.[57] By 1919, however, Holme had joined Haverfield in Serbia. Haverfield's judgement of the amount of assistance still needed by the Yugoslav authorities, especially for the support of orphaned children, led her first to reorganize an existing orphanage in Užice, then to found a new one in Bajina Bašta.[58] Yet almost immediately Haverfield fell ill with pneumonia, and died on 21 March 1920.

Holme remained at Bajina Bašta along with (and would go on to live with) Margaret Greenlees and Margaret Ker. Also present was Alexandra Onslow, who taught gymnastics and sport at the orphanage. Onslow was the connection between Holme and Rojc, having met the Croatian painter quite soon after the end of the war, probably during a summer vacation on the Adriatic coast in 1919. Onslow and Rojc started a lifelong relationship. It is to Rojc, rather than Holme, that one must turn for a biography of Onslow: a biographical text about her called 'Sjene, svjetlo i mrak' ('Shadows, light and darkness') appears as a separate sheet of paper among the Rojc documents in Zagreb. According to this biography Onslow had also joined SWH, but followed a different path until meeting the Holme–Haverfield circle in Dobrudja. After the war she went with them to Bajina Bašta, and, Rojc wrote, 'with her friends [...] raise[d] 60 orphans of different nationalities and religions'.[59] The Anglo-Yugoslav lesbian network would continue from this point primarily in artistic social circles, through Onslow and her relationship with Rojc – a woman whose significance for inter-war Yugoslav art has only recently been re-evaluated.

After the War: Rojc, Onslow and the Yugoslav Art Scene

The re-evaluation of Rojc in Yugoslav art history exemplifies how feminist art history might revise earlier dismissals of women's art. Though Rojc's work has typically been viewed as feminine and retrograde for a time when avant-garde movements were internationally at a peak, writers such as Leonida Kovač have revalorized it by analysing Rojc's self-representational strategies: Kovač thus argued 'not only [did] her portraits reject the concept of bourgeois femininity, but they deny the act of gender identification'.[60] Rojc's gender politics, unusual for her time and context, become visible through Kovač's ability to consult Rojc's papers in the Kovačić collection – though Kovač, similarly to Kisby's approach to Holme, was concerned more with Rojc's own life than with the transnational networks into which her papers also offer insights.[61] Among the documents Kovač cites are two autobiographies by Rojc, one ending in about 1918 and one written some time before Onslow's death in 1949. Writing in the third person, Rojc describes her childhood and personality in ways that establish her as a modern, autonomous and one might say feminist subject:

> She was born in 1883, in muddy and dusty little Bjelovar, where she went to gymnasium. There, besides various lectures on how to become 'a useful member of the community', she took part in many physical fights for women's rights. The smallest and youngest child in class, she despised male friends because of their stupidity and cowardice, and proved to them that a strong body did not mean much compared to a fast, courageous spirit – and that applies to both sexes; she fought her first battles for equality. [...] When she was 7, she rejected the knowledge of God as her elders taught her, and made her own thinking on the laws of nature. In that sense, she invented the program of her life as a program of an intelligent being with her own will, and she followed that conviction all her life: 'I will not be a blind follower of nature'.[62]

By arrangement with her father, Rojc married the painter Branko Šenoa (1879–1939), in return for her father providing the means for her to continue her artistic work. Art historians have described other relationships between Rojc and notable Croatian women, including the painter Dora Car,[63] and the greatest Croatian opera diva, Milka Trnina, who goes unnamed in Rojc's unpublished autobiography.[64]

In 1923, Rojc started living with Alexandra Onslow, travelling to England with her in 1924–5 and afterwards settling and living openly together in Zagreb. Their house at 6 Rokov Perivoj Street was an artists' studio and salon, which Kovač compares to the Parisian 'literary salons of that time run by Alice B Toklas and Gertrude Stein in Rue des Fleures, or the one by writer Natalie Barney and painter Romaine Brooks in Rue Jacob'[65] – the very salons Heather Love has described as an emblematic site of sapphic modernities. Rojc's contacts extended beyond the art world and also included important Croatian women writers such as Ivana Brlić Mažuranić and Marija Jurić Zagorka. Yet the significance of the Rojc–Onslow connection was not only social: it was a resource that stimulated the progress of Yugoslav feminist and women's art. Rojc's presence and work, the support and foreign connections Onslow offered her and their combined organizational skills offered female artists new possibilities for organizing and exhibiting their work as alternatives to the existing and almost exclusively male-dominated art market. Transnational connections were thus not only private affairs; they enabled networking and support which were probably crucial for women artists' self-organizing at the time.

Rojc had several exhibitions in England in the 1920s, the most important probably being her participation in a collective exhibition organized around the Women's Art International Club (WAIC). WAIC had been founded in 1899 and aimed to offer women of all nationalities the possibility of professional-standard exhibitions. The example of WAIC inspired Rojc to found the Klub likovnih umjetnica (Club of Women Painters), the first professional women's arts organization in the Balkans, in 1928. Rojc had help from Alexandra Onslow and her connections (one of these being the Queen of Yugoslavia, Marija Karađorđević, later to become patron of the club). The club's first exhibition opening received disdainful and mocking reviews from male critics, who wrote that 'our ladies' had decided to play with art; they had exhibited without any professional criteria; their work was outdated; and they were the only ones who dared not to have a jury select the works for exhibition (as was normal practice at the time). These reviews in *Narodne novine* and other newspapers were marked by misogyny and the attitude that those rare women who made 'good art' should not be mixed with the other female amateurs; they also reacted to the exhibition's alternative style, atypical for its time.

Rojc implicitly countered all these arguments in an article for Marija Jurić Zagorka's magazine *Ženski list* (*Women's Magazine*). Explaining how the exhibition had been organized, she emphasized that existing criteria – including selection of exhibits by jury, stylistic rigidity and repressive professionalism – could not apply to their work, which had been carried out in a spirit of solidarity, friendship and freedom, producing an alternative aesthetic:

> In the preparation of the exhibition there was no 'jury' or committee. All colleagues edited the show together, amicably, according to the best convictions. How this experiment of freedom, unity and collegiality turned out shows the top layout of the exhibition and the various criticisms of gentlemen critics. [...] without the jury – putting the paintings together so they look better together – we were all very satisfied.

[...]

The pavilion was in very poor condition and all of it was fixed and arranged with our devoted female care, avoiding city government and repairing the smashed glass roof through which rain was dripping into the hall. We, women, performed there together for the first time – in a wonderful harmony.[66]

Rather than excusing a badly reviewed amateur exhibition, Rojc was pointing to different criteria and an alternative relation to artistic and exhibitionary practice: clearly, Rojc and her friends and colleagues found collaborative working, support, solidarity and mutual respect to be more relevant for their exhibiting practice than juries, prevailing discourses of style or critics' judgement. They thus positioned themselves as the alternative to hierarchized structures and distribution of power in the art world. Although the critics who saw the exhibition as backward looking for the late 1920s were constituting themselves as part of an avant-garde by doing so, an exhibition which refused to follow even the conventions of a semi-institutionalized avant-garde was paradoxically *more* alternative than the critics were.[67] Rojc could thus be seen as the most visible representative of sapphic modernity and disturbing new sexual female identities in Yugoslavia – through her open sexuality, her clothing style, her cigarette smoking, her travel, her painting and her emancipation, but also her creation of female networks established through solidarity and mutual support.

Solidarity and mutual support likewise characterized the friendships Holme established and maintained through relief work, leisure time, letters and visits after the war, including her friendship with Rojc. After Haverfield's death, Holme moved back to Scotland with Greenlees and Ker, and according to Emily Hamer all three lived together until Ker moved out in the 1930s. Holme and Greenlees stayed together until Greenlees died.[68] However, Holme did remain tied to Yugoslavia: her papers testify to several trips with friends through the Mediterranean and Adriatic in the mid-1920s, sailing on the yacht *Festina Lente*. Rojc and Holme were exchanging letters throughout the Twenties, and Holme probably visited Rojc and Onslow in Zagreb.[69] She stayed in correspondence with Flora Sandes, and offered to work in a relief mission in Valona (Albania) in 1925,[70] all the while keeping up with affairs in Yugoslavia. Still connected with certain organizations and individuals, Holme, Ker and Greenlees visited Serbia again in the 1930s, and their visit gained attention from the press.[71] Apparently, the networks created in the war were too strong to be forgotten.

Even the Holme–Haverfield relationship, at the beginning of the 1930s, seemed to receive some unofficial recognition. On 3 September 1930, one Lena Joričić wrote to Holme that the Health Centre and one street in Bajina Bašta would bear Haverfield's name:

The League of Health in Belgrade was informed of these resolutions and has been asked if possible to communicate with any members of Mrs Haverfield's family [...] I think all this will interest you as you were so closely connected with Mrs Haverfield.[72]

The League of Health officially invited Holme to the opening ceremony.[73] There is no evidence Holme attended, but in 1933 Onslow and Rojc travelled together to Bajina Bašta to visit another ceremony in Haverfield's honour.[74] Anglo-Yugoslav lesbian networks thus began during the Great War, extended through post-war relief work, and were sustained through correspondence and occasional travel.

Beyond their significance for revealing the histories of individual lives, the Rojc and Holme collections can therefore also be used to reveal the level of SWH women's integration into wartime Serbia's high society and to cast light on the transposability and maintaining of unconventional lifestyles in a new context and environment. In this sense, the papers of Nasta Rojc contain an interesting photograph, taken by Onslow while she posed for Rojc, showing the painter painting the picture of her model. On the back is written: 'To captain Onslow, from your wild Yugoslav', with obvious sense for simultaneous irony and self-exoticization. 'Wild Yugoslavs' apparently found common language with British visitors within a mutually comprehensible set of signifiers known to historians of sexuality as 'sapphic modernities'.

Conclusion

The British volunteers were able to gain widespread acceptance in wartime Serbia through their ethnicity, their class, and the social and cultural capital they enjoyed as a result. Wartime conditions strengthened this, as their class alliance with the military elite enabled a redefinition of their own gender roles: the Serbian patriarchal order permitted them a privileged position where they could equally discuss political news with members of the elite and enjoy ordinary people's admiration and gratitude. One picturesque sentence allegedly circulated about Elsie Inglis: 'In Britain, they made her the doctor and we would have proclaimed her a saint.' Inglis, like Haverfield, would be among six British women volunteers commemorated on a set of Serbian stamps in 2015 – though without reference to their partnerships with women.[75] The British women had been allowed much that Serbian women were not, and that they themselves were not allowed in Britain.[76] Their proclaimed love for Serbia, their sacrifices, the money they collected and bombastic statements like Haverfield's deathbed cry of 'what will happen with Serbian children?'[77] must have their roots in this complex trade-off of ethnicized, class-marked and gendered positions.

While some SWH members, especially those outside the upper and upper-middle classes, faced a backlash after the Great War,[78] the changes war had brought also permitted some lesbians to expand their post-war networks and culture. Through the romantic and friendship networks described in this chapter, especially the partnership of Rojc and Onslow, part of that culture merged with part of the Yugoslav or at least the Zagreb art scene. The case of Rojc, Onslow and Holme thus presents a transposition of incipient modern sexual identities that influenced Yugoslav society, culture and art subtly but irrevocably, notably through a feminist politics of togetherness that women artists drew on in building an alternative model of knowledge production and creative esteem. The networks that developed around them were a transnational formation which needs to be recognized as such to provide a full context to this aspect of lesbian or queer history in Serbia *or* Britain, demonstrating that European gender history cannot be neatly separated into isolated eastern and western halves.

Notes

1. See, e.g., Laura Doan and Jane Garrity (eds), *Sapphic Modernities: Sexuality, Women and National Culture* (Basingstoke: Palgrave Macmillan, 2006); Ann T. Allen, *Women in Twentieth-Century Europe* (Basingstoke: Palgrave Macmillan, 2007); Ana Carden-Coyne (ed.), *Gender and Conflict since 1914* (Basingstoke: Palgrave Macmillan, 2012); Laura Doan, *Disturbing Practices: History, Sexuality, and Women's Experience of Modern War* (Chicago, IL: University of Chicago Press, 2013).
2. Inderpal Grewal and Caren Kaplan, 'Theorizing Transnational Studies of Sexuality', *GLQ* vol. 7, no. 4 (2001): 666.
3. Rojc's papers are part of the private collection of Dr Josip Kovačić, Zagreb. Holme's papers are held at The Women's Library (London School of Economics and Political Science Special Collections), ref. '7VJH' (archival references in this chapter beginning '7VJH' relate to these). Anna Kisby, 'Vera "Jack" Holme: Cross-Dressing Actress, Suffragette and Chauffeur', *Women's History Review* vol. 23, no. 1 (2014): 120–36 uses the Holme papers but is not primarily interested in Holme's encounters with the Yugoslav region.
4. Olga Dimitrijević is the primary author of this chapter. Catherine Baker has assisted with sections on the transnational history of sexuality, current British historical research on Holme, and final revisions.
5. Emma Donoghue, 'Doing Lesbian History, Then and Now', *Historical Reflections/ Réflexions Historiques* vol. 33, no. 1 (2007): 17.
6. See Ljiljana Kolešnik, 'Autoportreti Naste Rojc: stvaranje predodžbe naglašenog rodnog identiteta u hrvatskoj umjetnosti ranog modernizma', *Radovi instituta za povijest umetnosti*, no. 24 (2000): 187–204; Leonida Kovač, *Anonimalia: normativni diskurzi i samoreprezentacija umjetnica 20. stoljeća* (Zagreb: Antibarbarus, 2010).
7. Jelisaveta Blagojević and Olga Dimitrijević (eds), *Među nama: neispričane priče gej i lezbejskih života* (Belgrade: Heartefact Fund, 2014).
8. See Zaharijević, this volume; Baker, this volume.
9. See Doan, *Disturbing Practices*, 3.
10. Emily Hamer, 'Keeping their Fingers on the Pulse: Lesbian Doctors in Britain 1890–1950', in Franz X. Eder, Gert Hekma and Lesley A. Hall (eds), *Sexual Cultures in Europe: Themes in Sexuality* (Manchester: Manchester University Press, 1999), 154.
11. Terry Castle, *The Literature of Lesbianism* (New York: Columbia University Press, 2003).
12. Laura Doan and Jane Garrity (eds), *Sapphic Modernities: Sexuality, Women and National Culture* (Basingstoke: Palgrave Macmillan, 2006).
13. Nan Alamilla Boyd, 'The Materiality of Gender: Looking for Lesbian Bodies in Transgender History', *Journal of Lesbian History*, vol. 3, no. 3 (1999): 77. See also Judith Halberstam, *In a Queer Time and Place* (New York: New York University Press, 2005); Baker, this volume.
14. See Kovač, *Anonimalia*.
15. Jill Liddington, 'Britain in the Balkans: the Response of the Scottish Women's Hospital Units', in Ingrid Sharp and Matthew Stibbe (eds), *Aftermaths of War: Women's Movements and Female Activists, 1918–1923* (Leiden: Brill), 395–417; Olga Dimitrijević, 'Neočekivani savezi: britanske lezbejke u Srbiji i Prvi svetski rat', in Blagojević and Dimitrijević (eds), *Među nama*, 68–83.
16. Emily Hamer, *Britannia's Glory: a History of Twentieth-Century Lesbians* (London: Cassell, 1996).
17. Kisby, 'Holme'.

18. E.g. Hamer, *Britannia's Glory*; Doan, *Disturbing Practices*; Rebecca Jennings, *A Lesbian History of Britain: Love and Sex Between Women since 1500* (Oxford: Greenwood, 2007); Alison Oram, *Her Husband was a Woman: Women's Gender-Crossing in Modern British Popular Culture* (London: Routledge, 2007).

19. Oram, *Husband*, 3; Doan, *Disturbing Practices*.

20. Ana Stolić and Aleksandra Vuletić, "'...Brak je zajednica muškarca i žene...": koncept heteroseksualnosti, bračna politika i seksualne prakse u Srbiji 19. veka', in Blagojević and Dimitrijević (eds), *Među nama: neispričane priče gej i lezbejskih života*, 60–7.

21. Elisabeth Crawford, *The Women's Suffrage Movement: a Reference Guide 1866–1928* (London: UCL Press, 1999).

22. June Purvis, 'The Pankhursts and the Great War', in Alison S. Fell and Ingrid Sharp (eds), *The Women's Movement in Wartime: International Perspectives, 1914–19* (Basingstoke: Palgrave Macmillan, 2007), 141–57.

23. Doan, *Disturbing Practices*, 106.

24. Radclyffe Hall, *The Well of Loneliness* (Knoxville, TN: Wordsworth Classics, 2005 [1928]), 245.

25. Doan, *Disturbing Practices*, vii.

26. See Doan, *Disturbing Practices*, 21.

27. Judith Halberstam, *Female Masculinity* (Durham, NC: Duke University Press, 1998), 87.

28. Hamer, *Britannia's Glory*, 55.

29. Monica Krippner, 'The Work of British Medical Women in Serbia During and After the First World War', in John B. Allcock and Antonia Young (eds), *Black Lambs and Grey Falcons: Women Travelling in the Balkans* (Oxford: Berghahn, 2000), 73.

30. Liddington, 'Britain in the Balkans', 395; Hamer, 'Keeping their Fingers on the Pulse', 146.

31. Liddington, 'Britain in the Balkans', 395.

32. Katherine Storr, *Excluded from the Record: Women Refugees and Relief 1914–1929* (Bern: Peter Lang, 2010), 196.

33. Elsie Inglis, 'The Tragedy of Serbia', in Angela K. Smith (ed.), *Women's Writing of the First World War: an Anthology* (Manchester: Manchester University Press, 2000), 264.

34. Kisby, 'Holme', 127.

35. Martin Pugh, *The Pankhursts* (London: Allen Lane, 2001), 153; Katharine Cockin, 'Edith Craig and the Pioneer Players: London's International Art Theatre in a "Khaki-Clad and Khaki-Minded World"', in Andrew Maunder (ed.), *British Theatre and the Great War, 1914-1919: New Perspectives* (Basingstoke: Palgrave Macmillan, 2015), 133.

36. Kisby, 'Holme', 128. Monica Krippner, *The Quality of Mercy: Women at War, Serbia 1915–18* (Newton Abbot: David and Charles, 1980), writes (p. 73) that 'Mrs Haverfield's private life was unhappy' and of her two dissolved marriages, but does not mention Holme.

37. Bernard A. Cook, *Women and War: a Historical Encyclopedia from Antiquity to the Present* (Santa Barbara, CA: ABC-CLIO, 2006), 277.

38. Kisby, 'Holme', 131; see also Storr, *Excluded from the Record*, 205.

39. Liddington, 'Britain in the Balkans', 409.

40. Kisby, 'Holme', 132.

41. Doan and Garrity (eds), *Sapphic Modernities*.

42. Heather K. Love, 'Impossible Objects: Waiting for the Revolution in *Summer Will Show*', in Doan and Garrity (eds), *Sapphic Modernities*, 145.

43. 7VJH/2/5/06.
44. Jelena Petrović, 'Rod i žensko autorstvo u književnoj kulturi i javnim diskursima u Jugoslaviji između dva svetska rata' (PhD thesis, Institutum Studiorum Humanitatis, University of Ljubljana, 2009), 16.
45. Dubravka Stojanović, 'U senci "velikog narativa": stanje zdravlja žena i dece u Srbiji početkom XX veka', in Latinka Perović, Vera Gudac Dodić, Momčilo Isić, Dubravka Stojanović, Sanja Petrović Todosijević, Olivera Milosavljević, Andreja Šemjakin, Radmila Radić and Aleksandra Vuletić, *Srbija u modernizacijskim procesima 19. i 20. veka: žene i deca* (Belgrade: Helsinški odbor za ljudska prava u Srbiji, 2006), 163.
46. 7VJH/2/5/03.
47. 7VJH/2/5/03.
48. 7VJH/2/5/03.
49. 7VJH/2/5/06; Kisby, 'Holme', 130.
50. Crawford, *The Women's Suffrage Movement*, 289.
51. The *Women and War* encyclopedia claims that Yovitchitch was a lover of another unconventional SWH member in the Balkans, Olive Kelso King: Cook, *Women and War*, 341.
52. Dimitrijević, 'Neočekivani savezi'.
53. Julie Wheelwright, 'Captain Flora Sandes: a Case Study of the Social Construction of Gender in a Serbian Context', in Allcock and Young (eds), *Black Lambs and Grey Falcons*, 94.
54. Wheelwright, 'Sandes', 94.
55. Wheelwright, 'Sandes', 95.
56. 7VJH2/5/06; 7VJH2/5/07.
57. Kisby, 'Holme', 132.
58. 7VJH/3/2/04.
59. Rojc, 'Sjene, svjetlo i mrak'. Collection of Josip Kovačić.
60. Kovač, *Anonimalia*, 113.
61. Kovačić had bought Rojc's archive from her friend and later carer Jelena Puškarić.
62. Kovač, *Anonimalia*, 82.
63. Kolešnik, 'Autoportreti'.
64. Kovač, *Anonimalia*.
65. Kovač, *Anonimalia*. 87.
66. *Ženski list*, no. 11 (1928), 23.
67. See Kovač, *Anonimalia*.
68. Hamer, *Britannia's Glory*, 57.
69. 7VJH/3/4/06.
70. 7VJH/3/4/15.
71. 7VJH/2/1/05, 7VJH/2/1/06.
72. 7VJH/3/4/01.
73. 7VJH/3/4/33.
74. 7VJH/3/4/35.
75. The others were Sandes and three other medical women (Katherine MacPhail, Isabel Hutton and Elizabeth Ross): Milan Grba, 'Serbia Celebrates British Heroines of the First World War', *British Library: European Studies*, 14 February 2016, available at: http://britishlibrary.typepad.co.uk/european/2016/02/serbia-celebrates-british-heroines-of-the-first-world-war.html# (accessed 28 April 2016).
76. See Allcock and Young (eds), *Black Lambs and Grey Falcons*.
77. 7VJH/3/2/04.
78. Liddington, 'Britain in the Balkans'.

3

Creating 'New Soviet Women' in Armenia? Gender and Tradition in the Early Soviet South Caucasus

Jo Laycock and Jeremy Johnson

If in the previous chapter's example the political and social transformations of the Great War created conditions for renegotiating gendered 'modernities' among small, alternative circles, this chapter demonstrates that under state socialism notions of modernities, in tension with notions of tradition, were also a basis for the Communist Party and the state itself to reorder gender regimes. This would be visible in the USSR after the second Russian Revolution of 1917 and the Russian Civil War of 1917–22, a generation before eastern Europe, where state socialist regimes came to power in 1945–8. The size of the USSR also emphasizes an observation that should also be taken into account for eastern Europe: that gender regimes were and are not monolithic across the whole of society but rather stratified by other dimensions of identity and social hierarchy. Gender historians have demonstrated this for the USSR by turning their lens beyond Russia and the other so-called 'European' republics to study Soviet gender regimes in the Caucasus and Central Asia, where processes and outcomes were often very different. This chapter illustrates this approach through the case of efforts to create 'New Soviet Women' in Armenia and the rest of the South Caucasus – where more 'transnational formations' of humanitarianism and gender could be observed. At the same time, it raises problems about how historians might approach concepts of ethnic and national identity which will recur throughout the intersections of gender, ethnicity and nation in this volume.[1]

Indeed, the modern history of the South Caucasus has been an important case study for historical scholarship since the fall of the USSR which has sought to develop historical and theoretical perspectives on ethnic and national identities.[2] This focus on the national has dominated the field, with much of the recent historical literature addressing the construction of national identities in the early Soviet period and the rise of nationalism during and after the fall of the Soviet Union – even more for the South Caucasus than the historiography of the USSR in general. This is because the breakdown of the USSR in this region was dominated by the questioning of Soviet-defined national borders and competing claims to territory by titular nationalities and minorities. Much of the international scholarship on Armenia and Azerbaijan has sought to untangle the origins of the 'frozen' Nagorno-Karabagh conflict, while research on the Georgian case has addressed the related problems of ethnic and regional conflict and the emergence of de facto states. This context of conflict has meanwhile meant that local historiographies have been shaped by a perceived need to define and defend exclusive national histories, identities and traditions. Similar trends may be observed in the historiography of other regions which have experienced 'ethnic' conflicts since the fall of the Soviet Union, notably the Balkans.[3] However, this focus on the origins of contemporary conflicts has meant that other aspects of the region's social and cultural history, not least questions of gender and sexuality, have thus far been neglected.

Redressing the balance, this chapter takes the case of Soviet Armenia in the 1920s and examines the complexities of attempts by Soviet and international actors to transform the lives of women in the region during this period. It thus challenges the common perception that the history of gender in the South Caucasus is a straightforward narrative of Soviet 'modernization' versus indigenous 'tradition'. Although its particular geographical focus is just one of the Soviet Republics of Transcaucasia, Armenia, the analysis sheds light on questions pertinent to the broader region.

Indeed, gender and sexuality, although many historians neglect them, remain highly relevant in the region today. Both have recently been the subjects of intensive public debate and political activism in Transcaucasia and causes of social, cultural and political conflict. The 'transition' from state socialism there, as in other regions of the former Soviet Union, has been a gendered and unequal experience, with women in many ways faring worse: in the words of the scholar of post-Soviet Armenian society Armine Ishkanian, 'women have not only become the majority of the unemployed, but have also become depoliticized and are largely left out of the government, political parties, and the official public sphere'. At the same time, however, Ishkanian stresses that women are not simply 'victims' of the fall of the Soviet Union – they have found means to resist and partake in the public sphere, for example through non-governmental organization (NGO) activism.[4]

Contemporary conflicts around gender and sexuality have taken a variety of forms. In Armenia, the gendering of the process of 'transition' has been characterized by an increasing prevalence of discourses of feminine identity premised on domesticity, motherhood and female purity linked to notions of national and religious 'tradition'.[5] Local activists have also advocated vocally to improve the legal protections for Armenian women against the not uncommon, yet taboo, problem of domestic violence.[6] The fiercest conflicts have been, however, centred on homosexuality and LGBT rights.[7] In Armenia in 2013, the introduction of a new law 'On Equal Rights and Equal Opportunities for Men and Women', which defined gender as 'acquired and socially fixed behaviour of different sexes', produced a significant backlash among the Armenian public who argued that this was a European attempt to introduce 'immorality' – in particular homosexuality – to Armenia.[8] Yet these gendered discourses of family and tradition are not novel productions of the post-Soviet context. Rather, they are selective re-articulations of pre-existing gendered discourses of 'Armenian-ness' and a conception of the 'nation as family' in which women occupy the place of mothers and caregivers at national and familial levels.[9] This chapter argues that the concept of 'tradition' invoked in contemporary articulations of these discourses masks complex, contingent and contested sets of gender relations and identities past and present.

The dynamics of gender and sexuality politics in the three nations of the South Caucasus are framed by particular histories and social, political, economic and religious contexts. They cannot be reduced to a single 'problem'. Nonetheless there are common threads across national boundaries. Firstly, these issues are frequently framed as a conflict between indigenous 'traditions' and alien behaviours and practices emanating from 'the West'. These 'Western' incursions are frequently portrayed by political and/or religious elites as a threat to national integrity or authenticity.[10] Secondly, 'homosexuality' seems to have become the favoured symbol of 'immorality' and of the wider undoing of 'traditional' gender relations and moralities. In other words, expressions of intolerance of homosexuality are bound up with wider fears about the destabilizing of gender norms, hierarchies and the wider familial and social order.[11]

The discourses of 'tradition' which are invoked in response to these perceived threats in order to maintain the status quo and target those who transgress rely on conceptions of local gender norms and identities which are essentialist and ahistorical. Yet, as Ulrike Ziemer has demonstrated in her work on young Armenian women in Krasnodar Krai, resort to 'tradition' cannot provide a full explanation for specific sets of gender norms and relations, rather contemporary social and political contexts must be taken account of.[12] Unpicking gendered discourses framed as tradition, we suggest, demands paying attention to the historical specificities of their social and cultural construction. The 1920s, a period of social, economic and political change during which radical schemes were espoused to transform Armenian society, is an ideal period from which to begin. Our analysis focuses on the female population, as this was explicitly the object of attempts to transform gender roles and relationships during this period.[13]

Conceptualizing and Historicizing Gender in 'the Caucasus'

Although historical analyses of gender in the South Caucasus are relatively sparse, gendered stereotypes of the region abound, especially in popular journalism, literature and travel writing. These stereotypes have their origins in the Russian imperial encounter with the Caucasus and emphasize the wild, untamed and violent nature of the region and its inhabitants during the 19th century.[14] Western European representations of the region were produced in a different context yet share many common features of the Russian mode.[15] The Caucasus is represented as the crossroads of Europe and Asia, an unknowable and inaccessible region. Ethnically diverse and politically distinct regions are brought together in stereotypes which simultaneously homogenize and fracture the region into a patchwork of 'ethnic' identities prone to violence and conflict.[16]

These representations were inherently gendered. Local men were represented as untamed and brave, violent and lustful while local women were frequently represented in terms of well-worn orientalist tropes – exotic beauty, mystery and passivity. In the case of Armenians and Georgians, such stereotypes were complicated by the fact that these were Christian women, which tended only to amplify western European curiosities. While these 19th-century representations of the region have been re-articulated multiple times in the context of changing political and social circumstances, some of the gendered dimensions of these representations have endured. In terms of this chapter, more significant than the particularities of these representations is their overarching effect, the gendered construction of the Caucasus as 'other'. Despite recent scholarly attempts to deconstruct these discourses of Caucasian 'otherness', portrayals of the region as 'different' continue to proliferate.[17] Concurrent with this has been an assumption that it is the enduring and ahistorical power of tradition, understood as a product of a unique, isolated or liminal environment, which shapes local societies, cultures and politics – not least in terms of gender norms and relations.[18] Such dependence on stereotypes of tradition and 'otherness' is compounded by the still-influential assumption that Soviet rule in the region kept the 'traditional' identities, practices and conflicts of the Caucasus in check while the fall of the Soviet Union opened the floodgates for their resurgence. While recent scholarship has demonstrated that this approach is at best simplistic, its effects remain powerful.[19]

Narrating Soviet Armenia During the Soviet Period

Significant research has of course been carried out on the history of gender within Soviet Russia. Although local reception of Soviet projects to reform women's roles in Central Asia is the subject of a growing body of scholarship, Transcaucasia remains little studied in this regard. Much of the extant scholarship about the history of 1920s and 1930s South Caucasian social reform has been extrapolated from sources that address the Soviet Union at large. The main Anglophone source on Soviet social reforms in Armenia has long been Mary Matossian's groundbreaking *Impact of Soviet Policies in Armenia*, a text compiled mainly from secondary sources but also shaped by Matossian's three-week visit to the region in 1957. This source has been used by many scholars of Armenia to draw conclusions about the experience of women in contemporary Armenian society as well as Soviet Armenia. However, the extent to which Matossian's experience allowed her to understand the experience of average citizens in Armenia during her visit was limited, due to her restrictive guides and the extent to which she was monitored.

An examination of the most substantial piece of Matossian's text about women and the women's section of the Secretariat of the Central Committee, *Zhenotdel* (in Russian) or *Kinbazhin* (in Armenian), is necessary to locate the historiographical point of reference of contemporary scholars.[20] Most scholars who have made reference to women in Soviet Armenia have focused on the women's sector, the Kinbazhin. Matossian claims that the Kinbazhin helped reproduce the principles of the Communist Party among women, aided in the legal and educational support of women, helped with access to free abortion and provided women with employment opportunities.[21]

Matossian's description of a multifunctional organization that negotiated many spaces and identities raises a number of questions. The Kinbazhin was involved in the processes of the urbanization and industrialization of Armenia. It also had authority over women's bodies and served as a regulatory force shaping the notions of sexuality of women and men. As described, it would seem that this organization would have had a substantial impact on daily life until it was reduced in status in 1929.[22] However, Matossian's information about and analysis of women's position in Soviet Armenia in the 1920s derive primarily from sources describing the state of these issues in the early Soviet Union, or even Russia in particular, for example L. E. Luke's *Marxian Woman: Soviet Variants*.[23] The post-Soviet historiography of 1920s Georgia and Azerbaijan has been influenced by this scholarly tendency to extrapolate from general Soviet trends rather than regionally specific records, in part because of the lack of access to regional archival materials during the Soviet period.

Regional archival sources, however, allow us to paint a fuller picture of early Soviet life. Armenian women were able to move across Soviet categories, and Armenia's liminal position helped determine the multiplicity of forces inside and outside the Soviet Union that shaped gender as experienced, represented and embodied. Armenia was not merely a more traditional space on the edge of Soviet space, but a site of complex interactions between historically embedded ideologies of tradition and modernization which produced diverse and at times seemingly contradictory everyday experiences. Access to today's open regional archives allow scholars to better understand the roles of women in early Armenian Soviet society and the experienced realities of everyday citizens without unnecessarily extrapolating from data collected exclusively in Russia.

Soviet Women of the (Near) East

While the 'New Soviet Woman' provided a model for the reform of gender identities during the early Soviet period, the early Soviet state did not approach the population of the former Russian Empire as a uniform block. Rather, it attempted to negotiate the complexities and diversity of the female population through the use of categories such as 'women of the East', drawing on imperial discourses in order to frame understandings of backwardness and the path to Soviet progress. In theory, 'women of the East' described the population of the Southern peripheries of the Soviet Union. The case of Armenia, however, highlights some of the problems inherent in the deployment of this category and its consequences.

Soviet campaigns targeting the 'women of the East' sought to position women as specific targets of reform within a landscape of Muslim nations and societies lacking literate cultures and national histories. Armenia's position as a nation of the Near East with an already evolving history of national, cultural and political institutions made it an uneasy fit for such campaigns. The situation of women in Armenia was at times seen by central and local Soviet actors as analogous to the situation of women in Central Asia and at times as different. Armenian women specifically, and women of the South Caucasus more generally, were seen by the Zhenotdel as lead actors in a peripheral topography of 'Eastern' backwardness that stretched across the Caucasus and Central Asia. They were the group thought to be most capable of rapid progress from the imagined geography of backwardness towards the spaces of socialist modernity.[24]

Adopting these broad categories as the basis for schemes to transform the lives of women in reality presented a multitude of problems. For example, a pamphlet produced by the Transcaucasian women's sector about women of the East used the terms 'Near East' to describe the Caucasus and 'East' to describe other regions in the southern and eastern peripheries of the USSR, including Turkey.[25] The women of the East were invited to join forces with the women of the Near East (Caucasus) to overcome the oppressive forces of patriarchy, to become educated and resist the influence of the mullahs. But what if, as in the case of Armenia, there were not mullahs to resist? The non-Muslim populations of the 'Near East' were thus an uneasy fit for these emergent revolutionary categories. The uncertainty with which activists in the Caucasus used the category 'women of the East' is clear when they seek to imagine themselves within the new Soviet East.

The situation was further complicated by the fact that this geography of backwardness did not reflect the complexities of ethnic and religious identifications and conflicts on the ground in the Transcaucasian Republics. While Armenians and Turkic peoples inhabited the same regions and settlements, there was substantial conflict between the two groups as Armenians and Turks displaced during the events of World War I and its aftermaths made competing claims for land.[26] These divisions and conflicts were echoed in the sphere of the women's sector where, for example, there were very few cases where ethnic Armenian activists would be actively involved with Turkish women's projects, even in Yerevan where the women's sector largely supported Turkish theatrical and educational projects. The Armenian 'new woman' was therefore envisioned through a different and separate institutional framework than the Turkish new woman that she in reality lived alongside.

Meanwhile, local Armenian activists in regional and local publications usually referred exclusively to Turks and Kurds in discussions of 'women of the East'. This practice demonstrated that ethnically Armenian women at times did not recognize themselves as part of the category of 'women of the East' and saw themselves as distinct from the Turkish women who shared their national space. They would, for example, specifically request Turkish trainers to deal with the problems facing those ethnicities they viewed as 'women of the East' living among the Armenian population in Soviet Armenia. At times, questions regarding 'women of the East' would be addressed directly to the Muslim section in Armenia, bypassing the women's sector altogether.[27] Such practices demonstrated an awareness of ethnic or national difference on the part of the women's section at a local level which was apparently invisible at the centre.

The position of Armenian women within an overarching Soviet imagined geography of the East was therefore disrupted and re-articulated, at least in part by the perceptions of Armenian elites and the leaders of the Armenian women's section who saw themselves as more progressive and therefore less in need of reform then their neighbours. This self-understanding was in part informed by transnational discourses which had emerged in European 'Armenophile' circles in the final decades of the late 19th century in response to the politics of the 'Eastern Question' and concerns regarding the treatment of Christian minorities in the Ottoman Empire. Armenia was positioned as a civilized space in need of, and deserving of, 'rescue' from the 'less civilized' (and predominantly Islamic) cultures which surrounded it.[28] Such perceptions had come to the fore during World War I and not only shaped articulations of international responsibilities towards the Armenian people but also shaped Armenian elites' own self-understandings and visions of their national future. Sovietization did not simply erase these discourses. Thus, both long-standing notions of Armenian 'civilization' and their counterpart, stereotypes of Turkish barbarism or backwardness, informed the approaches local Soviet actors deployed when participating in Soviet projects of social reform.

The Veil of Unveiling

The campaign against the veil or chadra in Armenia provides a strong example of the ways in which Armenian activists sought to model both good Armenian women and good Soviet 'new women'.[29] In 1928, the campaign to unveil women stretched across the Soviet Southern periphery.[30] Women set ablaze their former facial garments and proudly displayed unveiled heads to Soviet society. Removing the veil was part of a larger Soviet project of modernization that labelled the veil as a site of gender inequality and factor inhibiting the building of socialism. In Armenia, veiling practices varied across regions, with some national minority populations covering the entire face while other groups covered only parts of faces or merely the hair and neck. The Kinbazhin sought out veiled Armenians and extended their understanding of what constituted 'the veil' to include pieces of fabric that covered the chin or hair coverings.[31] The justification for the removal of these traditional forms of dress was largely made through frequent public health concerns that these pieces of fabric were unclean and might spread disease.[32]

The Armenian woman was unveiled with great success in the late 1920s, in part because many women were not veiled (in a traditional sense) in the first place. Public performances of unveilings were conducted by activists, some of whom never actually wore veils in real life. Public performances of Armenian women sometimes involved performing Russian-language scripts for a Muslim audience. The public performances were often described in *Hayastani Ashkhatavoruhi* (*Armenian Worker Woman*) magazine and the newspapers *Communist* and *Soviet Armenia*. Donning veils to tear them off aligned Armenian women with the 'women of the East', but also demonstrated their ability to overcome this 'predicament' and provided a model of the good 'New Soviet Woman'. This 'performance' was particularly important given that most documentary evidence from the Armenian archives suggests that rural women's activists struggled to engage their communities in schemes for reform and social

missionary activities in the former Ottoman Empire and the value placed on hard work and self-improvement as part of a 'civilizing' process. It was also connected to moral readings of poverty and beliefs about the ill-effects of 'idleness' which shaped 19th-century charitable and philanthropic practice at 'home' in Britain. These discourses manifested themselves in a particular way in the aftermath of mass displacement, which was thought to be a breeding ground for 'idleness'. Self-help through 'constructive labour' was therefore prescribed as a means of avoiding personal and national 'degeneration'.[52] Refugee women were thought to be at particular risk and priority was placed upon finding them acceptable means of 'self-help', lest they turn to the unacceptable alternative of prostitution.

Such 'self-help' programmes were seen as a way to provide for basic needs and a means of safeguarding morality. The range of 'acceptable' work for women was, however, limited. 'Traditional' crafts, such as embroidery and spinning, had found favour as acceptable occupations for women in missionary settings in the Ottoman Empire in the 19th century.[53] During the war such methods had been adapted for the purposes of relief and idealized as a means of preserving Armenian culture. The LMF and NER continued this work in Soviet Armenia but also expanded the scope of acceptable women's work to nursing and teaching. The relief agents of the LMF and NER did not, however, espouse ideals for the construction of the 'New Soviet Woman' and the full participation of women in the world of work, instead maintaining a quite rigid belief in a gendered division of labour.[54] The education and training programmes that they provided for young girls and women focused almost exclusively on the domestic sphere, in contrast to education for boys and young men which was centred on cultivating physical fitness and practical vocational training.[55] The rationale for this was usually articulated in terms of the strength and significance of 'traditional' women's roles.

Although the NER and LMF accepted the fundamental principle that Armenian women belonged to the domestic sphere, they did not shy from critiquing the way in which this sphere functioned. In an unpublished account of NER's work, the former NER relief agent Randall McAfee observed that '[t]he lot of the peasant woman, a drudge in the home and a driven labourer in the fields, is different from that of the pampered favourite in the harem but the estate of neither offers any attractions to the woman of a free society'.[56] International relief organizations were not prepared to simply accept the Armenian domestic sphere in its existing form. Rather, they sought to improve upon the status quo by reshaping the lives of women, and the domestic sphere more broadly. James Barton characterized this as a:

> slow planting of better social ideas [...] in many of the 1,800 villages of the Caucasus, Syria and Greece [...] The social ideas cover principally: ways of working, home making, care of babies, changed attitude towards marriage, recreation, honest endeavour, co-operation, citizenship, human service and rural welfare.[57]

While it is tempting to frame the work of international humanitarian organizations among Armenian refugee women in opposition to the Soviet project – preserving traditional social roles and values in the face of radical change – the reality was more complex. Both the Soviets and international organizations sought to transform Armenian women in order to create an improved, 'modern' version of Armenian society. In the case of maternal health policy, their agendas overlapped and reinforced each other; in other cases, such as 'women's work' and the domestic sphere, they conflicted. In the context of post-war Transcaucasia, both projects were in reality limited by lack of resources and infrastructure. The transformation of Armenian women's lives therefore remained an uneven, incomplete process which opened up spaces in which local re-articulations and resistance were possible.

Conclusion

The practice of extrapolation from a general 'Soviet' experience onto the South Caucasus has meant that the unevenness and complexities of the process of local transformation and reform have been glossed over. Returning to the work of Mary Matossian reveals some of the flaws in this narrative of homogeneous transformation. Matossian painted a picture of a gradual but comprehensive transformation of the lives of women on 'Soviet' lines enacted through the Kinbazhin. Yet the travel notes from her 1957 trip create a rather different image of gender relations in rural Armenia:

> in certain remote districts of Armenia women still wear the national costume and cover the lower part of their faces [...] The repatriate girls claim that the local boys think a woman is only good for sex, and between the sexes there is little real friend-ship and camaraderie as we know it in the West [...] [there are] still vestiges of patriarchal customs even in Erevan [...] There are still some arranged marriages in Erevan [...] Soviet husbands *never* help with housework.[58]

Patriarchal structures remained powerful throughout the Soviet and post-Soviet period in the South Caucasus. The frequent use of the term 'traditional' to describe these structures reflects a common assumption that they are unchang-ing or inevitable. This chapter has demonstrated that the reality is more complex. The pre-Soviet social structures of the Ottoman and Russian Empires were themselves diverse, not characterized by a uniform set of gender norms and relations. During the Soviet period, the transformation of women's lives was not straightforward; throughout the 1920s multiple visions for the 'modernization' of women's lives circulated, competed and sometimes coexisted. 'Traditional' gender structures endured for a variety of reasons, including local resistance to Soviet reforms, a lack of local knowledge, influence and resources on the part of local and central Soviets and the interventions of international organizations. In later years, evolving Soviet gender policies and a renewed emphasis on motherhood and the traditional family would articulate a different version of 'traditional', patriarchal social structures.[59]

In the post-Soviet South Caucasus, the idea of an imagined pre-Soviet past characterized by 'traditional' gender roles and relationships serves to resist a failed Soviet reality and provide a foundation for national identities. Yet the contemporary impulse to embrace tradition in the shadow of a Soviet modern-izing past fails to address the lived experience of Soviet socialism and the extent to which Soviet ideals and norms changed over time. The idea of 'traditional' gender roles has been mobilized, attacked and reformulated repeatedly over the course of the 20th century by a range of actors in schemes for social transformation and reform, yet these schemes were rarely as comprehensive as they seemed. This chapter has revealed the conflicts and tensions inherent in them and the disparities between representations of reform and lived experiences.

Over the course of the 20th century, then, women were the objects of campaigns to transform or 'modernize' the South Caucasus, frequently instrumentalized as barometers of social change. In the early Soviet period, both the transformation of women's lives and images of this transformation were powerful signs of the building of socialism and the extent of Soviet control. However there is a tension between, on one hand, transformation as imagined in the rhetoric of reform and represented by secondary sources extrapolating from the Soviet Russian example and, on the other hand, the experienced reality revealed in local archival materials. The gap between the two reveals the extent to which the *representation* of transformation of women may in fact be more powerful than transformation itself. In a different way, the gap between representation and material transformation would be visible at the centre of the USSR, industrial Russia, through struggles over one of the fundamental concepts in any gender regime: motherhood.

Notes

1. Inderpal Grewal and Caren Kaplan, 'Theorizing Transnational Studies of Sexuality', *GLQ* vol. 7, no. 4 (2001): 666.
2. Two key examples are Ronald Grigor Suny, *Looking Toward Ararat: Armenia in Modern History* (Bloomington: Indiana University Press, 1993) and Razmik Panossian, *The Armenians: From Kings and Priests to Merchants and Commissars* (London: Hurst, 2006).
3. See, e.g., Wendy Bracewell, 'The End of Yugoslavia and New National Histories', *European History Quarterly* vol. 29, no. 1 (1999): 149–56; Keith Brown, *The Past in Question: Modern Macedonia and the Uncertainties of Nation* (Princeton, NJ: Princeton University Press, 2003); Isa Blumi, *Reinstating the Ottomans: Alternative Balkan Modernities, 1800–1912* (Basingstoke: Palgrave Macmillan, 2011).
4. Armine Ishkhanian, 'Gendered Transitions: the Impact of the Post-Soviet Transition on Women in Central Asia and the Caucasus', *Perspectives on Global Technology and Development* vol. 2, no. 3–4 (2003): 446–7.
5. On post-Soviet transformation of women's roles and its connection to nationalism more broadly, see Katherine Verdery, 'From Parent-State to Family Patriarchs', in *What Was Socialism and What Comes Next?* (Princeton, NJ: Princeton University Press, 1996).
6. Gayane Abrahamyan, 'Armenia: Activists Push for Domestic Violence Law amid Official Indifference', *Eurasianet.org*, 7 March 2014, available at: www.eurasianet. org/node/68115 (accessed 30 August 2014).
7. See also Baker, this volume.
8. Marianna Grigorian, 'Armenia: Fight Against Gender Equality Morphs into Fight Against EU', *Eurasianet.org*, 11 October 2013, available at: www.eurasianet.org/ node/67620 (accessed 30 August 2014). The conflict has sometimes become violent. In May 2012 the gay-friendly Yerevan bar 'DIY' was firebombed and the

perpetrators have not been brought to justice. The most dramatic events played out in the Georgian capital, Tbilisi, on 17 May 2013, when a peaceful rally by LGBT activists was violently attacked by anti-gay protesters, including significant numbers of Georgian Orthodox priests: Radio Free Europe Georgian Service, 'Antigay Protesters Disrupt Georgian Rights Rally', *Radio Free Europe/Radio Liberty*, 17 May 2013, available at: www.rferl.org/content/georgia-gay-rights-protests/24988972. html (accessed 30 August 2014).

9. On the family/nation concept, see Stephanie Platz, 'The Shape of National Time', in Daphne Berdahl, Matti Bunzl and Martha Lampland (eds), *Altering States: Ethnographies of Transition in Eastern Europe and the Former Soviet Union* (Ann Arbor: University of Michigan Press, 2000), 118.

10. Grigorian, 'Armenia'.

11. While sodomy was decriminalized in the revolution-era penal codes of both the Russian Socialist Federative Soviet Republic (RSFSR) and Armenia, it would later be criminalized. In Georgia and Azerbaijan, sodomy remained criminalized from the imperial period through the Soviet period. See: Dan Healey, *Homosexual Desire in Revolutionary Russia: The Regulation of Sexual and Gender Dissent* (Chicago, IL: University of Chicago Press, 2001), 159. Compare Takács, this volume.

12. Ziemer demonstrates that Armenian female identities are not simply a matter of 'cultural tradition' but have become means of 'boundary maintenance', differentiating the Armenian community from its Russian neighbours: Ulrike Ziemer, 'Tackling Tensions and Ambivalences: Armenian Girls' Diasporic Identities in Russia' *Nationalities Papers* vol. 38, no. 5 (2010): 693.

13. The majority of research on Soviet gender history still addresses women. A notable exception on the Russian case is Dan Healey, Barbara Evans Clements and Rebecca Friedman (eds), *Russian Masculinities in History and Culture* (Basingstoke: Palgrave, 2002). See also Fraser, this volume.

14. E.g., Susan Layton, 'Nineteenth-Century Russian Mythologies of Caucasian Savagery', in Daniel R. Brower and Edward J. Lazzerini (eds), *Russia's Orient: Imperial Peoples and Borderlands, 1750–1917* (Bloomington: Indiana University Press, 1997); more generally, Michael David-Fox, Peter Holquist and Alexander Martin (eds), *Orientalism and Empire in Russia* (Bloomington: Indiana University Press, 2006).

15. Jo Laycock, *Imagining Armenia: Orientalism, Ambiguity and Intervention* (Manchester: Manchester University Press, 2009), chapter 2.

16. See Bruce Grant, 'The Good Russian Prisoner: Naturalizing Violence in the Caucasus', *Cultural Anthropology* vol. 20, no. 1 (2005), 40. For a recent analysis of Caucasus stereotypes, see Sarah Kendzior, 'The Wrong Kind of Caucasian', *Al Jazeera English*, 21 April 2013, available at: www.aljazeera.com/indepth/opinion /2013/04/2013421145859380504.html (accessed 5 September 2014).

17. See, e.g., contributions to Bruce Grant and Lale Yalcin-Heckmann (eds), *Caucasus Paradigms: Anthropologies, Histories and the Making of a World Area* (Munster: LIT Verlag, 2007).

18. The issue of 'bride kidnapping' is a classic example here. For one recent attempt to interpret this phenomenon, see Elke Kamm, 'The Pride of Being Kidnapped: Women's Views on Bride Kidnapping in Tetriskaro, Georgia', *Caucasus Analytical Digest* vol. 42 (2010): 10–11.

19. The most obvious example of scholarship that has called into question such assumptions is that of nationalities policy and the way in which the USSR constructed rather than suppressed national identities. See Terry Martin, *The Affirmative Action Empire: Nations and Nationalism in the Soviet Union 1923–39* (Ithaca, NY: Cornell University Press, 2001).

20. The women's section of the Communist Party operated in the 1920s first as full Party sections on Soviet, Transcaucasian Socialist Federative Soviet Republic (TSFSR), Republic and sub-Republic levels. The women's section existed primarily at the republic level, the TSFSR level and the Soviet level. We use Kinbazhin here to refer to the Armenian case.

21. Mary Allerton Kilbourne Matossian, *The Impact of Soviet Policies in Armenia* (Leiden: Brill, 1962), 65–6. Her quoted phrase is taken from H. Hakobian, *Khorhrdayin Hayastan* (Paris: Gegharvestakan Hay Tparan, 1929), 217.

22. Matossian, *Impact*, 67.

23. Matossian, *Impact*, 64–5.

24. HAA (Hayastani Azgayin Arkhiv [National Archives of Armenia]), fund 1, list 3, file 262.

25. See HAA 1.3.276, and HAA 1.7.252.

26. Ronald Grigor Suny, *Armenia in the Twentieth Century* (Chico: Scholars Press, 1983), 35–52. For an in-depth discussion of the nature of displacement in the region during the revolutionary period, see Peter Gatrell, *A Whole Empire Walking: Refugees in Russia during World War I* (Bloomington: Indiana University Press, 2005).

27. HAA 1.2.141.

28. On European 'Armenophiles', see Laycock, *Imagining Armenia*, chapter 2.

29. The most common term for the veil used in the Caucasus during the early Soviet period was 'chadra'. The Persian term 'chador' was also used to a lesser extent.

30. See Douglas Northop, *Veiled Empire: Gender and Power in Stalinist Central Asia* (Ithaca, NY: Cornell University Press, 2004), 66–101.

31. SŠSSA (Saqartvelos šinagan saqmeta saministros arqivi [Ministry of Internal Affairs of Georgia Archive]) 13.7.196.

32. 'Chadran', *Hayastani Ashkhatavoruhi* no. 48 (January 1929): 11–12, HAA 1.9.213.

33. HAA 1.2.146; SŠSSA 13.3.542.

34. On Armenia between 1918 and 1920, see Richard Hovannissian, *The Republic of Armenia*, 4 vols (Berkeley: University of California Press, 1971–96). On patterns of displacement during the Armenian Genocide, see, e.g., Raymond Kevorkian, *The Armenian Genocide* (London: IB Tauris, 2011).

35. Both organizations returned to the region in 1921. NER's work continued until 1930 and LMF's until 1927.

36. On the longer-term context of the 'Armenian cause', see Laycock, *Imagining Armenia*, chapters 4 and 5; Michelle Tusan, *Smyrna's Ashes: Humanitarianism, Genocide and the Birth of the Middle East* (Berkeley: University of California Press, 2012).

37. Rockefeller Archive Centre (RAC), Near East Collection, Box 134, Report to Congress 1924.

38. James Barton, 'Near East Relief: Looking Backward and Forward', Report to Board of Trustees and Executive Committee of NER, 6 February 1930, RAC, Near East Collection Box 134.

39. Compare Jolluck, this volume.

40. For example, Eliz Sanasarian, 'Gender Distinction in the Genocidal Process: a Preliminary Study of the Armenian Case', *Holocaust and Genocide Studies* vol. 4, no. 4 (1989): 449–61.

41. The term genocide was not enshrined as a legal concept at this time.

42. Watenpaugh, 'The League of Nations Rescue of Armenian Genocide Survivors and the Making of Modern Humanitarianism, 1920–1927', *American Historical Review* vol. 115, no. 5 (2010): 1315–39; Lerna Ekmekcioglu, 'A Climate for Abduction, A Climate for Redemption: the Politics of Inclusion During and after the Armenian Genocide', *Comparative Studies in Society and History* vol. 55, no. 3 (2013): 522–53.

43. David Hoffmann, 'Mothers in the Motherland: Stalinist Pronatalism in Pan-European Context', *Journal of Social History* vol. 34, no. 1 (2000): 41.
44. 'News from the Stricken Lands', *The Record of the Save the Children Society* vol. 1, no. 2 (November 1920): 25.
45. Hoffmann, 'Mothers in the Motherland', 35.
46. On Soviet orphanages and childcare institutions, see Catriona Kelly, *Children's World: Growing Up in Russia 1890–1991* (New Haven, CT: Yale University Press, 2007), chapters 6–7. See also Kaminer, this volume.
47. Alexandropol was renamed Leninakan during the Soviet period and is now known as Gyumri.
48. Randall McAfee, 'Women and Children in the Near East', draft chapter manuscript, RAC, Box 132, 5.
49. McAfee, 'Women and Children in the Near East', 5.
50. The observation of Mabel Elliot, an American Red Cross doctor, from Armenia that '5,000 sick and dirty refugees huddled in a roped off street will divide the cobble stones into tiniest family-spaces' indicates the faith in and importance attached to the family unit: Mabel Elliot, *Beginning Again at Ararat* (New York: Fleming H. Revell and Co., 1924), 14–15.
51. Wendy Z. Goldman, *Women, the State and Revolution: Soviet Family Policy and Social Life, 1917–1936* (Cambridge: Cambridge University Press, 1993).
52. Save the Children's subscribers were told, 'Assistance to the adult refugees able to work takes the form of rations and a small wage in return for *constructive* labour' (authors' emphasis): 'The Appeal of Armenia: a Land of Destitute Children, Worthless Money and Widespread Destruction', *The World's Children*, no. 19 (15 June 1922): 296.
53. For an example of one such programme, see Michelle Tusan, 'The Business of Relief: a Victorian Quaker in Constantinople and her Circle', *Victorian Studies* vol. 51, no. 4 (2009): 633–61.
54. In his account of NER's work, its former director James Barton described 'diversified training covering all kinds of woman's work': James Barton, *The Story of Near East Relief* (New York: Macmillan, 1930), 242.
55. RAC Box 134, Misc. files. A scout group for example was set up at Alexandropol with an emphasis on athletic training. Boys were measured to monitor the results.
56. McAfee, 'Women and Children in the Near East', 2.
57. Barton, *The Story of Near East Relief*, 304.
58. Mary Allerton Kilbourne Matossian, *Soviet Diary, October 1957* ([Cambridge, MA]: [Harvard University Russian Research Center], 1958).
59. Compare Simić, this volume.

Part 2
Gender Regimes of Revolution and War

4
Mothers of a New World: Maternity and Culture in the Soviet Period

Jenny Kaminer

The relationship between mother and child was perhaps the aspect of Russian family life and intimate politics most profoundly transformed by the October Revolution. If, in pre-revolutionary Russia, religious and cultural codes proscribed a self-sacrificial, conciliatory and noble maternal figure (comparable with but not identical to the constructions of Czech motherhood seen in Chapter 1), then the Bolsheviks aimed to legitimize an entirely new kind of mother: unencumbered by the oppression of domestic bonds, she could dedicate herself – emotionally, physically and intellectually – to the construction of the new society rather than to the preservation of the hearth. The burden of child-rearing – and its attendant quotidian inconveniences – would be shouldered by the collective. Maternal sentiment would no longer be circumscribed by biological attachment to 'that piece of meat that is called [your] own child', as one Soviet mother of the 1920s so vividly put it, but would instead broaden to encompass all of the children of this reconstructed state.[1]

The history of motherhood in the remaining roughly 70 years of the USSR is characterized by the repeated reconciliation of these early, idealistic notions with the complicated and often tragic reality of Soviet family life. Mothers, early Bolshevik leaders came to believe, could not be trusted to give birth to and raise children properly and in accordance with Soviet ideals. From the campaign for obstetric enlightenment of the 1920s to the criminalization of abortion in the 1930s to the valorization of multi-child motherhood in the post-World War II period, the state repeatedly intruded into the mother–child relationship and attempted to assume a position of primacy. The mythology of the Great Family, emerging after Joseph Stalin consolidated power in 1929, symbolically excluded the biological father from the family unit, intensifying the burden placed on mothers and creating a crisis of fatherhood that continued into the post-Soviet period. At the same time, pre-revolutionary cultural ideals of maternity continued to resonate, as seen in the World War II-era utilization of iconic images of 'mother Russia' to galvanize individual and collective sacrifice.

This chapter charts the evolving ideals of maternity during the decades of the Soviet state, as well as the cultural media employed to disseminate them. The sources considered include novels, popular fiction and films that reached a large audience during the Soviet period, as well as those literary works originally unpublishable but heralding a re-evaluation of the legacy of Soviet motherhood after the collapse of the USSR in 1991. It sheds light on the complexities of the interplay between gender, cultural mythology and state policy that characterized not only the USSR but all of the countries of the former Eastern bloc, showing the place of cultural imagination and representation as well as lived experience in the formation of 20th-century gender regimes.[2]

Mothers to All, Mothers to None

The Family Code of 1918, one of the first pieces of legislation passed by the new Bolshevik government, was designed to impel the dissolution of the traditional, pre-revolutionary family. This new law negated the validity of religious marriages, giving legal status exclusively to civil marriages. It allowed divorce at the request of either spouse, without any grounds, and eliminated the concept of illegitimate birth, granting equal rights to children regardless of their parents' marital status.[3] Communal child-rearing would replace the individual family unit, which was deemed an oppressive bourgeois relic, and children would eventually be 'nationalized', as the wife of one prominent Bolshevik put it.[4] As early as 1899, Nadezhda Krupskaia (the wife of Vladimir Lenin), in her book *Zhenshchina–Rabotnitsa* (*The Woman Worker*), argued that women should naturally advocate communal child-rearing: 'The woman worker cannot fail to value all the benefits of socialized upbringing. Maternal instinct compels her to desire socialized upbringing.'[5] The concrete implementation of these abstract ideals was discussed during the 1919 All-Russian Congress for the Protection of Childhood in Moscow, where participants enthusiastically affirmed the ability of the state to raise children successfully as well as socialized child-rearing's power to free women from their domestic shackles.[6] Thus, freedom from the daily tasks associated with rearing children would allow women to attain the equality promised by the Russian Revolution.

It would also allow them to conquer the supposedly egotistical attachment to their own children in order to become, as Krupskaia articulated in a 1930 article, 'collective mothers'. 'Parental feelings do not have to degenerate into proprietorial ones', she contended, as is the case in capitalist countries, where parents selfishly obsessed with the well-being of only their biological children resemble 'dogs licking their puppies'. In the more highly evolved socialist society, Krupskaia argued, parental emotions can be raised to a 'higher level'; they could be expressed through 'especially attentive, caring relations to all children, not just to one's own [...] they can be sublimated'.[7] In other words, the transformation of Russian society propelled by the October Revolution necessitated significant shifts in maternal emotions as well.

This metamorphosis in motherly sentiment constitutes a central feature of one of the earliest classics of Soviet literature, Fedor Gladkov's 1925 novel *Tsement* (*Cement*). Serialized in the journal *Krasnaia nov'* (*Red Virgin Soil*) in

1925, *Tsement* is one of the earliest works of Soviet fiction to feature an exemplar of the new Soviet woman and to explore how the 1917 Revolution transformed Russian womanhood and the institution of the family. It would eventually serve as a prototype for the socialist realist novel, with its plot and positive heroes repeatedly imitated in later Soviet fiction.[8] Set after the end of the Civil War, at the beginning of the NEP (New Economic Policy) period, the work's central plot focuses on the return of the hero, Gleb Chumalov, to his hometown after a valiant fight for the Bolshevik cause. Alongside his efforts to resurrect the town's abandoned cement factory, Gleb struggles to adapt to a radically altered home life. His wife, Dasha – the formerly tender and selfless young wife and mother to their daughter, Nurka – now spurns her domestic role in favour of tireless activism for the collective. Nurka now resides in a communal children's home appropriately named 'Krupskaia'. Adhering neatly to the requirements of the collective mother, Dasha refuses to privilege the well-being of her biological daughter over that of other children: 'In what way is Nurka any better than the others?' she offers to Gleb by way of explanation for Nurka's abandonment.

During the course of the novel, Dasha undertakes a journey towards the goal of revolutionary enlightenment, but this necessitates the subsuming of her motherly emotions. Dasha's maternal sentiments for her daughter gradually deteriorate throughout the text, a process that Gladkov presents as complicated and painful. As Nurka slowly wastes away and eventually dies, Dasha senses her own responsibility keenly. Comparing her daughter to a group of wretched homeless children on the street, Dasha observes:

> Nurka was in the Children's Home, but was she happier than these naked little beasts? Dasha had once seen Nurka with the other children digging in the rubbish heap [...] It seemed to her then that her daughter was already dead, and that she, Dasha, was no longer her mother; that Nurka had been abandoned to hunger and suffering through Dasha's fault. [...] She had carried the little girl in her arms right to the Children's Home and her heart was ravaged with pain.[9]

Gladkov presents child abandonment as a necessary, if undeniably wrenching, prerequisite to the new woman's full participation in the construction of the society of the future.[10] If Dasha represented the new Soviet woman, then *Tsement* revealed the incompatibility of traditional maternal bonds and the society for which that woman toiled and sacrificed.

Popular responses to the widely read novel's reimagining of femininity and maternity varied. According to a study published in 1928, for example, *Tsement* elicited significantly more positive responses from male than from female readers: working-class women rated the novel favourably only 26 per cent of the time, compared with 50 per cent of men. These same female respondents reacted particularly negatively towards the character of Dasha, commenting, for example, that 'the working woman can learn nothing from Dasha's behaviour' and that 'a woman should not follow Dasha's example'.[11] At the same time, a questionnaire distributed to factory workers in the mid-1920s revealed more sympathetic responses, with some respondents affirming their belief that 'Dasha's attitude towards her personal life [is] perfectly correct'.[12] Although no definitive, quantitative measurement of the success of Soviet attempts to promote new cultural models of motherhood – such as that found in *Tsement* – exists, these varied responses testify to the challenges of disseminating such profoundly transformed notions of womanhood.[13]

Workers and Mothers

These challenges, in addition to daunting practical exigencies, ultimately doomed early Soviet experiments with communal child-rearing and collective motherhood to failure. The state, nonetheless, continued to insert itself into the relationship between mother and child, motivated, at least partially, by a suspicion that women's backwardness rendered them incapable of properly raising the citizens needed to construct the new society.[14] Throughout the 1920s, the Soviets waged a campaign for obstetric enlightenment that attempted to disabuse women of their traditional ways of childbearing and rearing, teaching them instead to rely on the proper and modern techniques advocated by the state's medical establishment.[15] This campaign to convince mothers to turn away from their traditional female networks and towards the expertise of medical science had a precedent in the West. Historians have identified the turn of the 20th century as the period when the ideology of 'scientific motherhood' first achieved prominence in Europe and the United States.[16] Scientific motherhood imparted the message to women that they could not successfully raise a healthy child without the intercession of scientific and medical experts, and that motherhood resembled a profession requiring the proper training and education.[17]

Through methods such as consultation, visiting nurses, birth homes for infants, and various forms of propaganda, the Department for the Protection of Motherhood and Infancy aimed to replace the unreliability of women's 'instinctual' ability to care for their own children with the certainty of scientific knowledge. Medical authorities maintained that high infant mortality rates were attributable not to poor conditions but to the incompetence and ignorance of Soviet mothers. In other words, the bad habits of mothers stood between Soviet society and the healthy new citizens needed to populate it. In line with this sentiment, propaganda of the period depicted women as incapable of performing even the most rudimentary childcare tasks without the guidance of medical experts.[18] Other propaganda demonized the rural folk healer (or *babka*), illustrating the glaring contrast between the clean, bright and healthy environment of the modern Soviet hospital and the unsanitary and ominous atmosphere of a birth attended by the *babka*. Soviet women who continued to give birth with the *babka*, according to the message these posters conveyed, invariably endangered the life of their child as well as themselves.[19] By clinging to traditional, rural ways, these mothers also imperilled the Soviet drive for progress and modernization and so posed a threat not only to themselves but to the entire collective.[20]

Throughout the 1920s, the state attempted to instil these ideals of maternal behaviour through enlightenment and education. After the Stalinist revolution of 1929, however, it resorted to much more coercive methods. By 1935, for example, birth in an officially sanctioned state institution became the only legal option, and state midwives were charged with the task of finding and denouncing folk midwives, who would then face arrest. This marked the end of the notion of childbirth as a 'private individual experience'; it would now occur exclusively 'under the watchful eyes of the state'.[21] A series of legislative reforms also had a profound effect on the lives of Soviet women. Notably, the 1936 Family Law codified a pro-natalist stance by outlawing abortions as well as by making divorce much more difficult to obtain and instituting harsh penalties for fathers who refused to pay alimony or child support. The prohibition on abortion did little to counteract a declining birthrate, but it did drive many women to seek the procedure underground, often at great personal peril. By resorting to illegal abortions, Soviet women rebelled against the imperative to produce and reproduce at the whims of the state.[22]

While increasing the levels of both state and individual male accountability for families, in exchange this law compelled mothers to shoulder the double burden of both work and motherhood. During the Stalinist regime's 'stabilizing accommodation with middle class values', to borrow Vera S. Dunham's phrase, Dasha Chumalova was replaced by the mother who fulfilled her duties both to the state *and* to her individual family.[23] The complete reversal of the early Bolshevik experiments with the 'withering away' of the traditional family was completed by the passage of the next comprehensive family law in 1944, which eliminated the most radical elements of the 1918 and 1926 Family Codes (for example, by withdrawing recognition of de facto marriages and reintroducing the category of illegitimacy).[24] Accordingly, the fiction of the post-war period increasingly stressed motherhood, which assumed priority over a woman's professional obligations. Works by writers such as the Stalin Prize-winning author Vera Panova extolled the virtues of women who embodied traditional female qualities – kindness and devotion to family and home, for example – while simultaneously succeeding as workers and as citizens. The balance of this female imagery was tipped, however, in favour of the joys of motherhood.[25] Parenting advice literature of the post-war period even presented working mothers (ideally those with large families) as raising the best children, since their positive example instilled self-sufficiency and proper behaviour in their offspring.[26] Thus, a woman's participation in the workforce enhanced her maternal effectiveness, and the regime expected that a woman excel in both the professional and the domestic spheres.[27] From the 1930s onward, women were expected to fulfil their duties both as workers and as reproducers, finding their ultimate satisfaction in the latter while never foregoing the former.

At the same time, after Stalin's death in 1953, several female authors embarked on the project of 'de-Stalinizing gender', as Catriona Kelly has aptly termed it.[28] Gradually, critical realists such as Irina Grekova began to reveal chinks in the armour of the indefatigable Soviet worker-mother, showing women who could not consistently and effortlessly 'soar above the tensions of home and work, as Stalinist heroines had done'.[29] The psychic and physical toll of this double burden was first fully explored in Soviet fiction, however, in Natalia Baranskaia's extremely successful and widely read novella *Nedelia kak nedelia* (*A Week Like Any Other*), originally published in the journal *Novyi mir* (*New World*) in 1969. Told in first-person narration, the work chronicled seven typical days in the life of Olga Voronkova, a wife and mother of two young children with an advanced scientific degree working in a research laboratory. Baranskaia thrusts the reader into the midst of Olga's breathless and unrelenting attempts to juggle the conflicting demands of family, household and career. Olga's female colleagues repeatedly identify her husband, Dima, as an enviable partner, since he helps her with the children and does not drink or commit adultery. Nonetheless, Olga's evenings are spent sewing and cooking while Dima reads technical magazines, and her repeated absences and tardiness to work because of her children's illnesses imperil her professional standing. Although Olga is as highly educated and qualified as her husband, her primary responsibility for home and hearth relegates her desire for accomplishment and intellectual stimulation to the background. The fear of an unwanted pregnancy – and the painful and dehumanizing abortion that may be its consequence – casts a pallor over her relationship with her husband. The frenetic pace of Olga's days underscored the exhaustion and psychological burden that this precarious balancing act required of her and her countless real-life Soviet counterparts.[30] This incitement to a dual sacrifice would remain part of official Soviet rhetoric until the 1980s.[31]

Return to the Motherland

As the Dasha Chumalova model of Russian motherhood receded into the background during the Stalin period, the pagan roots of the maternal archetype also resurfaced. In popular songs, poems and visual culture of the 1930s, a fertile, markedly feminine body replaced the 'neutered female image' of the earlier decade.[32] While actual agricultural productivity declined in the wake of the violent campaign for collectivization of the early 1930s, a 'pathos of fertility', as Hans Guenther terms it, emerged to fill the void.[33] Mothers once again assumed their symbolic association with the land and nation, as Soviet nationalism increased during the second half of the 1930s.[34] The word *rodina* (motherland) returned to prominence – a process that culminated during World War II with I. Toidze's famous *Rodina-mat' zovet!* (*The Motherland Calls!*) poster, which incited citizens to sacrifice on behalf of the nation allegorized as a mother. With a defiant arm cast upward against a backdrop of bayonets, the female figure evoked both the new Soviet mother and an older, peasant milieu far removed from the transformations of industrialization.[35] At the same time, the majority of artistic representations incorporating mothers during World War II portrayed them helplessly clinging to terrified children while under assault by fascists wielding menacing weapons.[36] Hence, the maternal archetype conveyed both strength and fragility as it inspired the valiant defence of the nation and sacrifice from its citizens and soldiers. Its utilization in wartime propaganda provided the link between the war and local loyalties, with an appeal to private emotions stimulating the call to public service.[37] Ironically, this gendered imagery also contributed to the underemphasis of Soviet women's substantial *actual* combat contributions, which received relatively little acknowledgement.[38] After the war, the same female archetype was deployed as part of what Susan E. Reid has termed the 'iconography of normalization'. 'The figure of woman', Reid explains, 'demobilized and restored to her supposedly natural, "essentially feminine" preoccupation with her own appearance, family and home' was meant to aid the citizenry in recovering from the multiple traumas of the Stalinist Terror and World War II. In other words, the iconic Russian mother was exhorted to turn back to her children in order to comfort the population and restore normalcy after a series of historical cataclysms.[39]

Meanwhile, the overt physical manifestations of a woman's childbearing abilities had returned from the margins to the centre of the cultural imaginary.[40] Alexander Deineka's 1932 painting *Mat'* (*The Mother*) encapsulated this shift in maternal representation from the 1920s to the Stalin era. Painted in warm, earthy hues, it depicts a small child sleepily perched in a mother's arms, basking in the glow of her adoring and reassuring gaze. The mother stands naked, with her back to the viewer, and the silhouette of her bare breast – symbolizing fecundity and nurturance – appears in the lower left of the canvas. Deineka foregrounds the intimacy and exclusivity of the mother–child bond, as well as its timelessness – the painting lacks any details (such as clothing or furnishings) that could situate it within an identifiable historical era. The sentiments evoked in *Mat'* contrast sharply with those exhibited in earlier works such as *Tsement*, which stress both the communality and the historical specificity of the relationship between mothers and children.

Alongside this celebration of a woman's fundamentally maternal nature, the myth of the Great Family was also introduced into Soviet culture during the Stalin period. With Stalin serving as the symbolic father of the nation, this myth cast Soviet citizens in the role of obedient, humble and unflaggingly loyal children. The mythology of the radiant Great Family united 'the young people, the earth mother, and the wise father'.[41] Images of joyous mothers and children abounded in the visual culture of the period, with Stalin hovering benevolently over the scene and leaving no doubt as to 'whose holy spirit has done the ideological inseminating'.[42] This symbolic union relegated actual fathers to the periphery of the Soviet family, where they could pose no challenge to Stalin's pre-eminence – a marginalization that would problematize familial relations throughout the Soviet period and beyond.[43]

Motherhood and Terror

Simultaneously, the Stalin era – characterized by housing shortages and arbitrary state violence – created increasingly difficult daily burdens for actual mothers. If official rhetoric under Stalin celebrated the ease with which maternal and professional commitments could be reconciled, the reality of most mothers' lives consisted of a much more mundane struggle for their own and their family's survival amid a climate of scarcity, mass arrests and unrelenting fear. The mothers depicted in the unofficial Soviet literature of the Stalin era, during the late 1930s in particular – such as Lidia Chukovskaia's novella *Sof'ia Petrovna* or Anna Akhmatova's famous poetic cycle *Rekviem* (*Requiem*) – reflect this cruel reality rather than the facile happiness of the Great Family with its infinitely fertile and joyous mother. The image of Dasha Chumalova and others like her attained an unintended irony in light of the involuntary separation of mothers and children that occurred on a massive scale during the Stalinist Terror and World War II.

Chukovskaia's *Sof'ia Petrovna*, written in 1939–40, has been widely acknowledged as one of the few texts to 'record and respond to the events of Stalinism where and when they occurred', consequently remaining unpublished in the Soviet Union until the perestroika period of the 1980s.[44] At the beginning of the text, its titular heroine embodies the effortless and uplifting synthesis of motherhood and professional accomplishment so touted during the Stalin period. After her husband's death, Sof'ia quickly acquires the training necessary to support her young son, finding such satisfaction in her job as a typist that she cannot imagine how she had lived without it for so long. Her son, Kolia – handsome, intelligent, kind and assured of a bright future – testifies to her success as a mother. Blithely unburdened by any critical awareness of the dark clouds of repression and violence gathering over Soviet society of the 1930s, Sof'ia seems to have stepped directly out of a propaganda poster celebrating Stalin's success in supposedly solving the Women's Question.[45]

The Terror of the late 1930s gradually encroaches upon Sof'ia's contented existence, however, eventually consuming her completely. After the inexplicable arrest of her upstanding son, Sof'ia swiftly encounters the indifference and brutality of the Soviet state. While clinging to an almost child-like belief in the justice of the system, she futilely attempts to navigate the bureaucratic labyrinth in search of information about Kolia. Sof'ia's journey into the prison underworld leads her to confront an alternative, almost exclusively female, society that flourished during the Stalin years – the prison line. These women, predominantly mothers, occupy a parallel space to the official world Sof'ia inhabited before her son's arrest. (Akhmatova's wrenching experiences as a part of this alternative, female community provided the inspiration for *Requiem*.) Chukovskaia's descriptions of this underworld highlight its ubiquity – government buildings are bursting from the throngs of women – as well as the seemingly unending nature of the women's quests. Despite her similar plight, however, Sof'ia remains isolated from this community of fellow sufferers, feeling no solidarity with them because they are the 'wives and mothers of poisoners, spies and murderers'.[46] Sof'ia does not extrapolate a wider phenomenon of unjust persecution from her innocent son's predicament. Rather, she clings to her facile acceptance of Soviet propaganda and thus imagines herself superior to the other mothers, rejecting any measure of comfort that this fellowship may have afforded her.

In the work's final chapters, Sof'ia's sanity gradually deteriorates as she writes naïve letters to Stalin and succumbs to the fantasy that Kolia receives a pardon, joyously awaiting his imminent return. The novella's concluding scene contains the symbolic severing of ties between Sof'ia and her son. Kolia's long-awaited letter finally arrives, and in it he begs his mother to intercede on his behalf with the authorities. Fear, however, compels Sof'ia to burn the letter. The reader understands that Kolia's desperate pleas will remain unanswered. Chukovskaia's novella reveals the ultimate impossibility of maternal ties for a woman who had seemed to embody the ideal qualities of Soviet womanhood, with its twin pillars

18. Tricia Starks, *The Body Soviet: Propaganda, Hygiene, and the Revolutionary State* (Madison: University of Wisconsin Press, 2008), 136, 145, 146.
19. Frances Lee Bernstein, *The Dictatorship of Sex: Lifestyle Advice for the Soviet Masses* (DeKalb: Northern Illinois University Press, 2007), 122–8.
20. Compare Laycock and Johnson, this volume.
21. Issoupova, 'From Duty?', 35.
22. Barbara Engel, *Women in Russia, 1700–2000* (Cambridge: Cambridge University Press, 2004), 180.
23. Vera S. Dunham, *In Stalin's Time: Middleclass Values in Soviet Fiction* (Durham, NC: Duke University Press, 1990), 14.
24. Goldman, *Women*, 336, 338.
25. Beth Holmgren, 'Writing the Female Body Politic (1945–1985)', in Adele Marie Barker and Jehanne M. Gheith (eds), *A History of Women's Writing in Russia* (Cambridge: Cambridge University Press, 2002), 231; Lynne Attwood, 'Rationality versus Romanticism: Representations of Women in the Stalinist Press', in Linda Edmonson (ed.), *Gender in Russian History and Culture* (Basingstoke: Palgrave, 2001), 170–1.
26. Greta Bucher, 'Stalinist Families: Motherhood, Fatherhood, and Building the New Soviet Person', in John W. Steinberg and Rex A. Wade (eds), *The Making of Russian History* (Bloomington, IN: Slavica, 2009), 141.
27. Dunham, *In Stalin's Time*, 14, 35, 214; Buckley, *Women and Ideology*, 131–3.
28. Catriona Kelly, 'Who Wants to Be a Man? De-Stalinizing Gender, 1954–1992', in Catriona Kelly, *A History of Russian Women's Writing, 1820–1992* (New York: Oxford University Press, 1994).
29. Kelly, 'Who Wants to Be a Man?', 358.
30. Natalia Baranskaia, *Nedelia kak nedelia: povest'* (Paris: Institut d'Études Slaves, 1988).
31. Engel, *Women in Russia*, 253–5. Although, by the Gorbachev period, official rhetoric enticed women with the prospect of choice, 'policy', as Engel explains, 'pointed in a different direction. Virtually every policy initiative aimed to encourage women to bear and raise children, rather than to help them advance on the job or combat discrimination at the workplace': Engel, *Women in Russia*, 255–6.
32. David Hoffmann, *Stalinist Values: the Cultural Norms of Soviet Modernity 1917–1941* (Ithaca, NY: Cornell University Press, 2003), 112.
33. Hans Guenther, '"Broad is My Motherland": The Mother Archetype and Space in the Soviet Mass Song', in Evgeny Dobrenko and Eric Naiman (eds), *The Landscape of Stalinism: the Art and Ideology of Soviet Space* (Seattle: University of Washington Press, 2003), 80.
34. Elena Baraban, 'The Return of Mother Russia: Representations of Women in Soviet Wartime Cinema', *Aspasia* no. 4 (2010): 122.
35. Linda Edmondson, 'Putting Mother Russia in a European Context', in Tricia Cusak and Síghle Breathnach-Lynch (eds), *Art, Nation and Gender: Ethnic Landscapes, Myths and Mother-Figures* (Aldershot: Ashgate, 2003), 53.
36. Victoria E. Bonnell, *Iconography of Power: Soviet Political Posters Under Lenin and Stalin* (Berkeley: University of California Press, 1997), 261; Irina Sandomirskaia, *Kniga o rodine: Opyt analiza diskursivnikh praktik* (Vienna: Wiener Slawistischer Almanach, 2001), 84–5. For more on female imagery in World War II posters, see also Jeffrey Brooks, *Thank You, Comrade Stalin! Soviet Public Culture from Revolution to Cold War* (Princeton, NJ: Princeton University Press, 2000), 178–79; and Susan Corbesero, 'Femininity (Con)Scripted: Female Images in Soviet Wartime Poster Propaganda, 1941–45', *Aspasia* no. 4 (2010): 103–20.

37. Lisa A. Kirschenbaum, '"Our City, Our Hearths, Our Families": Local Loyalties and Private Life in Soviet World War II Propaganda', *Slavic Review* vol. 59, no. 4 (2000): 838.
38. Engel, *Women in Russia*, 220; Bischl, this volume.
39. Susan E. Reid, 'The Khrushchev Kitchen: Domesticating the Scientific–Technological Revolution', *Journal of Contemporary History* vol. 40, no. 2 (2005): 292.
40. Keith A. Livers, *Constructing the Stalinist Body* (Lanham, MD: Lexington, 2004), 14.
41. Guenther, '"Broad Is My Motherland"', 92.
42. Eric Naiman, 'Historectimies: On the Metaphysics of Reproduction in a Utopian Age', in Jane T. Costlow, Stephanie Sandler, and Judith Vowles (eds), *Sexuality and the Body in Russian Culture* (Palo Alto, CA: Stanford University Press, 1993), 276.
43. See Sarah Ashwin and Tatyana Lytkina, 'Men in Crisis in Russia: The Role of Domestic Marginalization', *Gender and Society* vol. 18, no. 2 (2004): 189–206.
44. Beth Holmgren, *Women's Works in Stalin's Time* (Bloomington: Indiana University Press, 1993), 44.
45. See Buckley, *Women and Ideology*, chapter 3 ('The Stalin Years: the Woman Question is Solved').
46. Lidia Chukovskaia, 'Sof'ia Petrovna', in Lidia Chukovskaia, *Izbrannoe* (Moscow: Gorizont, 1997), 46.
47. I. Sofenov, 'Problema sinteza v metro', *Iskusstvo* no. 2 (1938): 40. Quoted in Hans Guenther, 'Archetipy sovetskoi kul'tury', in Hans Guenther and Evgeny Dobrenko (eds), *Sotsrealisticheskii kanon* (St Petersburg: Gumanitarnoe agenstvo 'Akademicheskii proekt', 2000), 778.
48. Amy E. Randall, '"Abortion Will Deprive You of Happiness!": Soviet Reproductive Politics in the Post-Stalin Era', *Journal of Women's History* vol. 23, no. 3 (2011): 18. See also Deborah A. Field, *Private Life and Communist Morality in Khrushchev's Russia* (New York: Peter Lang, 2007), chapter 4.
49. Engel, *Women in Russia*, 233.
50. Buckley, *Women and Ideology*, 171, 174.
51. Lynne Attwood, *Red Women on the Silver Screen* (London: Pandora, 1993), 127. For examples of 1970s films that explore this tension, see Attwood, *Red Women*, chapter 6.
52. Attwood, *Red Women*, 90–1.
53. Neya Zorkaya, *The Illustrated History of the Soviet Cinema* (New York: Hippocrene, 1989), 298. Quoted in Attwood, *Red Women*, 91.
54. *Moskva slezam ne verit*, dir. V. Menshov, perf. K. Tikhomirova, L. Gurina, and A. Batalov, Mosfil'm, 1979.
55. I. Grekova, 'Vdovii parokhod', in I. Grekova, *Vdovii parokhod: Izbrannoe* (Moscow: 'Tekst, 1998), 193–328.
56. Attwood, *Red Women*, 112. *Malen'kaia Vera*, dir. V. Pichul, perf. N. Negoda, A. Sokolov, and Y. Nazarov, Gorky Film Studios, 1988.
57. Jennifer Marie Utrata, 'Counting on Motherhood, Not Men: Single Motherhood and Social Change in the New Russia' (PhD thesis, University of California, Berkeley, 2008), 21, 71.
58. Issoupova, 'From Duty?', 39, 46.
59. Utrata, 'Counting on Motherhood', 93.
60. Ann Taylor Allen, *Feminism and Motherhood in Western Europe, 1890–1970: the Maternal Dilemma* (New York: Palgrave Macmillan, 2005), 184–5. The reasons that a woman chooses to have children are, of course, multifaceted and difficult to quantify. Utrata demonstrates how, during the Soviet period, women perceived the bond

between mothers and children as stronger than that between husbands and wives, and how children were seen as a more reliable source of rewarding love than husbands: Utrata, 'Counting on Motherhood', 66.

61. See, for example, the French scholar Elisabeth Badinter's *Mother Love, Myth and Reality: Motherhood in Modern History* (New York: Macmillan, 1981).

62. Michele Rivkin-Fish, 'Pronatalism, Gender Politics, and the Renewal of Family Support in Russia: Toward a Feminist Anthropology of "Maternity Capital"', *Slavic Review* vol. 69, no. 3 (2010): 721–2. Compare the introduction of homophobic and transphobic legislation under Putin in 2013 (Baker, this volume), arguably rolling back freedoms that had opened up in the 1990s.

5

Life and Fate: Race, Nationality, Class and Gender in Wartime Poland

Katherine R. Jolluck

The defining attributes of modern Eastern Europe were most consequential in World War II Poland: shifting borders, a population of mixed and increasingly differentiated ethnicities, at the mercy of outside powers seeking to conquer and dominate them. During the war the country endured occupation by two different ideologically driven regimes bent on complete domination. Individuals in Poland faced different treatment, restrictions, opportunities and life expectancy, depending on which occupier they fell under in 1939 and particularly on their ethno-national identity. Privation, brutality and the struggle for survival characterized the lives of nearly all Polish citizens, male or female. Under the Nazis, who occupied Poland for more than five years, Jews faced attempted annihilation, with confinement in ghettos, deportation to camps and execution as their most common fate. Some Jews, though, managed to remain on the 'Aryan side', either in hiding, passing as Christians or fleeing to the forests. These scenarios not only gave them a greater chance of survival but also the opportunity to actively resist the Nazis.

Polish Christians (for the sake of simplicity referred to hereafter as Poles) also faced tremendous hostility and cruelty from the occupying Germans. They were Slavs, whom the Nazis considered inferior and expendable, suited for slave labour or destruction; they also resisted Nazi domination, which elicited even greater wrath. Poles endured both arbitrary and targeted violence, imprisonment, and the concentration camps. Hundreds of thousands were executed or succumbed to the disastrous conditions in the camps. Most Poles, though, could carry on some semblance of a private life, as long as they conformed to Nazi strictures and were not in the wrong place at the wrong time. Living in this lesser degree of 'unfreedom', they worked, sought to care for their families and in large numbers contributed to the underground struggle against the Germans.

The inhabitants of Poland also twice endured invasion and occupation by the Red Army. In August 1939 Germany and the USSR signed the Molotov–Ribbentrop (Nazi–Soviet) Pact. It served as a non-aggression treaty between the two countries and an agreement to partition the Polish state. On 17 September 1939, after the Wehrmacht had already destroyed most of the Polish army following its 1 September invasion, the Red Army moved in to seize the Soviet portion. The inhabitants of eastern Poland faced a brutal attempt at Sovietization, which included mass arrests, executions and civilian deportations to the USSR. Ironically, deportation to the USSR, a tragedy that destroyed the lives of many Polish citizens, turned out to be a favour for many Polish Jews, as it took them out of the reach of the Nazis and made it possible for thousands of them to survive the war.

Though the Soviets were driven out of eastern Poland by the German army when it attacked the USSR in June 1941, they returned in 1944 as the tide of the war turned in their favour. The Red Army then eliminated the Wehrmacht from all of Poland, keeping troops there for the next 70 years. Liberation by Soviet troops occurred with a shocking level of violence against civilians; the defeat of the Nazis heralded peace in name only for the inhabitants of Poland. Soviet authorities, aided by local communists, arrested, executed and deported those they considered enemies. The transfer of eastern Polish territory to the USSR unleashed violent civil war between Poles and Ukrainians, capped by deportations and 'repatriations'. The transfer of eastern German territory to Poland (compensation by the Allies for its losses in the east) prompted brutal ethnic cleansing of Germans, many of whom were killed in the process. Surviving Jews faced violence as they tried to return to their homes. Ethnicity and location continued to be life-and-death matters for the people of Poland.

To what extent did gender matter in this cauldron of violence, in which people were slated for death because of their ethno-national identity or fell victim to indiscriminate violence meted out by conquerors with no regard for their humanity? Both the Nazis and Soviets waged war against entire populations; neither regime was content with simply annexing territory. Nor did they see enemies in men alone. The totality of their aims – to destroy or subjugate racial, ethnic and class enemies – required striking at females as well as males. Civil conflicts similarly engulfed both sexes. Most historical accounts of the treatment of Poles and, until the 1980s, of Jews, focus solely on racial/ethnic victimization.[1] That does not mean, however, that treatment of 'the enemy' was gender blind. Nor, in the struggle to survive or to resist the occupiers, did gender prove irrelevant. It played a role not only in how the occupiers treated their conquered populations but also in how individuals endured and interpreted their ordeals. Though the population of Poland included several ethno-national groups, this chapter will focus on the Poles and Jews, the main targets of the occupiers.[2]

Nazi Policy Towards the People of Poland

When Hitler sent his army eastward, in pursuit of *Lebensraum*, he had no pity for the populations of the territories he coveted. The Slavs and Jews, whom he despised as inferior, were slated for displacement, subjugation or destruction. The war with Poland was to be a war of liquidation. On the eve of the invasion, he sent his military commanders off with the order to 'kill, without pity or mercy, all men, women, and children of Polish descent or language'.[3] German forces engaged in *Blitzkrieg*, concentrating mobile ground units and air power against the cities, towns and villages of western and central Poland, specifically targeting the civilian population and strafing passenger trains and columns of fleeing refugees. Warsaw was besieged and heavily bombarded by German forces, causing 40,000 civilian deaths.[4]

After defeating the Polish army, the Nazis incorporated the western territories of Poland directly into the Third Reich, and began a process of Germanization which included executions and expulsions of non-Germans. The central part of Poland, designated the *Generalgouvernement*, fell under Hans Frank, a ruthless Nazi administrator. To the Nazis, the Poles were not only inferior but blocked German expansion to the east; subordinating them necessitated the annihilation of the Polish elite and the reduction of the remaining population to the status of slave labourers, who would ultimately be deported eastward. Immediately after the invasion, the Nazis began operations to eliminate the Polish intelligentsia.[5] This meant the mass murder of teachers, clergy, doctors, lawyers, artists, merchants, landowners – anyone able to carry on the political and spiritual leadership of the nation or direct resistance. Approximately 100,000 individuals were executed in these campaigns, while thousands more were sent to concentration camps. Gender made no difference to the Nazis when it came to destroying the Polish nation. Women as well as men were shot and buried in mass graves, or executed publicly, their bodies exhibited to demoralize the population.[6]

Men and women arrested for political crimes faced torture in Gestapo prisons and execution or confinement in concentration camps.[7] Auschwitz was originally built, in 1940, for Polish political prisoners; approximately 140,000 Poles were sent there, half of whom were either executed or died from starvation, beating or illness.[8] The Nazis ruled the territories of Poland by terror, indiscriminately striking men, women and children. Villages were wiped out in pacification operations. The Germans took hostages to ensure that local inhabitants refrained from acts of resistance or displays of nationalism; hostages were routinely executed in cases of non-compliance. Collective responsibility for resistance resulted in reprisal executions of thousands of innocent Poles, often seized in street round-ups known as *łapanki*. Frank, the ruler of the *Generalgouvernement*, decreed that 100 Poles be shot for each German killed. Comparing his regime to that of the Nazis' Bohemian–Moravian Protectorate, Frank stated: 'In Prague [...] large red posters were put up announcing that 7 Czechs had been shot today [...] If I wanted to have a poster put up for every 7 Poles who were shot, the forests of Poland would not suffice for producing the paper for such posters.'[9]

Other victims nabbed in *łapanki* were sent to concentration camps or to forced labour in Germany; in 1943 Frank bragged that his administration had supplied 1.3 million Polish forced labourers.[10] On Hermann Göring's orders, Polish girls were especially targeted for deportation to work in the Reich; he explicitly called for 375,000 of them to be employed in agriculture.[11] Young Polish (and Soviet) women were also attractive to German industries, as they received minimal compensation, had no protection under Nazi social legislation and were reputed to work well. Additionally, adhering to traditional stereotypes, firm managers anticipated females being more obedient and unlikely to cause trouble.[12]

Polish forced labourers in the Reich were subject to extremely harsh, and gendered, racial policies. Forbidden to have sexual relations with Germans, they faced differential treatment based on their sex and their purported 'racial fitness'. A Polish man deemed fit for Germanization typically ended up in a concentration camp for having sex with a German woman; one deemed unfit was hanged. A decree stipulated a three-month camp sentence for a Polish woman having sexual relations with a German man, suggesting she was less dangerous to the German race. There was also room for doubt in her sexual agency, and the decree ordered only 21 days' detention if a superior at work had taken advantage of her.[13] A 1943 decree permitted German doctors to perform compulsory abortions on Polish women. These abortions, done without anaesthesia and even in the eighth month, occurred not only by order of Nazi officials, but reportedly at the behest of the German wives of the men who impregnated them, out of fear of scandal or property claims.[14] In cases of childbirth, the infants were taken from their mothers. If judged to be of 'good racial stock', they were raised by German families; those considered 'inferior' were sent to special homes for foreign children.[15] One researcher contends that these homes 'were established to eliminate infants of Eastern European slave laborers' by starvation or the intentional feeding of spoiled milk.[16]

Though the Nazis prohibited sexual contact with people of 'alien races', women in Poland faced sexual enslavement by the regime. The view of Poles as an inferior race actually encouraged German men to look at the women as sexual objects at their disposal. Hitler initially forbade prostitution, but his military leaders convinced him of the need for brothels behind the front to satisfy the sexual needs of soldiers, keep them from seeking contact with local women, control the spread of venereal diseases and prevent homosexual relations. In the spring of 1940, Nazi authorities began setting up travelling brothels and bordellos in cities, towns and villages for the Wehrmacht and the SS.[17] At least 34,000 east European women, mostly Slavic, were forced to serve as sex slaves in these brothels.[18] Former prostitutes were compelled to serve in them, and some females agreed in hopes of saving their own or their family's lives, when threatened with death or the concentration camps. But women were often abducted for the brothels.[19] Once there, they endured state-sponsored serial rape, between 20 and 30 times a day.[20]

Concern for men's sexual outlet extended to the concentration camps, where separate brothels were created for the German and Ukrainian SS guards. Even some prisoners were given licence to sexually exploit female prisoners. Beginning in 1942, brothels were established in ten camp complexes, including Auschwitz, for privileged prisoners. Heinrich Himmler believed this would increase the productivity of male workers; female workers, the lowest of the low, thus had to serve their fellow inmates. As Elizabeth Heineman points out, this was an exchange between the state and men: 'these women could not opt out of the exchange or bargain for its terms. Men and the state could: the state could withhold access to brothels, and men could choose not to visit them.'[21] Women were either recruited with the false promise of an early release or simply forced into this role; they faced compulsory abortions or death in case of pregnancy.[22] Researchers have uncovered the names of 210 women who were assigned to brothels throughout the camp system; the majority were German or Polish, incarcerated as asocials or politicals.[23] There is evidence that Jewish women, too, were exploited in these brothels.[24]

Hitler considered Jews 'racially alien' and biologically dangerous to the German race. In occupied Poland, Jewish women, men and children were forced into ghettos, where cramped and squalid living conditions, combined with the deliberate dearth of food and medicine, and gratuitous violence, claimed thousands of lives daily. After the Wehrmacht invaded the USSR in 1941, *Einzsatzgruppen*, special mobile killing units, massacred Jews along the Eastern Front, including those in eastern Poland. Most were shot, sometimes by the tens of thousands. At the end of the year, Nazi leaders decided upon the Final Solution, which was then implemented in Poland, home to the largest Jewish population in Europe. Ninety per cent of them – three million individuals – were killed. Additionally, Jews from all over Europe were transported to the Nazi death camps in Poland to be gassed or worked to death.

Nazi anti-Semitism was uncompromising: Jewish men, women and children were all slated for death. 'We had to answer the question: What about the women and children?' explained Himmler:

> I did not feel I had the right to exterminate the men – that is to murder them, or to have them murdered – and then allow their children to grow into avengers, threatening our sons and grandchildren. A fateful decision had to be made: this people had to vanish from the earth.[25]

Owing to the primacy of race in the Nazi mind, Jewish females, far from being spared, were especially dangerous because of their capacity to reproduce their people.

Some scholars believe that more Jewish females were killed than males. Women had less opportunity to survive, Joan Ringelheim writes. In the ghettos, they were less likely to be among the privileged who could escape the transports by buying work certificates. Records from the Łódź ghetto in 1942 show that twice as many women of childbearing age were sent to the death camps as males of the same age. More camps existed for men, Ringelheim notes, where there was a chance to survive.[26] Upon arrival at Auschwitz or Majdanek, a woman who was pregnant or with a child was sent immediately to the gas chambers, whereas men – even fathers – had a chance of being selected for slave labour, with some hope of survival. Selections at Auschwitz were not gender neutral, emphasizes Mary Felstiner: only one-third of the total deportees selected for labour were female, and when Auschwitz was liberated in 1945, only 17 per cent of the surviving Jews were women. This was not simply a consequence of deeming men better labourers. The Nazi aim to 'obliterate the biological basis of Jewry' required that they wipe out females. Felstiner explains: 'Even within the lowest life-form – the anti-race – women ranked lower still, for spawning it.'[27]

As they had in Germany before the war, the Nazis used mass sterilization in the camps to prevent the procreation of peoples considered inferior. Acting with what Gisela Bock terms 'sexist racism', Nazi doctors forcibly sterilized thousands of women, mostly Jews, Roma and Sinti, from 1942–5.[28] Many of them were subjected to barbarous medical experiments with caustic injections, radiation and operations without anaesthesia.[29] The goal: to find fast and efficient ways to accomplish sterilization of people 'unworthy' to procreate.

From the perspective of the Nazis, abortions were not necessary for Jewish women, as they would simply be killed.[30] However, Jews performed secret abortions in the camps to save women's lives. Some inmate doctors also delivered babies and quickly killed them for the same reason.[31] Jewish women in hiding who were pregnant or in childbirth also endured abortions and infanticide: they could neither properly care for an infant nor allow its cries to alert hostile neighbours or Nazi officials to their presence.[32] The Nazis decreed a death sentence for anyone caught hiding a Jew in Poland, and it was applied to the offender's entire family. In the world deformed by the Nazis, conception and childbirth sometimes begot death rather than life, while abortion or infanticide became acts of resistance, offering some hope of survival.

Soviet Policy Towards the People of Poland

The Soviet system grew from a class-based ideology. Under Stalin's leadership, class hatred often overlapped with national enmity, leading entire peoples to suffer repressive measures. In Stalin's eyes, the Poles were anathema to the Soviet system, and he denounced them as effete nobles, militant nationalists, zealous Catholics and bourgeois exploiters. Soviet hostility towards Poland had deep historical roots, as Poles and Russians had struggled over the territory relegated to the USSR in the Nazi–Soviet Pact for half a millennium. 'Reclaiming' that land in 1939, Soviet leaders included the entire Polish population in the broader group of class enemies. The Red Army's professed intention when invading was to rescue the Ukrainians and Belarusians, fellow Eastern Slavs, from the 'yoke of the Polish lords'.

People of all ethno-national groups were subjected to the upheaval of the Soviet occupation, but many Jews, Ukrainians and Belarusians welcomed the fall of Poland and received favourable positions and opportunities in the new regime.[33] Stalin's policies, one Russian historian maintains, were 'aimed at undermining Polish statehood and the gene pool of the Polish people'.[34] Occupation authorities encouraged ethnic violence against the Poles, and targeted them for dispossession and repression. Both women and men suspected of violating Soviet law were dealt with harshly: arrested, brutally interrogated, incarcerated in prisons and sent to forced labour camps in the USSR, the infamous Gulag. In their recollections of prison, Polish men recall the harsh treatment of females with surprise: 'At night I often heard terrifying screams, even of women', writes one.[35] And women deride Soviet attitudes towards them. 'There is a lot one can say about the heroism of the Soviet army', declared one: 'I remember how [...] four soldiers from the NKVD, with revolvers and bayonets pointed, came to our apartment, and of whom were they afraid? Three women? Such things really are comical.'[36] Like the Nazis in western and central Poland, the Soviets aimed to completely transform the society of eastern Poland, by obliterating not just the military force, political power and economic system of the Poles, but also their culture and values. They thus viewed women as real or anticipated enemies, too.

The lack of expected respect for Polish women was reinforced by Soviet gender ideology. The Soviets continued a long revolutionary commitment in Russia to women's emancipation, primarily by freeing them from the 'shackles of the family' and promoting their role in the public sphere, particularly in labour.[37] 'If women were to be liberated economically and psychologically', historian Wendy Goldman explains, 'they needed to become more like men, or more specifically, more like male workers.'[38] Despite the fact that Stalin declared the 'woman question' solved in 1930, traditional gender stereotypes persisted in the USSR and were reflected in Soviet actions in Poland. Men seemed to pose the greatest danger, and it was the army and its reserves that Stalin had eliminated first. Captured Polish soldiers and officers were interned in camps inside the USSR, and over 22,000 of them were subsequently shot. Executions by the Soviets involved almost exclusively men.[39]

Males in eastern Poland were also arrested and incarcerated in prisons and Soviet labour camps at a greater rate than women, approximately 9:1. But women and children comprised the majority of those suffering the other type of mass repression: deportation of nearly 400,000 civilians deep into the USSR.[40] Most of the women fell victim because of their relationship to a man who had fled, been arrested or had a profession that categorized him as dangerous. One deportee noted, 'I was deported to Siberia for the "guilt" of my husband Adam', who worked in army intelligence.[41] Unless they violated Soviet law themselves (in which case they were accorded their own identity and punished like men), women were seen relationally – identified primarily through the men to whom they were linked. Like children, they bore the guilt – real, supposed or anticipated – of their husbands, fathers and sons. Despite Soviet claims of the equality of the sexes, the most salient aspect of a female's identity appeared to be that of her male relations. Additionally, Polish women were traditionally entrusted with maintaining Polishness – imparting Polish language, religion and culture to children, whom they strove to raise as patriots.[42] In order to break the Polish nation and keep it from rising again, women with a strong connection to it also had to be removed. In subsequent accounts women generally mention the reasons for their deportation matter-of-factly, for they identified themselves in family terms, as well; their own fate appears an anticipated consequence of being Polish and female.[43]

The exiled Poles joined Soviet citizens in an uncompromising system, demanding labour and obedience at minimal compensation, typically explained to them as: 'Whoever works eats, whoever doesn't drops dead.'[44] One of the most common complaints of the Poles – meant as an implicit condemnation of the Soviet system – was that 'women as well as men' were forced to work, assigned to the same heavy physical labour and made to fulfil identical demanding quotas. This accorded with the Soviet commitment to women's equality. But what the Soviets lauded as progress, the Poles denounced as 'against all the laws of nature'.[45]

The Soviets sought to turn the deported Poles into obedient labourers and subjects of the communist state. Like the Nazis, they strove to suppress all manifestations of Polish national identity. Poles bore vicious insults, along with assertions that Poland was dead and God did not exist. They were forbidden to gather for prayer or celebrate their holidays, to sing patriotic songs, read Polish books or impart their culture to offspring. These prohibitions threatened women's overlapping identities as Polish and female. Resisting Soviet domination, they ran clandestine lessons, teaching their children Polish language, history and literature, drawing directly from female ancestors who had taken on that task during previous periods of foreign domination.[46]

Unsanctioned Sexual Violence

Though sexual violence – outside the brothel system – was neither ordered nor *officially* condoned, it was nevertheless ubiquitous in Nazi-occupied Poland (and western USSR). The topic of sexual abuse of males remains understudied, but it is clear that German officials at all levels used sexual violence against females to assert power and control, to humiliate the occupied population, and to act out violent racist and misogynistic feelings.[47] In its less invasive forms, the abuse involved forced nudity, accompanied by voyeurism and jeering. Such humiliations were imposed especially on Jewish women in the camps, who also had to endure the shaving of their heads, touching, and gratuitous gynaecological searches.[48]

Untold numbers of women in occupied Poland found themselves forced into survival prostitution. Owing to the atrocious living conditions and strict legal regime, women and girls of all ethnicities resorted to this, in cities and villages, in the ghettos and camps. They bartered sex for food, shelter, documents and jobs. Any man with greater authority or access to goods or documents could demand payment in sex, regardless of nationality. In an account that expresses the dilemma of many females, a Jewish woman related that she had repeatedly slept with an SS officer in Auschwitz:

> I loathed him then; I knew that he was a criminal and a killer. But as the months went by I got used to him. He kept me out of the gas chamber. He gave me food [...] Whatever I did it was my way of surviving.[49]

As Maren Röger points out, the boundaries between survival prostitution, consensual relations and sexual coercion were quite fluid.[50]

Despite the Nazis' concern for racial purity and Himmler's decree prohibiting sex with women of different races, Germans raped women in the east, both non-Jews and Jews. The authorities did not order sexual violence but did little to prevent or punish it, for they did not consider it a 'primary crime' and they had no regard for victims considered 'alien'.[51] Röger found that soon after the invasion there were many gang rapes, highlighting the Poles' complete defeat, and the humiliation of the Jews included the rape of women and girls in front of male relatives.[52] Throughout the occupation, German men with power used sexual blackmail, while lower-ranking officials raped during searches and seizures of apartments.[53] Interrogators sometimes used rape as a way to extract confessions, or simply to punish their victims.[54]

Nazi notions of 'racial hygiene' did not protect Jewish women, considered the most dangerous source of defilement, from rape even at the sites of their destruction. They were raped in the ghettos and camps by police, SS men and Ukrainian guards, in some cases forced to perform in cruel sexual spectacles.[55] Camp and military commanders sometimes chose young Jewish women to serve as their sex slaves.[56] After attacking the USSR (which included eastern Poland), Germans began massacring Jews along the Eastern Front; men of the SS and Wehrmacht viciously raped and mutilated many females before killing them.[57]

Women in Nazi-occupied Poland also suffered sexual violence from local men of different nationalities and even from co-nationals. In four specific settings females – particularly but not exclusively Jews – were highly vulnerable to sexual abuse: in hiding, ghettos, camps and partisan units. Jewish women 'passing' on the Aryan side could be raped by any man who discovered their identity and threatened to betray them to the Germans. In hiding, they had no protection from the people concealing them, or their relatives.[58] Ghettos and camps became 'spaces of violence' against women, perpetrated not only by the men in charge but also by fellow inmates.[59] Women who fled to the forest, Christian or Jewish, were in danger of being raped or murdered. They often had to have sex with the commanders of partisan units to be admitted, or enter a 'forest marriage' for protection from other men and to obtain necessary supplies.[60] In each of these sites men – even those of persecuted peoples –took advantage of women's lesser physical strength and lack of weapons, which left them isolated, unprotected and dependent.

Soviet officials, soldiers and regular citizens also committed sexual violations. Women who were arrested or deported faced rape and other types of sexual abuse during interrogations, in camps and in Soviet exile.[61] Sexual violence reached its most brutal and extensive levels in the last stage of the war and its immediate aftermath, as the Red Army drove the Germans from Soviet territory, across eastern Europe and back to Berlin. Soviet soldiers raped staggering numbers of women, perhaps as many as two million, between April 1944, when they entered East Prussia, and late 1946. Females of all ages were raped multiple times, gang raped, beaten and murdered.[62] While German women were victimized the most, perhaps as a form of revenge, they were not alone. Soviet troops raped in every country they entered, whether the people were on the Axis side of the war or the Allied, like the Poles.[63] They raped Jewish survivors as they liberated them from Auschwitz, and even compatriots whom they freed from Nazi slave labour.[64] Neither nationality nor politics were important – only their female bodies. Stalin's response to complaints of his soldiers' behaviour was to dismiss it as trivial: 'And what is so awful in his having fun with a woman, after such horrors?' he reportedly asked Milovan Djilas, a Yugoslav communist.[65] With the tacit acceptance of their governments, many German and Soviet men acted as if they had a right to use any woman they wanted as they pleased, and women were left with no recourse.

Civil war and ethnic cleansing at the war's end also included brutal sexual violence. The conflict between Poles and Ukrainians became an ever-escalating bloodbath, in which rape and mutilation of women's bodies occurred on both sides. One Polish fighter recalled: 'There were no orders as regards non-combatants and those in the unit thirsty for more blood knew that they could kill and rape who they wanted and how they wanted. The Ukrainians were doing even worse to our people.'[66] Further west, rape occurred commonly as Poles and Soviets sought to drive ethnic Germans from the land ceded to Poland.[67]

Survival, Resistance and Collaboration

The daily lives of most people in occupied Poland focused on the struggle for survival.[68] Requisitioning of foodstuffs for the Wehrmacht meant severe rationing for the civilian population, just above starvation levels for Poles and lower for Jews. Most people had to turn to the black market in order to obtain the goods they needed. Peasant women proved particularly important in this economy, as they were able to hide contraband foodstuffs in their blouses and skirts, as well as their baskets, to sell in the cities. Women generally aroused less suspicion from German authorities than men, so were better able to transport concealed items. In Soviet territory, as well, shortages of food and other basic items meant that many Polish women spent a good portion of their days in lines. They also queued at prisons, trying to obtain information about arrested relatives or deliver them packages.[69] Since large numbers of men fled the country, went into hiding or were arrested, women, many of whom had never had paid employment outside the home, had to adapt to the new economic conditions and search for work. Some survived by sewing, giving lessons or selling off their possessions.[70]

Under the Nazis, Polish parents feared for the safety of their children, who could be snatched from the streets by the authorities at any time. The children were screened for their racial features, and those found to be of 'racially valuable stock' were sent to the Reich to be raised as Germans. In such cases parents lost all track of their offspring.[71] An estimated 200,000 children were kidnapped, and only 15–20 per cent returned to Poland after the war.[72] In Soviet exile, children whose parents died or could not earn enough to feed them were taken to Soviet orphanages, where they were raised as Russians. Many women agonized over this, and lamented: 'We want our children to be raised in our spirit, not to forget their language and their nationality.'[73] The inability to protect or provide for their children led some women to suicide.[74]

In occupied Poland, everyday life and resistance often went hand in hand. Poles built the most extensive resistance movement in all of wartime Europe, which was consolidated into the Home Army or AK (*Armia Krajowa*). The Poles also constructed a functioning underground state. Linked with the Polish government-in-exile in London, it strove to maintain the legal and moral continuity of the state and guide resistance. An estimated 500,000 individuals joined the AK alone; the 'secret state' enjoyed the support of millions of Poles who participated to varying degrees, from boycotting Nazi films to industrial sabotage. The leaders of the AK and the government were men, but women were involved in nearly all forms of resistance. They taught and studied in underground schools and universities, published in secret journals and acted in illegal plays. They wrote slogans of defiance on public walls, produced and distributed underground publications. Women laid flowers at places of executions, tenaciously replacing them when the Germans removed them. They also planned and participated in operations to extract resistance members from Gestapo prisons and to kill collaborators sentenced by the underground courts.[75]

The level of women's involvement in the resistance depended on their age and family status. Those with children or sick or elderly relatives to care for considered those duties paramount and played less perilous roles. Younger, unencumbered women put aside their personal lives and security, especially in the roles of liaison officers or couriers. These women ferried false documents, intelligence and ammunition. They excelled as guides, sneaking people illegally across wartime borders and leading male fighters through the sewers of Warsaw during the 1944 Uprising. Jan Karski, a renowned member of the Polish resistance, noted that the average lifespan of these women, often just teenagers, was only a few months. He continued:

> It can be said that of all the workers in the Underground their lot was the most severe, their sacrifices the greatest, and their contribution the least rewarded. They were overworked and doomed. They neither held high rank nor received any great honours for their heroism.[76]

In these roles, and in the fighting they engaged in during the Warsaw Uprising, Polish women often operated far outside traditional gender expectations. They simply considered themselves Poles fighting for their country's independence. And by all accounts they performed capably and courageously. Yet they were rarely considered on par with the men in the resistance, who often refused them weapons. 'It should be said, once and for all, that women fought too', stated Ida Kasprzak, an AK member, after decades of hearing the resistance described as male: 'we did the most tedious and most dangerous jobs. Women were injured and killed in action. Men just don't want to admit that we fought too.'[77] These women rarely saw themselves, or were regarded, as heroes, for this was reserved for men as well.[78]

The same can be said for women in the Jewish resistance, many of whom also served as couriers. They were especially valuable because of their greater ability to 'pass' as Christians. In Warsaw, females of the Jewish Fighting Organization (ŻOB) left the ghetto to operate on the Aryan side, concealing all signs of their Jewishness.[79] These women arranged hiding places for other Jews and regularly distributed money and fake identity cards; they maintained contacts with the AK and smuggled weapons and supplies into the ghetto. They courageously performed these tasks in a hostile environment, where not only Nazis hunted Jews but some Poles, either for material gain or from anti-Semitism.

Jewish women's participation in the resistance is even less known than Polish women's, for it is doubly obscured. For decades, the belief prevailed that during the Holocaust the Jews did not fight back; gender bias further marginalized the role of Jewish women. Although resistance by Jews was on a smaller scale, given their isolation, Jewish women also engaged in acts ranging from everyday defiance to outright combat.[80] Men have gained the most attention for leading uprisings against Germans in the ghettos (in Warsaw, Białystok, Częstochowa) and death camps (Treblinka, Sobibor, Auschwitz-Birkenau). Though little known, women also fought and died in the ghetto uprisings; several who survived later fought in the 1944 Warsaw Uprising. Irena Lewkowska served on the organizing committee of the Treblinka revolt; a small group of women, who were subsequently tortured and hanged, smuggled the gunpowder used in the Birkenau uprising.[81]

No collaborationist government was formed in Poland, though many public sector employees continued to work in administration. Most historians describe them as accommodating to the new regime, sometimes while resisting, and in fewer cases collaborating. Underground courts meted out punishment to over-zealous bureaucrats and policemen, compliant writers and actors, and anyone betraying members of the resistance. They also sentenced individuals identified as *Volksdeutsche*, as well as Ukrainians, for anti-Polish actions.[82]

In the east, Ukrainians, Jews and Belarusians have been accused of assisting in the Soviet oppression of Poles.[83] Recent research has uncovered greater Polish participation in persecuting Jews than hitherto acknowledged.[84] Such behaviour ranged from looting their property to betraying them to the Nazis; from refusing them admittance to partisan units to outright killing.

Collaboration in Poland has yet to be studied through the lens of gender. It seems clear that the majority of the police, bureaucrats and violent members of the ethnic minorities punished by the underground were male. Women were especially singled out as traitors for sexual crimes – consorting with German men. Patriots typically denounced them as whores, without questioning whether the relations were coerced or consensual. As in other parts of Europe, retribution included beating, head shaving or even execution.[85]

Conclusion

Both the Nazis and the Soviets invaded Poland in 1939 with broad and violent aims. The Nazis sought to destroy or dominate 'racial' enemies, Jews and Poles respectively; the Soviets aimed to eliminate class enemies, a label which only partly masked national enmity. The occupiers considered entire peoples as alien or inimical to their interests, and were willing to use the most extreme measures against them. All members, regardless of sex, thus became legitimate and even necessary targets.

Though racial, national and class ideologies dominated the policies of the occupiers, gender was not absent from their strategies. The Nazis considered Jews the greatest threat to the German nation; within that framework females were reduced to their reproductive and sexual functions. The ability to bear children – which guaranteed a future for the Jews – rendered them especially dangerous, and the Nazis made particular efforts to sterilize them, experiment on them and to quickly eliminate new and expectant mothers. The Soviets, in attacking the Polish nation, did not seek to kill Polish women. But as family members of men who had led or supported the Polish state and could continue to fight for its independence, females, too, were seen as 'socially dangerous elements', and therefore subjected to repressive measures. Additionally, their traditional function of raising patriotic children had to be curtailed.

Despite Nazi concepts of 'racial hygiene' and the prohibition on having sexual relations with women of 'inferior races', German men used both Jewish and Polish women to satisfy their sexual desires and their will to dominate and humiliate. It could be that the cloak of racial inferiority cast on the women of Poland unleashed sexual rapaciousness among many German men. But it is important to note that patriarchal gender views lay at the heart of their treatment of these women. Like men of the Red Army at the close of the war, many German men acted as if they had the right to force any female to submit to their sexual predations, acting brutally, even murderously, from feelings of anger, revenge, lust or misogyny. For Soviet soldiers who wanted to rape, nothing seemed to matter about the victim's identity but her sex – not her nationality, politics or recent past. They not only raped women of the enemy (Germans), but women of Allied nations (Poles) and women that they liberated from the Nazi camps (Jews). They even raped their 'own' (Soviet) women, as they freed them from slave labour in Germany. In an environment in which their leaders declared war on entire groups of people because of their identity, and sanctioned unrestrained violence against them, many men felt entitled to exploit women sexually. Gender was not erased in the ideological and indiscriminate violence in Poland during World War II, it was amplified.

The attacks on Jews and Poles as entire peoples led to a closing of ranks and an even greater sense of identification of many individuals with their own people. Even Jews who had assimilated to the dominant culture in their homeland could be only Jews under the Nazis. And Polish nationalism was only strengthened by German and Soviet oppression. Though nationality identified and motivated people in their struggles to survive and resist, gender did not recede. Males and females tended to play traditional roles ascribed to their gender. Even though females often transcended these roles and acted and fought in ways typically considered male, they were not seen as equals to men. They were left out of leadership roles, denied weapons for combat and excluded from the national depictions of heroism. The fact that they were female almost always seemed to matter, even to the women themselves, who rarely claimed credit, heroism or equality. The wartime experience, far from erasing or diminishing essentialized notions of gender in Poland, seems to have confirmed them, and may have made them a critical part of the post-war need for normalcy – particularly in the face of the new conqueror's attempt to import the Soviet answer to the 'woman question'.

Recent historiography on the war in western Europe has examined the gendered nature of state mobilization of civilians, particularly through propaganda and social welfare policies; the voluntary movement of women into 'male' jobs, giving them new skills and independence; the loosening of sexual mores; and bifurcated roles of men and women on the military front. A more comprehensive gender history of Europe at war must take into account the gendered *use of* and *reactions to* unparalleled violence – both targeted and arbitrary; the obliteration of citizenship and human rights; massive dislocation and involuntary labour; efforts to control reproduction and destroy ethno-national identities and cultures. It must incorporate the gendered aspects of disempowerment, privation, degradation and trauma – hallmarks of the wartime experience in the east.

Notes

1. For example, Józef Garliński, *Poland in the Second World War* (New York: Hippocrene, 1985); Richard C. Lukas, *The Forgotten Holocaust: the Poles Under German Occupation 1939–1944* (Louisville: University of Kentucky Press, 1986); Halik Kochanski, *The Eagle Unbowed: Poland and the Poles in the Second World War* (Cambridge, MA: Harvard University Press, 2012).
2. The other sizeable minority groups were Ukrainians, Belarusians, Lithuanians, Germans, Russians and Czechs.
3. Quoted in Tadesuz Piotrowski, *Poland's Holocaust: Ethnic Strife, Collaboration with Occupying Forces and Genocide in the Second Republic, 1918–1947* (Jefferson, NC: McFarland, 1998), 115. Ethnic Ukrainians on Polish territory, though also Slavs, were treated better than Poles by the Nazis, because 'the Germans hoped to play them off the Poles': John Connelly, 'Nazis and Slavs: From Racial Theory to Racist Practice', *Central European History* vol. 32, no. 1 (1999): 8.
4. On the Nazi invasion, see Alexander B. Rossino, *Hitler Strikes Poland: Blitzkrieg, Ideology, and Atrocity* (Lawrence: University of Kansas Press, 2003).
5. See Maria Wardzyńska, *Był rok 1939. Operacja niemieckiej policji bezpieczeństwa w Polsce. Intelligenzaktion* (Warsaw: Instytut Pamięci Narodowej, 2009).
6. In one case, 50 women were shot, including a 14-year-old girl. Rossino, *Hitler Strikes*, 79. See also Mark Mazower, *Hitler's Empire: How the Nazis Ruled Europe* (New York: Penguin Press, 2008), 448.
7. See Tadeusz Cyprian and Jerzy Sawicki, *Nazi Rule in Poland 1939–1945* (Warsaw: Polonia, 1961), 125–34.
8. Auschwitz-Birkenau: Miejsce Pamięci i Muzeum, available at auschwitz.org/historia/rozne-grupy-wiezniow/polacy/ (accessed 25 August 2015).
9. Quoted in Cyprian, *Nazi Rule*, 100, 104.
10. Quoted in Cyprian, *Nazi Rule*, 141.
11. Quoted in Cyprian, *Nazi Rule*, 136.
12. Ulrich Herbert, *Hitler's Foreign Workers: Enforced Foreign Labor in Germany under the Third Reich* (Cambridge: Cambridge University Press, 1997), 63, 392.
13. Birthe Kundrus and Patricia Szobar, 'Forbidden Company: Romantic Relationships Between Germans and Foreigners, 1939 to 1945', *Journal of the History of Sexuality* vol. 11, no. 1–2 (2002): 214–16.
14. Anna Rosmus, 'Involuntary Abortions for Polish Forced Laborers', in Elizabeth R. Baer and Myrna Goldenberg (eds), *Experience and Expression: Women, the Nazis, and the Holocaust* (Detroit, MI: Wayne State University Press, 2003), 78, 82.
15. Herbert, *Hitler's Foreign Workers*, 131–2, 270–1.
16. Rosmus, 'Involuntary Abortions', 86.
17. See Wendy Jo Gertjejanssen, 'Victims, Heroes, Survivors: Sexual Violence on the Eastern Front during World War II' (PhD thesis, University of Minnesota, 2004), 168–75.
18. Quoted in Nanda Herbermann, *The Blessed Abyss: Inmate #6582 in Ravensbrück Concentration Camp for Women* (Detroit, MI: Wayne State University Press, 2000), 34. Gertjejanssen suspects the number is much higher: Gertjejanssen, 'Victims, Heroes', 169, 223.
19. Cezary Gmyz, 'Seksualne niewolnice III Rzeszy', *Wprost 24* no. 17–18 (2007), available at web.archive.org/web/20110608174340/www.wprost.pl/ar/105285/Seksualne-niewolnice-III-Rzeszy/ (accessed 19 August 2015).
20. Gertjejanssen, 'Victims, Heroes', 177–86, 197–202, 216.

21. Elizabeth D. Heineman, 'Sexuality and Nazism: The Doubly Unspeakable?', *Journal of the History of Sexuality* vol. 11, no. 1–2 (2002): 54.

22. Gertjejanssen, 'Victims, Heroes', 232–4, 237–8.

23. Robert Sommer, 'Camp Brothels: Forced Sex Labour in Nazi Concentration Camps', in Dagmar Herzog (ed.), *Brutality and Desire: War and Sexuality in Europe's Twentieth Century* (Basingstoke: Palgrave Macmillan, 2008), 169–73, 175, 179.

24. Helene J. Sinnreich, 'The Rape of Jewish Women in the Holocaust', in Sonja M. Hedgepeth and Rochelle G. Saidel (eds), *Sexual Violence Against Jewish Women during the Holocaust* (Waltham, MA: Brandeis University Press, 2010), 115–16; Regina Mülhäuser, 'Between "Racial Awareness" and Fantasies of Potency: Nazi Sexual Politics in the Occupied Territories of the Soviet Union', in Herzog (ed.), *Brutality*, 207; Gertjejanssen, 'Victims, Heroes', 190–6, 229–30. Some scholars disagree: Sommer, 'Camp Brothels', 117; Nomi Levenkron, 'Death and the Maidens: "Prostitution", Rape, and Sexual Slavery during World War II', in Hedgepeth and Saidel (eds), *Sexual Violence*, 19.

25. Quoted in Eric Ehrenreich, *Nazi Ancestral Proof: Genealogy, Racial Science, and the Final Solution* (Bloomington: Indiana University Press, 2007), 165.

26. Joan Ringelheim, 'Women and the Holocaust: A Reconsideration of Research', in Carol Rittner and John K. Roth (eds), *Different Voices: Women and the Holocaust* (St. Paul: MN Paragon House, 1993), 391–400.

27. Mary Lowenthal Felstiner, *To Paint Her Life: Charlotte Salomon in the Nazi Era* (New York: Harper Perennial, 1994), 206–7.

28. Gisela Bock, 'Racism and Sexism in Nazi Germany: Motherhood, Compulsory Sterilization, and the State', *Signs* vol. 8, no. 3 (1983): 417.

29. See Lore Shelley, *Criminal Experiments on Human Beings in Auschwitz and War Research Laboratories: Twenty Women Prisoners' Accounts* (San Francisco, CA: Mellen Research University Press, 1991).

30. Bock, 'Racism and Sexism', 408–9.

31. Gisela Perl, *I Was a Doctor in Auschwitz* (Salem, NH: Ayer, 1997); Lidia Rosenfeld Vago, 'One Year in the Black Hole of Our Planet Earth', in Dalia Ofer and Lenore J. Weitzman (eds), *Women in the Holocaust* (New Haven, CT: Yale University Press, 1998), 281.

32. Adina Blady Szwajger, *I Remember Nothing More: the Warsaw Children's Hospital and the Jewish Resistance* (New York: Pantheon, 1990), 146.

33. Jan T. Gross, *Revolution from Abroad: the Soviet Conquest of Poland's Western Ukraine and Western Belorussia* (Princeton, NJ: Princeton University Press, 1988), 28–35, 50–6, 63–6.

34. N. S. Lebedeva, 'The Deportation of the Polish Population to the USSR, 1939–1941', *Journal of Communist Studies and Transition Politics* vol. 16, no. 1–2 (2000): 44.

35. Hoover Institution Archives (hereafter HIA), Władysław Anders Collection, 1939–1946 (hereafter AC), Box 48, vol. 19, no. R1355. See also AC, Box 54, vol. 37, no. R7911; Box 35, vol. 1, no. 1253.

36. AC, Box 36, vol. 2, no. 1976; Box 45, vol. 14, no. 14448.

37. See also Laycock and Johnson, this volume; Kaminer, this volume.

38. Wendy Z. Goldman, *Women, the State and Revolution: Soviet Family Policy and Social Life, 1917–1936* (Cambridge: Cambridge University Press, 1993), 11.

39. One woman, a Second Lieutenant in the Polish Air Force, was slain at Katyń; see *Lista Katyńska, Jeńcy obozów Kozielsk, Ostaszków, Starobielsk zaginieni w Rosji Sowieckiej* (Warsaw: Omnipress, 1989), 111. On gender and Stalin's purges, see Jehanne M. Gheith and Katherine R. Jolluck, *Gulag Voices: Oral Histories of Soviet Incarceration and Exile* (New York: Palgrave Macmillan, 2011), 130–1.

40. Katherine R. Jolluck, *Exile and Identity: Polish Women in the Soviet Union During World War II* (Pittsburgh, PA: University of Pittsburgh Press, 2002), 9–13; Lebedeva, 'Deportation', 33–44. The majority were ethnic Poles: Grzegorz Hryciuk, 'Deportacje ludności Polskiej', in S. Ciesielski, G. Hryciuk and A. Srebrakowski (eds), *Masowe deportacje radzieckie w okresie II wojny światowej* (Wrocław: Instytut Historyczny Uniwersytetu Wrocławskiego, 1994), 68.
41. AC, Box 53, vol. 34, no. R6856.
42. Jolluck, *Exile*, 87–141. Compare Paces, this volume.
43. Jolluck, *Exile*, 99.
44. AC, Box 51, vol. 27, no. R4565.
45. Jolluck, *Exile*, 45–86.
46. Jolluck, *Exile*, 120.
47. For brief discussions of the sexual abuse of males, see: Monika Flaschka, '"Only Pretty Women were Raped": the Effect of Sexual Violence on Gender Identities in the Concentration Camps', in Hedgepeth and Saidel (eds), *Sexual Violence*, 86–8; Gertjejanssen, 'Victims, Heroes', 107–14, 257.
48. Levenkron, 'Death and the Maidens', 22; Na'ama Shik, 'Sexual Abuse of Jewish Women in Auschwitz-Birkenau', in Herzog (ed.), *Brutality*, 229–31; Myrna Goldenberg, 'Memoirs of Auschwitz Survivors: the Burden of Gender', in Ofer and Weitzman (eds), *Women*, 330–1, 333, 336.
49. Quoted in Gertjejanssen, 'Victims, Heroes', 116; 89–120. And see more generally Levenkron, 'Death and the Maidens', 20.
50. Maren Röger, 'The Sexual Policies and Sexual Realities of the German Occupiers in Poland in the Second World War', *Contemporary European History* vol. 23, no. 1 (2014): 13.
51. Mülhäuser, 'Between "Racial Awareness"', 197–220; Gertjejanssen, 'Victims, Heroes', 286–9.
52. Gmyz, 'Seksualne niewolnice'; Röger, 'Sexual Policies', 10–11; Sinnreich, 'Rape of Jewish Women', 110; Gertjejanssen, 'Victims, Heroes', 313–14.
53. Röger, 'Sexual Policies', 16–17.
54. Mülhäuser, 'Between "Racial Awareness"', 201.
55. Gertjejanssen, 'Victims, Heroes', 303–10, 315–17; Levenkron, 'Death and the Maidens', 17.
56. Felicja Karay, 'Women in the Forced Labor Camps', in Ofer and Weitzman (eds), *Women*, 290–1; Anatoly Podolsky, 'The Tragic Fate of Ukrainian Jewish Women under Nazi Occupation, 1941–1944', in Hedgepeth and Saidel (eds), *Sexual Violence*, 96–7.
57. Podolsky, 'Tragic Fate', 96–102.
58. Zoe Waxman, 'Rape and Sexual Abuse in Hiding', in Hedgepeth and Saidel (eds), *Sexual Violence*, 124–35.
59. Levenkron, 'Death and the Maidens', 20; Sinnreich, 'Rape of Jewish Women', 111–15; Shik, 'Sexual Abuse', 233–5, 239; Karay, 'Women in the Forced Labor Camps', 290–1.
60. Nechama Tec, 'Women in the Forest', *Contemporary Jewry* vol. 17 (1996): 34–47; Tamara Vershitskaya, 'Jewish Women Partisans in Belarus', *Journal of Ecumenical Studies* vol. 46, no. 4, (2011): 567–72.
61. See Jolluck, *Exile*, 153–75.
62. Norman M. Naimark, *The Russians in Germany: a History of the Soviet Zone of Occupation, 1945–1949* (Cambridge, MA: Harvard University Press, 1995), 69–140.
63. Joanna Ostrowska and Marcin Zaremba, 'Kobieca gehenna', *Polityka*, 16 October 2013.

64. Antony Beevor, *The Fall of Berlin 1945* (New York: Viking, 2002), 65, 107–10; Laurence Rees, *Auschwitz: a New History* (New York: Public Affairs, 2005), 272–4; Ostrowska, 'Kobieca gehenna'.
65. Milovan Djilas, *Conversations with Stalin* (New York: Harcourt, Brace & Co., 1962), 110.
66. Waldemar Lotnik, *Nine Lives: Ethnic Conflict in the Polish-Ukrainian Borderlands* (London: Serif, 1999), 65–9.
67. Norman M. Naimark, *Fires of Hatred: Ethnic Cleansing in Twentieth-Century Europe* (Cambridge, MA: Harvard University Press, 2001), 126–8.
68. A voluminous literature exists on life in the ghettos and camps, so it will not be discussed here.
69. Compare Muller, this volume.
70. AC, Box 45, vol. 13, no. 14229.
71. Cyprian, *Nazi Rule*, 83–91.
72. Kochanski, *Eagle Unbowed*, 271.
73. HIA, Stanisław Mikołajczyk, Papers, 1938–66, Box 18, folder 'November–December 1941', 'Do Opieki Społecznej przy Ambasadzie w Kujbyszewie'.
74. AC, Box 42, vol. 10, no. 11638.
75. Jan Karski, *Story of a Secret State* (Boston, MA: Houghton Mifflin, 1944), 178–85, 219–29.
76. Karski, *Secret State*, 281.
77. Quoted in Shelley Saywell, *Women in War* (New York: Viking, 1985), 102. See also Weronika Grzebalska, *Płeć powstania warszawskiego* (Warsaw: Instytut Badań Literackich, 2013). Compare Bischl, this volume.
78. See also Muller, this volume; Jolluck, *Exile*, 104–11.
79. See Szwajger, *I Remember*, 67–177; Nechama Tec, *Resilience and Courage: Women, Men, and the Holocaust* (New Haven, CT: Yale University Press, 2003), 205–55. Jewish men were circumcised, unlike Polish ones, and could be identified quickly by a suspicious German.
80. See Tec, *Resilience and Courage*, 256–339.
81. See Zivia Lubetkin, *In the Days of Destruction and Revolt* ([n.p.]: Ghetto Fighters House, 1981); Yitzhak Arad, *Belzec, Sobibor, Treblinka: The Operation Reinhard Death Camps* (Bloomington: Indiana University Press, 1987), 219; Sobiborinterviews.nl, available at www.sobiborinterviews.nl/en/the-revolt/survivors-of-the-revolt (accessed 24 August 2015); Leni Yahil, *The Holocaust: the Fate of European Jewry, 1932–1945* (Oxford: Oxford University Press, 1987), 486.
82. Jan T. Gross, *Polish Society under German Occupation: the Generalgouvernement, 1939–1944* (Princeton, NJ: Princeton University Press, 1979), 125–33, 190–3; Marek Jan Chodakewicz, *Between Nazis and Soviets: Occupation Politics in Poland, 1939–1947* (Lanham, MD: Lexington Books, 2004), 76–9, 81, 85–6.
83. Piotrowski, *Poland's Holocaust*, 48–57, 144–7, 198–203; Gross, *Revolution*, 29.
84. Jan T. Gross, *Neighbors: The Destruction of the Jewish Community in Jedwabne, Poland* (Princeton, NJ: Princeton University Press, 2001); Jan Grabowski, *Hunt for the Jews: Betrayal and Murder in German-Occupied Poland* (Bloomington: Indiana University Press, 2013).
85. Stefan Korboński, *Fighting Warsaw: the Story of the Polish Underground State, 1939–1945* (London: Allen and Unwin, 1956), 140–1; Chodakewicz, *Between Nazis*, 138; Röger, 'Sexual Policies', 12, 16.

6
Female Red Army Soldiers in World War II and Beyond[1]

Kerstin Bischl

Between 1941 and 1945, around 800,000 Soviet women fought in the Red Army alongside Soviet men, in roles such as medical orderlies, radio operators, snipers and pilots. Though they only constituted between 2 and 3 per cent of Soviet forces, few other social groups within the Red Army have attracted as much attention: their status as soldiers, their carrying of arms and their front-line service in a state military made them a historical novelty in modern Europe, besides smaller numbers of women who served in partisan forces. Indeed, they have remained subjects of historical debate into the present day. The case of female Red Army soldiers not only demonstrates how Soviet gender regimes discussed in earlier chapters adapted to total war but also, as this chapter shows by analysing collections of these women's narratives produced at several points in Soviet and post-Soviet Russia, how the subject of gender relations in the past has consistently been open to struggle and reinterpretation as gender regimes are renegotiated in a given historical moment. The history of women in the Red Army contributes to an understanding of women's agency within state socialist and masculinist institutions not only during wartime but afterwards, when women's testimonies about wartime military service formed part of public memory of Stalinism and war.

Female Soviet soldiers were neither solely heroines of emancipation created by the Soviet state nor naïve victims deceived by Soviet propaganda and taken advantage of by male comrades. They were, rather, individuals with agency which they had to negotiate firstly within the contradictory setting of Stalin's USSR at war, then throughout later versions of Soviet Communism, and then after the collapse of the USSR itself. In fact, the re-evaluation and reinterpretation of the Red Army's female soldiers on which this chapter focuses began while the 'Great Patriotic War' of 1941–5 was still taking place: although the Soviet authorities had initially been reluctant to mobilize women, by 1943 – in circulated speeches to be read out in honour of International Women's Day before the one and only First All-Women's Volunteer Rifle Brigade – they promoted the idea that women's military service depicted the achievement of full gender equality in the USSR.[2] A state-sponsored textbook about heroic women and their deeds, *Sovetskaya Zhenshchina na frontakh velikoy otechestvennoy voyny – Sbornik vospominaniy i ocherkov* (*The Soviet Woman on the Fronts of the Great Patriotic War – A Collection of Memoirs and Reports*), containing fragments from reworked interviews conducted by the Commission for the History of the Great Patriotic War, was even planned for the aftermath of the war,[3] but never saw print: all commemoration of individual soldiers besides Stalin was halted after the war in order to prevent war heroes challenging Stalin's power. After Stalin's death in 1953, and especially under Leonid Brezhnev, several Soviet publications (including textbooks and female veterans' memoirs) gave women their share of the victory. Considering female Red Army soldiers as one homogeneous group, but with different tasks, they presented them as heroines, who had been educated and motivated in the Soviet Union and risked their well-being to save their country.[4] Several works in the West would later follow this perspective.[5]

The most sophisticated of these books is Anna Krylova's *Soviet Women in Combat: a History of Violence on the Eastern Front* (2010). Following Joan Scott in taking gender as a category of historical analysis and asking about its social meaning rather than viewing gender as a given fact, Krylova argues that a new generation of Soviet women emerged in the 1930s, when women as well as men were empowered to fulfil their civic duties, if necessary with weapons.[6] By pointing to the female soldiers as representatives of this new femininity, Krylova not only exposes gaps in depictions of the war that have continued to neglect women's presence and contributions in the Red Army,[7] but also challenges recent interpretations of the 1930s as a period of gender backlash in the USSR when women were once again bound to family duties.[8] She questions Thomas G. Schrand's argument that Soviet society was symbolically reared only in one gender, the masculine one of the worker.[9]

Krylova's rather heroic depiction of these women has, however, been rejected by Roger Markwick and Euridice Cardona. These historians have broadened their focus beyond Krylova's exclusive attention to the 120,000 well-trained female pilots, snipers and machine-gunners who had opportunities to publish their memoirs during and after the inflation of heroic depictions of the war and who could be considered the wartime female elite. Markwick and Cardona emphasize the high levels of sexual harassment in the army, by which the patriotism of those women serving voluntarily was 'betrayed',[10] and concentrate on their rather marginalized position in the Red Army. Unlike Krylova, Markwick and Cardona do not perceive them as representatives of a better and more gender-equal Soviet Union.

For Western scholars, dealing with female Red Army soldiers seems to be a way of making a judgement about female emancipation in the USSR, to provide their audience at home with a more or less encouraging example of social change carried out by or regarding women. In a strict historiographical sense, these arguments about the experience of fighting in the Great Patriotic War are plausible to some extent and supported by evidence – yet, when they are juxtaposed, very different interpretations and judgements of Soviet women's position in the social order of the Red Army emerge. Comparing evidence from oral history interviews from the 1940s, 1980s and 2000s, this chapter deepens the debate by asking how (former) Red Army women interpreted their gendered experiences concerning their military service, and what (narrative) strategies they applied in order to deal with their social position in the army during the war and afterwards.

Women's narratives about their experiences in oral history interviews varied. In the 5,000 transcribed and reworked interviews conducted by the state-organized Commission for the History of the Great Patriotic War in 1942–7, women's interviews stressed how eager they had been to be good soldiers and Soviet citizens, equal to their male comrades.[11] Several decades later, in oral history projects with former female soldiers, often conducted by female historians in a rather private setting, the tone had changed.[12] Now, they stressed that they had kept their feminine side even under front-line conditions, thus hinting at their precarious solutions to sexual harassment in the Red Army and challenging discriminations they had experienced after the war. Recent testimonies collected during a patriotic tide that has been sweeping Russia since the mid-2000s, however, condemn such feminine strategies of allure, instead presenting female soldiers who were capable of defending themselves without giving in to 'immorality'.[13]

By presenting these different narratives in testimonies from women of all ranks, each interviewed only for one body of sources, the chapter gives a more holistic and nuanced picture of their military service, avoiding over-simplistic ascriptions such as 'betrayed' or 'heroic'. By pointing to the different claims interviewees make about what it meant to be a good female soldier and about femininity at the front throughout the decades, it also reveals that women's position in the Red Army was tenuous and remained so. Hence, the chapter treats the changing narratives of (former) female Red Army soldiers as speech-acts and strategies in order to face different social realities and expectations and as an opportunity to act and to present oneself – be it to the Soviet system embodied by its historians, to (former) comrades, or to whomever they imagined to be their audience – thus confirming or challenging present-day discursive assumptions about what their experiences would have been. The memories they tell should therefore be seen as artefacts of the past and present, or, better, as a way to present one's own past according to the needs of the present, often establishing individual counter-narratives to assumptions that at a given moment have become mainstream.[14] These speech-acts are expressions of agency within larger public renegotiations of gender regimes.

Naivety and Vanguardism: Contemporaneous Testimonies by Female Soldiers

The most contemporaneous accounts by women serving in the Red Army are testimonies collected by Soviet historians in the 1940s for a planned *History of the Great Patriotic War*. Many were recorded during the war itself, sometimes within spitting distance of the battlefields. Because of the setting, one could say that they gave the respondents a chance to perform in the way that they wanted the Soviet system to perceive them. In their reworked interview transcripts, unsurprisingly, the women stressed their Soviet way of life and how closely they resembled the features of an ideal Soviet citizen: pointing to the very hard living and family conditions that had compelled them to work very hard since childhood, they had become compatriots impressed by Soviet propaganda, committed to sport, and part of the vanguard.[15] Their motivations to fight were articulated in the vocabulary being offered by the state, such as fighting for the motherland or taking revenge on the enemy. Sometimes, fighting was a family issue, as they and their husbands decided together to volunteer.[16] In any case, the description of task-fulfilment prevails in these testimonies.

The process of being called upon by the Soviet authorities, answering the call, was notably described by Galina Golofeevskaya, a reconnaissance soldier, who was interviewed in 1944 and 1947. She was first assigned to air defence in Moscow, where she had already felt herself to be a hero. She:

> ended up in the Army [when] there was the mobilization call-up [...]. The Komsomol informed us [...]. All the Komsomol girls wrote a request, some 75 people. It was a big upsweep [*podyem*], everybody wanted to go to the front so hard. [...]. After that month [of waiting for an answer] it became clear that they would take only two of us. [They] sent me and a nurse.[17]

Golofeevskaya and her fellow volunteers had very naïve ideas about how service would look:

> We remembered the example of the Civil War, when everybody defended the homeland with a rifle in his hands. There was a lot of romanticism. We spoke a lot about Anka from *Chapaev*, and for sure, we knew the fact that in the Civil War there were a lot of women at the front.[18]

Despite all these fantasies, however, she was sure: 'We were all patriots.' And so, when she was selected, 'there was so much happiness. "I will go to the front." I jumped out of the office, told [everybody] that I will go to the front. The girls got jealous: "How come? Why just two?".'[19]

Next, however, Golofeevskaya had to go through another stage of selection, where she was asked about her qualifications as a soldier, such as her training in shooting. She started to cry during the selection board as she had to confess she could do nothing except bandage a wound. It annoyed the officer in charge, who asked her why she was crying and what kind of soldier she thought she was, behaving the way she did. In the end, Golofeevskaya started her military career as a radio operator.[20]

Golofeevskaya's statement, like others by women soldiers with similar narratives, stressed that she and the other women saw their military service as a normal part of their biography, into which the war intruded. Or, better: they needed it to feel worthy in a society that had raised them with heroic (fictional) role models such as Anka and a sense of vanguardism from youth onwards. Thus, they could see the selections as a test and would be embarrassed if, as Golofeevskaya feared, they did not pass. This would confirm Krylova's argument that the USSR had indeed raised women who wanted to play their part in being of use for the country. But one could interpret it also as an effect of the Stalinism that had been implanted into them: that, in moments when they felt themselves under the surveillance of the Soviet system, they needed to show their devotion for the system. This occurred during the interviews themselves in the 1940s, as well as in most other situations during the reign of Stalin, whose carrot-and-stick system instilled a high level of distrust into its citizens through terror and surveillance. Showing their military eagerness could even be a means of washing off any possible stain that could have come across them or their families.[21]

For their aspirations to present their 'Sovietness', it did not matter much what gendered image the women had of themselves: they could equally have seen themselves as representative of (a new) femininity, being proud of their vanguard role and enjoying the disbelief and anger of Wehrmacht men being fired at by 'devushki' (young girls),[22] or instead have acted out of anti-feminine resentments, refusing allegedly female behaviour and company, and wishing to trespass the limits of their ascribed gender which was perceived as backward.[23] In any case, their service could be accompanied by taking up masculine habits such as smoking and cursing.[24]

The military authorities, unfortunately, were not always prepared to grant the women the fulfilment of these aspirations.[25] As Golofeevskaya's account has already shown, women's wish to serve was not received enthusiastically, owing to a gendered bias. Almost all women who talked about their Red Army experience mentioned that they had initially been rejected for service.[26] The highly skilled Irina Dunaevskaya, for example, had to wait for one year before she could join the army as an interpreter. By the time she arrived, her husband, with whom she wanted to serve, was already dead.[27] Others had to take the initiative into their own hands: when their requests were not granted, they 'deserted' from military schooling to the front.[28] As a rule, the authorities could find many arguments to discourage women: from their obligations to their families and the *kolkhoz* (collective farm) to the problems of accommodation alongside men[29] – most of these objections could also have been made against the military service of men, but were not. When the authorities could not change it, they, or male comrades, could even apply a boycott – turning their backs on the women and spitting on the ground – when women arrived at the front.[30] In accordance with Krylova, then, non-elite women like Golofeevskaya also epitomized the changing, and yet not clear-cut, gender order of the Soviet Union. For them, there were now new multi-layered roles by which to be of use for the state, and they strove for them, especially when talking to the state's representatives.

Expectations, Adjustments and Quarrels: Female Veterans Remember their Service

The young and eager women who passed the recruiting panels joined the war at a time when the fate of the Soviet Union hung in the balance. They encountered an army that was as incapable of waging war as its leaders were ambiguous about their service. Nevertheless, they had to adjust to wartime conditions that were neither easy for men nor women. For all of them military service within the German war of annihilation meant the very high risk of death, hunger, cold and other deprivations due to military unreadiness, the lack of materiel and sudden retreats. In the psychological realm, it meant trauma and fatalism as a result of chaos, haste and boredom, underlined by Soviet propaganda and Stalinist measures against defeatism and treason.[31]

Most of these topics were only brought up after the years of perestroika in the 1980s, when veterans inside and outside the USSR revealed features of their service that did not go along with the official story of heroism, capacity for suffering and comradeship. In addition to that, women's testimonies since that time, given in rather private settings, came up with other features of their service that had not been discussed before: their beauty habits at the front, their need to find a husband there and the quarrels there had been among women.

A representative account in this respect belonged to Klara Tikhonovich, who had operated an anti-aircraft gun.[32] For her there had been some confusion, because she and others at the front had been very eager to become:

> like men. At the beginning, oh yes. We had our hair cut very short, changed our movement when walking. But later on, no more, no. We wanted to wear make-up, we saved our sugar and used it for our hair. We were happy, when we found a cauldron of water for washing our hair. [...] We cleaned ourselves with grass. We had our specifics, we girls.[33]

Tikhonovich's statement can be taken as a description of how women were because of their 'nature', which overcame what she perceived as the misleading aspirations they had started with. Looking at other statements about femininity at the front, however, makes it clear that women emphasizing beauty habits there had a twofold agenda. Firstly, they challenged disrespectful assumptions, about 'army girls' having become vulgar and mannish, which had been revealed during and after the war, and, secondly, they disclose that physical beauty was a category that helped women to obtain a social position in the Red Army during wartime. This position meant being attached to a man and was negotiated in regard to men, but also in regard to other women and female soldiers, who had to be downgraded as possible rivals.

The first part of the agenda can be found in Tikhonovich's account itself. Her statement about 'we girls' as a collective was initiated by referring to the name calling she had endured after the war, by remembering painfully that people had doubted her sanity and her being a 'proper woman'[34] – accusations that had probably increased her problems in finding a husband at a time when the number of women of marriageable age exceeded those of men by about 18 million.[35] She needed to distance herself from allegedly mainstream features of war, such as dirt and vulgarity, which were supposed to be unwomanly. Indeed, such accusations were already in circulation during wartime. Asya Lavrova, a member of a political detachment, wrote a letter to her new boyfriend describing other female soldiers as follows:

> We had a rest at one base where military girls lived. [...] They grabbed paper and rolled papirossi [cigarettes] [...] as if they were in a contest. [...] I was shocked by this picture. How vulgar they were, they want to be like men in any case. [...] It is so disgusting.[36]

In contrast to Tikhonovich, who wanted to prove her femininity to her interview's late-20th-century audience at a time when the femininity of female Red Army soldiers had been challenged by public slurs, Lavrova's strategic aim in her contemporaneous letter had been more concrete: by pointing to the other women as vulgar, she was presenting herself as decent and feminine, not vulgarized by the war, and worthy to be chosen for a relationship by the letter's addressee.

Lavrova was joined in these aspirations by a former nurse, Mariya Aripova. When being interviewed in 2006, Aripova described how she had met her husband-to-be for the first time and returned late at night to the dormitory where she was living with other army women.

> The girls ask me: 'Have you worked two shifts today?' 'No, [...] I met a pilot.' 'What, a pilot?' 'He wants to see me again, but I won't go to the meeting. [...] I have nothing to wear. Here [in Lipetsk] there are young girls, here there was no front. Should I go in this army shirt?' I had just bought this new skirt for 200 grams of bread...[37]

In short, Aripova, too, tried to distance herself from being an army girl when she was about to meet her groom-to-be again, and she invested bitterly needed resources into her beautiful appearance.

Unfortunately, the need to find a husband at the front was not only the result of a wish for love, romance or lust; rather, it was the only sufficient protection against the high levels of sexual harassment there. A former radio operator, Zoya Gorokhova, described this in her interview:

> And the men around us were also horrible. [...] And every one of them, he wanted something warm, you know, tender from life. He needed a woman. But there were only a few of us, we struggled to fight our way out, it was very hard for us to exist in that zone. For that reason many of the girls got together with one single guy, in order to protect themselves from advances from the rest of them.[38]

At the front, this getting together with one single man, which Gorokhova explains and collectively excuses for most if not all military women, even had a name: becoming a *PPZh*, (*Pokhodna-Polevaya Zhena*, marching field-wife). *PPZh*s were attached to commanders or high-ranking officers with the power to protect their wives from sexual harassment by others. In this kind of relationship, beauty was a resource.[39] However, beauty gained its value not only through a woman investing in it, but also rhetorically and symbolically in comparison to other (army) women who were downgraded. Unfortunately, the accusations Lavrova had uttered only privately in a letter during wartime seem after the war to have become public accusations for Tikhonovich, forcing her (and others) to stress her beauty habits in her testimony even decades later. But this emphasis on beauty was not the only category liable to be used for quarrels among and discrimination against female soldiers. Soon it would also publicly be replaced by an emphasis on morals.

The moral conduct of women at the front had already been an issue in women's testimonies during wartime, even though it was only hinted at in the contemporaneous sources. Only in the mid-2000s did accounts of discrimination against *PPZh*s for being 'loose women' and gaining personal advantages by unfair means become especially prominent. Most descriptive is, however, a slightly older account by Vera Malakhova, a former military doctor who was interviewed in 1994. She viewed *PPZhs* as an entire group, although she had only one example at hand:

> We didn't like them. We [...] behaved honorably. [...] They got special privileges. [One of them] was an excellent surgical nurse. [...] But if he [her field-husband] summoned her, she would drop everything, and others had to do her work. [...] When he died, she immediately began to live with the head of the 'special section' [...] What sort of person are you [...].[40]

Malakhova showed no understanding that her female comrades might have acted in this way because of the structural need to be protected by an officer, especially when serving as young untrained rank-and-file medical orderlies or radio operators among hundreds of men. The 'logic' behind her judgement, that women themselves were responsible for what was happening to them, was, however, not her invention: it had already been expressed in testimonies given to the Commission for the History of the Great Patriotic War, but without any context, that is, without mentioning the *PPZhs*.[41] Such a perspective meant individualizing the problem of sexual harassment and blaming the victim while disapproving of what was supposedly the only sufficient protection. Thus, becoming a *PPZh* was not an all-encompassing solution, neither in historical reality nor in the later discussions about the female Red Army soldiers, but rather a symbol of the highly precarious position of women in the Red Army, who were discriminated against because of assumptions related to their bodies and criticized when using their bodies to negotiate this situation.[42]

This criticism is embraced in testimonies by former female soldiers collected since the beginning of the 21st century, a time when a patriotic tide of heroic vocabulary was sweeping Russia. Interviews for the prominent 'I Remember' project condemned the *PPZhs* even more than Malakhova had done. Here, no interviewees would confess to having been a *PPZh* or show the kind of comprehension Gorokhova had shown for them. These narratives (and probably the audience perception that the speakers anticipated) exhibit the greatest possible distance to the *PPZhs*. One former gunner, Nina Smarkalova, whose testimony was published in 2012, told the following story when being interviewed:

> One day I behaved like a hooligan: our commander from the regiment [*kompolka*] came together with his girl, or, with his *PPZh*. The kompolka said: 'There is a new soldier, show her how the mortar works, make her familiar with the situation.' [....] I decided to make some fun of her. It was in April, the earth was wet, and water was everywhere. When the mortar fires, all the dirt and the water [...] went up like a fountain. I ordered her to stand right there where all this stuff would go to and ordered: 'Fire!' She did not know what to cover [from the mud].[43]

In this cohort of interviews, some women even dared to present themselves as filthy and dirty in order not to be mistaken for a *PPZh*.[44] Describing themselves as not having been feminine at that time seemed to be a way for them to present themselves as having been real soldiers, in contrast to the *PPZhs* and to the women who had spare time to take care of their outer appearance. Again, hair

24. Interview with Nina Shinkarenko (18 October 1946), NA IRI RAN f. 2, s. 10, o. 7, d. 38, p. 3; Interview with Aleksandra Shlyakhova (16 March 1944), NA IRI RAN f. 2, r. 10, o.7, d. 8, p. 9.
25. For the ambivalent mobilization politics of the Soviet state, see Krylova, *Soviet Women in Combat*, 110–20.
26. In addition to Golofeevskaya, see, for example, Mariya Morosova, quoted in Alexijewitsch, *Der Krieg hat kein weibliches Gesicht*, 2004, 34–5, and interview with Nina Shinkarenko (18 October 1946), NA IRI RAN f. 2, r. 10, o. 7, d. 38, p. 2.
27. Dunaevskaya, *Ot Leningrada do Kenigsberga*, 19–34.
28. RGVA f. 38694, o. 1. d.55, p. 60; RGVA f. 38964, o. 1, d. 43, p. 20; RGVA f. 38964, o. 1, d. 29, p. 7.
29. RGVA, f. 38694, o.1, d. 3, pp. 16, 29.
30. Alexijewitsch, *Der Krieg hat kein weibliches Gesicht*, 229; RGVA, f. 38964, o. 1, d. 38, p. 25.
31. See (despite a neglect of gender) Merridale, *Ivan's War*.
32. Other, numerous, examples concerning female habits at the front: Noggle, *A Dance with Death*, 57, 81, 112, 136; Alexijewitsch, *Der Krieg hat kein weibliches Gesicht*, 49, 55, 79, 86–90, 104f.
33. Alexijewitsch, *Der Krieg hat kein weibliches Gesicht*, 214.
34. Alexijewitsch, *Der Krieg hat kein weibliches Gesicht*, 214.
35. These statistical numbers were established by a population census in 1959: 'Ni v odnoy strane voennye poteri ne priveli k takomy narusheniyu polovych proportsiy, kak v CCCR', available at: demoscope.ru/weekly/2013/0559/tema02.php (accessed 4 April 2015).
36. Nikolay N. Inozemtsev, *Frontovoy dnevnik*, 2nd ed. (Moscow: Nauka, 2005), 420–1.
37. Interview with Mariya Aripova (by author), 6 May 2006, Lipetsk, Russian Federation.
38. Interview with Zoya Gorokhova, 'Intervyu', available at: http://wmw.gender-ehu.org/Intervews.htm (accessed 30 August 2014).
39. Franziska Exeler's research on gender relations in the Red Army has pointed to the *PPZh* phenomenon and women's use of their feminine beauty as a resource to gain a superior's protection against harassment by male comrades: Franziska Exeler, 'Gewalt im Militär: die Rote Armee im Zweiten Weltkrieg', *Zeitschrift für Geschichtswissenschaft* vol. 60, no. 3 (2012), 228–47.
40. Vera I. Malakhova, 'Four Years as a Frontline Physician', in Barbara A. Engel (ed.), *A Revolution of Their Own: Voices of Women in Soviet History* (Boulder, CO: Westview Press, 1998), 175–218, 197.
41. Interview with Aleksandra Shlyakhova (16 March 1944), NA IRI RAN f. 2, r. 10, o.7, d. 8, p.5.
42. The term *PPZh* is applied in most sources primarily as a descriptive and discriminatory term against other women; to what extent the women themselves would agree with it remains doubtful. This chapter uses it mainly for the necessarily pragmatic relationships at the front. It should be mentioned that some relationships from wartime service, whatever they were based on, could be stable: some officers wished to marry their subordinates officially when the war ended, and relationships resulting from mixed-gender military service could last for years after the war. RGVA f. 32925, o. 1, d. 528, p. 252; Evgeni Bessonov, *Tank Rider: Into the Reich with the Red Army* (Philadelphia, PA: Casemate, 2005), 242f.
43. Interview with Nina Smarkalova, 'Smarkalova Nina Arsentevna: Ya pomnyu. Geroy Velikoy Otechestvennoy Voynnoy. Uchastniki VOV. Kniga pamyati', available at:

http://iremember.ru/memoirs/minometchiki/smarkalova-nina-arsentevna/ (accessed 25 January 2015).

44. Interview with Evdokiya Nesterova-Chirimisina, 'Nesterova (Chirimisina) Evdokiya Yakovlevna: Ya pomnyu. Geroy Velikoy Otechestvennoy Voynnoy. Uchastniki VOV. Kniga pamyati', available at: http:iremember.ru/memoirs/svyazisti/nesterova-chirimisina-evdokiya-yakovlevna/ (accessed 25 January 2015).

45. Luferova Kira Ivanovna, in: Artem Drabkin and Bair Irincheev (eds), 'A zori zdes gromkie'; zhenskoe litso voyny (Moscow: Eksmo, 2012), 35.

46. Malakhova, 'Four Years as a Frontline Physician', 187; interview with Mariya Galyshkina, 'Galyshkina (Kleymenova) Mariya Aleksandrovna: Ya pomnyu. Geroy Velikoy Otechestvennoy Voynnoy. Uchastniki VOV. Kniga pamyati', available at: iremember.ru/snayperi/galishkina-mariya-aleksandrovna; Interview with Nina Afanaseva, 'Afanaseva Nina Fedotovna: Ya pomnyu. Geroy Velikoy Otechestvennoy Voynnoy. Uchastniki VOV. Kniga pamyati', available at: http://iremember.ru/memoirs/nkvd-i-smersh/afanaseva-nina-fedotovna/ [sic] (both accessed 25 January 2015).

47. See especially Andrey Kovalevskiy, 'Nychne u nas peredyshka: frontovoy dnevnik', *Neva* no. 5 (1995), 63–108, 85–90. For the purpose of the men's storytelling, see: Kerstin Bischl, 'Telling Stories: Gender Relationships and Masculinity in the Red Army 1941–45', in Maren Röger and Ruth Leiserowitz (eds), *Women and Men at War: a Gender Perspective on World War II and its Aftermath in Central and Eastern Europe* (Osnabrück: fibre, 2012), 117–33.

48. Oleg Budnitskii, 'Muzhchiny i zhenshchiny v Krasnoy armii (1941–1945)', *Cahiers du Monde Russe* vol. 52, no. 2–3 (2011), 405–422, 410.

49. Maurice Halbwachs, *Das kollektive Gedächtnis* (Frankfurt am Main: Fischer, 1991 [1967]), 31.

50. Compare Jolluck, this volume, on eastern Europe 1939–45.

51. See Raewyn Connell, 'The State, Gender, and Sexual Politics: Theory and Appraisal', *Theory, Culture and Society* vol. 19, no. 5 (1990), 507–544, 523.

7

Soviet Masculinities and Revolution

Erica L. Fraser

Revolution, as well as war, permits gender historians to seek both continuity and change in gender regimes at moments of crisis, violence and rupture. This chapter offers an example of how gender historians might approach revolution by remaining with the topic of Soviet gender history but focusing on the construction of Soviet masculinities during and after the Russian Revolution, especially on how the concepts of revolution and masculinity might have been linked. Links between these concepts, or what could simply be called 'revolutionary masculinity', have already gained the attention of historians looking to explain the peculiar power dynamics and governmental cultivation of gender regimes in a variety of other global post-revolutionary settings, including 18th-century France and 20th-century Latin America. And yet – despite the USSR's self-identification as a revolutionary state and the leading Bolsheviks' self-identification as a revolutionary vanguard – revolutionary masculinity has not been systematically explored for the Russian Revolution. Indeed, the Soviet Union has largely been left out of broader discussions in European and global gender history, because the complexities of its gender ideology and outcomes have not easily fitted prevailing models elsewhere – and still do not.

In the USSR, the concept of revolution drove Soviet ideology from the early Bolshevik intelligentsia all the way until the late 1980s. It changed in form and definition over the course of the century, from its initial goals of seeking power for the workers, to the Stalinist terror campaign to purge supposed enemies of the true revolution, through the defence of a Russian-centric revolution in World War II, and finally to Mikhail Gorbachev's project of reimagining and reinvigorating revolutionary consciousness for the coming 21st century. One could say therefore that, despite changes in its meaning, the idea of 'revolution' remained part of Soviet gender regimes long after the Bolshevik period, or the period most likely to be thought of as 'revolutionary'.

In a variety of forms – some Soviet, some not – revolutionary ideology also informed post-war recovery in eastern Europe.[1] In a newly partitioned East Germany in the late 1940s, 'revolution' might have looked less like radical change and more like a return to stability and even (briefly) political plurality; in Poland, it wore the face of Russian imperialism; and in Yugoslavia, the concept of revolution came to define and narrate a way forward out of fascism and monarchism, one that did not involve German or Russian control. In Russia, however, the Bolshevik revolutionaries of the early 20th century embodied a particular consciousness that drew on older revolution models while also forging a new path as the basis of the world's first socialist state. This heavy sense of the historical significance of their task imbued the Bolsheviks, under Vladimir Lenin's leadership, with masculinized notions of privilege, duty and honour.

This chapter's discussion of Soviet 'revolutionary masculinities' has two goals. First, it measures the suitability for historians of applying the conceptual framework of revolutionary masculinity to the Bolsheviks by comparing the Russian Revolution to two other revolutionary models in world history, the French and Latin American, using secondary literature and some contemporary voices observing their countries' revolutionary projects. Second, however, it argues that Soviet revolutionary masculinity is useful as a 'working concept' precisely *because* it does not fit comfortably into global patterns, producing a discomfort which itself underscores the value of Soviet experiences in forging new historical queries and models. Historians must take ideas of Soviet revolutionary masculinity seriously both in order to complicate the standard story of the Bolshevik revolutionaries, which has ignored masculinity, and to better integrate Soviet experiences into European and global gender histories.

Although historians of imperial Russia and the Soviet Union have begun studying masculinity in the past 20 years with important results, Russian and Soviet masculinity still remains a vastly understudied field, especially in comparison to the amount of research in Russian women's history.[2] Pairing the concepts of masculinity and revolution in Soviet history illuminates one of the main goals of historical masculinity studies: that masculinity is never static, fixed or constant but is dynamic and ever changing, and that it must continually be remade, renegotiated and reworked by historical actors. What it means to be 'a man' is historically specific, in other words, not constant through time and place. The Bolshevik revolutionaries argued that what it meant to be a 'revolutionary' was historically specific as well, and required constant re-education and re-evaluation. Bolshevik ideology held that the business of revolution was never complete; the Soviet people and government would have to continually work to enact, defend and adapt the October 1917 revolution as time went on. In this cycle of making and remaking the self, Bolshevik ideology opens a space for forging the particular consciousness of revolutionary masculinity, because if the process of revolution was never complete, then the 'process' of masculinity, or masculinization, was never complete either. Historians of the Russian revolutionary moment need to consider it as foundational to the ensuing Soviet gender regime.

The standard revolutionary model, both in European history and globally, has been the French Revolution of the late 18th century. Indeed, it is not only historians who have compared the French and Russian Revolutions; the Bolsheviks themselves were acutely aware of the French revolutionary symptoms, behaviours and outcomes. The first part of the chapter will evaluate the usefulness of the model of French revolutionary culture for studying Russian and Soviet revolutionary masculinity. Triggered by a series of financial crises in the 1780s but bringing forth long-standing grievances of the politically voiceless French people against an opulent king and queen, the French Revolution and its 'stages' have occupied historians for centuries now, including gender historians. Was the beheading of the country's metaphorical mother and father in Marie Antoinette and Louis XVI an act of belligerent children against an oppressive patriarchal authority? Was the terror phase an inevitable fratricide among revolutionaries? Historians of Russia have discussed many of the comparisons between France in 1789 and Russia in 1917, including the persistent reign of an autocratic monarch against the wishes of an increasingly dynamic population, the remaking of society from the ground up by a 'people's government', and the eerie similarities between the Jacobin terror of the 1790s and Stalin's purges of the 1930s. When we examine these revolutions through the lens of masculinity, however, the similarities do not hold up.

The chapter then turns to another part of the world and a different historiography on gender and revolution, this time in Latin America. If the French model of masculinity in a revolutionary context does not quite work for studying gender in Russia, will the leftist fighters of 20th-century Latin America? Unlike the comparison to the French Revolution, which was undertaken by the Bolsheviks themselves, a conversation about the possibilities of finding a Fidel-style *machismo* among the Bolsheviks is based on historians' theories of gender and revolution. Socialist politics in Mexico, Cuba, Brazil, Chile and other countries often pitted the guerrilla against the bureaucrat for ownership of the Marxist revolutionary voice: a rifle, beard and fatigues against a Party *apparatchik*.[3] Imperial Russian and Soviet history does not often engage in such dialogues and conversations with other historiographies and historical models, nor vice versa, to the detriment of all sides.[4]

The Bolshevik Revolution,[5] from the early 20th century through the consolidation of power in the Civil War of 1918–21, was a time when one's revolutionary consciousness was constantly measured, when the (shifting and unreachable) ideal of an authentic revolutionary self adjudicated Soviet masculinity and models that would influence the 20th century in the USSR, eastern Europe, and indeed the rest of the world, were formed. At the same time, Soviet revolutionary masculinity set its own path – eschewing the notion of 'brotherhood' and including women revolutionaries; believing the message itself would carry more weight than the personal charisma of the men delivering it; and stripping sexuality from its discourse. Historians of masculinity must always be aware that discussions of men's gendered identities and men's relationships to power and privilege risk inadvertently bolstering the very 'great man history' tropes we seek to dismantle. In turning the lens back on some famous revolutionary actors in world history, however, this chapter deepens our understanding of gender and revolution and shows that mapping Soviet masculinities into and among European and global revolutionary models benefits all fields.

The French Revolution Model: an Exclusionary Brotherhood

The idea of studying revolution through family motifs was first introduced to cultural history by Lynn Hunt's pathbreaking 1991 book, *The Family Romance of the French Revolution*. Hunt conceived of the French revolutionaries as a band of brothers, arguing that drawing on family motifs was a way for individuals in revolutionary France to understand their place in the social order, especially at that particular 18th-century moment when Europeans 'thought of their rulers as fathers and their nations as families writ large'.[6] To begin theorizing about Bolshevik masculinity as an ingrained part of the broader project of revolution, it is worth examining the ideal of 'brotherhood' among Lenin and his colleagues. In many ways the concept is useful for understanding revolutionary masculinity in Russia, but in other ways it places limits on our understanding of the particular circumstances and ideology of the Bolsheviks.

The goals, actions and identity formation of the early Bolshevik revolutionaries has occupied historians of Russia for more than half a century, providing one of the most written-about topics in Soviet history. Historians have long debated whether the Bolshevik leaders were eager and thoughtful revolutionaries acting on behalf of the workers to stage a Marxist revolution, or a criminal gang who stole power in a *coup d'état* and continued to rule Russia illegitimately for the rest of the century. Both of those assessments were heavily influenced by New Left and Cold War politics from the 1950s to the 1970s, in which ideological imperatives about the promise, or the evils, of Communism polarized academics.[7] Although not framed as such by most historians, these fierce debates about Bolshevik motives, acts and legitimacy were also implicitly debates about the kinds of people – the kinds of *men* – who would engage in them. The model of a cooperative, egalitarian brethren rising up against an aged, stagnant and ineffective father-king paints a portrait of a particular type of manhood that has endured in revolutionary myth from the 18th century through the 20th, representing a populist struggle to wrest some semblance of civil rights from absolutist oppressors. Its Cold War-era opposite for Soviet history, emphasizing the illegitimacy, trickery, bloodthirstiness and violence of the same group, has the potential to rewrite revolutionary masculinity in a different way – as criminal rather than righteous, as having seized power ignobly rather than proceeding as an honourable populist vanguard. While most historians now agree that the Bolshevik Revolution was far more complicated than this assessment, and Cold War politics have given way to more nuanced studies of revolutionary actors and their motivations, the Cold War characterization lingers. Hunt's 'band of brothers' motif draws on the Shakespearean usage of the term as well, which is rooted in military camaraderie. The broader US understanding of the term as a heroic World War II-inspired soldiering ethos, popularized by Steven Spielberg, might also explain the reluctance of Western historians to use this terminology for the Bolsheviks. As a result, the French revolutionary brotherhood persists as a noble group pursuing equality and liberty, while the Bolshevik revolutionaries have been largely cast in history as violent thugs undeserving of the honour that a righteous 'brotherhood' label implies.

A second reason why revolutionary masculinity has not been defined in Russia by the ideal of a brotherhood is because of socialist (or Marxist) ideology. In particular, the Marxist goal of abolishing the dominant, bourgeois family structure and the official ideology of women's equality and emancipation need to be taken seriously in any discussion of Bolshevik masculinity.[8] The French revolutionary brotherhood largely defined itself not only in generational terms, as the fresh leaders bringing down the old monarchy, but also in distinctly masculinized terms. Its calls for universal citizenship boldly forged a new future by eliminating restrictions based on race or religion, thus sanctioning in particular the rights of black men in the French colony of Saint-Domingue (now Haiti) and Jewish men in France. But as commenters such as the writer Olympe de Gouges pointed out sharply at the time, the revolutionaries' conceptions of *liberté, egalité, fraternité* deliberately omitted women. 'Having become free, [man] has become unjust toward his companion. Oh women! Women, when will you cease to be blind? What advantages have you gathered in the Revolution?' de Gouges wrote in her scathing critique of the revolutionaries' *Déclaration des Droits de l'Homme et du Citoyen* (*Declaration of the Rights of Man and Citizen*) in 1789, which denied women's basic rights in the new republic.[9] The revolutionaries' very sense of masculinity was defined in opposition to femininity, othering women and insisting – when women were recognized at all – that they were not part of the revolution.

The Bolsheviks' Marxist–Leninist philosophy did not follow the French model, and in fact actively worked against it. Further, women were not just accepted as tokens in the Bolshevik party (and in other Russian socialist parties at the time); rather, socialist ideology fully sought to abolish what it saw as the twin injustices of capitalism and patriarchy that denied women opportunities as workers and equal members of the proletarian collective.[10] Alexandra Kollontai, a feminist and socialist revolutionary who held several posts in Lenin's government after 1917, wrote of women under socialism:

> In place of the old relationship between men and women, a new one is developing: a union of affection and comradeship, a union of two equal members of communist society, both of them free, both of them independent and both of them workers. No more domestic bondage for women. No more inequality within the family. No need for women to fear being left without support and with children to bring up. The woman in communist society no longer depends upon her husband but on her work. It is not in her husband but in her capacity for work that she will find support.[11]

The fact that women's equality was embraced as a specific part of Bolshevik ideology was significant for the development and definitions of Bolshevik masculinity. However, the primacy of socialist ideology in producing narratives of gender equality in the Bolshevik Revolution has obscured some of the continued discrimination Soviet women faced after 1917 and the ways in which Bolshevik masculinity was also premised on excluding the feminine, if more covertly, just as it was for French revolutionary masculinity. Professing a social revolution does not automatically make it so, and historians have found that women faced continued challenges from masculinized worker cultures on the shop floor in the 1920s and from Stalinist political culture in the 1930s, despite nominal equality.[12]

Still, the specific context of Marxism's call to reject and indeed abolish the traditional family creates quite a different framework than the French model if we are to understand Bolshevik masculinity using the language of revolutionary brotherhood. The Bolsheviks did not generally refer to themselves as a brotherhood, for instance. A core component of Leninist philosophy, and one that separated Lenin from the Mensheviks and other social democrats, was his insistence that the revolution in Russia could not wait for Russian workers to develop sufficient consciousness to enact it *en masse*, but that it must be introduced to them 'from without', by a core group of professional revolutionaries.[13] This implicit hierarchy was one unique hallmark of revolutionary masculinity in Russia in comparison with other fields. For Lenin, the worker and the party were the primary categories of identity, with the gender-neutral 'comrade' delineating class-based ties that did not cater to family motifs. Lenin himself wrote about his emerging understanding of revolutionary hierarchies as a young activist at the turn of the 20th century, when he and another junior colleague were rebuffed by the 'grand old man of Russian Social Democracy', Georgii Plekhanov:[14]

> Had we not been so in love [with Plekhanov]... we would not have experienced such a crash in the literal sense. This was the most severe, the most painfully severe, painfully brutal life lesson. Two young comrades 'courted' an older comrade because of their great love for him, and, all of a sudden he injects into this love an atmosphere of intrigue, and makes them feel – not like younger brothers – but like idiots who are being led around by the nose, like pawns that can be moved around at will.[15]

From the late 19th century through the 1917 revolution and into the 1920s, Bolshevik leaders deliberately avoided motifs about biological family, which for them was tainted by bourgeois power dynamics. Reforging the lexicon of the Soviet family (and its accompanying legal codes that emphasized marriage and motherhood for women) would only come with Stalin's retreat from Bolshevik ideology in the early 1930s.

And yet, in other ways the flattened hierarchy of Bolshevik political culture did lend itself to a 'brotherhood' metaphor, with gendered identities shaped according to cooperation and comradeship, not to the power of some men over others. In a scenario like France as well as Russia in which some element of 'the people' overthrew an old-regime king, it is useful for masculinity scholars to take seriously the framework of a newly empowered brotherhood coming together to remake political power in its own image. In doing so, the brotherhood in this model disconnected its masculinity from that of the deposed hegemonic father, who was no longer idealized or influential in the revolutionaries' gendered identity formation. Eliot Borenstein has characterized the early Bolshevik state this way, as embodying and practising 'fratriarchal communism'. He writes that 'the chaos of the Russian Civil War could easily be understood as the struggle for power among "sons" now that the father was gone'.[16] Brotherhood in this sense also suggests a family not necessarily born but chosen, a fraternity of like-minded individuals who opt into their communal allegiance, rather than being trapped into it by an accident of birth. With this in mind, the model of a Bolshevik revolutionary brotherhood could be more useful than it first appears, with the revolutionaries rejecting their tsarist family ties as part of their dismissal of the governing father of the old regime.

Ideology also influenced the division between bourgeois and proletarian masculinities in the Russian case. For many historians, the French Revolution in fact produced the type of bourgeois masculinity in the revolutionaries that would become the primary acceptable and endorsed form of manhood in modern Europe. This form is called *hegemonic* masculinity, a term coined by sociologist Raewyn Connell in the 1990s to refer to the masculine identity in any given society that enjoys the greatest privilege; for many modern Western societies this includes men who represent physical fitness, military service, wealth, political power and so on.[17] 'The [French] revolution consolidated bourgeois ideas about male respectability and honour, especially with regards to individualism, merit, and property', but one must be cautious in assuming uniform masculinized attributes based on ideology. Although the 'bourgeois' actors of the French Revolution are often seen as a unified group with similar goals, they were much more diverse and acted according to a variety of scripts.[18] A similar plurality could be found in socialist masculinity. The Bolshevik Revolution was pursued in the name of the worker, privileging a masculinity defined by labour, activism and one's revolutionary 'consciousness', or commitment to ending class-based oppression. Yet to label Bolshevik masculinity as 'monolithically proletarian', gender historians have already argued, would obscure the plural identities that were possible even among the revolutionaries themselves.[19]

Historians and literary theorists, as well as contemporaneous writers, have argued that the ways the Bolsheviks disrupted and attempted to manipulate history and even modernity itself transcended any simple gender dichotomies. As part of a revolution intended to become universal, men and women alike were meant to overcome gender and exist solely as workers. To this end, for example, the *Zhenotdel*, or Women's Section of the Communist Party, was founded in 1918 to pursue women's emancipation, but its timeline to accomplish this rather abstract goal was finite; by 1930, the Section was closed, its project was declared complete and women were presumed, ideologically, to have overcome the need for distinct institutions or treatment.[20] However, those ideals of a universal human-worker quickly devolved back to man as the default human, with rhetoric about gender equality or even post-gender reality only masking newly resurgent hierarchies that rendered women's contributions invisible. Metals, machinery and cement all spilled from revolutionary ideology to the cultural terrain of the early 1920s: literature favoured machines over men, and a sense that the revolution really had remade all of society and culture in a new image was pervasive.[21] In this context, the men of the revolutionary vanguard could not rely on older models of masculine power or virility to lead them into this new world. Historians of gender and revolution should look to Russia to see that the Bolsheviks in fact invented an entirely new lexicon for gender and masculinity, in which the leader of the workers was a philosopher, the 'sons' did not so easily overthrow the father and – in the most important difference from the French or American Revolutions – granting full citizenship and legal equality to women in fact removed from the Bolshevik worldview the standard opposing identity against which masculinity defines itself.

The Latin American Revolution Model: Charisma and Rogue Masculinity

If the French revolutionary concept of 'brotherhood' as a window onto the actions and ideologies of revolutionary masculinity produces mixed results for Russia, what other models might we use for analysing Bolshevik masculinity? Historians of Latin America have examined gendered revolutionary moments in Mexico, Cuba, Chile and Brazil (among other countries) and might offer an important way forward. For one, the Latin American revolutionaries were socialist as well, providing a similar base for analysing masculinity as opposed to the French revolutionary 'bourgeois' model. Although not toppling old-regime monarchs as in France or Russia, the Latin American revolutionaries of the 20th century embodied elements of brotherhood while also performing rogue, individualistic charisma that gained purchase against the faceless bureaucrats in the corrupt governments they sought to overthrow. But should historians talk about Lenin, Trotsky or even a young Stalin in the same conversation about revolution and masculinity as Che Guevara or Fidel Castro? As young *barbudos*, Florencia Mallon has written, the latter figures personified 'the bearded and long-haired young romantic' with personal charisma that 'relied substantially on the youth, good looks, and revolutionary moustache that so deeply resonated with the young idealists of the time'.[22] The Cuban revolutionaries in particular were defined by American observers of the revolution as warriors for rough heterosexuality and machismo, drawing on Castro's hyper-masculinized 'bombastic personality, with his black-framed spectacles, cigars, curly whiskers, and olive-green fatigues complemented by a sniper's rifle'.[23] While this image of the Latin American revolutionary has become almost stereotypical and has indeed been critiqued as being too 'obvious', it has endured in the global mythos of revolutionary masculinity and continues to inform historical studies.[24] It remains a useful benchmark for evaluating Russian revolutionary masculinity, particularly in terms of investigating why the Bolsheviks did not achieve the same legendary status as masculine icons.

Personal leadership played a significant role in many Latin American revolutions as well as for the Bolsheviks. For a revolutionary like Castro, the trajectory from pre-revolution *barbudo* to creating hegemonic masculinity in power might signal a key moment of a masculinized identity shift. Lenin, however, consistently positioned himself as disciplined and professional, especially when compared to his less regulated, commune-dwelling colleagues in the turn-of-the-century socialist movement. The historian Nina Tumarkin has written that 'the juxtaposition of radicalism with utter self-control, an unusual blend for his milieu, made him appear at once revolutionary and responsible'. His contemporaries wrote that while in exile before the revolution, 'Lenin exuded an air of "purity." He did not drink or smoke. He loved brisk walks, chess, ice skating, and hunting. In his work Lenin was organized [and] self-disciplined.'[25] Even after the Bolsheviks seized power in October 1917, Lenin's wife, the revolutionary Nadezhda Krupskaia, recalled that 'nobody knew Lenin's face at that time. In the evening we would often [...] stroll around the Smolny, and nobody would ever recognize him, because there were no portraits then.'[26] His focus had been on the work, not on the performance of rifle-toting, rebellious masculine authority.

Led by Lenin, the young workers who joined the Bolshevik cause were also meant to be disciplined even while seeking to incite chaos. The rank-and-file diarist Eduard Dune described the establishment of the Red Guard in the summer of 1917 as a careful process:

> Recruitment to the workers' militia was as strict as to any other organization. The candidacy of each prospective member was discussed at a session of the factory committee, and applicants were often turned down on the grounds that they were regularly drunk or engaged in hooliganism or had behaved coarsely with women. The volunteers numbered 150 and were all drawn from among the young workers, with the exception of some three dozen older men. Twice a week we lined up and were taught military drill, tactics, camouflage, and the rifle manual. We had no weapons, so we learned the rifle manual using wooden staves.[27]

One major challenge for Lenin and his cadre of professional revolutionaries was to train and unleash workers such as Dune in order to incite change, but then to contain them afterwards. The violence of the ensuing Civil War from 1918–21 (committed on all sides, not only by Bolshevik fighters) suggests that the careful training of units such as the Red Guard might not have held in the face of political and social chaos. While Lenin's iconic revolutionary leadership at first glance places him on a similar playing field to the rough, charismatic authority of several Latin American revolutionaries, his personal asceticism contrasted sharply with their *machismo*.

Lenin's successor, the future dictator Joseph Stalin who was also part of the early Bolshevik cause before and after 1917, displayed a more personality-driven, charismatic leadership style that might better compare with the revolutionary masculinity of Latin American leftist fighters. Historians have explored his Georgian roots in particular in seeking to explain his later political actions and his role in directing state violence.[28] Ronald Suny has identified Stalin's demand for loyalty from a small circle of friends, for example, as 'a necessity in the highly competitive world of Georgian men where one's status depended on associations – family, friends, patrons, clients'.[29] Alfred J. Rieber has also investigated Stalin's Georgian heritage, playing up Stalin's roots in a 'warrior culture' in which fealty to one's 'warrior brothers' trumped all other allegiances.[30] Ruling over an inner circle Rieber describes as a 'band of brothers', Stalin after the revolution 'acted out the role of the traditional Georgian pater familia [sic]'.[31]

Not quite the modern American militarized 'band of brothers' and not quite Lynn Hunt's male-dominated third estate seeking a political voice, Rieber's use of the term appears to represent Stalin's bureaucrats (again, male-dominated). It positions Stalin as a new version of the tsarist father-king and uses his Georgian heritage to locate Stalinist revolutionary masculinity not in Lenin's many books or in the cacophonous meetings of St Petersburg factory workers, but rather in the villages of the Georgian borderlands. Stalin never wore fatigues or slung a rifle across his chest, but playing up his heritage in the North Caucasus mountains suggests a way historians could put his legacy in conversation with Latin American revolutionaries like Che or Fidel. Even though Stalin consciously adopted a Russian identity to pave the way for further success as a revolutionary, his personality, for Rieber, was centred on his 'Georgian accent, style, and proletarian gruffness'.[32] Still, Stalin's heritage alone did not inform his masculinity or his revolutionary actions, and emphasizing it too much risks essentializing and exoticizing Georgian masculinity.

As a final point of comparison, sexuality, a major component in analyses of Latin American masculinity, also looked different for the Russian revolutionaries. Latin American gender history overall has led the field since the 1990s in innovative research into the ways in which masculinity is defined in Latin cultures by one's sexual acts. The term *macho*, for example, although constantly shifting according to historical circumstance, suggests an identity shaped by sex with women.[33] Sexual identity did not define the Bolshevik revolutionaries. The revolution against bourgeois family constructs promised by socialist ideology, as previously discussed, even in the permissible 1920s never reached the heights of frank talk about sexuality nor the revolutionary leaders demonstrating their own sexual fluidity or open sexual appeal like Guevara or Castro. The Bolshevik revolutionaries carefully contained sexuality in their own families and cultivated their images as responsible married men. Lenin's wife, Nadezhda Krupskaia, was portrayed as an intellectual partner for him, not fitting the usual Western archetypes for femininity – the sexual conquest, the mother or the pious innocent. Today, young people engaged in the wonders of social media seem determined to overcome the sexual reserve of the Bolshevik revolutionaries, as evidenced by any Internet search for 'young Stalin'. The leader's now-famous portrait as a 20-something *barbudo*, bearded and tousle-haired – a 'proper' revolutionary much more like Guevara's famous image than the elderly dictator photographed years later with the similarly aged Churchill and Roosevelt at Yalta – appears front and centre along with sites devoted to sexualizing his image.

The *machismo* of Latin American revolutionary masculinity thus does not fully resonate in the Bolshevik context. Certainly, the language of Marxism permeated both revolutionary traditions and the individual charisma of many Latin American leaders seems more familiar to us in analysing Lenin, Trotsky or Stalin than the broad populist category of revolutionaries in 18th-century France. But the charismatic leadership of the Latin American revolutionaries of the 20th century, as well as their heightened attention to sexuality as a defining marker of revolutionary masculinity, diverge significantly from the Soviet experience.

Conclusion

How, then, should historians proceed if we are to bring Soviet revolutionary history more fully into European and global masculinity conversations? Like gender identities more broadly, Soviet conceptions of masculinity that were shaped by notions of revolution constantly shifted not only as part of the seizure of power in 1917 but throughout the 20th century. Scholars of Russian masculinity have argued, in fact, that it would be unwise to 'conceive of the Russian Revolution as a culminating moment in the creation of a new masculine identity'.[34] At the same time, however, fully understanding this self-declared revolutionary state and its leaders, the proclaimed revolutionary vanguard, requires understanding the revolutionaries as gendered beings who positioned themselves as men experiencing and indeed driving a particular historic moment.

Since World War II, however, Europe has been less certain about how to adjudicate revolutionary moments. The Nazi rise to power, dismantling of the German old regime and gruesome war aims shattered any lingering romantic European ideals from 1789, 1848 or 1871 about the nature of revolution and the nobility of the men engaged in radical political reinvention. It would take several decades of recovery for a new generation of European activists in Czechoslovakia, Yugoslavia and Poland to renew revolutionary discourse. Widespread political protests across Europe from Paris to Prague (as well as elsewhere in the world, including Mexico City) in 1968 gestured to a renewed revolutionary spirit there in the post-war era, at the same moment that the Soviet Union's revolutionary fervour and masculinized fortitude were waning in the wake of the war's widespread destruction of male bodies and soldiering ethos.

Yet scholars have remained uncertain about how to characterize or define Soviet revolutionary masculinity, and the Soviet Union is generally left out of conversations within and between fields regarding these constructions. In comparison to French and Latin American revolutionary traditions, we have seen that Soviet revolutionary masculinity forged a path apart. Its ideology largely included women and de-emphasized 'brotherhood' labels in favour of a workers' collective; personal charismatic appeal was not always fostered; and Bolshevik masculinity mostly ignored sexuality. These ideals also seem to have influenced the Bolsheviks' antithesis, the anti-Communist revolutionaries in Russia and eastern Europe in the late 20th century. When Lech Wałęsa addressed a Gdańsk shipyard in 1976 or Boris Yeltsin stood on a tank in front of the Moscow White House in 1991, did they think they were acting in a particular revolutionary tradition – deposing an autocratic monarch figure like the French revolutionaries, taking up arms for community and nation like the Cuban revolutionaries, or even enacting the business-like, asexual, professional revolutionary script of Lenin himself? Or were they forging their own revolutionary moment, one that would influence future models for masculine identity formation and comportment during moments of monumental political and social change?[35] And will future historians consider these revolutionaries' gendered subjectivity alongside the *sans-culottes* of the French Revolution or the Che Guevaras of the Cuban?

Dwelling on Russian exceptionalism can be dangerous, of course. Policy makers have cited it many times in past centuries as well as in recent politics to argue that Russia's unique history, geography and society sets it apart in Europe and the world, leading to the insistence by some that Russia does not need or cannot support democratic institutions or universal civil rights. But European and global gender historians must consider Bolshevik masculinity as a major part of any discussion of revolutionary gender regimes. With the world now watching Russia regarding issues of gender, sexuality, leadership, privacy, individual rights, legality and dissent,[36] gender historians have the opportunity to emplot these themes as masculinity issues with a long history in Soviet politics and culture. Rethinking the Soviet experience of revolution through masculinity, and testing some of the ways in which that experience can be put into conversation with global revolutionary moments elsewhere, offers a new way forward for gender history in all fields.

Notes

1. See also Simić, this volume.
2. Some of the most salient recent work on Russian and Soviet masculinities includes: Barbara Evans Clements, Rebecca Friedman and Dan Healey (eds), *Russian Masculinities in History and Culture* (Basingstoke: Palgrave Macmillan, 2002); Dan Healey, 'Comrades, Queers and "Oddballs": Sodomy, Masculinity and Gendered Violence in Leningrad Province of the 1950s', *Journal of the History of Sexuality* vol. 21, no. 3 (2012): 496–522; Dan Healey, *Homosexual Desire in Revolutionary Russia: the Regulation of Sexual and Gender Dissent* (Chicago: University of Chicago Press, 2001); John Haynes, *New Soviet Man: Gender and Masculinity in Stalinist Soviet Cinema* (Manchester: Manchester University Press, 2003); Lilya Kaganovsky, *How the Soviet Man was Unmade: Cultural Fantasy and Male Subjectivity Under Stalin* (Pittsburgh, PA: University of Pittsburgh Press, 2008); E. Thomas Ewing, '"If the Teacher Were a Man": Masculinity and Power in Stalinist Schools', *Gender and History* vol. 21, no.1 (2009): 107–29; Ethan Pollock, '"Real Men Go to the Bania": Postwar Soviet Masculinities and the Bathhouse', *Kritika: Explorations in Russian and Eurasian History* vol. 11, no. 1 (2010): 47–76; Claire E. McCallum, 'The Return: Post-War Masculinity and the Domestic Space in Stalinist Visual Culture, 1945–53', *Russian Review* vol. 74, no. 1 (2015): 117–43.
3. Jocelyn Olcott, *Revolutionary Women in Postrevolutionary Mexico* (Durham, NC: Duke University Press, 2005), 19; Florencia Mallon, '*Barbudos*, Warriors, and *Rotos*: the MIR, Masculinity, and Power in the Chilean Agrarian Reform, 1965–74', in Matthew C. Gutmann (ed.), *Changing Men and Masculinities in Latin America* (Durham, NC: Duke University Press, 2003), 191.
4. New research in cultural history is beginning to put Soviet and Latin American history in conversation. See Anne E. Gorsuch, '"Cuba, My Love": The Romance of Revolutionary Cuba in the Soviet Sixties', *American Historical Review* vol. 120, no. 2 (2015): 497–526.
5. Historians have long debated the timeline this phrase covers, including Sheila Fitzpatrick who has persuasively argued that it must include the 'terror phase' in 1937–8, which represented Stalin consciously honouring the French revolutionary timeline. See Fitzpatrick, *The Russian Revolution*, 3rd ed. (Oxford: Oxford University Press, 2008).
6. Lynn Hunt, *The Family Romance of the French Revolution* (Berkeley: University of California Press, 1993), xiii–xiv.
7. On the Cold War politicization of Soviet history, see Sheila Fitzpatrick, 'Revisionism in Retrospect: a Personal View', *Slavic Review* vol. 67, no. 3 (2008): 682–704.
8. See also Kaminer, this volume.
9. Olympe de Gouges, 'The Declaration of the Rights of Woman' (September 1791), in Lynn Hunt (trans. and ed.), *The French Revolution and Human Rights: a Brief Documentary History* (New York: St Martin's, 1996), 124–9. See also Joan Landes,

'Republican Citizenship and Heterosocial Desire: Concepts of Masculinity in Revolutionary France', in Dudink et al. (eds), *Masculinities in Politics and War*, 96–115.

10. See Karl Marx and Friedrich Engels, 'The Communist Manifesto', especially chapter 2, 'Proletarians and Communists' (1848), reproduced in *Avalon Project: Documents in Law, History and Diplomacy*, available at: http://avalon.law.yale.edu/subject_menus/mancont.asp (accessed 7 April 2016); Friedrich Engels, 'Origin of the Family, Private Property, and the State' (1884), reproduced in *Marx and Engels Internet Archive*, available at: https://www.marxists.org/archive/marx/works/1884/origin-family/ (accessed 7 April 2016); Alexandra Kollontai, 'Communism and the Family' (1920), reproduced in *Marx and Engels Internet Archive*, available at: www.marxists.org/archive/kollonta/1920/communism-family.htm (accessed 7 April 2016). See also Barbara Evans Clements, *Bolshevik Women* (Cambridge: Cambridge University Press, 1997).

11. Kollontai, 'Communism and the Family'.

12. See Diane P. Koenker, 'Men against Women on the Shop Floor in Early Soviet Russia: Gender and Class in the Socialist Workplace', *American Historical Review* vol. 100, no. 5 (1995): 1438–64; Thomas G. Schrand, 'Socialism in One Gender: Masculine Values in the Stalin Revolution', in Clements et al., *Russian Masculinities*, 194–209; Eliot Borenstein, *Men without Women: Masculinity and Revolution in Russian Fiction, 1917–1929* (Durham, NC: Duke University Press, 2001).

13. Alan Shandro, 'Lenin and Hegemony: the Soviets, the Working Class, and the Party in the Revolution of 1905', in Sebastian Budgen, Stathis Kouvelakis, and Slavoj Žižek (eds), *Lenin Reloaded: Towards a Politics of Truth* (Durham, NC: Duke University Press, 2007), 308.

14. Nina Tumarkin, *Lenin Lives! The Lenin Cult in Soviet Russia* (Cambridge, MA: Harvard University Press, 1997), 37.

15. Quoted in Tumarkin, *Lenin Lives!*, 37. See also Leopold H. Haimson, *The Russian Marxists and the Origins of Bolshevism* (Cambridge, MA: Harvard University Press, 1955), 139–41.

16. Borenstein, *Men without Women*, 276.

17. On hegemonic masculinity, see the work of Raewyn Connell, especially *Masculinities*, 2nd ed. (Berkeley: University of California Press, 2005).

18. Sean M. Quinlan, 'Men Without Women? Ideal Masculinity and Male Sociability in the French Revolution, 1789–99', in Christopher E. Forth and Bertrand Taithe (eds), *French Masculinities: History, Culture and Politics* (Basingstoke: Palgrave Macmillan, 2007), 31.

19. Clements et al., *Russian Masculinities*, 232.

20. Compare Laycock and Johnson, this volume.

21. See Rolf Hellebust, *Flesh to Metal: Soviet Literature and the Alchemy of Revolution* (Ithaca, NY: Cornell University Press, 2003); Kaminer, this volume.

22. Mallon, '*Barbudos*, Warriors, and *Rotos*', 180.

23. Van E. Gosse, '"We Are All Highly Adventurous": Fidel Castro and the Romance of the White Guerrilla, 1957–58', in Christian G. Appy (ed.), *Cold War Constructions: The Political Culture of United States Imperialism, 1945–66* (Amherst, MA: University of Massachusetts Press, 2000), 242. Castro's bearded, virile image was not only meaningful to American observers but Soviet as well. For the Cuban revolutionaries' reception in Soviet culture in the 1960s, see Gorsuch, '"Cuba, My Love"', especially 513–14.

24. On the critique, see Krissie Butler, 'Deconstructing an Icon: Fidel Castro and Revolutionary Masculinity' (PhD thesis, University of Kentucky, 2012), 9–10.

25. Tumarkin, *Lenin Lives!*, 40.
26. Quoted in Tumarkin, *Lenin Lives!*, 79.
27. Eduard M. Dune, *Notes of a Red Guard*, ed. and trans. Diane P. Koenker and S. A. Smith (Urbana: University of Illinois Press, 1993), 51.
28. Biographies of Stalin are legion, of course, although historical treatments of him as a gendered subject are not.
29. Ronald Grigor Suny, 'Beyond Psychohistory: the Young Stalin in Georgia', *Slavic Review* vol. 50, no. 1 (1991): 54. On tradition, compare Laycock and Johnson, this volume.
30. Alfred J. Rieber, 'Stalin, Man of the Borderlands', *American Historical Review* vol. 106, no. 5 (2001): 1660.
31. Rieber, 'Stalin', 1661.
32. Rieber, 'Stalin', 1677. Unfortunately, Suny and Rieber do not discuss masculinity or treat the personality traits they are investigating in Stalin as part of his gendered identity.
33. On the peculiarities of the term and its shifts, see Matthew C. Gutmann, *The Meanings of Macho: Being a Man in Mexico City* (Berkeley: University of California Press, 1996), especially chapter 9.
34. Clements et al., *Russian Masculinities*, 232.
35. See Muller, this volume.
36. See Baker, this volume.

Part 3
Gender Politics and State Socialist Power

8

Gender and Youth Work Actions in Post-War Yugoslavia

Ivan Simić

The transnational circulation of models of gender, seen in the last chapter's rethinking of Soviet masculinities, was also visible in the new gender policies intrinsic to the social changes initiated by the Communist parties that secured power in eastern European countries between 1945 and 1948. Scholars usually argue these gender policies were based on Stalinist ideals, transferred to eastern Europe and slightly modified to fit local conditions.[1] Once applied, Stalinist gender policies were a radical challenge to existing gender norms. They created new opportunities for men and women to work and invent new identities, while the implications of Stalinist gender policies were very broad – affecting domains from labour policy to family relations.[2] The circulations of these ideas require historians to reconsider the models that informed national gender histories as well as their long-term effects.

Of all the east European countries, Yugoslavia can offer the best insights into how Stalinist gender policies were transferred, domesticated and applied, even though Yugoslav Communism would break with Stalinism in 1948. The Yugoslav Communist Party (KPJ) was Stalinized during the 1930s and had already developed a programme for gender policies based on Soviet models in 1940,[3] while during the war (which in Yugoslavia started in 1941) the KPJ spearheaded much resistance against Nazi occupation, established a new government and began to enact radical reforms to transform Yugoslav society. The Soviets did help the Yugoslav Partisans to liberate the country, but the war legitimacy that the KPJ acquired among the population empowered it to secure power faster than other Communists in east European countries. By late 1945, the KPJ was already the only political power in Yugoslavia, able to import many new models for organizing politics, economics and social practices directly from the USSR.[4]

The desire to rely on Soviet models was not simply due to the Soviet presence in Yugoslavia, since the Soviet military presence was ensured only through special advisors rather than a mass presence of Red Army troops. Strongly supported by the Soviets during the war, inexperienced in ruling the state and with only limited reliable information about Soviet policies, Yugoslav Communists seem truly to have believed in the correctness of the models that came from the USSR. The transfer of Soviet ideas and practices was ubiquitous; it occurred through the media, the KPJ's schools for ideological education, the mass organizations ruled by the KPJ, different state institutions, regular schools and, on the lowest level, local communities. However, the conflict with Stalin that began in 1948 led Yugoslavia to proclaim its own path to socialism in 1949: some Soviet models were abandoned as new economic and foreign policies began to be crafted. Even though Yugoslavia's trajectory started to differ from the Soviet bloc at this point, many social practices inspired by the USSR remained unaltered. One set of these practices was Yugoslav gender policies, where Soviet influences could be traced for the subsequent decade.[5]

Using the example of Yugoslavia, this chapter analyses how eastern European Communist parties constructed gender policies towards youth by focusing on the first four years after the end of World War II. This formative period of Yugoslav socialism allows insight into how Soviet models were transferred and domesticated in Yugoslav surroundings in an era when Yugoslav gender policies witnessed a series of significant changes that were influenced by both classical Marxism and the Soviet model. At the same time, this chapter also underlines the political agency of the periphery. In this case, the Yugoslav government utilized its large volunteer projects designed for youth (*Omladinske radne akcije* – Youth Work Actions) to impose ideas about socialist gender roles that were seemingly very ambiguous.[6] The KPJ fully encouraged gender equality on one hand but retained certain traditional practices on the other, often related to domestic chores and 'motherly duties' for women.[7] However, this did not conflict with Stalinist gender roles.

In exploring which Soviet models were domesticated in Yugoslavia and how, the chapter also offers insights into how the social and political environment changed as a result of the transfer. New ideas about socialist work, and especially *udarništvo* ('shock-work'), together with socialist sport events and initiatives, contributed to establishing new gender roles and relations, and they were followed by new ideas concerning the body and fashion. The Youth Work Actions are particularly well suited for such an analysis: they were state-led projects that aggressively intended to change ideas, identities and the behaviours of young people, and indeed a significant number of young people were affected.[8] Though the personal experience of men and women at the Youth Work Actions varied from person to person, this chapter analyses what the system attempted to produce, how certain norms were established as hegemonic, and how state policies attempted to define what it meant to be a young man or woman. While in the articulation of these hegemonic identities many people were excluded, evidence about the frameworks that the KPJ offered to the people is nonetheless valuable because they offered meanings, ideas and information to young people.

Particularly useful sources for studying these frameworks are newspapers published for the Youth Work Actions, *Omladinska pruga* (*Youth Railway*, 1946) and *Borba na Omladinskoj prugi* (*The Struggle on the Youth Railway*, 1947). Volunteers read these widely in their camps after the work day (there were even organized group readings where devoted activists read news aloud). These were produced by KPJ officials, controlled and published in order to inform volunteers and the general public about ongoing projects. Since the newspapers were following KPJ policies to intervene in existing gender relations, the gender identities and relations offered by the KPJ press also mattered on the level of daily practices. Through them the KPJ defined the most honoured modes of being a man or a woman and the most honoured forms of relations between genders. At the same time, KPJ officials were not just attempting to produce a desirable reality through the promotion of positive texts; rather, they relied on actual events in their work, so they covered the same problems that also appear in internal archival reports.

Yugoslavia's first mass federal work action was the construction of the Brčko–Banovići railway in 1946, when approximately 90,000 young people built a 90 km-long railway connecting a coal basin in Bosnia with industrial centres. Guided by the freshly announced Five Year Plan, the KPJ organized an even bigger action in 1947 in which 217,000 young people worked on the Šamac–Sarajevo railway (constructing 243 km of railway, nine roads and many large bridges in Bosnia), making the success of the Youth Work Actions crucial for the Yugoslav economy. These two large actions also provided models for all later volunteer-based projects.[9] During their stay at these projects (one month for young people who came from urban centres and two for those from the countryside), young people were offered the chance to gain some education through the courses and an option to be employed in industry later. For the KPJ, however, the most important tasks were to separate young people from their habitual surroundings and to use volunteer work to educate a new generation of loyal Communists adapted to the new socialist values.[10]

Changing these young people's values was one of the crucial components of the socialist modernization project,[11] particularly because they came from all over the country and varied in their religious beliefs and social and family backgrounds; they even came from regions which had had different legislation on gender relations until the KPJ declared a new Law on Marital Relations in 1946. Until then, women's position in Yugoslavia had been regulated by four different sets of legislation: Serbian civil law, Sharia law for the Muslim population and old Austrian and Hungarian civil laws in the areas that had previously belonged to Austria-Hungary. For example, the previous Serbian civil law had stated that a woman was practically the private property of her husband. Husbands were declared to be the head of the family who would thus represent women in all affairs. Women were obliged to obey their husbands' orders, to serve them, and take care of the children and the house. Women were not allowed to inherit real estate nor did they have any political rights. Legally, women were equal to minors.[12] The majority of youth volunteers were, therefore, predominantly male (for instance, 80 per cent male in the case of the Šamac–Sarajevo railway),[13] as traditional norms and huge illiteracy were the main obstacles hindering female peasants' engagement in activities outside their homes and farms. At the same time, Yugoslavia was largely a rural country, with over 75 per cent of the population living in the countryside, where the majority of volunteers came from as well. Therefore, for the KPJ, the Youth Work Actions were an opportunity to work with these young people and to create a modern image of rural youth, ready to accept women as equal.[14]

The personality cult of Yugoslavia's leader Josip Broz Tito was widely used in this process, and was particularly important in challenging traditional family relations. The youth media invested a lot of effort in portraying Tito as part of the imagined family, a father, a friend and a teacher at the same time. Tito took on the role of a traditional father who was capable of making the right decisions in the name of youth.[15] He was depicted as someone who knew what was best for young people and the state, but also had certain expectations of his children. As with traditional families, children were expected to unconditionally obey and trust him. The KPJ tried to build on Tito's paternalism with a rhetoric of love, contrasting with traditional families in which the father was usually feared. Nevertheless, just as with traditional fathers, the new father also had full rights over the minds and bodies of young people.[16]

Once the KPJ had established such a framework, gender identities were altered through various means. A new attitude towards physical work and sport was essential. Work was a crucial component in constructing the new socialist society and its modernization project, since, owing to a deficiency of other resources, industrialization would depend on mass manual work. The KPJ thus intended to carry out mass industrialization alongside a cult of work and physical strength. In that sense, the Youth Work Actions were a testing ground where the KPJ could continuously transfer its ideas into practice. Any physical job conferred particular 'honour' and 'pride', and was understood to be of the highest value; this was a pervasive feature of the volunteer actions, as young people, both men and women, were expected to be very enthusiastic and were encouraged to develop a genuine love for work.[17] Shock-work was the pinnacle of this idea, taken from the Soviet 'Stakhanovite movement' of the 1930s (named after the emblematic Soviet shock-worker Alexei Stakhanov) and applied in the very first Youth Work Actions. The KPJ's intention to create its own shock-workers went wider than the volunteer projects, but the heroic shock-worker was still a particularly useful model in an isolated environment. The press disseminated ideas about how Stakhanovites had behaved in the USSR and what was expected from Yugoslav youth. The traits of these imagined Stakhanovites were a precise indicator of how the KPJ defined a desirable young person in general and how the Soviet model was domesticated to suit Yugoslav needs.[18]

In the immediate post-war period, under powerful Soviet influence, sex and intimate love among shock-workers were taboo topics, immoral even to discuss. The Soviets never discussed the sexuality of their shock-workers, which suited the very prudish Yugoslav Communists well. The very strict moral code of the wartime Partisans was carried forward to youth volunteer projects. The Communist officials actually lacked language for writing about sexuality: even when several women were expelled from their brigades for 'immorality' (and not a single man was punished for this reason),[19] the youth newspapers never published any articles regarding proper sexual behaviour for young people or even mentioned these incidents. The sole exception seemed to be a two-page health pamphlet on syphilis from 1946, urging young men to refrain from intercourse before marriage and telling them 'people of strong will can restrain themselves, only weaklings cannot!'.[20] In the 1950s, the officials of the KPJ youth organization were still struggling to find adequate terms to discuss sexual activities during work actions. Although their meetings were closed to the public, the officials used vague terms and clumsy descriptions to criticize the reckless behaviour of young people that was 'appalling' the rural population next to a construction site. None of this was published in the youth newspapers, as young people (or at least young women) had to stay chaste.[21] An even deeper silence surrounded non-heterosexual practices. The KPJ's gendered understanding of shock-workers was inherently heterosexual, as no other sexuality was considered as a possibility.

Yugoslavs received basic ideas on shock-workers from the translation of the Soviet press, and adapted these representations for their own needs. This process had already started during the war, while in peacetime the shock-work system encompassed all spheres of society.[22] Some characteristics ascribed to shock-workers in media were shared by both genders. Shock-workers were supposed to go about their tasks tirelessly and enthusiastically, and always be ready to learn and adapt to new techniques of work. They fully supported the KPJ, regularly participated in sport and cultural events and cared about hygiene and health. Nevertheless, they had to stay focused and intent, prepared for possible new 'struggles' in the face of time, norms, nature, enemies and a variety of other obstacles. In the end, the new young people in Yugoslavia had to be humble; yet, according to most newspaper reports, this attribute was mostly reserved for women, setting just one of many significant differences in how shock-work was used in defining the masculinity and femininity of the KPJ's youth.[23]

Much of the social power of masculinity is typically dependent upon a belief in the natural physical superiority of men,[24] and Yugoslav Communist masculinities were no different.[25] For a young man, being a shock-worker was a crucial constituent of masculinity, as it showed his physical strength and commitment to the country's reconstruction. The KPJ youth press disseminated a completely masculine discourse that emphasized a new socialist man who could achieve anything, but also put additional pressure on the masculinity of those who were not working hard enough. It was always complemented with an ideal of sacrifice, especially because of the harsh working conditions. With all these characteristics, the identity of the male shock-workers was constructed as dominant and hegemonic, one that should be accepted by everyone and that presumed subordinating the masculinity of people without strong physical skills. Consequently, shock-work was presented as harder to achieve for women. The media insisted that women had to show stronger persistence and to draw on the social resources of the rest of the brigade. They were expected to reach the norms set by the men, and not to be norm-setters themselves.[26] Women who managed to become shock-workers were also praised for being pleasant women who always smiled, and who remained humble even when they were the best in the brigade. Women's work would be recognized widely, but it was up to their male comrades to acknowledge their success.[27]

Similar gendered differences existed in defining 'innovators', as well as in deciding who could control machinery. Just as in the USSR, shock-workers had to invent new methods of work, fuelled by their high enthusiasm as expressed in 'socialist competition' with others. These new methods would increase workplace norms and break world records in productivity.[28] However, almost all of the 'new innovators' were men. This illustrates a recurrence of old patterns of behaviour and, indeed, the reluctance to accept women as equal in highly technical fields. Additionally, control of machines, mining of tunnels and conquest over nature defined a significant component of being a male shock-worker, as the conquest of nature was always perceived as masculine, especially with the use of large machines such as bulldozers that were expensive and scarce.[29] For men, control of such machines designated prestige but also showed a lack of trust in women's skills. Moreover, members of the most celebrated mining brigades were almost exclusively men.[30] Their masculinity had to contain both physical and technical skills. This created a situation in which specific occupations were reserved for men already in the first years of Yugoslav socialism and shows that oppressive gender hierarchies were only changing slowly.[31] Nevertheless, it would be wrong to neglect the agency of women. There were young women who operated less expensive machines, and some dug out tunnels with drilling machines, despite the idea that control over those machines was not of great importance in defining a new socialist femininity.[32]

The KPJ nevertheless invested a lot of efforts to show the 'normality' of female work. Notable young women were praised, either individually or together with their comrades from the brigades, as newspaper editors often tried to show that young women were capable of completing the same amount of work as young men and distinguishing themselves. The visibility of women was a significant way of changing old perceptions towards women's work, while many texts about female shock-workers were designed to increase all women's self-confidence. This policy was intended to change pre-war patterns of behaviour, when women were expected not to gain any credit for their hard work, especially in the countryside.[33] Men had to accept that women were about to enter the workforce and that they should work together.[34] A few female shock-workers even became brigade commandants, probably the highest position one could obtain during work actions, so this was used as yet another example that in the new socialist society a woman could move up the hierarchy.[35]

There was, however, a clearly gendered division of labour in brigades' everyday life. In many brigades, men would carry out most of the hardest physical work, while women were particularly active in educational roles and in taking care of brigade hygiene and health issues.[36] 'Domestic work' was always left to women – fully reflecting Stalinist gender policies in the USSR.[37] These women were not always youth volunteers, but could also be activists from the KPJ women's section (*Antifašistički front žena* – Antifascist Front of Women (AFŽ)),[38] who had been sent to work in brigade kitchens and wash laundry. The AFŽ gave them a directive to use their 'maternal and domestic experience' to help young people organize their personal lives. A particular task was to make sure that young women were 'always clean and properly dressed, with brushed hair, and that they were not to do hard physical work or to work in damp places when they were on their period'.[39] Although the majority of young women did not work in the kitchens and a lot of them did the same jobs as men, in the brigades without AFŽ activists the KPJ advised that once a week a certain number of 'female comrades' should stay in the camp and wash laundry for everyone.[40] This was a clear message to all young women that they would have to carry the burden of housework as well as the burden of the reconstruction of the country. Since it was never questioned, the practice of female domestic labour remained naturalized. Scholarship has usually referred to this as a specifically socialist 'double burden' imposed by socialist industrialization and the demand for a larger workforce. More recent gender historians, such as Małgorzata Fidelis, have disputed this, arguing that the double burden was not novel to state socialism since many women had been expected to work and do unpaid domestic chores before the war as well.[41] Nevertheless, newspapers regularly used gender-sensitive language that marked comrades working in the kitchen as 'drugarice' ('female comrades') while not always using such language in other contexts.[42] Humour sections of the newspapers also tackled this issue, for instance in a 1946 article mocking young men having to wash their own plates. One of them blamed the new equality that socialism had brought women, while the other explained that it was women's fault, because they were always pretending to be busy at conferences just to avoid domestic chores.[43]

Another field in which gender relations were renegotiated, besides ideas about socialist labour, was participation in sports events. Yugoslav Communists took sport very seriously, establishing federal institutions to monitor, organize and promote sport activities. The basic concepts for Yugoslav sports were taken from the USSR, but in interwar Yugoslavia (and within several central European nationalist movements) there had already been a similar youth sport movement called the Sokols, which utilized sport associations for political purposes.[44] The KPJ built on that tradition, not allowing sport to be independent and free of political influence. Instead, sport was strictly controlled and devoted to a common goal: to prepare young people 'for building and defending the homeland' and for maintaining high productivity and fertility.[45] As Georg Starc notes, ascribing such features to mass socialist sport was a bio-political project with the intention of disciplining people's morality and mentality through their bodies.[46] Once again, the Youth Work Actions were the testing ground for the KPJ.

Sport became a semi-militaristic policy, promoted as 'one of the indispensable requirements for the all-round upbringing of the railroad builders'.[47] New socialist sports were planned through 'physical culture' programmes, with the idea that every socialist man and woman had to participate. Besides traditional sports, such as football, the KPJ also organized competitions in volleyball, basketball and light athletics, open to women as well. However, the most important were the daily morning exercises and pre-military training that were mandatory for everyone.[48] The morning exercises, seen as a means to train the mind and morality of youth, created a new reality in gender relations, since there was no gender-based division during this training. In that process, the KPJ's bodily policies were crucial. Shirtless men would do exercises not just in the youth camps but also in villages and cities in front of larger crowds, while the young women who exercised always wore more clothing. The KPJ used their bodies to convey ideological messages to communities, and to show the discipline and commitment of youth. The 'muscular, tanned' bodies of men were not promoted as sexually attractive but as proof of the productive force of the working class. This was a significant change to the gender norms of participation in sport compared to pre-war Yugoslavia: apart from women living in urban areas, women had not participated in any sport at all, and especially not with men. Accordingly, sport organizers explicitly wanted to include rural youth at any cost, not just to engage them in competitions but also to train them to become sport organizers themselves who would spread the new 'sport culture' when they returned home.[49]

As the KPJ and its youth organization wanted to show that socialist sport was open to everyone, the newspapers published many articles praising young Muslim women for outstanding sport results in addition to their physical work. Since the largest volunteer projects were organized in areas with Muslim majorities in Bosnia, the KPJ insistence on Muslim women's participation was not a coincidence. This was related to broader attempts to penetrate Muslim communities, 'modernize' them and engage them in the socialist project.[50] The KPJ insisted that these young women should successfully practise sport with men from other social backgrounds. As a result of their efforts, they were invited to demonstrate their skills at the central youth rally in the capital, Belgrade, featuring the best sportsmen and sportswomen from the work actions. While they were writing Tito's name with their bodies, none of these Muslim women wore the veil any more.[51]

The clothing of these Muslim women constituted a site for some of the KPJ's biggest experiments with people's values, but other young people were targeted as well. Their bodies were central in shaping gender relations, particularly as the body and clothing embodied gender, as well as ethnic, regional and religious identity. Dress is fundamental to the social presentation and understanding of the body, being an arena for the performance and articulation of identities.[52] Clothing in Bosnian villages next to the construction site was very different from, for example, the clothing of students from Zagreb who arrived at the camps wearing trousers and make-up. The local peasants helping these volunteers wore traditional clothing, including headscarves and sometimes the veil. However, the Youth Work Actions allowed the KPJ to construct unifying norms of what was acceptable (or not) to wear, and to instigate a process of attenuating the expression of individual subjectivity by focusing on collective identities.[53] This was sometimes policed by issuing direct orders, but more often through media. Media representations of the Youth Work Actions produced significant differences in defining male and female bodies, closely connected with differences in moral codes.[54]

The model for a male body was directly taken from the dominant style in socialist realism, yet another instance of a direct transposition of a Soviet model. It was a cult of a muscular and 'healthy body', capable of any physical work and endurance. It defined the core of the new socialist masculinity and shock-work policy: the volunteers had to become strong young men, builders of socialism, capable of making any sacrifice on the road to a brighter future. A man's body was disciplined, thus marking out a material space through which the KPJ exercised its power. As clothing is inseparable from bodily practices, it is crucial to note that in the media men were always half-naked. This was everyday practice at the construction sites and, although it was a consequence of poverty and very warm summertime weather, the KPJ gave it a certain symbolic value. A young male body had to be visible to show its strength and health, as the KPJ transformed impoverishment into desirable behaviour.[55] The KPJ made sure that such visions of men's bodies disseminated through the press were also vigorously applied in practice, as even men unwilling to cut their hair short were expelled from the actions.[56]

Bodily policies regarding young women and their visibility were also new to Yugoslavia, making female bodies more visible than in pre-war times or in rural areas just after the war. Young women had to live in the same camps as men, which was already a huge transformation for many. Their lives became more public, and, even if they did not share tents or barracks with men, they did share a daily routine – they ate, practised fitness and sport, and worked together. The bodies of young people were visible not just in their camps, but also all across the construction sites and nearby areas. Furthermore, their bodies were exposed in all available media, since newspaper images and newsreels from the work actions circulated throughout the whole country.[57]

Some restrictions regarding the visibility of female bodies owing to different moral codes still applied to men and women. Unlike their male comrades, young women were not allowed to be 'inadequately clothed'. This was the case during work, but also in the morning, as women were expected to be fully dressed when they got up and left their barracks. The morning exercises that followed were the same for everyone, but clothed women trained with shirtless men; the directive ordering that sport should be practised wearing as little clothing as possible had not been addressing women. Young women at work wore more clothes than men, and many wore long skirts, with only their hands visible. Their decorum was to be preserved from early morning until they went to sleep at night.[58] To ensure that, another directive was issued to stop the practice of women working at the construction site in swimming costumes or 'half-naked'.[59]

Female bodies were hidden on other occasions as well. When attending to personal hygiene women were separated from men. Collective bathing and swimming in the rivers was acceptable for men, but no images suggest that this was allowed for women.[60] In medical situations, too, the female body was also conceived as something that should not be publicly visible, allowing women more privacy. For example, male bodies were more exposed in the promotion of medical exams, and male-oriented posters exhibited shirtless men taking a vaccine from male doctors. Young women were never represented in these situations, although they too were all examined and vaccinated. Similarly, menstruation was expected to be hidden, or at least discussed only among women themselves.[61]

Conclusion

The history of the Youth Work Actions in early Communist Yugoslavia shows that Yugoslav Communists were actively transforming and reinterpreting Soviet models, adapting them to the Yugoslav situation and altering them where necessary. Even when some ideas were just a direct transposition, they still had to fit the KPJ's needs or they would not have been transposed. The Youth Work Actions highlighted the complexity of Yugoslav gender policy, formulated on the basics of Stalinism. On one hand, it was a radical shift from the pre-war position. The KPJ included young women in physically very demanding projects of building infrastructure, just as they believed Soviet women had participated in industrialization earlier. Following the idea of shock-work read through Soviet pamphlets and magazines,[62] the KPJ created the image of a young woman able to compete with men, even in hard physical work, while practices that the KPJ considered as gender-based discrimination were strictly forbidden. This was a significant change not only for young women but also for young men, who had to accept this new policy and challenge to their masculinity. To be praised as a shock-worker was the highest acknowledgement that one could earn at that time, bringing both fame and material benefits to these young women. Furthermore, the KPJ leadership believed that women could achieve further emancipation through employment and offered many women a chance to learn necessary skills on the courses alongside men, which prepared them to work in heavy industry later. Although that transition to employment in industry was hard for many women who complained about unequal treatment from factory managers, the KPJ supported them and pledged to solve the problem.[63]

Conversely, the Communists considered it a given that some duties were reserved exclusively for women. Young women were expected to pay more attention to their personal hygiene than men, but also to be concerned about other workers' hygiene. Some young women would do additional jobs that young men were supposedly 'incapable of', in addition to being shock-workers doing heavy physical labour. Many of these women would take on what were traditionally considered to be maternal roles, and were praised for the selfless help given to their male comrades. Women would stitch their comrades' shirts, sort out their laundry and even check to see whether they were covered with blankets at night. At the same time, the newspapers would praise them for being 'cultured' and nice to everyone.[64] Others would do physical work besides working as nurses. This was all in addition to other expectations that were exclusively for young women such as being modest, and chaste in intimate relationships. The KPJ's moral purity was enforced through the control of women's sexuality, with women being the only ones who were punished for breaking the moral codes regarding sex. The Youth Work Actions showed that the KPJ did not intend to change these patterns of behaviour. The policing of young people's sexualities and bodies was, in fact, strengthened by daily practices and Stalinist discourse, demonstrating the broad repercussions of Stalinist gender policies once they were adapted and applied in eastern Europe.

Notes

1. On Soviet gender policies, see, for instance: Elizabeth A. Wood, *The Baba and the Comrade: Gender and Politics in Revolutionary Russia* (Bloomington: Indiana University Press, 1997); Frances Lee Bernstein, *The Dictatorship of Sex: Lifestyle Advice for the Soviet Masses* (DeKalb: Northern Illinois University Press, 2007); Karen Petrone, *Life Has Become More Joyous, Comrades: Celebrations in the Time of Stalin* (Bloomington: Indiana University Press, 2000); see also Fraser, Laycock and Johnson, and Kaminer, this volume. For the transfer of Soviet models into other east European countries, see, among other works: Małgorzata Fidelis, *Women, Communism, and Industrialization in Postwar Poland* (Cambridge: Cambridge University Press, 2010); Shana Penn and Jill Massino (eds), *Gender Politics and Everyday Life in State Socialist Eastern and Central Europe* (New York: Palgrave Macmillan, 2009); Éva Fodor, *Working Difference: Women's Working Lives in Hungary and Austria, 1945–1995* (Durham, NC: Duke University Press, 2003).
2. This argument is convincingly put forward by Fidelis, *Women, Communism, and Industrialization*, 9.
3. Vida Tomšič, 'Referat na V Zemaljskoj konferenciji', 1940, Collection 141 AFŽ, box 10, The Archives of Yugoslavia.
4. For more on Yugoslav–Soviet relations, see: *Ljubodrag Dimić, Agitprop kultura: agitpropovska faza kulturne politike u Srbiji: 1945–1952.* (Belgrade: Rad, 1988); Goran Miloradović, 'Staljinovi pokloni: tematika jugoslovenskog igranog filma 1945–1955', *Istorija 20. veka* vol. 20, no. 1 (2002): 97–114; Goran Miloradović, 'U traganju za "novim čovekom": vrhunac kulturne saradnje Jugoslavije i Sovjetskog Saveza 1944–1948', in Aleksandar Životić (ed.), *Oslobođenje Beograda 1944: zbornik radova* (Belgrade: Institut za noviju istoriju Srbije, 2010), 419–36.
5. For a general overview of Yugoslav gender policies, see: Sabrina P. Ramet (ed.), *Gender Politics in the Western Balkans: Women, Society, and Politics in Yugoslavia and the Yugoslav Successor States* (University Park, PA: Pennsylvania State University Press, 1999); Renata Jambrešić Kirin, 'Žene u formativnom socijalizmu', in Jasmina Bavoljak (ed.), *Refleksije vremena: 1945.–1955.* (Zagreb: Galerija Klovićevi dvori, 2012), 182–201; Milica G. Antić and Ksenija H. Vidmar, 'The Construction of Women's Identity in Socialism: the Case of Slovenia', in Jelisaveta Blagojević, Katerina Kolozova and Svetlana Slapšak (eds), *Gender and Identity: Theories from and/or on Southeastern Europe* (Belgrade: Women's Studies and Gender Research Center, 2006), 291–307.
6. For the Soviet usage of volunteer works, see William Chase, 'Voluntarism, Mobilisation and Coercion: Subbotniki 1919–1921', *Soviet Studies* vol. 41, no. 1 (1989): 111–28.
7. Compare Muller, this volume; Adamson and Kispeter, this volume.
8. In 1946–52, more than 1 million young people worked on 70 significant projects: Slobodan Selinić, 'Omladina gradi Jugoslaviju: savezne omladinske radne akcije u Jugoslaviji 1946–1963', *Arhiv* vol. 6, no. 1–2 (2005): 87–101.
9. See Selinić, 'Omladina gradi Jugoslaviju'.
10. 'Gradimo prugu - izgrađujemo sebe', *Omladinska pruga* no. 3 (25 May 1946): 6.
11. Industrialization and electrification were supposed to facilitate this 'modernization', and to foster changes in people's living habits, moral norms and worldview. This was based on the Soviet idea of modernism; see: Stephen Kotkin, *Magnetic Mountain: Stalinism as a Civilization* (Berkeley: University of California Press, 1995); Richard Stites, *Revolutionary Dreams: Utopian Vision and Experimental Life in the Russian Revolution* (New York: Oxford University Press, 1989); Sheila Fitzpatrick, *The Russian Revolution*, 3rd ed. (New York: Oxford University Press, 2008).

12. Neda Božinović, *Žensko pitanje u Srbiji: u XIX i XX veku* (Belgrade: Dvadesetčetvrta, 1996), 29; Violeta Achkoska, 'Lifting the Veils from Muslim Women in the Republic of Macedonia Following the Second World War', in Miroslav Jovanović and Slobodan Naumović (eds), *Gender Relations in South Eastern Europe: Historical Perspectives on Womanhood and Manhood in 19th and 20th Century* (Belgrade and Graz: Udruženje za društvenu istoriju; Institut für Geschichte der Universität Graz, 2002), 183–95; Karl Kaser, *Porodica i srodstvo na Balkanu: analiza jedne kulture koja nestaje* (Belgrade: Udruženje za društvenu istoriju, 2002).

13. Selinić, 'Omladina gradi Jugoslaviju', 91.

14. Olga Kovačić, 'O prosvetnom radu medju ženama', 19 June 1945, Collection 141 AFŽ, box 1, The Archives of Yugoslavia.

15. On Tito's personality cult, see: Olga Manojlović-Pintar, '"Tito je stena": (dis)kontinuitet vladarskih predstavljanja u Jugoslaviji i Srbiji XX veka', *Godišnjak za društvenu istoriju* vol. 11, no. 2–3 (2004): 85–100.

16. Published letters often addressed Tito as 'our dearest comrade Tito'. This is the closest translation of a very unusual form: 'Naš rođeni druže Tito'. The word 'rođeni' signifies closeness for family relatives. There were many similar examples: 'Dobro doš'o mili druže Tito, da nam vidiš djelo plemenito [Welcome Dear Comrade Tito, To See Our Noble Deed]', *Omladinska pruga* no. 22 (29 September 1946): 3; 'Opravdajmo povjerenje druga Tita [Let's Justify Comrade Tito's Trust]', *Omladinska pruga* no. 3 (25 May 1946): 1; 'Vođi i učitelju naroda Jugoslavije, drugu JOSIPU BROZU TITU [To the Leader and the Teacher of Yugoslav People, Comrade JOSIP BROZ TITO]', *Omladinska pruga* no. 1 (6 May 1946): 2.

17. Mihajlo Švabić, 'Omladinska pruga: ponos Narodne omladine Jugoslavije', *Omladinska pruga* no. 27 (7 November 1946): 2; Brato Pavlović, 'Kako se Blagoje popravio', *Borba na Omladinskoj pruzi* no. 79 (July 1947): 4.

18. Dušan Popović, 'Sovjetska omladina: naš uzor', *Omladinska pruga* no. 27 (7 November 1946): 4; O. J., 'Ko je udarnik taj ne sustaje', *Omladinska pruga* no. 1 (6 May 1946): 6; 'Stahanov i stahanovski pokret', *Omladinska pruga* no. 16 (31 August 1946): 7. Stakhanovism in the USSR has been well researched; see, for instance, Lewis H. Siegelbaum, *Stakhanovism and the Politics of Productivity in the USSR, 1935–1941* (Cambridge: Cambridge University Press, 1990).

19. 'Dopis Glavnom štabu Omladinskih radnih brigada', 28 June 1947, Collection †14 – SSOJ, Box 128, The Archives of Yugoslavia.

20. 'Zdravstvena poruka br. 6', 1946, Collection 114 – SSOJ, Box 127, The Archives of Yugoslavia.

21. 'Savetovanje članova CK Narodne omladine republika po pitanju rada u srednjim školama u narednoj godini', 16 August 1952, Collection 114 – SSOJ, Box 58, The Archives of Yugoslavia.

22. For instance: 'Plodovi Oktobra', *Žena u borbi* no. 5–6 (November 1943): 14–15.

23. Mihajlo Švabić, 'Sednica pretsedništva Centralnog veća Narodne omladine Jugoslavije', *Omladinska pruga*, no. 21 (27 September 1946): 1; O. J., 'Takmičenje je počelo', *Omladinska pruga*, no. 3 (25 May 1946): 5.

24. See: Gay Mason, 'Looking into Masculinity: Sport, Media, and the Construction of the Male Body Beautiful', in Jacqueline Low and Claudia Malacrida (eds), *Sociology of the Body: a Reader* (Don Mills, ON: Oxford University Press, 2008), 272.

25. See Fraser, this volume; Bischl, this volume.

26. For example: Kemal M., 'Kako mi povišavamo normu našega rada', *Omladinska pruga* no. 4 (1 June 1946): 2.

27. 'Najboljem radniku prve banjalučke brigade: Drugarici Božici Petković', *Omladinska pruga* no. 6 (15 June 1946): 1.

28. P. Č., 'Povodom novih normi', *Borba na Omladinskoj pruzi* no. 82 (5 July 1947): 2.
29. 'Naši drugovi savladali su mašine', *Omladinska pruga* no. 12 (26 July 1946): 4; Dragomir Tošić, 'Buldozeri na Omladinskoj pruzi', *Omladinska pruga* no. 16 (24 August 1946): 5.
30. Ilija Zekić, 'On zna šta znači svaka mašina na našoj pruzi', *Omladinska pruga* no. 17 (31 August 1946): 7; Đ. Č., 'Vrandučki mineri razvili su ofanzivu', *Borba na Omladinskoj pruzi* no. 18 (20 April 1947): 1.
31. 'Na kursu automehaničara u Brčkom', *Omladinska pruga* no. 16 (24 August 1946): 7.
32. Luka Banović, 'Probjen je gornji potkop tunela "Majevice" za 16 dana prije roka, a tri dana prije date obaveze', *Omladinska pruga* no. 17 (31 August 1946): 7.
33. The Youth Work Actions were also used to affect gender relations in nearby villages, both by involving the local men and women in the work, and by organizing educational courses for them and their children: 'Primorsko-goranska brigada otvorila je drugi analfabetski tečaj za seljačku djecu', *Omladinska pruga* no. 7 (22 June 1946): 6.
34. N. S., 'Milija i Cvijeta: ponos Bijeljinske brigade', *Borba na Omladinskoj pruzi* no. 66 (15 June 1947): 5.
35. 'Po kvalitetu rada varaždinska brigada je jedna od najboljih', *Omladinska pruga* no. 7 (22 June 1946): 7.
36. Being a nurse could also bring a shock-work badge: Cvetanka Organdžijeva, 'Omladinska ambulanta u Bukinju', *Omladinska pruga* no. 23 (5 October 1946): 6.
37. Even a magazine designed for women published an article by Lenin criticizing domestic chores as 'unproductive labour' that made 'women stupid', but similar magazines never questioned the established division of labour. See Vladimir Ilyich Lenin, 'Pravo oslobođenje žene', *Radnica* no. 5 (December 1948): 12.
38. The AFŽ had only a minor role in the Youth Work Actions, but the organization was crucial in formulating and implementing the KPJ's policies towards women. It had been established during the war in 1942 to mobilize women for the Partisans, and was abolished in 1953.
39. Lj. M., 'Glavnom odboru AFŽ', 22 May 1948, Collection 141 AFŽ, box 32, The Archives of Yugoslavia.
40. 'Uređenje logorskog života', *Borba na Omladinskoj pruzi*, no. 6 (6 April 1947): 4.
41. See Fidelis, *Women, Communism, and Industrialization*.
42. Živan Šijački, 'Takmičimo se za bolju organizaciju posla', *Omladinska pruga* no. 2 (13 May 1946): 4.
43. 'Kad drugarice konferišu', *Omladinska pruga* no. 16 (24 August 1946): 8.
44. Dejan Zec, 'The Sokol Movement from Yugoslav Origins to King Aleksandar's 1930 All-Sokol Rally in Belgrade', *East Central Europe* vol. 42, no. 1 (2015): 1–22.
45. Todor Bulja, 'Zadaci i forme fiskulturne aktivnosti na pruzi', *Omladinska pruga* no. 27 (7 November 1946): 16.
46. Georg Starc, 'Sportsmen of Yugoslavia, Unite: Workers' Sport between Leisure and Work', in Breda Luthar and Maruša Pušnik (eds), *Remembering Utopia: The Culture of Everyday Life in Socialist Yugoslavia* (Washington, DC: New Academia Publishing, 2010), 264.
47. 'Proljetni kros Omladinske pruge', *Borba na Omladinskoj pruzi* no. 11 (12 April 1947): 1.
48. An exercise known as the Soviet 'Zarjadka' was most popular, although it was no different than usual calisthenics. The youth organizers emphasized its Soviet origin for ideological reasons. See 'Proslava Dana fiskulturnika Omladinske pruge', *Borba na Omladinskoj pruzi* no. 80 (3 July 1947): 6.

49. 'Savjetovanje fiskulturnih rukovodilaca sa sekcija na Omladinskoj pruzi', *Borba na Omladinskoj pruzi* no. 12 (13 April 1947): 5.
50. See also Laycock and Johnson, this volume.
51. B. C., 'Nosimo mladost, polet i snagu...', *Borba na Omladinskoj pruzi* no. 63 (15 June 1947): 7.
52. As argued by Joanne Entwistle, 'The Dressed Body', in Joanne Entwistle and Elizabeth Wilson (eds), *Body Dressing* (Oxford: Berg, 2001), 33–58.
53. 'Naši mišići, naša tela i naš um sve za izgradnju', *Omladinska pruga* no. 11 (20 July 1946): 3.
54. 'Mladost naše domovine', *Borba na Omladinskoj pruzi* no. 8 (8 April 1947): 4. See also Gustav Gavrin's film *Život je naš* (*Life is ours*) (Avala film, 1948).
55. Ljubica Smiljanić, 'Sa prvih predavanja', *Omladinska pruga* no. 3 (25 May 1946): 6.
56. 'Dopis Glavnom štabu Omladinskih radnih brigada'.
57. Gavrin, *Život je naš.*
58. J. O., 'Kako izgleda jedan dan u radnoj brigadi', *Omladinska pruga* no. 7 (22 June 1946): 5.
59. Batrić Jovanović, 'Odluka Glavnog štaba Omladinskih radnih brigada na gradnji Omladinske pruge Šamac–Sarajevo. Broj 8583', 10 July 1947, Collection 114 – SSOJ, Box 128, The Archives of Yugoslavia.
60. All those who drowned during the Šamac–Sarajevo project were men: 'Izveštaj Centralnom vijeću Narodne omladine Jugoslavije', 1947, Collection 114 – SSOJ, Box 128, The Archives of Yugoslavia.
61. See the poster published on the front page: 'Pozdrav trećem kongresu', *Omladinska pruga* no. 2 (13 May 1946): 1; Josip Konforti, 'Zadaci sanitetske službe', *Omladinska pruga* no. 19 (14 September 1946): 2.
62. See Kaminer, this volume.
63. S. Ćerović, 'Masovnim stupanjem u industriju omladina daje doprinos ispunjavanja zadataka Petogodišnjeg plana', *Borba na Omladinskoj pruzi* no. 74 (26 June 1947): 2; Danica Perić, 'Materijali o radnoj ženi iz BiH', 1955, Collection 117, Savez sindikata Jugoslavije, box 235, The Archives of Yugoslavia.
64. '*Biti kulturan*' ('being cultured'), or '*kult'urnost*' in Russian, was yet another element of the Stakhanovite movement. This concept concerned the construction of cultivated individuals, who were supposed to behave in a polite manner and had supposedly developed a taste for Soviet art. See Amy E. Randall, '"Revolutionary Bolshevik Work": Stakhanovism in Retail Trade', *Russian Review* vol. 59, no. 3 (July 2000): 425–41, and, in the Yugoslav case, 'Iz zidnih novina naših brigada', *Omladinska pruga* no. 8 (29 June 1946): 7.

9

Listing Homosexuals since the 1920s and under State Socialism in Hungary[1]

Judit Takács

Histories of gender, sexuality and the body can employ comparison across space, as in the last chapter, but also over time. The example used in this chapter, historical evidence about 'lists of homosexuals' compiled for official state use in Hungary from the early 20th century onwards, reveals what can be gained by studying a topic such as the control of homosexuality under different political regimes rather than beginning and ending every study at points of political rupture such as the establishment or fall of state socialism. At the centre of the chapter is a special list of 993 alleged homosexuals, found annexed to correspondence between the Hungarian security services and the Minister of Defence in 1942 which contemplated whether to use homosexuals as forced labourers within the wartime Labour Service System. This discussion took place under the authoritarian right-wing regime of Miklós Horthy. Yet the practice of special state surveillance on homosexuality both persisted after the Communist takeover of Hungary – when compiling 'homosexual inventories' of potential blackmail victims who could be coerced into becoming police informers was part of regular police work in urban areas, especially in the capital, Budapest – and dated back to the police practice of late Habsburg Hungary. The complexities of this history would not be seen in research that concentrated only on state socialism.

At the beginning of the 20th century, Hungary was still part of the Habsburg Empire, which had been divided into Austrian and Hungarian halves since the Austro-Hungarian Compromise of 1867 inaugurated the so-called 'age of dualism'. Hungary thus had complete independence regarding domestic policy, but surrendered state sovereignty in foreign and military policy to the Empire.[2] Hungary's 1878 Penal Code (created by one secretary of state at the Ministry of the Interior, Károly Csemegi) was part of this system. Paragraph 241 of the Csemegi Code rendered unnatural fornication – or literally 'perversion against nature' (*természet elleni fajtalanság*), a term with unspecified content – an illegal act punishable by up to one year's imprisonment.

Hungary's 1878 Penal Code would outlast World War I and Habsburg rule itself. After the last Habsburg emperor, Charles I of Austria (Charles IV of Hungary), abdicated in November 1918, the first Hungarian Republic was formed in the spring of 1919, leading to the first 'Communist experiment' in Hungary (a Soviet-type republic with proletarian dictatorship) and then a counter-revolution that lasted until March 1920. Miklós Horthy, whose regime re-established the monarchy without a king but with Horthy as regent, remained in power until 15 November 1944.[3] The Csemegi Code of 1878 was still in place in March 1944, when the Germans occupied Hungary.

Even after the liberation (or occupation) of Hungary by the Red Army, the Code remained in place. It was in force between 1945 and 1948, when 'tentative democracy' turned into Communist rule; during the Rákosi era, a 'totalitarian reign of terror' between 1948 and 1956,[4] named after the General Secretary of the Hungarian Communist Party, Mátyás Rákosi, who liked to refer to himself as Stalin's best pupil;[5] and during the 1950s, even during the 1956 revolution, the greatest attempt at destalinization in the region. It was only in 1961, early in the era of János Kádár (General Secretary of the Hungarian Communist Party between 1956 and 1988), that the unnatural fornication clause changed. The 1960s seem to have brought the aggressive prosecution of homosexuals to a halt; however, the long tradition of specialized state surveillance of homosexuality was still able to continue after 1961.

By rendering homosexual activities illicit, 20th-century Hungarian legislation provided a sufficient basis for developing a state-run system of social control and surveillance of homosexual people or, more precisely, of people who could be suspected of being homosexual. Representations of same-sex desires were rare under state socialism in Hungary, as they were in other '*iron-curtained*' countries,[6] at least in public – though certain kinds of representations of same-sex desires were quite well documented in secret police and state security files. Historical recollections of same-sex desire were often sporadic and piecemeal, reflecting the desires of men more than those of women, whose same-sex identifications and practices left few detectable marks in the public realm. The state's recognition and representation of same-sex desire, through the practice of police keeping lists of male homosexuals, show that in this semi-public, semi-private setting, same-sex desires were already being both recognized and misrecognized during the first half of the 20th century, and that these processes were not discontinued at all for most of the rest of the century.

Policing and Listing

Soon after the establishment of the Budapest Metropolitan Police in 1873, when the formerly independent municipalities of Pest, Buda and Óbuda were unified, a Criminal Investigation Department (*Detektív Osztály*) was formed in 1885 and introduced a local criminal registry system on the basis of detectives' private notes. The registry initially had four main sections (records of ex-offenders and wanted criminals; records of those on conditional release; a list of stolen items; and a collection of police bulletins), while in 1887 a portrait register of convicted criminals was also added. It took about two decades to create the National

Office of Criminal Records (*Országos Bűnügyi Nyilvántartó Hivatal*) on 1 January 1909: by this time the local criminal records included 148,273 individual profiles and 18,563 fingerprint files.[7] Fingerprinting as a means of identifying criminals started to come into effect in Budapest in 1902.[8] In 1914, when the First International Criminal Police Congress was organized in Monaco, the participants adopted the principle of creating a *casier central international* (centralized international record system), leading to the establishment of INTERPOL in 1923.[9] Representatives of the National Office of Criminal Records took part in the Monaco congress, which also reflected the office's increasing professionalization. Hungarian criminal records were now also part of an international system of control.

In 1926, one of the first books to be fully devoted to the modern aspects of the 'homosexuality problem' was published in Budapest. Its author, Dr György Pál, described homosexuality as having recurred suddenly after World War I as a mass phenomenon and as a 'burning issue of the modern era' that could not be ignored in Hungary either.[10] In the view of the author,[11] whose work can be interpreted as pleading against the criminalization of homosexuality, the broader context of these developments was a reflex-like reaction to the overexerted maleness of the war: the male world had thus become over-feminized, while the female world had become over-masculinized by trying to exhibit the modern boyish image, recognizing that 'it is in fact the boy who is the real ideal of men'.[12] The rapid expansion of homosexual life, the 'great homosexual tide flooding Budapest',[13] was presented as an inherent feature of global urbanization and as a parallel development to those shaping Budapest into a world-class metropolis. In Pál's estimate, by the 1920s the number of *urnings,*[14] (a reference to men who loved other men, belonging to a transitional third gender) was more than 10,000 in Budapest. They had several venues to meet and interact at, including bath houses and steam baths, as well as inner-city locations (such as Kálvin Square, Erzsébet Square, Emke Corner or the Buda side of the Margaret Bridge), most of which would remain popular cruising areas for several decades.

In comparison to villages, Pál explained, Budapest and other big cities could provide a more inciting environment for homosexuals to shift away from introverted passive sexuality and start exploring an extroverted active sex life. The main urban advantage was the immense ease of disappearance that could protect one from the dangers of blackmail in a city of a million people. The post-war shortage of housing was another reason that could leave the family-like cohabitation of same-sex partners unremarkable, as rooms for rent were often advertised for two gentlemen together. Additionally, the density of monosexual contact characterizing work–life socialization in some occupations, when most of the work time was spent in an exclusively same-sex environment (such as in the case of footmen and servants or seamstresses), could be identified as a hot bed for homosexualization – especially when access to potential different-sex partners was very limited for class-specific as well as financial reasons.

A few years later, a group of journalists and police officers published a two-volume work on 'modern criminality' (*A modern bűnözés*).[15] Here, in the section 'Circumstances That Promote Crime', a whole chapter was devoted to homosexuality, or more precisely its punishment and cure.[16] Following the aetiology of the psychiatrist Richard von Krafft-Ebing, the authors distinguished between acquired and inborn forms of homosexuality, and pointed out that at the beginning of their homosexual career people with acquired homosexuality did not yet have that 'unbelievable and unexplainable skill with which they are able to recognise each other'. Thus sometimes they wrongly pursued 'normal men', who would be 'naturally repulsed' or even report them to the police: 'These unsuccessful attempts bring them to those well-known places, where the pathologically inclined ones and especially their scum' gather – public toilets, parks and public bath houses – where they could find suitable partners; however, they could also fall into the hands of extortionists and male prostitutes.[17] Men with congenital homosexuality could be categorized into active *urnings* and passive effeminate homosexuals who could live together in a household as husband and wife; however, 'their family life can last only up to a maximum of two or three years', because they were unable to remain faithful.[18]

The authors of *A modern bűnözés* estimated that the proportion of homosexuals used to be 0.5 per cent of the population, but, owing to the Great War and the accompanying long terms of internment for prisoners of war, this rate had recently increased to 1 per cent. In modern big cities the homosexual rate could be even higher. For example, the male population of Budapest was 438,456 in 1925, while the number of homosexual men could be estimated at more than 5,000,[19] or at least 1.14 per cent.

A modern bűnözés also presented a statistical register, compiled between 1926 and 1929, of 2,000 homosexual men living in Budapest 'whose homosexuality is undeniable'.[20] This contained information on their ages, marital status, occupations and whether they had criminal records.[21] The authors claimed that no data had been collected previously and so the increasing proportion of homosexuals since the war could not be exactly determined. Even though no exact details were provided on how the reported information was gained, it can be assumed that police files were used as main sources of information, but the exact procedures are not at all clear.[22] The authors referred to the fact that out of the 2,000 examined men 345 already had a criminal record, and additionally there were a few hundred cases pending – however, they also added that 'even though perversion against nature was committed by all of them, there were only a few who were convicted on this basis',[23] as there had been very few reports of perversion against nature. Homosexuals reported each other to the authorities only because of revenge, the authors explained, and homosexuals approached 'normal men' only very rarely because they could sense whom they could approach. Even if a homosexual man did approach a normal man, they added, it would in any case be unsuccessful – so legally it would be defined only as attempted perversion against nature, on the basis of which convictions were rarely made in court.[24]

Additionally, it was made clear that the 2,000 homosexual cases did not include any prostitutes. The police had a separate file on cases of homosexual prostitution: since 1924 more than 400 men had such a police record, including 281 recidivists. The problem with homosexual prostitution was presented in a way that emphasized its dangers: 'Today there are homosexual prostitutes in all big cities, who are involved in much more criminality and cause much more trouble than their female colleagues. Male prostitution is secretive, uncontrollable and thus specifically in need of persecution.'[25]

In 1933, a practising doctor of the Royal Hungarian Public Health Institute published a study that was fully devoted to the issue of homosexual male prostitution: his Hungarian data source was a secret police file of 1932, containing a list of 1,695 male homosexual prostitutes.[26] The secret police file listed mainly men aged between 18 and 30, but also 64 boys younger than 18, though the author added that the number of those younger than 18 did not reflect reality. Their number was apparently much higher, but 'for philanthropic reasons [the authorities] try to defer the registration of juvenile homosexuals until they see no hope that they can improve by leaving this lifestyle behind'.[27]

The author of this study, Jenő Szántó, used a broader definition of prostitution than the legal definition then in force in Hungary, and defined it as a person making their body available for the lust of others in order to gain financial profit or social advantage or both. However, it should be observed that in a social context where, as Szántó stated, homosexual activities 'clash with the dominant moral views, being despised and detested by heterosexuals, persecuted by the state, proscribed by religious rules and punishable by the law',[28] the luxury of having a same-sex sexual partner was reserved for those with greater social advantages. The study distinguished two main groups of male homosexual prostitutes: the first one was the group of 'honest' homosexual prostitutes, recruited from among homosexual men, led by the same desire as their clients, with whom their interaction was characterized by 'the economically stronger party supporting the economically weaker one'.[29] It also pointed out that, in contrast to female prostitution, return to respectable society was possible for those who have become too old for that job but were being provided for by their friends, so for them plenty of other career options were still open. The second homosexual prostitution category was that of the '*Strichjunge*' or profit-seeking boys, whose main profit was made in fact not from actual prostitution but from blackmail. Homosexual prostitution could be linked to certain localities, including popular clubs, cafés, pubs and bars, as well as steam baths, beaches and the promenades on the banks of the Danube, and squares with busy public toilets (for example, at Kálvin Square, Berlini Square (now Nyugati Square), Erzsébet Square and Emke Corner).

In the same year, the same author published another study on homosexuality in Budapest in *Bőrgyógyászati, Urologiai és Venerologiai Szemle* (*Review of Dermatology, Urology and Venereology*). This included a list of 3,425 homosexual men,[30] gathered through 'special data collection', the exact nature of which was not detailed.[31] However, it can be assumed that the sources of data were police files, as the author points out that the number of known homosexuals had almost doubled since 1929, when the police superintendent József Vogl (author of the chapter on homosexuality in *A modern bűnözés*) had reported on the personal data of 2,000 homosexual men living in Budapest.

In 1934, Zoltán Nemes-Nagy, a Hungarian psychiatrist and neurologist, devoted a whole chapter of his study of sexual pathology to 'Homosexuals in Budapest', as well as a chapter on 'Homosexual Women' and another one on

'Punishment of Homosexuals in the Past and Today'. The 'Homosexuals in Budapest' chapter listed well-known homosexual meeting places, including bath houses, public beaches with separate cabins, the surroundings of public toilets and steam chambers with limited lighting.[32] In fact, this part of the book resembles a present-day gay guide, providing detailed information on venues such as Erzsébet Square, where homosexuals gathered in groups on benches around the public toilet; bath houses with steam chambers such as the Rác, Király, Lukács and Kazinczy Baths, and previously (before too many light bulbs had been installed) the Császár Bath; the public toilets at Kálvin Square, the corner of Teréz Boulevard and Király Street, Emke Corner; the little park at the Elisabeth Bridge on the Buda side around the fountain and under the bridge; at the Keleti railway station on the departures side; and the Sasfészek, a homosexual restaurant in Buda. However, the author also emphasized that Budapest was 'the first metropolitan city in the whole world where semi-official records [had been] compiled on homosexuals' for about 15 years, and thus Budapest police had data on about 5,000 men, including 'mainly passive homosexuals and those, who commit unnatural fornication for material interest'.[33] The author estimated 'the real number' of homosexual men in Budapest at about 15,000, most of whom would never be detected as they belonged to 'upscale circles, carefully trying to avoid publicity and any kind of scandal leading to the police'.[34] Social phenomena consisting of disorders of people's sexual life as well as the rise of various perversions were interpreted by another contemporary Hungarian neurologist, Sándor Feldmann, as features of a grave crisis.[35] The great extent to which homosexuality developed in the case of both sexes was seen by him to be caused by the very serious economic situation and the 'painfully limited social freedom of the sexes': thus, he explained, it was not surprising that people tried to 'find relief in excessive work and the pursuit of artificial pleasure'.[36]

By the 1920s, the population of Budapest had already grown to over a million and the city faced metropolitan problems related to its fast growth, such as having inappropriately functioning political institutions and a physical infrastructure that to a large extent derived from the disproportion characterizing the relations of the capital city and the rest of the country. Urban historians explain this disproportionate relationship by pointing to historical facts: 'The savage dismantling of the territory which had been Hungarian before the [First World] War, reducing the country to a third of its former size, was to leave Budapest as a hydrocephalus, at least 15 times larger than the next largest Hungarian town.'[37] In the 1930s Budapest became a spatially ordered modern city; that is, it was characterized by specialized uses of public space, serving mainly the interest of the higher middle classes.[38] While for most urbanites meeting – cultural and biographical – strangers, coming from previously separate real and symbolic worlds was merely an unavoidable concomitant of living in a modern city, for homosexual life the emergence of the unique social psychological space of the public realm provided a previously unknown dynamic.[39] In big cities such as Budapest with established meeting places and patterns of decodable behaviour, a same-sex attracted person could submerge in the world of strangers, and could try to act more openly as a homosexual – not just to be one.

Continuity During and After the Second World War

A document from 1942 recently recovered in the Hungarian War Archive (*Hadtörténelmi Levéltár*) contributes to the still very scarce historical evidence that during World War II homosexuals were also targets of life-threatening state control in Hungary: it is a list of altogether 993 alleged homosexuals that was attached to the correspondence between the State Security Centre and the Minister of Defence contemplating whether or not to use them as forced labourers within the wartime Labour Service System.[40] The obligation of home-defence-related labour service (*honvédelmi munkakötelezettség*), a special phenomenon of the Horthy regime, had originally been introduced by Act No. II of 1939 on Home Defence, and in 1942 the 69059/1942 Decree of the Minister of Defence extended the scope of the law to all Jewish men aged between 18 and 48. The aim of the wartime Labour Service System was to keep the politically unreliable elements of society – primarily Jews, but also Communists and members of non-Hungarian ethnic groups – away from armed military service and at the same time to force them to take part in the war effort. This is how the unarmed home defence labour service came into being, leading to the death of thousands of forced labourers who were sent to the front lines without sufficient equipment and supplies.

The correspondence, consisting of altogether four letters and two attached lists, started on 7 November 1942 with a proposal on behalf of the State Security Centre (part of the Ministry of Home Affairs),[41] addressing the Minister of Defence as follows:

> Please, call up into the home defence labour service the homosexual individuals, being unreliable regarding public morality, located within the territory of the capital, Budapest, listed in the attached register. Please, inform us about your Honour's decision.

High-ranking officers at the Ministry of Defence disagreed with the proposal that homosexuals, being residents of and registered by the police at Budapest, should be called into the 'home defence labour service' by pointing out that:

> it would not be desirable to look for solutions in the military line: this issue requires an explicit policing (administrative) solution as there is no hope of changing the character of these degenerated neurotic individuals.

It was also added that there was:

> an increasing tendency to offer the scum of the population for military use, while these procedures would hurt the feelings of those other impeccable individuals who participate in the war, when they see that the [military] service has primarily a punitive character.

Additionally, one officer made the following note in handwriting: 'It is undoubtedly useful, if mainly the nationally useless elements decay...'. Another lieutenant referred in a handwritten comment to the possibility of collecting homosexuals into special labour force companies and employing them outside the country's borders; however:

> in this case they would get into the same category with those being unreliable regarding national loyalty, thus the question emerges: "would it be useful to make all these men meet and get to know each other more closely? *I certainly wouldn't advise that*" (my emphasis).[42]

Nevertheless, on 11 November 1942 another short letter arrived from the State Security Centre, addressed again to the Minister of Defence, requesting similar treatment for an additional 184 men besides those 810 alleged homosexuals whose data had already been sent on 7 November. The two lists consisted of data on altogether 993 men, including their names, places and dates of birth, religious denominations, family status, occupations, fathers' first names (or indications of illegitimacy), mothers' names and (possibly their last known) addresses. Data on two further individuals is literally missing because the paper part of their records had been cut out with scissors 'on the basis of a conversation with the Chief Commissioner', as handwritten margin notes testify.

Most of these men were in their late 20s (with an average age of 29, ranged between the age of 16 and 48), and worked as manual labourers (about 160 of them were farm hands and about 80 worked in commerce); there were only a very few intellectuals and artists among them (for example, three actors, eight musicians and only one journalist). Of the 993 men, 29 were married, 46 had been illegitimate children and 37 had their address given as prison. Regarding religious affiliation there were 629 Roman Catholics, 167 Jews, 127 Calvinists, 24 Evangelicals and 19 Greek Catholics – these numbers are in line with the division of denominations in the population of Budapest in the early 1940s.[43]

It is a matter of concern that the origin of these lists cannot be established. It can be supposed, however, that they came from police files, and the phrase 'officially registered homosexuals' used in the correspondence supports this supposition. The final item of the correspondence, as far as it has come to light, is a reply of 3 December 1942 from the Minister of Defence to the Minister of Home Affairs, stating that 'I have no means to follow your Honour's recommendation to take these homosexual individuals into military service'. So far, these are the only known documents that can provide a link between the history of homosexuality in Hungary and the Holocaust, and this link is not a very strong one because at present, apart from archival documents about criminal court cases, there is no historical data available to find out what happened in Hungary during the 1940s to alleged homosexuals in general and these 993 listed men from Budapest in particular.

The practice of specialized state surveillance of homosexuality, meanwhile, persisted after World War II, especially during the rise of the Hungarian state socialist political system. Compiling 'homosexual inventories', which provided potential blackmail victims who could be coerced into becoming police informers, was part of regular police work in urban areas and especially in Budapest. These practices are reflected in archive documents of the Historical Archives of the Hungarian State Security, including the National Police Headquarters instructions from 1958 on how to keep criminal records.[44] According to these instructions there were 13 types of criminal records, and data on homosexuals had to be kept in at least three of them, including the 'Preliminary Records of Persons Suspected of Crime'; the 'Record of Regular Criminals' and a photo register of convicted homosexuals. Preliminary records of homosexual persons suspected of crime were kept only in the capital city; this was not required in the countryside or in smaller cities and towns.

The goal of keeping a register of 'regular criminals' was to collect data on criminally active, socially seriously harmful persons with a criminal record. Regular criminals were defined as recidivists and those whose personal circumstances or the mode of perpetration could project repetition of crime, such as (in the case of homosexuals) prostitutes, offenders committing thefts against drunk people, swindlers and vagabonds. During the 1950s, the Police Chief of Budapest therefore had access to a special data set of persons with 'proved homosexual inclinations', including the circles of their friends who were also participating in perversion against nature, their photos, their nicknames and also their female nicknames, if they had any, as well as their 'method' of committing perversion against nature.

By the end of the 1950s, however, a change in official attitudes to homosexuality had emerged. Recently discovered archival records show that in 1958 the Health Science Council (*Egészségügyi Tudományos Tanács*) within the Ministry of Health unanimously supported a proposal to decriminalize unnatural fornication between consenting adults. The Council based its support on a medicalizing approach that defined homosexuality as a biological phenomenon which was not logical to persecute under the law, and it also acknowledged the increased vulnerability of homosexual men to blackmail, created and sustained by criminalization.[45] These arguments were reflected in the official ministerial standpoint, which emphasized that homosexuality was:

> either an inborn sexual perversity rooted in a developmental disorder or such acquired anomaly that develops mainly within neurotic people as a result of some sort of sexual impression during childhood, adolescence or at a young age [...] and can therefore not be handled legally as a crime. Finally, in the course of its legal regulation the practical point should be considered that criminalization of such behaviour would provide a wide scope for blackmailing.[46]

Homosexual activity between consenting adult men became decriminalized in 1961. Nevertheless, different ages of consent were set for heterosexual and homosexual relationships, and this remained the case until 2002: while the age of consent for heterosexual relationships became and remained 14 in 1961, the age of consent for homosexual relationships was set at the age of 20 in 1961 and at 18 between 1978 and 2002.[47] Additionally, the circle of potential perpetrators and victims also changed in 1961. Men and women could now equally be prosecuted for 'perversion against nature', as long as the conduct had been with another person ('perversion against nature' conducted with an animal was no longer penalized). Furthermore, a special clause was introduced to cover 'perversion against nature conducted in a scandalous manner', carrying up to three years' imprisonment. The law did not specify what counted as 'scandalous', though court reports suggested that judges applied the clause if, among other circumstances, a third party could have witnessed the 'perversion'. The age of consent and potential public scandal clauses, in particular, provided good opportunities for state authorities such as the police – as well as extortionists at an interpersonal level – to keep (alleged) homosexual practices under close control. With the compilation of 'homosexual inventories' providing information on potential blackmail victims (and potential police informers) having been part of regular police work, especially in urban areas, since at least the 1920s, the long tradition of specialized state surveillance of homosexuality could even continue after 1961.

Evidence also shows how the collection of incriminating data could be put into practice, for example in the process of recruiting police informers. In a textbook from 1965 used by the Department of Political Investigation of the Police Academy, the whole process of police informant recruitment was described in a way reminiscent of a truth-producing therapeutic session:[48] the more incriminating evidence, the higher the chance of success. It was important for the recruiting officer to give an impression of expertise, with thorough knowledge of the incriminating details against the informer candidate and the relevant pieces of legislation (an example was given: that of a priest informer who had had sexual relationships with five women, with the police having firm evidence about two). The informer candidate had to be invited for a private talk but it had to be left open exactly what kind of crime they were suspected of. During this session, the recruiting officer had to avoid reacting snobbishly, triumphantly or sarcastically to the admissions, self-struggles and problems of the candidate. Instead, officers should present themselves as if they appreciated the candidate's honesty and current difficult situation, and declare that the law provided for the punitive process to be stopped if the candidate gave their full admission and repentance. The candidate would then be asked to give testimony about his/her companions' hostile behaviour, providing the authorities with additional incriminating data about others.

These incriminating details, the candidate's first 'minor task', had to be given in writing and could be of major assistance in future police work. Complete discretion – at least towards the candidate – was assured. The recruiting police officer would condemn the acts the candidate had committed but at the same time show understanding of their situation, while the candidate could feel that it was not the main goal of the interrogator to send them to jail. At the end of the session, the candidate prepared a declaration in which it was emphasized that 'I repent the committed crimes and in order to make reparations I agree to cooperate with the political investigatory bodies. I understand that in return they will waive any punishment.' The process of recruiting an informant was complete. However, becoming a successful, fully fledged informant also involved doing the work not (only or mainly) because there was incriminating evidence against oneself but because of (political) conviction and commitment.

Besides its value in recruiting future police informers, incriminating data about alleged homosexuals could also be used for supposedly 'protecting the community' in criminal investigations. For example, attached to the police reports of one 1961 murder case was a list of 187 alleged homosexuals.[49] Official records showed the investigating detectives' main assumption was that the 71-year-old homosexual man (living in an elegant neighbourhood of Budapest) had been murdered by another (probably younger and poorer) homosexual. Thus the police could argue that they needed these practical homosexual lists to map the network of homosexuals known by the police, in order to speed up the investigations in the homosexual underworld of Budapest. This approach was based on a semi-hidden and semi-closed subcultural image of urban homosexuality, within which participants could quite easily navigate.

Conclusion

This chapter has presented historical evidence about the existence of 'lists of homosexuals' compiled for official state use in Hungary from at least the 1920s, and has introduced a special list of 993 alleged homosexuals from 1942 that can provide the only – currently known – link between the history of homosexuality in Hungary and the Holocaust. It has shown that before and after the world wars, in different political regimes, homosexuality was controlled in 20th-century Hungary by quite similar means. Even after the general criminalization of homosexual acts ceased to exist in 1961, homosexuality carried such a heavy social stigma that it could still be used as an incriminating personal detail in recruiting potential police informers for at least two further decades. Homosexual lists could be used not only by the secret police but also by ordinary police detectives in their investigations, especially in homosexual murder cases, when looking for perpetrators to be caught and additional victims to be protected in a gloomy homosexual underworld. According to informal police reports and interviews conducted with elderly Hungarian gay men, this latter practice continued even after the change of political system in 1989–90.

Regimes of all different stripes in Hungary's turbulent 20th-century history, then, appeared to have made use of secret lists of sexually non-conforming men in order to oppress them and recruit them to perhaps spy on others as well. What becomes visible through the State Security archives, and what remains more difficult to perceive, has several implications for historians. Firstly, since women who had non-heteronormative desires and sexual practices were not persecuted in the same way as men, there are no such secret lists of them as far as we can tell today; nevertheless, their narratives remain a very much under-researched topic in Hungary and elsewhere.[50] Secondly, while the 20th century appears dominated by cisgender homogeneity for the most part, records suggest that requests to permit a change of gender on official records were apparently being granted even in the 1950s, at the height of Stalinism in Hungary, and these remarkable facts deserve to be further investigated. Thirdly, the extent and durability of Hungarian surveillance of homosexual men would make it worthwhile to investigate this topic in a wider central and eastern European context. The Hungarian records show that the lives of gay men in 20th-century Hungary were not as wholly invisible as one might think; in the eyes of the state, both before and during Communism, their lives were very visible indeed, another tension between public and private in the intimate politics of gender history.

Notes

1. This research was supported by Grant 105414 from the Hungarian Scientific Research Fund. The author gratefully acknowledges inspiring suggestions from Catherine Baker and the reviewers of this volume.
2. Zoltán Fónagy, 'The Age of Dualism', in István György Tóth (ed.), *A Concise History of Hungary* (Budapest: Corvina–Osiris, 2005), 425–35.
3. This period of Hungarian history is often described as a kingdom without a king, ruled by an admiral without a fleet, in a country without a coastline. The powers of the Regent were comparable to the legal position of a moderately powerful president – but as the 'Chief Warlord' the Regent had great influence over the army: Ignác Romsics, 'Hungary in Two World Wars', in Tóth (ed.), *A Concise History*.
4. György Gyarmati, 'Hungary in the Second Half of the Twentieth Century', in Tóth (ed.) *A Concise History*, 570.
5. Árpád Pünkösti, *Rákosi, Sztálin legjobb tanítványa* (Budapest: Európa Könyvkiadó, 2004).
6. See, for example: Francesca Stella, *Lesbian Lives in Soviet and Post-Soviet Russia* (Basingstoke: Palgrave Macmillan, 2015); Josie McLellan, *Love in the Time of Communism: Intimacy and Sexuality in the GDR* (Cambridge: Cambridge University Press, 2011).
7. János Baksa, *Rendőrségi Almanach* (Budapest: A Rend kiadása – Stephaneum Nyomda és Könyvkiadó, 1923), 108.
8. Lajos Rácz, 'A modern nagyvárosi rendőrség kialakulása és működése', in N. Kollár (ed.), *A fővárosi rendőrség története (1914-ig)* (Budapest: BRFK, 1995), 253–320.
9. Baksa, *Rendőrségi Almanach*, 127.
10. György Pál, *A homoszexuális probléma modern megvilágításban* (Budapest: Mai Henrik és Fia Orvosi Könyvkiadó, 1926), iii.
11. It cannot be determined precisely whether Pál was a legal or a medical expert; however, in light of the fact that the book was published by a 'medical publishing house', as stated on its cover, it seems to be more likely that he had a medical background.
12. Pál, *A homoszexuális probléma modern megvilágításban*, 78.
13. Pál, *A homoszexuális probléma modern megvilágításban*, 60.
14. The term, inspired by Plato's *Symposium*, was coined by the German jurist Karl Heinrich Ulrichs.
15. Gyula Turcsányi (ed.), *A modern bűnözés* (Budapest: Rozsnyai Károly Kiadása, 1929).
16. In the same section, other chapters were devoted to Prostitution, Drugs and Alcoholism.
17. Turcsányi (ed.), *A modern bűnözés*, 121.
18. Turcsányi (ed.), *A modern bűnözés*, 129.
19. Turcsányi (ed.), *A modern bűnözés*, 133.
20. Turcsányi (ed.), *A modern bűnözés*, 134.
21. According to marital status, 76 per cent of them were single, 18 per cent married, 3 per cent were widowers and 3 per cent were divorced. Regarding the occupational statistics, the authors voiced their view that among the 2,000 men they had examined there were exceptionally high numbers of those doing 'feminine work' such as cooks, confectioners, tailors, bakers, valets and nurses – as well as those who dealt with men in their work, such as barbers, men's tailors, waiters, bank clerks, masseurs, footmen, shop assistants specialized in menswear, teachers in boys' schools, and music teachers with male pupils. They also referred to the concordant

view of medical specialists in sexual pathologies that sedentary workers tended to have a greater libido and committed most of the sexual crimes. Turcsányi (ed.), *A modern bűnözés*, 138–40.

22. In a study published in 1933, this set of data is referred to as 'statistics published by police superintendent József Vogl during the years of 1926–1929': Jenő Szántó, 'A homosexualitásról, különös tekintettel a budapesti viszonyokra', *Bőrgyógyászati, Urologiai és Venerologiai Szemle* no. 3 (1933), 43.

23. Turcsányi (ed.), *A modern bűnözés*, 142.

24. According to the authors there were several milder crimes that homosexuals did tend to commit, including theft and fraud, while crimes with physical harm were rarer. It was also emphasized, in a taken-for-granted sexist manner, that most homosexuals had a workless, inactive, slothful lifestyle and in general a lot of feminine characteristics.

25. Turcsányi (ed.), *A modern bűnözés*, 143.

26. Jenő Szántó, 'A homosexualis férfiprostitutio kérdése', *Népegészségügy* no. 20–1 (1933), 7.

27. Szántó, 'A homosexualis férfiprostitutio kérdése', 9.

28. Szántó, 'A homosexualis férfiprostitutio kérdése', 3.

29. Szántó, 'A homosexualis férfiprostitutio kérdése', 5.

30. This list, similarly to the list in *A modern bűnözés* in 1929, contained information on the age, marital status, occupation and the criminal record of persons. A new element of the 1932 list was information on religious affiliation.

31. Szántó, 'A homosexualitásról, különös tekintettel a budapesti viszonyokra'; Jenő Szántó, 'A homosexualitásról, különös tekintettel a budapesti viszonyokra', *Bőrgyógyászati, Urologiai és Venerologiai Szemle* no. 2 (1933).

32. Zoltán Nemes-Nagy, *Katasztrófák a szerelmi életben*, vol. 2. of *Sexualpathologiai tanulmányok* (Budapest: Aesculap Kiadás, 1934), 75–9.

33. Nemes-Nagy, *Katasztrófák a szerelmi életben*, 73. The collected data included the following elements: name, place and date of birth; religious affiliation; marital status; occupation; address; place apprehended; nationality; knowledge of languages; female name; inclination; company; height; way of speaking; eyes; mouth; nose; ears; face; hands; hair; moustache; beard; special distinguishing marks; previous criminal record; and three photographs: Nemes-Nagy, *Katasztrófák a szerelmi életben*, 73–4.

34. Nemes-Nagy, *Katasztrófák a szerelmi életben*, 73.

35. Sándor Feldmann, *Idegesség és ösztönélet* (Budapest: Novák Rudolf és Társa Tudományos Könyvkiadó, 1928).

36. Feldman quoted in Kálmán Ruttner, 'A szekszualitás befolyása a bűnözésre', in E. Wulffen, W. Steckel and K. Ruttner (eds), *Szekszuális abnormitások és büntettek* (Budapest: Sándor József és társa kiadása, [c. 1930]), available at: http://mtdaportal. extra.hu/books_kulf/wulffen_erich_szekszualis_abnormitasok_es_buntettek.pdf (accessed 5 May 2015).

37. Helen Meller, *European Cities 1890–1930s: History, Culture and the Built Environment* (Chichester: John Wiley and Sons, 2001), 102.

38. Lyn H. Lofland, *A World of Strangers: Order and Action in Urban Public Space* (New York: Basic Books, 1973).

39. On the public realm as a unique social psychological space, see Lyn H. Lofland, 'The Morality of Urban Public Life: the Emergence and Continuation of a Debate', *Places* vol. 6, no. 1 (1989): 18–23.

40. 'Homoszexuális egyének bevonultatása munkaszolgálatra (benne névjegyzék a fővárosi lakosokról)', 1942, Hungarian War Archive HM 68763/Eln.1b. – 1942.

41. The State Security Centre was established within the Ministry of Home Affairs in 1942.

42. All quotations from this correspondence relate to the following document: 'Homoszexuális egyének bevonultatása munkaszolgálatra (benne névjegyzék a fővárosi lakosokról)', 1942, Hungarian War Archive HM 68763/Eln.1b. – 1942.

43. I would like to thank Péter Tibor Nagy for sharing this data with me on the basis of a contemporary yearbook of statistics (*Budapest székesfőváros statisztikai évkönyve 1944–1946* (Budapest: Budapest Székesfőváros Statisztikai Hivatala, 1948)).

44. 'Bűnügyi nyilvántartási utasítás', 1958, Állambiztonsági Szolgálatok Történeti Levéltára (Historical Archives of the Hungarian State Security), Ikt. szám 50–6/5–1958 ABTL.

45. Judit Takács and Tamás Ptóth, 'Az "Idegbizottság" szerepe a homoszexualitás magyarországi dekriminalizációjában', *Socio.hu Social Science Review* no. 2 (2016), available at http://socio.hu/uploads/files/2016_2/takacs_ptoth.pdf (accessed 29 July 2016).

46. Országgyűlési irományok, 1958, vol. 1, 270. (Parliamentary documents – original unpublished document, access provided by the Országgyűlési Könyvtár (Library of the Hungarian National Assembly.)

47. Judit Takács, *How to Put Equality into Practice?* (Budapest: New Mandate, 2007) 35. Since 2002, the age of consent has been set at 14 for same-sex as well as mixed-sex sexual relationships.

48. Dr Balázs Tibor, 'A terhelő vagy kompromittáló adatok alapján végrehajtott beszervezések néhány tapasztalata', 1965, BM Központi Tiszti Iskola Rendőrtiszti Akadémia, Politikai Nyomozó Tanszék (Ministry of the Interior, Central School for Officers, Police Academy, Department of Political Investigation), Állambiztonsági Szolgálatok Történeti Levéltára (Historical Archives of the Hungarian State Security) ABTL A–3802.

49. Budapest Főváros Levéltára (Budapest City Archives), BFL XXIV-1 BRFK.

50. Exceptions include, e.g., Anna Borgos, 'Secret Years: Hungarian Lesbian Herstory, 1950s–2000s', *Aspasia* no. 9 (2015): 87–112; Stella, *Lesbian Lives*.

10

Everyday: Intimate Politics under Communism in Romania

Maria Bucur

Six o'clock in the morning: Cold – they haven't turned the heat up again, gotta put on two, maybe three layers. I can see my breath ... What can I fit under the uniform before it bursts? Tights, pants, two pairs of socks. OK, that will do. What is there for breakfast? Gotta find my way to the kitchen and the candle, I can't see anything in the pitch dark hallway. So quiet ... just the morning trams and construction trucks nine floors below. I fumble through the darkness – the matches. Now let's see if there is any gas pressure or I won't be able to warm up at all with tea. Out of luck. Let's see what's on the balcony – a bit of milk. Well, at least one good thing about this cold weather, the food won't go bad as quickly out here. Where is the bread and jam? Oh, in the fridge, of course, with all the other groceries that don't need to be kept cold.

[...]

OK, ready to go, but I have to pee first, there is no knowing when I'll get a chance again in a decent place all day ... hmm, what do I need to take with me – bags to make sure I can buy food if there is anything out there, some toilet paper, and maybe a bottle, if I can find some oil, to exchange for a full container if I get lucky ... Fshhhh! Oh crap, I flushed the toilet. Stupid. Now I'll have to use the water for cooking and cleaning to flush down tonight. Damn it, I can never remember NOT to do this early in the morning.

[...]

This was the interior dialogue of an average urban young woman, aged 16–35, in Romania during the 1980s. It is a remembered dialogue, as it was mine. It is also a typical set of habits and thoughts many other people had at that time. I reproduced this fragment to set the mood for my comments on 'everyday citizenship' or 'intimate politics'. In recent years I have become more and more interested in the quotidian aspects of life that are often evanescent, difficult to measure, yet crucial for understanding both the lives of *individual* average (and extraordinary) people, as well as historical processes. Everyday practices are a nexus of structures of habit, discrete personal choices, our personalities and milieu. These practices mould our paths through life even as we give more conscious thought to the big stuff – education, career, lovers, children, parents – and are in turn the product of both thoughtful and routine repetitions.

Scholars such as Maureen Healy, Belinda Davis and Sheila Fitzpatrick have demonstrated the importance of paying attention to such unremarkable details and repetitions in studies focusing on life in World War I Vienna and Berlin, and in Soviet Russia.[1] Their research has creatively sought to connect intimate details with societal shifts and challenges, to show the impact on social trends and politics of choices made by women in matters from cooking and cleaning to concealing and supporting their families. For instance, the impact of preserving routines or breaking them in times of war bore important consequences for both the women shouldering these responsibilities and the men who were away from home, fighting and being exposed to unprecedented forms of physical and psychological trauma. And when the state becomes the vehicle for violating every type of intimate routine – from having meals as a family, to dating – just for the sake of showing its prowess, a person's ability to hold on to any sort of choice, no matter how (in)visible, gains a very different significance, a deeper meaning than the simple routine of brushing one's teeth at a certain point in time every day. Historians have written a lot more about the ways in which inmates in concentration camps in Nazi Germany between 1933 and 1945 were psychologically traumatized through the imposition of absurd routines (bed making, cleaning of all supplies, etc.) that were not born out of necessity or personal preference.[2] The struggle between state socialist government authorities and individuals over controlling their lives followed a similar dynamic of psychological manipulation of lived environments on the part of the state, with individuals seeking authenticity, choice and real intimacy through dissimulation and duplicity.[3]

Most people would not dispute the notion that such everyday practices are in fact a large part of what we do on a daily basis as human beings. Where different knowledge makers part ways is on the issue of what these practices mean for the larger world – human, institutional, political, economic, cultural, and so on.[4] This is where my encounters with the work of Alf Lüdtke and his *Alltagsgeschichte* school,[5] as well as my readings in feminist theory (philosophy and anthropology in particular),[6] have been important for where I stand. Lüdtke, whose ethos is closely connected to that of many Marxist labour historians of the 1970s (among them E. P. Thompson and the early work of Joan W. Scott),[7] insisted that the lives of workers and the actions of such unprepossessing people were indeed worth examining as intrinsically interesting and socio-politically relevant. Lüdtke's work reinforced my own interest in those who are socially marginal – in my case, women and peasants, the two most populous categories of people in the pre-1945 history of Eastern Europe.[8]

Fundamentally, if history is the study of change over time, it needs to take into account not only major visible shifts in institutions, intellectual elites' discourse, art or borders. When human communities or entire societies, as was the case with the Communist bloc, were in effect living duplicitous lives, their reality was never just the visible part of human interactions, or just the public actions they undertook. To give just one vivid example: if for some people their religious identity had to be expressed through crossing oneself with one's tongue, inside one's closed mouth, out of fear they or their families would suffer severe consequences, one can imagine the myriad of significations of small or invisible everyday routines that are intimately connected to the context of the one-party state and of living with fear all the time.

Trying to probe into the lives of people without an interest in or resources for marking their passing through life through written documentation drove historians of everyday life into different directions, one of them being oral history, and another important focus being material culture. Though the early work of everyday historians focused on the working classes, they were fortunate to dwell among people who had a higher level of literacy than the people I was interested in. Historical traces linked directly, rather than conjecturally and relationally, to the historical agents to be studied were sometimes available.[9] Living in an urban environment also placed such historical actors more often in the presence of others who wrote about them, drew them or recorded their actions and words in some fashion (e.g. social reformers going into the slums).[10]

However, for rural, barely literate (in some places until the mid-20th century) societies such as those of Romania, Bulgaria, Poland, Russia, Serbia, Greece and so on, many of these avenues to explore everyday life are not available.[11] Few written records from and about these populations have survived, and material culture traces are also sparse. Ethnographic research, ethnographic collections, oral history and personal collections have provided a wider array of nuanced information about everyday practices.[12] Overall, cultural anthropology has been most helpful in suggesting useful ways to read the relationship between material culture – food-ways, rural architecture, rituals of passage, clothing, for example – and human actions in the past.[13] Questions of agency, scale and motivation or meaning are difficult to derive from such pluriform types of historical evidence. To find out who produced an artefact and in what way (agency), for instance, one needs to possess deep locally based knowledge about technology and artisanship in that locale. The meaning of a set of ritual practices in a village beyond that location (scale) requires knowledge about religious dogma and institutions and their local history. Anthropological methods of observation and engagement with local cultures offer better means to achieve such knowledge than reading the scholarship and primary sources on the political and intellectual history of these countries.

As I began using the methodological insights of cultural anthropologists in my search for useable historical evidence, I also turned to the work of feminist scholars such as Ann Oakley and Sandra Harding for a better appreciation of what an empathetic approach can mean in social studies.[14] Historians tend to be weary of the false hope that we can somehow fully understand the past on its own terms; that we can identify with historical actors on their own terms. A healthy dose of self-reflexivity is always welcome when embarking upon grandiose intellectual expeditions such as explaining the lives of dead people to those around us. Yet intellectual distance doesn't do much more than to point to the holes in this very human quest of giving voice and trying to fully understand how people led their lives in times that preceded us. The desire to empathize and our ability to think of daily choices people had to make as a matter of survival and leading a normal anonymous life is a powerful tool for moving beyond that which seems solid but isn't particularly concrete in our everyday life, such as politics, identities or ideology. These big concepts find concretization in our quotidian reality in barely perceptible ways, through small choices that may not be visible or seem too insignificant to take into account. It is their repetition, however, and their articulation as personalized choice, that makes them truly significant and connects them to the more abstract polis; that is the heart of everyday life and intimate politics under Communism.[15]

An additional important element in considering the limited usefulness of traditional historical methods is the difficulty of placing women into masculinist categories of analysis (political, economic, sociological, cultural, etc.) that preclude understanding the gendered nature of historical agency and, in particular, women's everyday lives through anything else other than exceptional or derivative narratives.[16] The work of Ruth Lister, in particular, is framed through an ethic of deep respect towards difference and marginality, celebrating diversity in thought and deed, and eschewing any linear explanation/analysis.[17] As a gender historian working on eastern Europe this approach has become more appealing to me over time, as a matter of personal satisfaction in being able to place what seems invisible, yet ever present – everyday habitual practices – into a framework that allows us to understand and appreciate them. In the east European context, this approach also opens up the possibility of considering gender analysis significant more broadly for better understanding the societies we study, and not just as an exotic sidebar. In particular, by focusing on topics such as mourning rituals, smoking or consumer practices, gender historians have made women visible to an extent unknown previously, while also drawing attention to women's agency in shaping their families, cities, professions and other communities in which they dwell.[18] In a region with a lack of democratic traditions, with power (and implicitly wealth, political authority, visibility, etc.) concentrated in small pockets of society until the second half of the 20th century, and even then under the auspices of authoritarianism, to adopt a position that celebrates the marginal seems essential for a more nuanced understanding of these societies. The ethics of respect proposed by Lister also acknowledge our own humanity as knowledge makers and the contexts that bind us to our surroundings and each other, rendering us historical agents in time and space.

Being able to observe and appreciate everyday life occurrences requires another important departure from the theories and practices of many historians today: using psychology to analyse behaviour in a historical setting.[19] In order to understand how routine frames a sense of the self and how, in turn, people are (or not) conscious of such routinization and the way it conditions them, psychology offers important tools. Even more pertinent to studying the history of Communist regimes/societies is the question of how fear – potential, actual, reactive, proactive, direct, indirect, and so on – pervades the quotidian.[20] Fear is a dominant force present in other types of modern regimes, and thus my comments are not pertinent for only one kind of historical experience. But the specifics of how fear operates in daily life are deeply contextual and thus need to be understood both in terms of psychological mechanisms (e.g. how a person becomes traumatized and then conditioned by fear in general), as well as essentially in terms of cultural specificities that trigger fear in daily life. For instance, the unpredictability in an urban setting of available utilities necessary to produce food, keep warm and have clean clothes is a condition that may be present in many settings, like a post-natural disaster area.

In the case of Romania in the 1980s, this unpredictability was manufactured and entirely orchestrated by the Communist regime as a means to control the lives of every citizen in the country at the whim of its leadership, under the guise of developing autarchic means of dealing with the energy crisis at that time.[21] The energy crisis was an everyday reality for many in eastern Europe, owing to the rising prices that followed the oil embargo of the late 1970s. Governments found themselves unable to sustain the rising prices of imported consumer goods and oil without borrowing massively, which eventually forced those regimes to take more drastic measures in terms of cutting energy consumption. However, in Romania, which was a producer of oil rather than just an importer, the choice was not born out of necessity. In the 1980s Ceauşescu grew obsessed with the goal of economic autarchy, especially after establishing close relations with North Korea, one of the regimes he held very close to his notion of what a leader should be.

The choice to cut off electricity or gas in apartment buildings without any other means for heating, cooking or pumping water, especially on the higher floors, was entirely out of the hands of individual citizens and placed them at the mercy of a system that people understood to be the source of their fears. Coping with this system required being aware of the unpredictability of these services and finding ways to control the few means of collecting water, keeping warm and preparing food. Any mistake, such as flushing the toilet when no additional water would be available at any predictable moment in the near future, would translate into both frustration and guilt about such a mistake. By virtue of the myriad of choices related to the use of water, electricity and heating that a person in an urban 20th-century setting needs to make as a matter of daily activities, fear of squandering the few available resources or of being unable to prepare for the unpredictable became part of the fabric of everyday life.

The one general aspect of fear that bears remembering in any context is the issue that, once internalized, fear tends to become undifferentiated as a physiological and psychological reaction: regardless of how great or petty the actual condition that prompts the fear, the result at the personal level is a build-up of a sense of insecurity, of powerlessness, of frustration and diminishment of personal agency. In a recent history of fear, Joanna Bourke identifies it as changing with the wider societal anxieties of the time, and thus as a function of both politics and culture more broadly.[22] The example of absence of gas or flushing the toilet is a good one – they are not life-threatening circumstances, they are simply small repeated inconveniences that can be resolved usually through expenditure of time and effort. Yet, there is a continuum on which such fears are placed and identified by most people as connected to the unchecked power of the party and its attendant institutions (in areas from economic planning and education to law enforcement). Thus, the frustration of not finding enough food to put on the table in the daily hunt, or using up precious water that one does not control but badly needs every day, were experiences that psychologically connected with people's awareness of the greater structure that made individual lives powerless in relation to the regime and to one's personal or familial intimate needs.

Given the complexity of these forces in the daily lives of people who lived through the Communist period in eastern Europe, it is important to listen carefully and understand how small everyday actions interweave with weighty ideological frameworks such as Communism, post-totalitarianism and neoliberalism. My goal is to redefine politics to include not only unambiguous actions such as voting and marching in protest. Based on what I understand to be a strong linkage between ideology and political regimes on the one hand, and quotidian actions on the other hand, I want to suggest the need to analyse the history of intimate or everyday citizenship in modern societies. My focus is on the post-1945 regimes of eastern Europe (Romania in particular), but I believe and hope to show in a future transnational segment of my project that other regimes – postcolonial, social democratic, autocratic, neoliberal, for example – of the modern and post-modern world can also be understood in a significantly more nuanced manner through the lens of everyday citizenship.

Let me return now to the interior dialogue narrated at the outset of this essay. The everydayness of the experiences and choices described there is self-evident. The question for someone interested in the notion of 'everyday citizenship' or 'intimate politics' is whether this is a set of political or politically minded actions; and if so, what makes them political and not just mundanely social. Waking up in a dark cold apartment represents something so routine and unspecific as to suggest very little of explicit historical relevance. Yet both physiologically and psychologically it describes a moment of 'coming to', albeit a routine one, into a reality that is unpleasant and uncomfortable, regardless of how used one is to it. Therefore, though routine, it is still a significant marker for one's mood at the beginning of the day and possibly for other actions to be undertaken in the course of that day. Moreover, knowing that the apartment is likely to be cold and dark because of an absence of electricity and central heating is a sensory trigger with cognitive elements that reminds the person experiencing the cold and darkness about what is producing this discomfort. If one lives in an apartment outfitted with central heating elements and with electrical wiring, yet is unable to enjoy these presumed benefits of living in an urban area, this is a constant reminder of the substandard modernity of the regime (the Communist Ceauşescu one in this case) that produced both the structure and its substandard implementation. Thus, I consider this to be a moment of political mindedness, in which the person sensing the discomfort has also a political object of resentment easily identifiable in mind as she prepares for the day. She is reminded of her powerlessness (to keep herself warm other than by putting on more clothes) as a citizen of a land of substandard provisions of basic goods who has nobody to complain to about such issues, because to complain would bring about additional fears of being reprimanded by the secret police for speaking negatively about the regime.

Citizenship is generally defined as the relationship between individuals and the political structures that frame our rights and obligations in the public arena in relation to the polis and other citizens. Many historians and political scientists have easily dismissed citizenship under Communism as devoid of any 'real' value, as no rights supposedly existed under such regimes.[23] With no rights there could be no 'buy in' for people to invest themselves in any active fashion in relation to Communist regimes. We now know that is not the case. Just because Western theorists and frustrated dissident intellectuals, such as Alexander Solzhenitsyn, saw the Communist regimes as illegitimate, totalitarian and unwilling to create political structures that would treat citizens as both obedient subjects and active participants with rights to be protected, it doesn't mean that those individuals did not participate actively in shaping their relationship with the state, sometimes to their personal benefit, other times to their own detriment.[24] Such moments are not necessarily the result of some intentional actions on the part of the one-party state; but they are real, conjectural and deeply meaningful for those able to create and take advantage of them. The joke 'they pretended to pay us and we pretended to work' is a good summation of such negotiations of agency.[25]

What is particularly difficult to appreciate then is the actual quality of historical agency or empowerment in such moments, as they are often not marked by any great social change or by measurable acquisition of goods or privileges. Being able to negotiate a position of autonomy as a citizen under Communist Romania was often an affair of the mind – the ability to work around the fears that dominated everyday life; finding loopholes around the overburdening of everyone's life by asinine obligations; duplicity; dissimilation; or lying.[26] The face value of such small actions is practically invisible, but the contextual personalized meaning in terms of quality of life is far greater. And it is this kind of invisible qualitative difference that everyday life historical analysis can bring back into the picture of how people managed to live under Communism (or 'coped with' Communism, as a Bulgarian colleague identified it).[27]

With the goal of finding narrative threads about everyday citizenship and in particular its gendered aspects, in 2009 I embarked upon an oral history project with a team of colleagues from Romania, seeking to connect the stories of 100 women from the Hunedoara County with the question of how one's personal life connects to the rights and obligations of citizenship, and how these women understand how things have changed at the everyday level for them from the Communist into the current regime.[28] Our subjects were a mix of rural-urban inhabitants, Romanians, Hungarians and Germans, professionally educated women, peasants, doctors, entrepreneurs, unemployed service workers, pensioners and young graduates, thus representing a broad cross-section of Romanian society. Regardless of their station in life (economically and socially), all women described themselves as deeply involved and tied to obligations to their families that limited their ability to think about other relations of responsibility and empowerment in the polis. Yet many of them identified these obligations as politically contingent, since the absence of basic goods under Communism was a politically controlled reality and not simply the result of poverty.

The same awareness of the political aspects of education and professional training pervaded their narration of parental responsibilities.[29] Being able to see their children grow up to have a good education and job was important for all the women we interviewed, and many spoke with great pride about being able to contribute to that by working hard and adding to the economic well-being of their family, as well as their efforts in doing well by teachers, private tutors, potential employees and other people who embodied in one way or another the Communist regime. Being able to secure the right tutor to enter a good high school or college in town was a matter of both savings (how to secure a daily existence and put away money was no small matter for most employees) and also connections (though illegal, private tutoring was pervasive and such tutors were often party members, wives of prominent party members or vetted by party members).

Another interesting element emerged in our discussions with these women. Everyday citizenship is not only a matter of wriggling through the many oner-ous obligations imposed by a police state, but also of finding ways to build loyalty with others in your predicament, building a sense of community out of marginalization and dearth. All of the people we interviewed talked about family, friends and neighbours as essential to preserving humanity and a sense of hope and support during the Communist period. In the face of the pervasive fear and powerlessness most of them experienced as a matter of daily life, espe-cially in any relationship with the political institutions of the Communist state, people felt the compulsion of banding together with those with whom they shared such fears and who could become a buffer. Such communities of hope were often gendered, as they were built around the daily routines that men and women respectively shared. Women spent time together around familial chores (pickling, canning, house cleaning, sewing, knitting), while men did some of the same as well as other socializing activities (queuing for food, fixing cars, playing backgammon, watching/playing soccer games). Though such activities seem to have little in common with the rights or obligations of citizens in relation to the state, my contention, based on the ways our subjects narrated these relation-ships, is that communities of kinship and friendship were crucial to how people found resources to cope with the Communist regime's politicization of everyday life. The scarcity of food, money and trust in relation to the regime was over-come through informal networks that enabled people to simply go on, and sometimes even thrive around the obstacles set up by the state.

These informal networks seem to be the element of greatest focus when the women we interviewed talk about changes since 1989. Freedom and the free markets have meant open competition for resources. There is nothing against which these women have found a way to band together around, as the economic, political and other concerns of the day have become diffuse. Mass media has done a fine job of creating a pervasive sense of fear not about the state's policing of everyday life, but rather about the explosion of violence and lawlessness in society in general. I had the strange experience of having to explain to an 85-year-old woman about reality shows, as she was convinced that what she was seeing on TV was some sort of plot to connect violent criminals with every person in the land, and she was afraid one of the people she watched on TV was going to come and rob her in the middle of the night. In reality, this woman lives in utter poverty, save for access to cable TV, in a remote village without any public transportation.

Therefore, despite free elections and many other identifiable ways in which one could easily argue for a real growth in citizenship rights, I heard few celebratory stories about post-Communism. Most women do not see their needs reflected in the local, regional and national electoral contests and often abstain from voting based on such premises or non-representation. They see corruption, as well as a general absence of civility and care, in how elected officials act, and therefore have little interest in working with them as citizens or potential representatives. Most of the women we interviewed thought that in principle the presence of women in city councils and parliament would elevate how politics is conducted, especially the management of resources. Yet they also acknowledged that women are not well suited for the dirty political games of elections or appointments to a seat of political power, and thus concluded that only those who are willing to become corrupt can succeed.

In the meantime, the communities of kinship and friendship that buffered these women against the daily grind of fear and scarcity during the Communist regime (whether real or not, as some of the nostalgia is also about building up a romantic view of the past to cope with a gruelling present) have diminished. The deep transformation of Romanian society in the past 25 years has also meant that the everyday practices of that period are largely different and have helped reshape how individuals think of themselves in relation to the state and other citizens. Between mass media – especially the Internet – mass communication and the ability to travel freely, interpersonal relations have changed dramatically and nothing of the sort narrated by old pensioners (e.g. sitting around in the evening in front of the apartment building and talking politics while knitting) can be sustained, even by those who remember those days and try to replicate such communities. Everyday citizenship has become a globalized, virtualized identity, with links across the world, but often lacking in connection to the local community from which many try to escape through the computer screen or various hand-held devices. These new means for connecting and escaping reinforce, however, how revealing intimate politics and everyday routines can be for the historian interested in modern societies.

Notes

1. From the vast literature on everyday life, I offer the following as a starting point: Paul Steege, Andrew Bergerson, Maureen Healy and Pamela E. Swett, 'The History of Everyday Life: a Second Chapter', *Journal of Modern History* vol. 80, no. 2 (2008): 358–78; Belinda J. Davis, *Home Fires Burning: Food, Politics, and Everyday Life in World War I Berlin* (Chapel Hill: University of North Carolina Press, 2000); Sheila Fitzpatrick, *Everyday Stalinism: Ordinary Life in Extraordinary Times; Soviet Russia in the 1930s* (Oxford: Oxford University Press, 1999); Michael R. Ebner, *Ordinary Violence in Mussolini's Italy* (Cambridge: Cambridge University Press, 2011); Harry Harootunian, *History's Disquiet: Modernity, Cultural Practice, and the Question of Everyday Life* (New York: Columbia University Press, 2000); Maureen Healy, *Vienna and the Fall of the Habsburg Empire: Total War and Everyday Life in World War I* (New York: Cambridge University Press, 2004).
2. See, for instance, Harold Marcuse, *Legacies of Dachau: the Uses and Abuses of a Concentration Camp, 1933–2001* (New York: Cambridge University Press, 2001).
3. The best study on this is Gail Kligman, *The Politics of Duplicity: Controlling Reproduction in Ceausescu's Romania* (Berkeley: University of California Press, 1998).

4. Steege et al., 'The History of Everyday Life'.
5. Alf Lüdtke, ed., *The History of Everyday Life: Reconstructing Historical Experiences and Ways of Life*, trans. William Templer (Princeton, NJ: Princeton University Press, 1995); *Alltagsgeschichte* is the term coined by Lüdtke to define his methodology and site of research interest in the banal, routine, the everyday occurrences that seem insignificant. The term literally means 'everyday history'.
6. Ruth Lister, *Citizenship: Feminist Perspectives* (Basingstoke: Macmillan, 1997); Chantal Mouffe, 'Feminism, Citizenship and Radical Democratic Politics', in Judith Butler and Joan W. Scott (eds), *Feminists Theorize the Political* (New York and London: Routledge, 1992), 369–84; Susan M. Okin, *Justice, Gender and the Family* (New York: Basic Books, 1989); Nira Yuval-Davis, *Gender and Nation* (London: Sage, 1997); Wendy Sarvasy, 'Beyond the Difference Versus Equality Policy Debate: Post-Suffrage Feminism, Citizenship and the Quest for a Feminist Welfare State', *Signs* vol. 17, no. 2 (1992): 329–62.
7. E. P. Thompson, *The Making of the English Working Class* (London: Victor Gollancz, 1963); Joan W. Scott and Luise Tilly, *Women, Work and Family* (New York: Holt, Rinehart and Winston, 1978).
8. Maria Bucur, Rayna Gavrilova, Wendy Goldman, Maureen Healy, Kate Lebow and Mark Pittaway, 'Six Historians in Search of Alltagsgeschichte', *Aspasia* 3 (2009): 189–212.
9. Songs were a crucial source for some of the historians aiming to revive the voice of the lower classes. See, for instance: Catherine Bowan and Paul Pickering, 'Singing for Socialism', in Laurajane Smith, Paul A. Shackel and Gary Campbell (eds), *Heritage, Labour and the Working Classes* (Abingdon: Routledge, 2011), 192–215. Many songs were collected by others, such as ethnographers, but also passed down in written form through published collections that were read and embraced by both the higher and lower classes.
10. Judith Walkowitz, *City of Dreadful Delight: Narratives of Sexual Danger in Late-Victorian London* (Chicago, IL: University of Chicago Press, 1992).
11. The rate of literacy should also be differentiated between men and women, as well as rural versus urban populations. Public education was funded differentially for boys and girls until after World War I, when efforts to eliminate illiteracy in the countryside also started. It is also true that in eastern Europe different ethnic and religious groups placed different emphases on literacy. That is why, in a country such as Romania, in 1930 the rate of literacy in a city such as Braşov (in 1930 with very large German and Jewish communities, which valued education a great deal more than the Romanian state until the 20th century), less than 100 miles from Bucharest, was 90 per cent, while the capital (ethnically very heterogeneous, but proportionally much more dominated by ethnic Romanians at that time, together with a large Roma population) had a less than 50 per cent rate of literacy. Overall, women tended to have a much lower rate of literacy, sometimes up to three times lower than men's. In Romania's 1930 census, women had a 50 per cent level of literacy, and men's was 75 per cent. See archive.org/stream/recensamntulgene02inst#page/n1/mode/1up (accessed 9 January 2014).
12. A visit through any local museum in this area reveals the uneven and rather poorly inventoried collections that have survived since the 19th century, when the earliest of these museums were started. Ethno-nationalism was an important impulse during that time for tracing national origins and building a narrative of continuity and cultural accomplishments. One of the most impressive early practitioners in Romania was Simion Florea Marian, who authored an impressive number of books and other studies on many aspects of folklore and cultural practices in Romania,

including *Sărbătorile la români: studiu etnografic*, vol. 1, *Cârnilegile*, vol. 2, *Păresimile* and vol. 3, *Cincizecimea* (Bucharest: Ed. Academiei Române, Institutul de arte grafice Carol Göbl, 1898–1901). A recent discussion of the development of ethnography and cultural anthropology in the region can be found in: Gheorghiță Geană, 'Discovering the Whole of Humankind: the Genesis of Anthropology through the Hegelian Looking-Glass', in Han F. Vermeulen and Arturo Alvarez Roldán (eds), *Fieldwork and Footnotes: Studies in the History of European Anthropology* (New York: Routledge, 1995), 60–74; Julie Scott-Jones and Sal Watt (eds), *Ethnography in Social Science Practice* (New York: Routledge, 2010).

13. Among the growing number of cultural anthropologists who have shaped our understanding of everyday life in Romania, I would like to identify: Mihai Pop, Sabina Ispas, Smaranda Vultur, Katherine Verdery, Mircea Vintilă, Gail Kligman and Enikö Magyari-Vincze.

14. Ann Oakley, 'Interviewing Women: a Contradiction in Terms', in Helen Roberts (ed.), *Doing Feminist Research* (London: Routledge and Kegan Paul, 1981), 30–62; Sandra Harding, 'Rethinking Standpoint Epistemology: What is "Strong Objectivity"?', in Ann E. Cudd and Robin O. Andreasen (eds), *Feminist Theory: a Philosophical Anthology* (Oxford: Blackwell, 2005), 218–36; Clare Hemming, *Why Stories Matter: The Political Grammar of Feminist Theory* (Durham, NC: Duke University Press, 2011).

15. Bucur et al., 'Six Historians in Search of Alltagsgeschichte'.

16. Sandra Harding, *Whose Science? Whose Knowledge? Thinking from Women's Lives* (Ithaca, NY: Cornell University Press, 1991).

17. Lister, *Citizenship*.

18. Some of these studies include: Mary Neuberger, *Balkan Smoke: Tobacco and the Making of Modern Bulgaria* (Ithaca, NY: Cornell University Press, 2012); Susan E. Reid and David Crowley (eds), *Style and Socialism: Modernity and Material Culture in Post-War Eastern Europe* (Oxford: Berg, 2000); Maria Bucur, *Heroes and Victims: Remembering War in Twentieth-Century Romania* (Bloomington: Indiana University Press, 2009).

19. Michael Roth, *Psychoanalysis as History* (Ithaca, NY: Cornell University Press, 1987).

20. James R. Millar (ed.), *Politics, Work and Daily Life in the USSR: a Survey of Former Soviet Citizens* (New York: Cambridge University Press, 1987); Vladimir Shlapentokh, *Public and Private Life of the Soviet People: Changing Values in Post-Stalinist Russia* (New York: Oxford University Press, 1989); Zygmunt Bauman, *Liquid Fear* (Cambridge: Polity, 2006).

21. On the energy policies under Ceaușescu, see Cornel Ban, 'Sovereign Debt, Austerity, and Regime Change: the Case of Nicolae Ceausescu's Romania', *East European Politics and Societies* vol. 26, no. 4 (2012): 743–76.

22. Joanna Bourke, *Fear: a Cultural History* (London: Virago; Emeryville, CA: Shoemaker and Hoard, 2005).

23. Vladimir Tismăneanu, *Stalinism for All Seasons: a Political History of Romanian Communism* (Berkeley: University of California Press, 2003); Anne Applebaum, *Iron Curtain: the Crushing of Eastern Europe 1944–56* (New York: Allen Lane, 2012).

24. Hilde Coffé and Tanja van der Lippe, 'Citizenship Norms in Eastern Europe', *Social Indicators Research* vol. 96, no. 3 (2010): 479–96; Lewis Siegelbaum and Andrei Sokolov, *Stalinism as a Way of Life: a Narrative in Documents* (New Haven, CT: Yale University Press, 2000).

25. I am not sure when this joke first surfaced, I just remember growing up with it in the 1970s.

26. Kligman, *The Politics of Duplicity*; Siegelbaum and Sokolov, *Stalinism as a Way of Life*.

27. Bucur et al., 'Six Historians in Search of Alltagsgeschichte', 206.

28. See the following working paper as summary of the project and initial findings: Maria Bucur, 'Citizenship, Gender and the Everyday in Romania since 1945: Work and Care', Working paper (Seattle, WA: National Council for Eurasian and East European Research, 2011), available at: www.ucis.pitt.edu/nceeer/2011_825-16n_Bucur-Deckard.pdf (accessed 19 January 2014).

29. All of our subjects were or had been at some point in a relationship with another man, and an overwhelming majority of them either contemplated having a child or had had children. We encountered no lesbian subjects, or at least nobody self-identified as such, and nobody even brought up same-sex intimacy. In Romania, the category of lesbian/homosexual is barely developing as a subject of public discussion today, and even though there is some visible grass-roots activism in that area, homophobia is still mainstream and goes unpunished. For a very recent controversy on this, see the case of Mihaela Rădulescu Schwartzenberg's homophobic blog and reactions to it: Mihaela Rădulescu Schwartzenberg, 'Adam şi Eva?!' (Toleranţa pe la spatele normalităţii)', available at: http://www.mihaelaradulescu.ro/traieste/adam-si-eva-toleranta-pe-la-spatele-normalitatii/?src=soc_fcbks (accessed 8 April 2015); Oana Băluţă, 'Normalitatea homofobă a Mihaelei Rădulescu', *Adevărul Blog*, 7 April 2015, available at: adevarul.ro/entertainment/celebritati/normalitatea-homofoba-mihaeleiradulescu-1_55238c60448e03c0fd4d1510/index.html (accessed 8 April 2015).

Part 4
Gender During and After the Collapse of Communism

11
Masculinity and Dissidence in Eastern Europe in the 1980s

Anna Muller

'I think we will learn a lot, and I know that it won't be opportunism or anything of that sort. I have already learned English, among other things, and how to make good tomato salads and play chess', wrote Jacek Kuroń to his wife Gaja in April 1966 from his prison cell.[1] Between 1955 and 1984, Kuroń – one of the leaders of the anti-Communist opposition in Poland – spent a total of almost ten years in prison. Gaja was imprisoned only once: on 15 December 1981, two days after the Polish authorities introduced martial law, which ended the legal existence of Solidarność (Solidarity) – the largest anti-Communist movement in eastern Europe. Solidarność was banned and many of its members were either imprisoned or interned. Kuroń was arrested on 13 December, the day martial law was introduced. 'As a result of this story [his imprisonment], we have gained something absolutely essential – internal courage and an awareness of the strength for everything that awaits us', Kuroń continued in the letter.[2] Using the lens of gender to explain how Kuroń and other imprisoned dissidents made sense of prison culture not only reveals much about the construction of dissident and prisoner masculinities in 1980s Poland but, continuing the previous chapter's theme of intimate politics, offers insights into the gendered nature of agency, empowerment and disempowerment in late state socialism.

The Kurońs' world outside prison was rich in oppositional activities. Their apartment functioned as a centre where anyone could report Communist abuses of power, exemplifying one dimension of the interrelatedness of intimate, private and public space under state socialism. However, the oppositional circles in which the Kurońs operated extended beyond private households into, as openly as possible, disseminating information and demonstrating dissatisfaction with the state, believing that a politically and socially engaged society could be created despite state socialism curtailing individual freedoms. Many opposition members who felt that neither their universities nor workplaces provided them with space to act and speak freely gained a sense of empowerment from activities such as demonstrations, distributing clandestine publications and finally signing proclamations with their name. The authorities often responded with a 48-hour detention sentence for encroaching on the public domain, and more serious offences carried prison terms of several years.

For many political prisoners, imprisonment required strength and character that was understood in very masculine terms. It required courage, separation from domestic life, a tolerance for pain and discomfort, and a mental acuity that had the power to emancipate an individual from the restrictions and limitations imposed by prison. Thinking about his imprisonment, Kuroń wrote: 'This is a time of iron discipline [...]. Here one needs to work. And not work in general, but work on realizing a concrete task which you set for yourself.'[3] Adam Michnik, one of the leaders of the Polish opposition, sardonically noted that his friends had joked that he ought to be put in prison to facilitate his writing.[4] This understanding of imprisonment as a space and time of self-mobilization extended beyond Polish borders. Václav Havel, the Czechoslovakian activist and long-time political prisoner, wrote in a letter to his wife: 'And it also seems to me that the only way for someone like me to survive here is to breathe his own meaning into the experience.'[5]

This chapter examines prison as a site where Polish political prisoners reflected on who they were through interactions both with their cellmates (often criminal prisoners) and with the women who were the recipients of their letters and, as the link between the inside and outside world, stepped into roles of caregivers. (All the men who appeared in the sources on which this chapter is based were heterosexual, and none of the sources dealt with experiences of homosexual or bisexual male prisoners.) Situated between hypermasculinity (understood as a way to mark domination among men in prison) and a femininity that connoted traditional order as a counterbalance to cell life, political prisoners treated prison not only as a site that either hindered or facilitated their political engagement, but also as a site of becoming – growing as men, husbands and fathers. This interpretation reveals a complex picture of the genealogy of gender roles, and as such invites us to rethink the post-1989 gender order, which is often said to have been characterized by a reversion back to traditional gender norms – manifested, in Poland, through a new gender contract that called for women's return to their 'more natural roles' and private spheres. Viewing this as a post-1989 reversion is based on the assumption that Communism, with its notions of gender equality, skewed gender norms. Yet looking at how some opposition activists constructed their masculinity shows that the opposition had started to reinforce the traditional gender norms long before Communism failed – suggesting that the change in gender regimes after 1989 was less of a rupture, rather a continuation of what the 1980s opposition had begun.

Since access to prison correspondence remains limited, this chapter is instead built around the letters that three prisoners (Zbigniew Gluza, Czesław Bielecki and Jacek Kuroń) wrote to their wives. While Kuroń's letters cover almost three decades – from the 1960s to the early 1980s – the letters by Gluza and Bielecki offer a glimpse into the men's prison cells in 1985–6. All the letters are from published collections, though Gluza indicated in the introduction that he had altered his letters before publishing them. The chapter also uses a collection of 1980s prison recollections published underground in 1988, titled *Polityczni* (*Politicals*),[6] and a book by Marek Kamiński, a sociology student imprisoned in

1985 in Warsaw for distributing illegal publications. Kamiński spent five months in prison analysing the life around him and smuggling out his notes from his cell-based 'fieldwork'. 'Partially I was a revolutionary, but I was thinking about becoming a scholar', he said in the introduction to his work, which provided a fascinating look into the world of criminal prisoners.[7] These writings are important evidence for the history of masculinities in late state socialist Poland, but must be read in the context of Poland's specific relationship between gender, political opposition, imprisonment and nationhood.

Political Imprisonment in Poland

In modern Polish history, shaped by its struggle for independence between the partitions of the Polish Commonwealth in 1772–95 and the formation of a Polish republic in 1918, imprisonment represents an important intersection of nationhood and gender: for Poles to endure imprisonment was a test of strength of character and devotion to Poland, putting their manliness and patriotism on trial. For instance, the dissident and writer Adam Michnik, reflecting on the place of prisons in Poland's history in a volume of prison letters and other essays published in 1987, quoted Poland's first head of state, Józef Piłsudski, who said: 'In Poland, prison is an everyday companion of human thought. It is a part of consciousness, political culture, and everyday life.'[8] Many Polish insurgents and revolutionaries in the period between partition and independence had paid for their political involvement with isolation, either in prison or exile. Prisons thus occupied a significant place in the Polish historical imagination, and functioned figuratively as a site of an almost uniquely masculine transformation into a mature warrior. The exemplary romantic figure of the Polish political prisoner, the protagonist of Adam Mickiewicz's 1822 play *Dziady* (*Forefathers' Eve*) (a romantic lover named Gustav who in prison transforms into a revolutionary fighter named Konrad), was himself imagined in the prison cell where the Russian authorities had sent Mickiewicz in the 1820s.[9]

Political imprisonment continued to carry heavy weight in 20th-century Polish history. In the early 1930s, for instance, the interwar Polish regime dealt with its own political opponents by imprisoning them. World War II brought mass arrests from the Nazis.[10] The decade that followed the end of the war was as harsh in Poland as in other eastern European countries,[11] and the post-war Communist regime imprisoned an estimated 65,000 people between 1944 and 1956.[12] Throughout the 1960s and 1970s, political imprisonment was also common. However, the tide of arrests and imprisonment rose in the 1980s, the decade of Solidarność and martial law, when the authorities created 52 internment camps for Solidarność members during the martial law period of 1981–3.[13] Solidarność would remain illegal even after martial law was suspended at the end of 1983.

The conflict between the authorities and the opposition entered a new phase at the end of 1983 after the suspension of martial law when Solidarność remained illegal and the opposition went underground. In December 1983, the leader of Solidarność, Lech Wałęsa, received a Nobel Prize and Adam Michnik wrote to the Minister of Internal Affairs, Czesław Kiszczak, from his prison cell, criticizing Kiszczak's proposition to grant freedom to imprisoned oppositionists provided that they left Poland upon their release. The moral power of Solidarność grew, as did the numbers of political prisoners. In the first half of 1984, the number of people imprisoned grew by 3,000 every month.[14] It was not uncommon to be detained for several months or years for carrying illegal publications, possessing an offset printer or criticizing the political situation.[15] Oppositional recollections presented prison as a rite of passage that led to the internal crystallization of ideas and intellectual activity, a school of life that taught lessons about human behaviour and individual reactions. Marek Kulczyk, who spent two-and-a-half years in prison, said:

> For me prison was undoubtedly a test of my own character [...]. It was both an experience of my own helplessness as well as a source of strength that comes with the rejection of an absurd reality. It was finally a process of self-discovery.[16]

Polish oppositional discourse, though viewed by some scholars as 'deeply individualistic',[17] was also based on collective participation in a common historical and moral community. Participation in a collective struggle provided an individual with agency and empowered one through deeds for a nation. Imprisonment encompassed both: it was individual and collective. It meant sacrifice for a common struggle. But it also required virility and perseverance, features that were considered very masculine. Not surprisingly, most of the male opposition activists considered a political prisoner's ethos to be a heritage inherited from his forebears. Both Kuroń's father and grandfather, for instance, had been imprisoned as socialist revolutionaries. Prison handcuffs were a source of pride and 'the most precious jewellery'. As Kuroń recalled, his father had taught him to think of life as a struggle for Poland and socialism – a struggle that required sacrifice and pain, but also the ability to persevere despite difficulties.[18] Yet political imprisonment, despite this ethos, in reality meant inadequate nutrition, physical abuse and no recourse for relief.[19] Indeed, Havel, in Czechoslovakia, also confessed that in prison his prior expectations had turned into illusions. He hoped for more freedom and free time, but experienced more intense surveillance.[20]

Imprisonment also meant confinement in an ultramasculine world where political prisoners had to engage with criminal prisoners. As gender studies scholars already recognize, prisons are among the key sites for the expression of hegemonic masculinity, something which is 'apt to take shape in any homosocial setting' where male cultural lore and hierarchical relations among men emerge.[21] In Poland, and in other state socialist countries, this masculine space contained both criminal and political prisoners. Political prisoners thus had to learn how to find a practical compromise with criminal prisoners, a search that would push them to draw on their own more feminine sides in creating distinctions between their own subjectivities and others. Their understanding of masculinity and femininity was constituted by their past and present social interactions, including those mediated through letters.

The men discussed in this chapter presented themselves as vigorous, but also as rational fighters. They were brave and committed, but often rational in their assessment of the opponent they were facing: the state that imprisoned them. They were fighting not *for* the nation, but rather *against* an oppressive state that was disrespecting human dignity: these men presented themselves as physically tough and morally uncompromised, but also sensitive to the 'other' (meaning criminal prisoners) and open to having emotional interactions with women.[22] Deprived of the right to publicly criticize the Communist state (since their letters were censored), the political prisoners focused in their letters on their daily life and the most immediate demands of prison existence, which they understood in terms of self-improvement, negotiation, compromises and responsibility to others. In prison their oppositional activities shrank into the private sphere, as opposed to their more public engagements before prison. This led to a growing appreciation for domestic life and hence allowed for more permeability of the public and private sphere, of male and female. Though appearing to safeguard the traditional gender order, this redefined masculinities and opened up spaces for women's agency.

Historiography

The history of men dominates Polish historiography. The last two centuries of Polish history have been overshadowed by national uprisings and wars, through which 'the greatness of the Polish soldier became the foundation of the national code'.[23] Although many scholars have made direct links between nationalism and the formulation of modern masculinities,[24] for which studies of Polish masculinities would be salient, historians did not start exploring Polish masculinities until recently, once interest in gender and women's history had developed.[25] Historically, the dominant model of a Polish man was that of a brave soldier – ready to sacrifice his youth, health and life for the Polish cause.[26] Similar to the Western model of masculinity, the Polish model underwent what George Mosse defined as 'militarization': masculine fulfilment meant a search for a higher goal, such as serving the nation.[27] However, Polish soldiers rarely had the luxury of fighting in open combat or under their own state, distinguishing them significantly from models of masculinity developed for western European gender history.

From the 19th-century insurgents to the underground Home Army during World War II, the dominant model of a Polish fighter was instead that of an underground insurgent or soldier. Illegality granted these fighters exceptional legitimacy, while, for the members of underground groups, operating underground not only created an alternative model of soldiering but also functioned as a substitute for a role in public life. However, living and acting in conspiracy had significant implications for gender dynamics, producing a national struggle that was normatively based on homosocial ties among men (which still deserve more extensive research) despite the mass participation of women in every phase.[28]

Studies of gender and opposition to Communism during the 1980s, however, have focused instead on the place of women. Most scholars imply that women, who were successfully able to cross from private to public example, sustained the underground.[29] Shana Penn's book on Solidarność, for instance, focused on the women who created and sustained the flagship underground newspaper

Tygodnik Mazowsze (*Mazowsze Weekly*), organizing its distribution while caring for opposition members in hiding. Penn shows how women concealed their public engagements through private roles associated with motherhood and domesticity, which made them invisible as members of the opposition.[30] Padraic Kenney, on the other hand, extended the focus towards masculinity in a seminal article on workers' strikes in post-war Poland which argued that the Polish state and opposition shared a 'culture of masculinity and political logic'.[31] Kenney drew on scholarship that conceptualized Communism as masculine: its founding myth was based on a heroic and male struggle.[32] Early Communism had been enchanted with masculine physical strength and the virility of the male worker,[33] while late socialism was best defined as paternalistic. Throughout this period, despite the official call for gender equality, the social (private) realm remained feminine and the political (public) masculine.[34] The opposition thus functioned within this shared culture of masculinity that socialism developed and the tradition of national struggles maintained.

Prison Correspondence

The prison well captured the fluidity of private and political. With the exception of the martial law years of 1981–3, when larger groups of women were imprisoned alongside men, in general male activists were more often imprisoned. Meanwhile, women tried to provide them with food packages that were nutritious, suited their husbands' tastes and were permitted by the prison authorities – an effort that was especially burdensome in the 1980s shortage economy. These women worked as liaisons between the private and public: delivering important – and at times also illegal – information and letters from the prison into public space.[35] The letters were private, often intimate, and yet many were shared. In 1965, during one of Kuroń's first imprisonments, whenever his wife Gaja received a letter she would call Natalia Modzelewska, the wife of Karol Modzelewski (an activist and prisoner), to read the letters together.[36] Reading a message from prison was an event, an opportunity to meet and talk, and sometimes even to cry together over shared misfortune.[37]

The significance attached to prison correspondence, as well as the rituals involved in receiving, smuggling out and sharing information, made the private and public closely intertwined. Women were gaining political agency, not only as women who supported their husbands, but also as sustainers of the community-based resistance. This shift resembles what happened to 19th-century Polish gender roles, when the absence of a Polish state meant public institutions were replaced with informal kinship relationships and women gained an opportunity to play public roles.[38] Opposition circles centred on creating a conscious and informed society through informal kinships – and those informal networks were especially fruitful for women's activism. Interestingly, some women who were imprisoned during the first days of martial law, in cooperation with family members and local parishes, managed to create a support and information network while still in prison.[39]

Censorship and self-censorship both affected the content of letters. The men censored themselves: the stories they conveyed as well as their worries and anxieties regarding a life occurring outside prison. The letters were also subject to official censorship, but it is not entirely clear how strict the censorship was. Commenting on the work of Czechoslovakian censors, Václav Havel complained that they usually scolded him for being too philosophical. And yet Havel believed that writing in a convoluted way helped him get his letters passed through censorship. For Havel, writing turned into a game during which he tested censors' understanding of his ideas.[40] Letter writers often criticized the censorship and commented on the slow delivery of the correspondence – 'the magic pipe' that often got backed up because of the difficulties censors had reading long letters.[41] From his cell, Gluza requested a register of all his letters, which, surprisingly, the prison authorities granted him. He learned that it took up to nine days for his letters to reach his wife.[42] The speed of delivery depended on a prisoner's status as well as his relationship with the authorities; occasionally prisoners were punished with the prohibition of correspondence. Bielecki continued sending letters to his wife, even when at some point she was being held in the same prison. Of the 50 or more letters that he sent, she received around 20.[43]

In a Cell Among Men...

Most political prisoners experienced a sense of discomfort at their first encounter with criminal prisoners.[44] Everything set them apart: the cause of their imprisonment and the approach to their confinement, their lifestyles and experiences, and their attitudes towards the opposite sex and their own bodies. Regardless of the existing class differences among political prisoners, they perceived themselves as one group defined by their anti-state outlook. This created a basis for their attitudes towards the criminal prisoners, whom they perceived as different in terms of social position, values and life commitments. This sudden immersion in an alien homosocial cell stirred in Kamiński repulsion mixed with fascination: 'Rapes, knife duels, suicides, verbal offences, self-mutilation, and brutal sex appear to be the main activity of its habitants. [...] Life rushed in leaps and bounds, then congealed, reduced to eating and defecation.'[45] For Gluza, the first striking difference was their physical appearance. 'They feel my difference,' he noticed after walking into his cell, '[my] long hair and beard distinguish me from this medley of people.'[46] Andrzej Machalski also experienced the difference: 'My first companion ... he was from Solidarity – without a doubt, at first sight. Restless, nervous, of course: beard, moustache, fire in his eyes.'[47]

The ultimate test for the cell relationship between political and criminal prisoners was *grypsera* – a set of rules already established by prisoners that dictated a hypermasculine order in the cell, encompassing language and social and bodily practices among *grypsera* users, such as daily cell hygiene and the usage of a toilet. It tested one's strength, mental resistance and loyalty to the group through various rites of passage. According to Kamiński, at least in two Warsaw prisons – Białołęka and another on Rakowiecka Street – the majority of criminal prisoners (around 70–80 per cent) practised *grypsera*.[48] Kamiński argued that *grypsera* functioned as a 'foreign language' that marked life in a cell as different from life outside.[49]

One feature of *grypsera* was a strict ban on certain sexual phrases and practices, such as uncontrolled masturbation.[50] Some more experienced *grypsera* groups (those who had been imprisoned for longer) practised self-imposed celibacy as a way to control one's body. The subculture accepted occasional acts of homosexual rape or even homosexual relationships – as long as the *grypsera* user assumed an active role (he was the rapist). Prisoners who let themselves be raped as a punishment received feminine names and were forced to dance in the evening while wearing feminine dresses made out of blankets.[51] Through such gestures, criminal prisoners were reinventing gender divisions in a same-sex group: they created a weaker (more feminine) group. They differentiated life in prison from that outside, as Kamiński suggested, yet they tried to reinvent traditional divisions in order to more effectively control the space and their prison life.

Political prisoners maintained that few of them practised *grypsera*. They also never recollected whether or not they had been able to make that decision on their own without pressure (or even violence) from criminal prisoners. One person who did practise *grypsera* was Leszek Moczulski – an oppositional activist from an older generation, who, during the 1980s, spent almost six years in various prisons. Moczulski believed that understanding the secrets of the prison underworld could help protect the weaker inmates.[52] But, as Kamiński argued, the majority of political prisoners refused to obey the rules of *grypsera*.[53] In general, political prisoners distanced themselves from criminal prisoners, whom they saw as accepting violence as a means of achieving their goals. Gluza saw criminal prisoners as vulgar, lazy, brutish and bereft of values and morals.[54] 'They do not even understand what life in captivity means', he wrote in a letter to his wife.[55] 'Merciless war. [...] Everything happens mainly in order to harm the hateful enemy, i.e. the prisoner from the opposite camp', Stefan Niesiołowski wrote in his prison memoirs about the relationship between political and criminal prisoners.[56]

In contrast to many other prisoners, Gluza spent most of his sentence in one cell, where he and his cellmates had to work out rules of cohabitation. He noticed that they accepted his refusal to adopt their practices and his right to work (writing and reading). 'They began making sure I have space for this; they even try to be quieter', he wrote to his wife.[57] He helped them write appeals and letters of complaint, taught them how to treat women and punished them with 'silent days' when they did something of which he did not approve.[58] 'And besides that,' he wrote to his wife, 'I feed them, which perhaps adds to my authority the most. I serve the role of the food trustee.'[59] While rejecting ultramasculinity, Gluza used skills that made him important to cell life. But he also adapted the cell to his needs. This element of prison recollection is common for other prisoners as well. 'Plastic knives and forks, a cutting board, and dishwashing detergent domesticated the cell.'[60] He used a tablecloth to make meals more pleasant. Through very feminine and parental gestures, he turned it into a more familiar space.[61]

Working out their 'ways of living' with people different from them, Gluza and many other political prisoners presented themselves as observers who maintained their distance in order to be able to better negotiate their social position in their cells and learn something about Polish society. Gluza even pondered how many criminals (meaning unreflective individuals) and politicals (reflective individuals) Polish society consisted of.[62] This understanding was very much in accordance with the political prisoners' view of prison time not as a break from life, but rather as work and a life lesson. In his letters to his wife, Kuroń often emphasized that in prison he was 'studying' others to learn how to build bridges between different people and learn how to love them despite differences. Based on prison observations, he concluded that political protest was not constructive enough.[63] But the compromise that most political prisoners tried to form with criminal prisoners was of a different nature. Rather than sharing Kuroń's ideal of building bridges through acceptance, Gluza presented himself as wise through the benefit of hindsight and hence capable of achieving compromises even with vulgarity and aggressiveness.

The difference between political and criminal prisoners encompassed different understandings of what imprisonment was. This understanding in turn affected their understanding of masculinity. Many political prisoners emphasized that, in contrast to criminal prisoners, they dedicated themselves to work, self-reflection and self-improvement. Prison enabled self-mobilization and discipline. But it also allowed a certain flexibility while negotiating one's position in an ultramasculine group; a role that encompassed more feminine and domestic roles as protector (for weaker inmates), but also caregiver and teacher.[64]

'A More Manly Man Will Come Back to You...'

According to the political prisoners, the most salient divider between them and the criminal prisoners was the fact that criminal prisoners neglected their bodies. 'They do not exercise, nor do they care about their physical well-being', complained Gluza.[65] 'Thieves do not usually ask for [...] toilet paper, soap, or toothpaste. They only have pieces of grey soap they found somewhere', added Bielecki.[66] Though many political prisoners saw this as a sign of hypermasculinity and criminals' lack of culture, Kamiński explained it in terms of *grypsera* and a different understanding of cleanliness. 'One of the foundations of this subculture is the myth of a mystical kind of impurity, which a male member is a carrier of.'[67] Daily hygiene meant, for example, washing hands after any contact with one's intimate parts (and in the morning after a night's sleep).[68] Daily hygiene was thus important among criminal prisoners as well; but in contrast to political prisoners, who understood it in terms of an individual's well-being, for criminal prisoners hygiene was an element of the rules of co-existence.

Both political and criminal prisoners used their bodies as weapons in the struggle with prison authorities. Political prisoners manifested disagreement with the prison authorities through hunger strikes that could last from a few days to months.[69] Throughout his imprisonment, Bielecki was on hunger strike for nearly 11 months, during which he demanded prisoner of conscience status for all the political prisoners.[70] Criminal prisoners also used their bodies in order to exert pressure on prison authorities, but did this through self-mutilation: they swallowed objects, stuck wires into their carotid arteries or practised controlled hangings to fake suicide. The goal of this dangerous game was the improvement of prison life, but according to Kamiński it also brought respite from the overwhelming prison boredom.[71] The body was becoming a source of violence, but also an instrument in a constant struggle between submission and subordination. In contrast to the severe self-mutilations of the criminal prisoners, political prisoners' hunger strikes provided them with a chance to observe their own bodies and their gradual reactions to changes that the lack of food inflicted on them.

Prisoners' letters confirmed that the body was an important concern and, indeed, suggested that the body was becoming an important source of identity. Overall control over one's body, through both physical strength and mental perseverance, meant empowerment and resistance to the state. Kuroń emphasized that in prison everyone had an obsession with manliness.[72] Kuroń, Gluza and Bielecki regularly exercised, doing leg lifts, push-ups and bends. Physical activity helped them become more masculine, which they often mentioned in letters to their wives with pride, as if trying to convince them to wait for their imprisoned partners. While describing the daily push-ups, Gluza wrote to his wife: 'A more manly man will come back to you, somebody who does not look like a member of the state administration.'[73] Demasculinized state officials embodied a weak state. In contrast, the political prisoners were becoming more masculine through physical prowess and control over their physicality.

The body in a prison cell was a source of agency and physical and mental prowess. But it was also a source of emotions that provided prisoners with means to transcend the prison cell. 'I received a package from you,' wrote Gluza to his wife. 'And inside this package, there was coloured, perfumed soap…! The smell was pleasant. Later on, I felt that something is interrupting me in my reading…This smell!'[74] The list of items that the prisoners were allowed to receive in a package was limited to simple food items and basic necessities. However, almost any ordinary object sent from home could become an impulse to reimagine home – with its smells, comfort and physical intimacy. For both Gluza and Bielecki, this object was soap. The sensual stimulation that originated from home was so strong that it interrupted the mental work to which Gluza was so committed.

The letters rarely dwell on a longing for home, as if stating the obvious could have opened a Pandora's Box of emotions which would be difficult to control. Instead, the authors often expressed a growing appreciation for women's daily obligations and struggles. Though sexual abstinence and annoyance about the misogynistic attitudes of criminal prisoners was certainly part of this longing, Kuroń, Gluza and Bielecki often emphasized the dialogic nature of their manhood based on relationships with women: not only did they share their intellectual ideas and worries, but they also seemed deeply affected by the reactions, worries and joys that their women shared with them. 'I've always demanded from my beloved woman spirit and education, without even knowing that what is most important is a woman's ability to respond to what constitutes *logos* in me', Bielecki stated in one letter.[75] 'Among the twigs of thyme, leaves of laurel, oak, and ash, you leave what is most important: my understanding of your femininity and your understanding of my masculinity. Isn't this the most important for every sex?' he asked his wife in a different letter.[76] Bielecki constructed femininity as a balance for masculinity. His words implied an understanding of femininity as a force that could mobilize masculinity both by an appeal to intellect as well as nature.

Zbigniew Gluza considered himself a revolutionary and for that reason decided not to have children with his long-time girlfriend, Alicja, whom he had recently married. 'This country does not deserve to get citizens. Thinking about a baby raises an instinctive resistance in me: I do not want it to live in this country, in such circumstances', he wrote.[77] In prison, he learned that Alicja was pregnant.[78] Though the importance of a father's role had begun changing in the 1970s, raising a child remained a woman's task. This was partially because long work hours and small, multi-generational flats impeded men experiencing fatherhood first-hand.[79] Officially, socialist Poland was based on the principles of gender equality and incorporating women into the workforce, ideologies that challenged the traditional model of family and women's roles.[80] However, as many authors emphasize, earlier models of the 'Polish Mother' prevailed – and indeed even merged with the Communist model of new socialist women, as both models shared an 'idea of devotion and sacrifice' as a gendered duty.[81] Additionally, despite the existence of state institutions such as nurseries and kindergartens that supported women's professional work, the regime's levels of interest towards families and women were 'unbalanced', with state policy frequently shifting as the political and economic situation changed. The so-called 'double burden' on women under state socialism affected women who had to combine professional work with service to their families in Poland's shortage economy.[82]

Gluza's reluctance to have a child, however, was more the political decision of a revolutionary who rejected the norms of a patriarchal state, combined with his fear of losing his former lifestyle, especially the 'spiritual life'.[83] But in prison he grew into the idea of fatherhood. 'Fatherhood will be more difficult than being in prison', he wrote at one point.[84] With time, however, his wife's 'motherly words' began awakening a father in him:[85] 'Now nature will have to introduce some sort of order which will affect mostly you.'[86] Gluza soothed his anxieties by drawing on a traditional argument about the natural divisions between women and men.

Affecting Gluza most deeply was the information he received about the physicality of his future child; the fact that his life also continued 'outside' him disturbed him, causing problems 'with gathering any thoughts':[87] 'Our child moved, giving the first sign of its existence. You cannot understand how strongly this message affected me. It was almost a physical sensation.'[88] He began considering his future child (he assumed it was going to be a son) not to be a 'compromise' with his wife (and society) but a new experience and life impulse.[89] Fatherhood became an exercise in responsibility and a way to prove to the world that being a mature father was possible for a revolutionary. It was an element of consciously becoming and growing as a man. 'My feelings [...] become more manfully, more mature, and more willing to take responsibility for their impulses.'[90]

Both Gluza and Bielecki felt comfortable in a traditional gender order: men were viewed as strong and constantly in the process of active and conscious 'becoming', while women were deprived of such agency and defined, at least partially, by the dictates of nature. Gluza, Bielecki and many other political prisoners situated themselves between the hypermasculinity of criminal inmates and the natural and feminine world of their partners: between aggressiveness as a sign of mental and emotional weakness and the comforts of domestic life ruled by women. In this case, as elsewhere, gender is relational – men and women construct their identity based on the particularities of their social interactions. Thus, while negotiating their position in the cell, the prisoners were composing an image of their masculinity as dialogic – a more fluid and complementary image, the product of a search for equilibrium between hypermasculinity on the one hand and a femininity understood as natural and complementary to masculinity on the other.

In Poland, political imprisonment therefore strengthened the value of traditional divisions between women and men but also introduced more fluidity into masculine self-definition. The women were treated as a spark for masculine mobilization, which included respecting not only women's 'natural' skills but also their agency and ability to become a partner through various difficulties. Male oppositionists, meanwhile, did not belong to any of the categories of male activists (disciplined soldiers, rational bureaucrats and vigorous warriors) that had existed in the 19th and early 20th centuries – even if Gluza had wanted to perceive himself as a vigorous warrior at first. In prison they presented themselves as constantly 'becoming' while adapting to conditions and stepping outside the boundaries defined by traditionally masculine qualities.

Debates about women's and men's roles in the opposition have continued in Poland since the fall of Communism in 1989. In general, 1989 disappointed women.[91] The Polish literary critic Maria Janion, for instance, summarized 1989 as follows: 'It turned out that in free Poland, a woman is not an individual, but "a family being", who instead of being involved in politics should have been concerned with her household.'[92] According to Agnieszka Graff, one of the most prominent Polish feminists, Solidarność and opposition became a rite of passage: it allowed men to be who they were supposed to be, meaning 'real men', while excluding women.[93] But this was not something that suddenly happened with the fall of Communism; rather, the opposition of the 1980s was already embracing, and even reinforcing, traditional understandings of femininity and female gender roles.

The case of dissidents as political prisoners in Poland also shows that permeability between the private and public realms, which gender historians of state socialism have usually associated with women (ascribing them greater capacity to cross between public and private), also characterized the masculinities they formed in prison – even though the result was 'a more manly man'. The permeability of private and public and the embracing of more feminine aspects of the self (such as attention to nature and the emotions) empowered imprisoned male dissidents in their relations with criminal prisoners, but also empowered them beyond the prison walls, in their relations with the state and in their sense of control over the world they were separated from. Their understandings of how to personify dissident masculinity in prison both drew on and fed back into a specifically Polish framing of the intersection between gender, resistance and nationhood, suggesting that further research on the gender regimes of late state socialism could usefully inform studies of gender and the nation after 1989, for Poland but also elsewhere. Within the gender history of political activism, meanwhile, the dissidents' construction of masculinities can be contrasted with the struggles over patriarchy and nationalism that post-Yugoslav feminists faced in the 1990s as they confronted the breakdown of Yugoslav socialism and the violence of the Yugoslav wars.

Notes

1. Jacek Kuroń to Gaja Kuroń, 10 April 1966, *Listy jak dotyk: Gaja i Jacek Kuroniowie* (Warsaw: Ośrodek Karta, 2014), 105.
2. Jacek Kuroń to Gaja Kuroń, 10 April 1966, *Listy jak dotyk*, 105.
3. Jacek Kuroń to Gaja Kuroń, 28 April 1982, *Listy jak dotyk*, 273.
4. Adam Michnik, *Letters from Prison and Other Essays* (Oakland: University of California Press, 1987), 164.
5. Václav Havel, *Letters to Olga* (New York: Henry Holt, 1989), 44.
6. *Polityczni: opowieści uwięzionych w Polsce, 1981–1986* (Warsaw: Przedświt, 1988).
7. Marek Kamiński, *Gry więzienne: tragikomiczny świat polskiego więzienia* (Warsaw: Oficyna Naukowa), 14.
8. Michnik, *Letters from Prison and Other Essays*, 78.
9. Maria Janion and Marta Zielińska (eds), *Style zachowań romantycznych, Propozycje i dyskusje: sympozjum* (Warsaw: PIW, 1986), 8–9, 63.
10. See Jolluck, this volume.
11. The scale of repression in eastern Europe in the 1950s is relatively well researched; see, for example: Kevin McDermott and Matthew Stibbe (eds), *Stalinist Terror in Eastern Europe: Elite Purges and Mass Repression* (Manchester and New York: Manchester University Press, 2010); Jaroslav Cuhra, 'In the Shadow of Liberalization: Repressions in Czechoslovakia in the 1960s', *Cahiers du Monde Russe* vol. 47, no. 1–2 (2006): 409–26. The scale of repression in the 1970s and 1980s in eastern Europe needs more research. In the Czech Republic, the problem is currently being studied by researchers at an organization called 'Political Prisoners' (see www.political prisoners.eu, accessed 16 April 2015).
12. Tadeusz Wolasz, *Więzienia stalinowskie w Polsce: system, codzienność, represje* (Warsaw: Wydawnictwo RM, 2013), 8.
13. Andrzej Friszke, 'Introduction', in Władysław Bartoszewski, *Dziennik z internowania* (Warsaw: Świat Książki, 2006), 11. Some other estimates suggest up to 67 camps. Grzegorz Wołek, 'Internowanie Działaczy Opozycji w Stanie Wojennym', *Komentarze Historyczne IPN*, available at: ipn.gov.pl/__data/assets/pdf_file/0019/70750/1-34121.pdf (accessed 20 January 2015), 83.
14. Liberiusz, 'W promieniach więziennego cienia', *Praworządność: pismo o prawie i bezprawiu* no. 13 (1986): 113.
15. Bogdan Dariusz, 'Małolat', *Praworządność*, no. 9 (1985): 72–5. Moreover, Helsinki Watch considered sentences were becoming more stringent, with average sentences rising from 'just over one year' in the mid-1970s to 'two years and three months' by 1988: Human Rights Watch, 'Prison Conditions in Poland: a Helsinki Watch Report' (Washington, DC: Human Rights Watch, 1988), 2.
16. Marek Kulczyk, [untitled], in Zbigniew Gluza (ed.), *Polityczni: opowieści uwięzionych w Polsce*, 51.
17. Robert Brier, 'The Roots of the "Fourth Republic": Solidarity's Cultural Legacy to Polish Politics', *East European Politics and Societies* vol. 23, no. 1 (2009): 71. Brier follows the Polish sociologist Jerzy Szacki: Jerzy Szacki, *Liberalizm po komunizmie* (Warsaw: Fundacja im. Stefana Batorego, 1994).
18. Jacek Kuroń, *Wiara i Wina* (London: Aneks, 1989), 5–18.

19. On physical violence in prison, see Human Rights Watch, 'Prison Conditions in Poland', 27–8.
20. Václav Havel, *Zaoczne przesłuchanie: rozmowy z Karelem Hvížďalą*, trans. Jacek Illg (Warsaw: Wydawnictwo Krytyki Politycznej, 2014), 189.
21. Don Sabo, Terry A. Kupers, and Willie London, 'Gender and the Politics of Punishment', in Don Sabo, Terry A. Kupers and Willie London (eds), *Prison Masculinities* (Philadelphia, PA: Temple University Press, 1996), 5.
22. The term of a vigorous soldier (as opposed to disciplined soldier) comes from Claudia Kraft, 'From Noble Knight to Polish Warriors: Reconfigurations of Masculinities and Femininities in Polish Revolutionary Warfare and During the Times of Partitions', *Rocznik Antropologii Historii* no. 2 (2014): 33.
23. Maria Janion, *Płacz Generała: esej o wojnie* (Warsaw: Wydawnictwo Sic!, 1998), 41.
24. George Mosse, *The Image of Man: the Creation of Modern Masculinity* (New York: Oxford University Press, 1996), 7. See also John Horne, 'The Age of Nation-States and World Wars', in Stefan Dudink, Karen Hagemann and John Tosh (eds), *Masculinities in Politics and War: Gendering Modern History* (Manchester and New York: Manchester University Press, 2004), 27.
25. See, for instance, the work of Weronika Grzebalska on the 1944 Warsaw Uprising. Grzebalska asks new questions about the cultural and social factors that structured women's roles in the Uprising. While focusing on gender identities during World War II, as well as in the immediate post-war period, Grzebalska analyses the language of various documents issued during the war in order to understand how they impacted women and men differently. Weronika Grzebalska, *Płeć powstania warszawskiego* (Warsaw: IBL PAN, 2013).
26. See, for instance, Bohdan Cywiński, *Rodowody niepokornych* (Warsaw: Świat Książki, 1996), 10–11.
27. George Mosse, *The Image of Man*, 44.
28. Grzebalska, *Płeć powstania warszawskiego*, 33. See also Mosse, *The Image of Man*, 7.
29. See, for instance, Kristi Long on the household in the Polish culture of resistance, or Shana Penn on women's role in Solidarność: Kristi Long, *We All Fought for Freedom: Women in Poland's Solidarity Movement* (Boulder, CO: Westview Press, 1996); Shana Penn, *Solidarity's Secret: the Women Who Defeated Communism in Poland* (Ann Arbor: University of Michigan Press, 2005).
30. Penn, *Solidarity's Secret*.
31. Padraic Kenney, 'The Gender of Resistance in Communist Poland', *American Historical Review* vol. 104, no. 2 (1999): 408.
32. Examples of scholarship that Kenney draws on are: Ferenc Fehér, 'Paternalism as a Mode of Legitimation in Soviet-Type Societies', in T. H. Rigby and Ferenc Fehér (eds), *Political Legitimation in Communist States* (New York: Palgrave Macmillan, 1982), 64–81; Katherine Verdery, *What Was Socialism, and What Comes Next?* (Princeton, NJ: Princeton University Press, 1996).
33. Compare Simić, this volume.
34. See Padraic Kenney, 'The Gender of Resistance', 404–5.
35. Compare Kaminer, this volume.
36. Jacek Kuroń to Gaja Kuroń, 1–2 May 1965, *Listy jak dotyk*, 31. Kuroń and Modzelewski had written an open letter in March 1965 criticizing the Communist Party and calling for its liberalization; they received the longest sentences in the history of post-1956 Poland. On Modzelewski, see: 'Karol Modzelewski, Friszke i Koczanowicz o Liście otartym do partii', transcript from conference held on 14 December 2009: 6, available at: lassalle.org.pl/wp2/wp-content/uploads/2011/06/OSML-1964-2009-Modzelewski-Friszke-i-Koczanowicz.pdf (accessed 25 December 2014).

37. Many women recalled trips to visit their husbands in prisons and internment camps, which women organized together and which brought them very close to one another: Natalia Jarska, 'Po drugiej stronie: żony i matki internowanych w stanie wojennym', in Natalia Jarska and Jana Olaszka (eds), *Płeć buntu. Kobiety w oporze społecznym i opozycji w Polsce w latach 1944–1989 na tle porównawczym* (Warsaw: IPN, 2014), 326–8.

38. Kraft, 'From Noble Knight to Polish Warriors', 18.

39. Interview with Anka Kowalska, Warsaw, 2004.

40. Paul Wilson, 'Introduction', to Václav Havel, *Letters to Olga*, 1 and 7.

41. Czesław Bielecki, *Z celi do celi: listy do żony* (London: Wydawnictwo Plus, 1990), 21.

42. Zbigniew Gluza, *Epizod, Epizod – dziennik zamknięcia* (Warsaw: Przedświt, 1988), 86, 94.

43. Maciej Poleski, *Z więzienia* (Warsaw: Wydawnictwo CDN, 1986), 63.

44. In one underground publication (published under a pseudonym), Bielecki implied that the authorities hoped such a cell composition would contribute to cell conflicts: Poleski, *Z więzienia*, 56.

45. Marek Kamiński, *Gry więzienne*, 16.

46. Zbigniew Gluza, *Epizod: dziennik zamknięcia*, 7.

47. Andrzej Machalski, *Polityczni*, 101. See also Tadeusz Rzeszótko, *Polityczni*, 67. Interestingly, at the beginning of the 1980s, while male oppositionists had long hair, women involved in the opposition wore long hair and long skirts. It was a 'na Maryjki' (Mother Mary) look, according to the Polish sociologist (and former opposition member) Inka Skłodkowska: interview with Inka Skłodkowska, Warsaw, 2004.

48. Kamiński, *Gry więzienne*, 47.

49. Kamiński, *Gry więzienne*, 124.

50. Gersz, *Polityczni*, 19.

51. Kamiński, *Gry więzienne*, 66.

52. Gluza, *Epizod*, 114.

53. Conversation with Marek Kamiński, Warsaw, 2014.

54. Gluza, *Epizod*, 100, 143, 113.

55. Gluza, *Epizod*, 113.

56. Stefan Niesiołowski, *Wysoki Brzeg* (Poznań: W Drodze, 1989), 106.

57. Gluza, *Epizod*, 97–8.

58. Gluza, *Epizod*, 101, 109.

59. Gluza, *Epizod*, 99.

60. Gluza, *Epizod*, 112.

61. See also Henryk Wujec, *Polityczni*, 10. Rzeszótko gave criminals gifts at Christmas: Rzeszótko, *Polityczni*, 69.

62. Gluza, *Epizod*, 113.

63. Jacek Kuroń to Gaja Kuroń, 19 September 1965, *Listy jak dotyk*, 75.

64. Gluza, *Epizod*, 50.

65. Gluza, *Epizod*, 100–1.

66. Bielecki, *Z celi do celi*, 99.

67. Gersz, *Polityczni*, 21.

68. Marek Kamiński, *Gry więzienne*, 97.

69. For more examples of hunger strikes, see: Anonymous, 'Świadectwa', *Praworządność*, no. 12/13 (1986): 153–4; Rzeszótko, *Polityczni*, 71–2. In 1981, the Committee of Defending Those Imprisoned for Their Opinions (Komitet Obrony Więzionych za Przekonania) published a newsletter that included names of prisoners on hunger strike, their letters and letters sent from abroad in their defence. See, for example, *Biuletyn Informacyjny Gdańskiego Komitetu Obrony Więzionych za Przekonania* (May 1981).

70. His wife, Maria Twardowska, was imprisoned at the same time: Human Rights Watch, 'Prison Conditions in Poland', 48–9.
71. Kamiński, *Gry więzienne*. See also Human Rights Watch, 'Prison Conditions in Poland', 37.
72. Kuroń, *Listy jak dotyk*, 70.
73. Gluza, *Epizod*, 116–17.
74. Gluza, *Epizod*, 60.
75. Bielecki, *Z celi do celi*, 69.
76. Bielecki, *Z celi do celi*, 68.
77. Gluza, *Epizod*, 23–4.
78. Interview with Alicja Gluza, Warsaw, 2005.
79. Ewa Mazierska, *Masculinities in Polish, Czech, and Slovak Cinema: Black Peters and Men of Marble* (New York: Berghahn, 2010), 90. Justyna Stacherzak, 'Miłość 'nowych ojców': przemiany społecznych oczekiwań', in Bożena Płonka-Syroka (ed.), *Miłość mężczyzny*, (Wrocław: Arboretum, 2008), 489. See also Piotr Perkowski, 'Kulturowe wzorce przeżywania miłości u polskich mężczyzn po drugiej wojnie światowej', in Płonka-Syroka (ed.), *Miłość mężczyzny*, 396–7.
80. See for example, Małgorzata Fidelis, *Women, Communism, and Industrialization in Postwar Poland* (Cambridge: Cambridge University Press, 2010).
81. Agnieszka Zembrzuska, 'The Socialist Model of Woman in Poland and its Soviet Prototype', in Dorothy Rogers, Joshua Wheeler, Marína Zavacká and Shawna Casebier (eds), *Topics in Feminism, History and Philosophy: IWM Junior Visiting Fellows Conferences*, vol. 6 (Vienna: IWM, 2000), p. 8. Available at: www.iwm.at/wp-content/uploads/jc-06-02.pdf (accessed 26 April 2016).
82. Peggy Watson, 'Eastern Europe's Silent Revolution: Gender', *Sociology*, vol. 27, no. 3 (1993), 471–87. On the 'double burden', see also Slavenka Drakulic, *How We Survived Communism and Even Laughed* (New York: W. W. Norton, 1993).
83. Gluza, *Epizod*, 23.
84. Gluza, *Epizod*, 70.
85. Gluza, *Epizod*, 142.
86. Gluza, *Epizod*, 23.
87. Gluza, *Epizod*, 23–4.
88. Gluza, *Epizod*, 94.
89. Gluza, *Epizod*, 111.
90. Gluza, *Epizod*, 114. Bielecki expressed a similar understanding of masculinity as growing when he talked about how his sons' willpower and hard work would turn them into men: Bielecki, *Z celi do celi*, 59.
91. See also Zaharijević, this volume.
92. Maria Janion, 'Za wolność waszą i naszą', *Gazeta Świąteczna*, 3–4 July 1999, 25.
93. Agnieszka Graff, 'Patriarchat po seksmisji', *Gazeta Wyborcza*, 19 June 1999, 20.

12

What is Political in Post-Yugoslav Feminist Activism?

Adriana Zaharijević

In contrast to countries such as Poland where the 'transition' to democracy and/ or capitalism was a peaceful process and national borders were not altered, Yugoslavia's experience of the fall of state socialism was very different. Instead, a flurry of militant nationalisms produced several violent conflicts, and in the states that had used to form the Socialist Federative Republic of Yugoslavia, SFRY (Bosnia-Herzegovina, Croatia, Serbia, Slovenia, Macedonia and Montenegro[1]), the transition process therefore had a specific dynamic. This dynamic would go on to structure the ways in which issues, goals and specific understandings of what was a 'political' matter developed in post-Yugoslav feminism. The case of post-Yugoslav feminist activism can be usefully compared with others – in this volume and elsewhere – to illustrate how political and economic ruptures alter the material contexts for activism, the programmes and strategies activists might use, and the relationships between feminism, capital, democracy and the state.

Yugoslavia in the late 20th century could exemplify several things: a nation that embodied differences in unity, a European socialist state that differed in many ways from the other states behind the Iron Curtain and a state that would dissolve in bloodshed in the quest for absolute congruence between states and ethnic communities. In each respect, it was a 'laboratory of citizenship', a space where citizenship was used as a tool for making and un-making social and political ties in different 'citizenship regimes'.[2] With the shifts in citizenship regimes, under-standings of feminist activism would also undergo a paradigm shift.

Scholars have already demonstrated how the profound political and social changes after the dissolution of Yugoslavia affected gender, as society was re-patriarchalized and women were repositioned in relation to the state, nation and war.[3] Many of these emphasized the feminist movement's role in sustaining and forging ties, and in furthering anti-war politics across newly established borders.[4] New research on the difficulties of grassroots mobilization within civil society complements those early accounts.[5] The 2000s, however, saw the former parts of Yugoslavia finally on their way to becoming post-conflict, post-socialist, (future) EU societies. A new generation of activists and new settings required certain redefinitions of feminist activism, which have only begun to be researched in more depth.[6] Issues relating to social citizenship, injustices of transition and unequal redistribution accompanying the severe austerity measures introduced at different times in various post-Yugoslav states, prompted analyses with a different focus and a different political framework, even a different understanding of what 'political' in feminist activism might mean.

From Socialism to Nation Building

Unlike most east European countries, where socialism was succeeded by a post-socialist/transitional regime, Yugoslavia experienced not only transition from socialism but also a gruesomely violent disintegration. Although discourses of transition and its political, social and economic mechanisms were already in place before 2000, the dissolution of the socialist federation through violent conflicts meant that the transition from war to peace had a central, sometimes even an exclusive, position, in understanding post-Yugoslav social relations, while other aspects of transition were less prominent and less discussed. The violence of Yugoslavia's disintegration also accentuated the dramatic shifts in what Jo Shaw and Igor Štiks refer to as 'citizenship regimes' that the Yugoslav space underwent after 1989. A citizenship regime, comparable to Raewyn Connell's concept of a gender regime,[7] can be defined as a complex cluster of state governance, the state's responsibilities towards its citizens, citizens' rights and duties, and a broad informal set of practices of belonging.[8] The shift in citizenship regimes not only introduced deep legal and political changes but also strongly impacted on the lived dimensions of citizenship,[9] that is, the possibilities for the new nation states' citizens to realize their full human and political capacities.

To understand the specific Yugoslav path to post-socialism, two different phases have to be distinguished. Under the first, 'nation building' or ethno-nationalist citizenship regime, the citizens of the former socialist Yugoslav state became the bearers of distinctive ethno-national identities, according to which they were fought against, internally displaced, tortured, raped and mutilated; under the second, strictly 'transitional' citizenship regime, they became transformed into the rightful citizens of new nation states that were undergoing an unsettling transition to free-market democracy. It can be argued that the end of the socialist citizenship regime and the beginning of the ethno-nationalist citizenship regime coincided in all successor states of Yugoslavia, despite the differences between them. However, the specific territorialization of violence (most strongly felt in Bosnia-Herzegovina, Croatia and Kosovo), the differences in management of violence and the different dynamics of development of the SFRY's former republics meant the transitional citizenship regime began at different times in different states.

The transformation of citizenship regimes was accompanied by deep changes in gender regimes. The emergence of Yugoslav feminism was closely related to the socialist gender regime. As in other state socialist countries, the Yugoslav

Communist Party had introduced equality and special provisions for women as (working) mothers after World War II,[10] though in the Yugoslav case this would later be supplanted by the uniquely Yugoslav economic model of 'workers' self-management'.[11] The Yugoslav feminism that emerged in the 1970s was a specific Eastern variant of feminism, quite unique during the Cold War era even in comparison to the feminisms of other state socialist countries. It wanted to integrate feminist issues into socialist self-management by bringing the issues of the private sphere into the fore: to paraphrase Mirjana Morokvasic, feminism wanted to have the socialist revolution cross the threshold of the family.[12]

These rather modest early feminist attempts to critically examine the drawbacks of the revolutionary promises for women came to a halt when the nation-building citizenship regime began to replace the socialist citizenship regime after 1990. The shift to nation-building processes did not just bring profound constitutional rearrangements but also changed the ways in which communities functioned. It enhanced certain features of belonging while depreciating others, and endangered some rights while augmenting some duties. Gendered aspects of rights and duties also came to be redefined.

Before the 1990s, feminists had wanted to make gender inequality in socialism overt, by showing that there was a difference between comrades and that that difference was heavily gendered. With the citizenship regime change, however, this very difference became the most prominent feature of the new gender regime. Woman in socialism was construed as a working mother – both as a natural and social being – and the role of the socialist state had been to protect her naturality and to encourage her full sociality.[13] The dominant narratives of the post-socialist return to nature aimed to restore the significance of the nuclear family, which in some states' constitutions, for example Slovenia's and Croatia's, even became a subject with its own rights.[14] Most often contrary to reality itself, women were now figured as 'non-working mothers', that is exclusively natural, reproductive beings. Placing motherhood on a pedestal served to discredit the 'debilitating "mothering" of socialism',[15] to denounce women's emancipation 'as a salient and disgraceful trait of "so-called" socialist societies',[16] and to 'struggle against the anti-life mentality... [which was part of] the laws of the time of communist single-mindedness'.[17]

Despite this overwhelming rhetoric, the social dimension of womanhood that had been apparent under state socialism did not, in fact, disappear. Instead, it was transformed and profoundly 'naturalized'. Instead of being represented as equal workers operating under the so-called 'double burden' of labour outside and inside the home, women were now to be represented primarily as mothers of the nation and reproducers of its longevity, only secondarily as participants in paid labour or public life, despite the promises of the newly introduced post-socialist *democratic* regime. In the nation-building processes especially, as they were organized around ethnic communities, perpetuating the birth of the nation went hand in hand with the shaping of the nation in terms of wanted and unwanted populations.[18] This 'demographic transition',[19] which expected ethnic majority women to give birth more and coerced minority women to reproduce less, privatized and depoliticized women's membership in the community, denying them agency and making them personifications of the nation they accidentally belonged to. As real or potential producers of ethnically 'wrong' kin, women were treated as the naturalized gate to the existence of future ethno-national communities. In this context, most of all in Bosnia-Herzegovina, wartime rape was the ultimate form of gendered and ethnicized objectification. Maja Korać has described war rapes as a gendered weapon used to advance a systemic demographic transition along ethnic lines, where wombs acted as 'occupied territory'.[20] The wars produced a rhetorical opportunity for the use of women's bodies not only as a site of revenge but also as a vessel for future 'members', that is, ethnically moulded prospective citizens.[21]

Feminism in Nation-Building Times

In the last decade of the 20th century, when the post-Yugoslav wars were the key to understanding the reality of the post-Yugoslav space, feminism was organized around – as Vesna Kesić put it – 'women as bodies in pain'.[22] During socialism, feminists had argued, the private sphere had been seen as the domain where practising equality could be somehow overpassed. During the post-Yugoslav wars, private sphere took a new form which constructed all women, for the purposes of nation building, as natural rather than social beings. The patriarchal construction of 'our' and 'their' (women's) bodies as the means for shrinking and enlarging national communities redefined the space of privacy. The politics that post-Yugoslav feminism chose to nurture was centred on those bodies, regardless of the ethnic group they belonged to – accidentally, by birth or by marriage, or by the side of the newly established frontier they remained at.

These bodies thus became symbols of both patriarchal oppression and feminist resistance to nation-building processes. Feminists insisted on supporting, as Rada Borić put it:

> women regardless of their nationality, ethnicity, religious belief, education, age, sexual affinities. Those were not mere statements. We lived by those principles. Our aim was to recognize and oppose (on a daily basis) male-dominated ethics/politics/structure which disrespects difference.[23]

The politics of anti-war post-Yugoslav feminism were a conscious project of countering the essentialisms imposed by the ethno-nationalist agenda. To do so, anti-war feminists had to resist the dominant understanding that women should be differently valued as either 'ours' or 'theirs', and to choose (public) activism as a counter-image to the image of all women being privatized (by 'their' nation) and essentialized (to their wombs). Being a feminist activist meant making political decisions which ran counter to the prevalent narratives of war, hatred and victims/aggressors. Instead, feminists would emphasize the politics of solidarity and disloyalty to the nation, state, Church and the army, which were all epitomized by men and fathers.[24]

The politics of solidarity also rested upon a conscious and active politics of mobility. It incorporated both the active construction of alternative narratives, insisting on a continuity of memory that would run counter to the immobile and ahistoric politics of nationalism, and the politics of determined crossing of physical borders, which for a long time functioned as an emblem of feminism. The strategy of border crossing was most forcefully actualized in 2002, when 47 women from all parts of the former Yugoslavia and Albania spent two weeks together crossing the real and imagined borders that had been put up between them. As one prominent participant, Lepa Mlađenović, described their campaign (Women Activists Cross the Borders): 'The cities are divided, but some activists speak many languages.'[25]

From Nation Building to Post-Socialism: Feminism in Transition

By 2000, the decade of post-Yugoslav nation building through conflict was over, and the ensuing transition was instead represented as a transition to peace, democracy or a 'new way of life'.[26] The new nation states began their EU accession processes, and the integration of Slovenia (joining in 2004) and later Croatia (in 2013) proved successful, while the other states remained in negotiations to join. Europeanization, democracy and, to a lesser extent, human rights became the top keywords in the processes of a planned social transition, which had had institution building, comprehensive reforms and a solid civil society defined as its main goals.[27] However, the narrative of the advent of democracy symbolizing the end of violent conflicts successfully hid other dimensions of transition. The Romanian feminist philosopher Mihaela Miroiu's observation about transition in central and eastern Europe, that 'the free market was taken as an epistemology rather than as an ideology',[28] became a glaring lived reality of the post-Yugoslav space after 2000. The economic side of transition, which until the global financial crisis of 2008 was rarely debated in public, involved massive privatization, restructuring, market liberalization and the deep transformation of social citizenship.

During the 2000s, or the first decade of the 'transitional' citizenship regime, feminist activism ceased to organize around 'women as bodies in pain'. It also changed its attitude towards the state. The Yugoslav wars were over, and the newly established states ceased to epitomize inimicality towards women in women's organizations' eyes; rather, women's organizations in the Yugoslav successor states now saw the state as a partner in a common struggle to reach European values and the state of democracy and human rights as the final point of transition. The difference between ethno-national 'democracies', which in essence fought against ideas of democracy and human rights, and transitionally produced democracies, which publicly promoted them, shaped the grounds on which feminist action would take place from now on. Democracy in which all participants had an equal share, where the power of their collective action might prevent any future bloodshed because it would be shaped by the vision of human rights to equality, and where women and men would be on equal footing in broadly defined decision-making processes was a concept worth fighting for. Feminists had seen themselves as part of a larger commitment to releasing this spirit, through fostering tolerance towards differences and fighting for women's rights and human rights; the values of this new citizenship regime, they considered, would release the true spirit of democracy. Some of the earlier alternativeness or oppositionality of feminism had to be compromised in this process, because of the gradual – if somewhat reluctant – state acceptance of the policy framework of gender mainstreaming, a gender equality strategy favoured by the EU.[29]

Civil society, which during the nation-building citizenship regime had often acted in opposition to the newly established states, also changed during this period. During the first years of the Yugoslav wars, the wide-ranging space hidden behind the term 'civil society' had acted as a loose network, an 'alternative scene' and an aspiring frame for activism, with immense contributions from post-Yugoslav feminists described above.[30] Civil society organizations had cooperated, or at least tried to cooperate, across post-Yugoslav borders even when their respective states were at war. Post-Yugoslav civil society in the 1990s tended to have an oppositional relationship towards the state, especially but not only in Serbia. This attitude altered after 2000 for civil society in general just as it did for women's organizations in particular. In the 2000s, civil society and the state reached better mutual understanding, while the international donors who funded civil society organizations increasingly encouraged (and institutionalized) their activities bridging gaps between post-Yugoslav states. Processes of 'NGO-ization' therefore transformed activism into an organizational structure where donors' agendas structured what action was taken and how[31] a problem that Kristen Ghodsee, commenting on feminism in eastern Europe as a whole, has termed 'feminism-by-design'.[32]

If feminist activists had earlier sought to understand themselves as part of a transnational, border-crossing social movement, 'projectization' and professionalization now began to successfully preclude the collective action that a politics of solidarity would have needed. The relentless production of project language, project data and changeable project staff became a goal in itself, sometimes quite detached from the population it professed to cater for. Mobility, the frequent crossing of the post-Yugoslav national borders which once used to be a sign of courage and solidarity during and after the Yugoslav wars, was now facilitated as a matter of fact, but its beneficiaries were mainly young, urban, educated, English-speaking, elite members of civil society rather than women marginalized by their age, class, educational resources or location.[33]

Both the acceptance of feminism-by-design policies and the overly close proximity of feminist non-governmental organizations (NGOs) to the state helped in furthering the omnipresent discourse of transitional reforms. Feminists drew closer to the state by organizing women's parliamentary caucuses, insisting on women's impact on politics (without questioning the political frames they were operating in), educating women for leadership positions and introducing various mentoring processes. On the other hand, community-based projects in areas such as social work, domestic violence, health and care more often than not acted as more or less visible adjuncts of the state in its work – and indeed, as Ghodsee argues, feminist NGOs performing public care activities that had used to be a state duty perhaps inadvertently aided 'the neoliberal state to dismantle its social programs and shift the responsibility for these services to the grass roots'.[34]

Thus, while civil society had once been perceived as a rare space for enacting the alternative politics of solidarity and mobility, and as a relatively autonomous space for expressing feminist politics, by the mid-2010s it had become the channel for declaring what the adequate problems, approved topics and appropriate organizations were. This structuring of needs, but also knowledge, skills and available (legitimate and recommendable) discourses through which those needs would become mainstreamed into governmental actions or public languages restrained the visibility of certain forms of political activism. Even more importantly, it removed the dimension of collectivity and wiped out the broadness of a movement.

This final change in citizenship regime saw changes in the gender regime being followed by unrelenting social stratification. Transition, as this phase made apparent, was thus not only (or not for the most part) a passage from authoritarianism and ethno-national single-mindedness to militarism-free democracies: it also had a neoliberal side, which has generally been neglected and downplayed. Life in a war-free society has by all means curtailed the amount of pain, fear and uncertainty. But, by the end of the 2000s, many destructive structural traits that were integral to transition had already become clear, including the spread of poverty, deindustrialization, privatization, clientelistic employment opportunities, social insecurity, decreasing public expenditure in the social and cultural sectors and precarization of the rights that constituted social citizenship. As comparative studies of the gender-specific aspects of the transition to post-socialism (including the restructuring of healthcare, pensions, the labour market, childcare and social security) have suggested,[35] the socialist gender regime was much more generous than the transition gender regime towards women, whose daughters now lead incomparably fragmentary and precarious lives.

Disillusionment with the promises of the smooth transitional institutionalization of post-socialism would therefore create foundations for new forms of feminist political thought and action. If feminism had been organized around 'women as bodies in pain' during the 1990s context of war and nationalism, its central tenet now became to critique the system that had produced what Larisa Kurtović termed a specifically 'postsocialist pseudo-democracy'.[36] This critique enabled the return of an old feminist question: was feminism solely about bettering the position of women (and which women?), or was it also about changing the economic, political and social structures which incessantly perpetuate inequalities?

Conclusion: What Can We Learn from Post-Yugoslav Feminism?

Recent post-Yugoslav history, this chapter shows, provides several valuable lessons for feminist historians more widely. Even within a very short period of time, between the collapse of the Yugoslav Communist Party in 1990 and the present day, the political dimensions of feminist activism went through two important sets of changes as the defining frames of national politics in the post-Yugoslav successor states changed. This is more than just the notion of 'the political' proving malleable; rather, it emphasizes that understanding the structural contexts in which feminists can define an issue or strategy as 'political' is essential for historicizing feminist activism. When these contexts endure profound change, feminist definitions of the political will also change.

Post-Yugoslav feminism, therefore, was shaped both by war and by transition, and each should be seen as a different source of the political, accounting for the different emphases of feminist activism in the 1990s compared to the 2000s.

Speaking more theoretically, the shifts in feminist activism's political paradigms described in this chapter would be accounted for by shifts in citizenship regimes – the clusters of state governance, state responsibilities, citizens' rights and duties, and informal practices of belonging that constitute the relationships between states and individuals at any given time. Contextualizing feminist activism using the concept of citizenship regimes demonstrates that the history of feminism cannot and should not be detached from the various transformations of the world it takes part in. The history of post-Yugoslav feminism can show that women's position did not automatically improve with the collapse of state socialism, as exposure to the nation-building citizenship regime weakened their social and intimate autonomy in comparison to the socialist past. Simultaneously, it also shows that while feminism is deeply implicated in and affected by shifts in the constitutional, legal, communal and civic aspects of citizenship regimes, shifts in their *economic* aspects are just as important for explaining the history of feminism. This observation is particularly useful for gender histories of eastern Europe, because it emphasizes seismic changes in the social, political and first-hand lived dimensions of the world after 1989, which would not have been felt the same way outside countries which had not experienced state socialist rule.[37]

Post-Yugoslav post-socialism nevertheless had a specific character as a result of the break-up of Yugoslavia into successor states and the effects of the Yugoslav wars. As this chapter has demonstrated, the region went through two distinguishable phases of citizenship regimes, with consequent changes in the gender regimes linked to them. Instead of one monolithic 'East European post-socialism', therefore, we must discuss *varieties* of post-socialisms. To avoid a one-sided view of citizenship regimes and gender regimes since the fall of state socialism, we need to ascertain the similarities of these post-socialisms but also their many differences; we need to see how they have communicated with each other, but also how they have not. One form of one-sidedness has occurred because communication between varieties of post-socialism has materialized mostly in and through the English language, in conversations between east Europeans and Westerners, rather than directly between east Europeans in the region's languages (or in another language widely spoken in the region, such as Russian). This requires asking critical questions about how we have used the most widely available and, until recently mostly Western, ideas and models of what being Eastern means, and all the more so today, when the designation 'Eastern' might mainly be understood as relating to the Middle Eastern region. We have used and borrowed concepts and ideas which might or might not have been part of our own legacies; sometimes rightly, sometimes not. In relation to this particular region, we theorists should not let ourselves become petrified by the relative decline of foreign (particularly Western) research interest in the post-Yugoslav region compared to the amount of research about it during the Yugoslav wars: instead, it should compel us to develop our own standpoints and notions, and not just to borrow them. But we also need to be wary of another type of one-sidedness: one which dismisses the feminism engendered by anti-war and antinationalist politics in the 1990s in order to fit neatly into more recent post-austerity discourses that tend to brush aside the contributions of feminist activism around 'bodies in pain'.

Understanding feminist activism, therefore, requires a critical appreciation of both temporal and spatial 'politics of location'. Belonging to certain generations equips us with different tools for memorizing, historicizing and analysing certain phenomena – and, more importantly, enforces a specific way of living through those memories and their interpretations.[38] Historians as well as activists must, therefore, accept that their stances are partial, situated, and immersed in specific interpretations of the political.[39] Claiming that paradigm shifts in understandings of feminist activism occurred after the dissolution of Yugoslavia and again after 2000 does not, therefore, call for the erasure of previously dominant memories. Quite the contrary: it calls for a critical understanding of the contexts in which these very memories had to be constructed, but also for an appreciation of the difference in parameters which enabled different facets of the political in feminist activism to emerge.

This specific vantage point offers two potential directions. One is imaginative. For example, when describing the political trajectory of the usage of 'transition', Boris Buden claimed that, when the word first appeared in relation to politics in the 1960s, it implied solely a passage from authoritarianism to another form of community, without pre-determining what form of community that would be. After 1989 'transition' would become reserved exclusively for the post-Communist transitions to free-market democracy, rather than for transition to any other form of government.[40] In other words, it was taken for granted – as an epistemological rather than as an ideological given – that democracy was the best model and that there was only one model of it. Yet in the context of the paradigm shifts this chapter has described, it seems reasonable to ask whether this passage was really as smooth and uncomplicated as it had been anticipated to be. Questioning this one-dimensionality, we may as well join Kristen Ghodsee in asking: what would have eastern Europe, and feminist activism in it, looked like if democracy could have been conceivable *without* capitalism?[41] And then we might think further about the fortunes of feminism in a Yugoslav democracy without capitalism.

Another direction that feminist historians might take is to try to revise the notions taken for granted in interpreting our own histories. Revisiting Yugoslav histories, with a deeper and more nuanced understanding of what they have to offer, complicates the ready assumptions about the heritage and the prospects we have. The many political meanings that feminism has had in this 'laboratory of citizenship' may well compel us to rethink the extant definitions and categorizations of feminism itself. Meanwhile, the need to complicate assumptions about gender regimes during and after state socialism that this chapter demonstrates does not just affect the history of feminist activism or of the Yugoslav region; it is an essential analytical observation for any gender history research about the area(s) covered by this volume, as will also be seen from the next chapter's illustration of a comparative methodology in the study of gender and women's participation in professional work.

Notes

1. Kosovo declared independence from Serbia unilaterally in 2008.

2. Igor Štiks, 'A Laboratory of Citizenship: Shifting Conceptions of Citizenship in Yugoslavia and Post-Yugoslav States', in Jo Shaw and Igor Štiks (eds), *Citizenship after Yugoslavia* (London: Routledge, 2012), 15–37.

3. See, for example, Renata Salecl, *The Spoils of Freedom: Psychoanalysis and Feminism after the Fall of Socialism* (London: Routledge, 1992); Rada Iveković, 'Women, Nationalism and War: Make Love Not War', *Hypatia* vol. 8, no. 4 (1993): 113–26; Žarana Papić, 'Women in Serbia: Post-Communism, War and Nationalist Mutations', in Sabrina P. Ramet (ed.), *Gender Politics in the Western Balkans: Women and Society in Yugoslavia and the Yugoslav Successor States* (University Park: Pennsylvania State University Press, 1999, 153–69; see also other chapters in this volume); Julie Mostov, '"Our Women "/"Their Women": Symbolic Boundaries, Territorial Markers, and Violence in the Balkans', *Peace and Change* vol. 20, no. 4 (1995): 515–29; Dubravka Žarkov, *The Body of War: Media, Ethnicity, and Gender in the Break-Up of Yugoslavia* (Durham, NC: Duke University Press, 2007).

4. For example, Sonja Licht and Slobodan Drakulić, 'When the Word for Peacemaker was a Woman: War and Gender in the Former Yugoslavia', *Research on Russia and Eastern Europe* vol. 2 (1996): 111–39; Donna Hughes, Lepa Mladjenovic and Zorica Mrsevic, 'Feminist Resistance in Serbia', *European Journal of Women's Studies* vol. 2, no. 4 (1995): 509–32.

5. See Orli Fridman, '"It Was Like Fighting a War With Our Own People": Anti-War Activism in Serbia during the 1990s', *Nationalities Papers*, vol. 39, no. 4 (2011): 507–22; Elissa Helms, 'The "Nation-ing" of Gender? Donor Policies, Islam, and Women's NGOs in Post-War Bosnia-Herzegovina', *Anthropology of East Europe Review* vol. 21, no. 2 (2003): 85–92; Cynthia Cockburn, 'Against All Odds: Sustaining Feminist Momentum in Post-War Bosnia-Herzegovina', *Women's Studies International Forum* vol. 37 (2013): 26–35; Ana Miškovska Kajevska, 'Taking a Stand in Times of Violent Societal Changes: Belgrade and Zagreb Feminists' Positionings on the (Post-) Yugoslav Wars and Each Other (1991–2000)' (PhD dissertation, University of Amsterdam, 2014); Mirjana Adamović, et al. (eds), *Young Women in Post-Yugoslav Societies: Research, Practice and Policy* (Zagreb: IDI, 2014).

6. See, for example, Adriana Zaharijević, 'Dissidents, Disloyal Citizens and Partisans of Emancipation: Feminist Citizenship in Yugoslavia and Post-Yugoslav Spaces', *Women's Studies International Forum*, vol. 49 (2015): 93–100; Ankica Čakardić, 'Women's Struggles and Political Economy: From Yugoslav Self-Management to Neoliberal Austerity', in Srećko Horvat and Igor Štiks (eds), *Welcome to the Desert of Post-Socialism: Radical Politics After Yugoslavia* (London: Verso, 2015), 223–342.

7. See R. W. Connell, 'The State, Gender, and Sexual Politics: Theory and Appraisal', *Theory, Culture and Society* vol. 19, no. 5 (1990): 523.

8. Shaw and Štiks (eds), *Citizenship After Yugoslavia*.

9. Jelena Vasiljević, 'Citizenship as Lived Experience: Belonging and Documentality after the Break Up of Yugoslavia' (Edinburgh: University of Edinburgh, CITSEE Working Paper Series 2014/36, 2014).

10. The first post-war constitution (1946) guaranteed suffrage to all citizens regardless of sex; women were proclaimed equal with men in all domains of economic, state and social life, while their place in the processes of production, as working women and mothers, was especially protected by the constitution. Subsequent laws proclaimed equality in parenthood (granting both parents the right to parental leave), inheritance and economic independence. Abortion laws were introduced as early as 1951.

11. Milica Antić and Ksenija Vidmar, 'The Construction of Woman's Identity in Socialism: the Case of Slovenia', in Jelisaveta Blagojević, Katerina Kolozova and Svetlana Slapšak (eds), *Gender and Identity: Theories from and/or on Southeastern Europe* (Belgrade: Belgrade Women's Studies and Gender Research Center, 2006), 219–38; Neda Božinović, *Žensko pitanje u Srbiji u XIX i XX veku* (Belgrade: Devedesetčetvrta i Žene u crnom, 1996).

12. Mirjana Morokvasic, 'Being a Woman in Yugoslavia: Past, Present and Institutional Equality', in Monique Gadant (ed.), *Women of the Mediterranean* (London: Zed, 1986).

13. See also Kaminer, this volume.

14. Milica Antić, 'Yugoslavia: the Transitional Spirit of the Age', in Chris Corrin (ed.), *Superwoman and the Double Burden: Women's Experience of Change in Central and Eastern Europe and the former Soviet Union* (London: Scarlet Press, 1992), 155–79.

15. Katherine Verdery, *What was Socialism and What Comes Next?* (Princeton, NJ: Princeton University Press, 1996), 80.

16. Jacqueline Heinen, 'Clashes and Ordeals of Women's Citizenship in Central and Eastern Europe', in Jasmina Lukić, Joanna Regulska and Darja Zaviršek (eds), *Women and Citizenship in Central and Eastern Europe* (Aldershot: Ashgate, 2006), 83.

17. Vesna Kesic, 'From Respect to Rape', *Warreport* no. 36 (1995): 37.

18. While some women were urged to give birth for patriotic reasons, others (of 'unwanted' ethnic origin) were vilified for procreating too much: see Vjollca Krasniqi, 'Feminism and Nationalism', *Profemina*, Special Issue, no. 2, Summer/ Autumn (2011): 53–7; and Staša Zajović, 'Birth, Nationalism and War' (1995), available at: http://www.hartford-hwp.com/archives/62/039.html (accessed 9 February 2015).

19. Rada Drezgić, *'Bela kuga' među 'Srbima': o naciji, rodu i radjanju na prelazu vekova* (Belgrade: IFDT i Albatros plus, 2010).

20. Maja Korać, 'Ethnic Nationalism, Wars and the Patterns of Social, Political and Sexual Violence against Women: the Case of Post Yugoslav Countries', *Identities: Global Studies in Culture and Power* vol. 5, no. 2 (1998): 153–81.

21. Karmen Erjavec and Zala Volčič have persuasively described what actually happened to the offspring of women raped in war in Bosnia-Herzegovina. Treated as 'children of ethnic cleansers', 'children of the enemy' or 'children of hate', they were either forgotten or manipulated for political ends, they were less likely to be adopted, and were often socially ostracized and stigmatized. Erjavec and Volčič identify four recurrent themes in their respondents' stories: the continuation of the war through permanent hostility of the communities they belonged to, internalized guilt and self-hate, role reversal (acting like mothers to their mothers), and to some extent the potential for agency in reconciliation. See Karmen Erjavec and Zala Volčič, 'Living With the Sins of Their Fathers: an Analysis of Self-Representation of Adolescents Born of War Rape', *Journal of Adolescent Research* vol. 25, no. 3 (2010): 359–86.

22. Vesna Kesić, 'Muslim Women, Croatian Women, Serbian Women, Albanian Women', *Eurozine*, 9 May 2003, available at: www.eurozine.com/articles/2003-05-09-kesic-en.html (accessed 9 February 2015).

23. Rada Borić, 'Nešto moramo učiniti', *Zarez* no. 106 (2003).

24. Staša Zajović, 'Ne u naše ime!', in Staša Zajović, Marija Perković and Miloš Urošević (eds), *Women for Peace* (Belgrade: Žene u crnom, 2007), 79–83.

25. Lepa Mlađenović, 'Svedočenja učesnica karavana', *Profemina* no. 31–32 (2003): 132.

26. Zagorka Golubović, 'Tranzicija u Srbiji posle 2000. godine: lavirinti tranzicije', in Zoran Stojiljković (ed.), *Lavirinti tranzicije* (Belgrade: Friedrich Ebert Stiftung and Centar za demokratiju, 2012), 26.

27. Srećko Mihajlović (ed.), *Dometi tranzicije od socijalizma ka kapitalizmu* (Belgrade: Friedrich Ebert Stiftung, 2011).
28. Kristen Ghodsee, 'On Feminism, Philosophy and Politics in Post-Communist Romania: an Interview with Mihaela Miroiu', *Women's International Studies Journal* vol. 34 (2011): 305.
29. Barbara Einhorn, 'Citizenship in an Enlarging Europe: Contested Strategies', *Sociologický časopis* vol. 41, no. 6 (2005): 1023.
30. Paul Stubbs, 'Networks, Organisations, Movements: Narratives and Shapes of Three Waves of Activism in Croatia', *Polemos* vol. 15, no. 2 (2012): 11–32; Bojan Bilić, 'A Concept that is Everything and Nothing: Why *Not* to Study (Post-) Yugoslav Anti-War and Pacifist Contention from a *Civil Society* Perspective', *Sociologija* vol. 53, no. 3 (2011): 297–322.
31. See Elissa Helms, 'The "Nation-ing" of Gender?'; Zhivka Valiavicharska, 'Culture, Neoliberal Development, and the Future of Progressive Politics in Southeastern Europe', in Jonathan Harris (ed.), *Globalization and Contemporary Art* (Malden, MA: Wiley-Blackwell, 2010), 85–92.
32. Kristen Ghodsee, 'Feminism-by-Design: Emerging Capitalisms, Cultural Feminism, and Women's Nongovernmental Organizations in Postsocialist Eastern Europe', *Signs* vol. 29, no. 3 (2004): 727–53.
33. Paul Stubbs, 'Civil Society of Ubleha?', in Helena Rill, Tamara Šmidling and Ana Bitoljanu (eds), *20 Pieces of Encouragement for Awakening and Change* (Belgrade and Sarajevo: Centre for Nonviolent Action, 2007), 221. This overall trend does not, of course, mean that there is no internal critique towards its pervasiveness, as well as attempts at restoring and sustaining alternativeness of the movement. See 'Kuda ide feminizam danas?', *Žene za mir* (Belgrade: Žene u crnom, 2012).
34. Ghodsee, 'Feminism-by-Design', 738. See also Cockburn, 'Against All Odds'.
35. See, for instance, Chiara Bonfiglioli, 'Gendered Citizenship in the Global European Periphery: Textile Workers in Post-Yugoslav States', *Women's Studies International Forum* vol. 49 (2014): 57–65; Krassimira Daskalova, Caroline Hornstein Tomic, Karl Kaser and Filip Radunovic (eds), *Gendering Post-Socialist Transition* (ERSTE Foundation Series, 2012); Mariya Stoilova, 'Post-Socialist Gender Transformations and Women's Experiences of Employment: Movements Between Continuity and Change in Bulgaria', *Journal of Organizational Change Management* vol. 23, no. 6 (2010): 731–54; Adamson and Kispeter, this volume.
36. Larisa Kurtović, 'Istorije (bh) budućnosti: kako misliti postjugoslovenski postsoci-jalizam u Bosni i Hercegovini?', *Puls demokratije*, 17 August 2010: 1–15, available at: https://web.archive.org/web/20101120132339/http://pulsdemokratije.ba/index.php?id=1979&l=bs (accessed 16 April 2015).
37. See Susan Gal and Gail Kligman, *The Politics of Gender after Socialism: a Comparative–Historical Essay* (Princeton, NJ: Princeton University Press, 2000).
38. On 'generations' in feminism, see Claire Hemmings, *Why Stories Matter: the Political Grammar of Feminist Theory* (Durham, NC: Duke University Press, 2011).
39. Having in mind Adrienne Rich's challenge, I would situate myself as belonging to the post-2000 generation of feminists, from Belgrade (at the time the capital of SFRY, and afterwards the capital of several other states, most recently the Republic of Serbia), born only a month before the famous *Drug-ca žena*, the first feminist conference behind the Iron Curtain, took place. The first time when I, as a feminist, crossed the borders of the new nation states which used to be republics of SFRY, I was crossing them with a Serbian passport. I would refer to myself as an academic feminist, but with a steady activist 'training' in Belgrade Women in Black. By insist-ing on this type of description, I do not wish to perpetuate the activist/theorist

divide, but to evoke the relevance of the academic agency which is all too often taken for granted. (See Adrienne Rich, 'Notes toward a Politics of Location (1984)', in *Blood, Bread, and Poetry: Selected Prose 1979–1984* (New York: W. W. Norton, 1986); see also Moya Flynn and Jonathan Oldfield, 'Trans-National Approaches to Locally Situated Concerns: Exploring the Meanings of Post-Socialist Space', *Journal of Communist Studies and Transition Politics* vol. 22, no. 1 (2006): 3–23. The short outline of my own partiality is included in the text because the locatedness of the author who attempts to cover the whole post-Yugoslav region will doubtless be noticeable. I am grateful to Ana Miškovska Kajevska, who in many different ways pointed to the significance of appreciating one's own politics of location.

40. Boris Buden, *Zona prelaska: o kraju postkomunizma* (Belgrade: Fabrika knjiga, 2012).
41. Kristen Ghodsee, 'Revisiting 1989: the Specter Still Haunts', *Dissent* no. 7 (2012): 7.

13
Gender and Professional Work in Russia and Hungary

Maria Adamson and Erika Kispeter[1]

A key question for historians of gender relations in late 20th-century eastern Europe is how far one can draw conclusions about the effects of state socialism and its demise on the scale of the whole region, and how far factors specific to each country are of importance here. The Yugoslav wars, discussed in the last chapter, present one setting that illustrates the need to balance these levels of analysis. This chapter illustrates a complementary approach in gender history – comparison – by comparing the histories of women's advancement in professional work in 20th-century state socialist Hungary and Russia (the largest republic of the USSR). In both countries, the dramatic increase in the number of women in paid labour under state socialism had been heralded as a major achievement: for instance, women constituted 51 per cent of the workforce in Soviet Russia and 41 per cent in Hungary in 1970.[2] Moreover, women in state socialist countries seemed to have achieved the holy grail of Western feminist pursuit by gaining access to professions such as law, medicine and engineering, traditionally dominated by men in most Western countries.[3] By the mid-1970s, 60 per cent of workers in professional occupations in the USSR were women.[4] By focusing on comparing the changing gender regimes of professional work in Hungary and Russia,[5] this chapter demonstrates a complexity of gender histories that would be obscured if all state socialist societies were viewed, on the basis of their politics and policies, simply as one 'Eastern bloc'. It also considers how far these gender regimes and these achievements would be preserved after the collapse of state socialism.

The concept of the 'bloc' derives from the end of World War II, when Hungary as well as Bulgaria, Romania, Hungary, Poland, East Germany and part of Czechoslovakia were in the so-called zone of 'Soviet influence'. These countries plus Yugoslavia and Albania formed the 'Soviet bloc', a group of countries expected to follow the leadership of the Communist Party of the Soviet Union and on the whole adopt Soviet models of ideology and policies, including those related to gender equality.[6] However, the adoption of Soviet policies (on gender equality at work and other matters) was a complex process;[7] moreover, gender-related labour policies underwent much change even in Soviet

Russia itself.[8] A nuanced and contextual understanding of the comparative histories of gender and professional work requires seeing women's position in the professions in relation to varieties of state socialism. That is, it must take into consideration the specific historical, structural and cultural contexts of individual countries. This chapter's comparison of Russia and Hungary demonstrates how this might be done.

After comparing the state socialist histories of Russia and Hungary, the chapter gives an overview of the development of the professions in socialist societies and discusses socialist policies on women and professional work. It then turns to Éva Fodor's concept of women's limited inclusion in the world of paid work to explore women's position in medical and law professions in Hungary and Russia.[9] As the chapter demonstrates, there were many similarities in the patterns of Russian and Hungarian women's inclusion in and exclusion from the professions in these two contexts, but the gendered work histories of the two countries were by no means the same.

The Russian and Hungarian Contexts

When attempting to compare women's participation in professional work in Russia and Hungary, the two countries' paths to socialism, and the relationship between them, must be understood. Soviet Russia was the largest republic of the USSR and a flagship of radical Communist policies. After the Bolshevik Revolution in October 1917, the Russian Communist Party came to power and the country embarked on dramatic and large-scale social, political and economic transformations, including the abolition of private property, nationalization of industries, mass-scale industrialization, agricultural collectivization and centralized economic planning.[10] The history of socialism in Russia was characterized by several periods, from the 1917 Bolshevik regime and New Economic Policies in 1921, followed by Stalin's rule and repressions between 1922 and 1952, Khrushchev's thaw in 1953, Gorbachev's perestroika of 1985 and the eventual dissolution of the USSR in 1991.[11] During these periods, work-related gender agendas inevitably also varied – from genuine excitement in and enforcement of equality policies in the revolutionary years and an unprecedented increase of women in paid work to declarations that 'the woman question' had been resolved in the 1960s and a resurgence of domesticity rhetoric in the late 1980s.[12]

The context of Hungarian state socialism, meanwhile, began at the end of World War II when Hungary was in economic chaos. After a brief period of multi-party democracy, the Hungarian Communist Party gained power in 1949 and a new, 'Soviet-style' constitution came into force. The country embarked on rapid and extensive industrialization, which lasted until the early 1960s, a period often referred to as the 'classical', Stalinist model of socialism in Hungary.[13] The curtailment of personal and political freedoms and poverty stirred resentment, contributing to an uprising against Communist rule in 1956. Although the revolution was overpowered by Soviet military invasion and followed by severe retaliation, the new regime, led by János Kádár, sought to reconstruct Hungarian Communism rather than restore the Hungarian variant of Stalinism.[14] Economic reforms after 1966 led to improved standards of living. At the same time, a new, unwritten social contract between the leadership of the Hungarian Communist Party and the population emerged: Communist rule was not to be criticized or opposed openly, and in return individuals were allowed more freedom from state interference than before 1956.[15] As a result, the Hungarian version of state socialism is often termed 'goulash communism' and the country was seen as the 'happiest barrack' of the Eastern bloc.[16]

Professions in State Socialism

Another dimension of context for comparing women's participation in the professions is the specific nature of professional structures and arrangements under state socialist regimes, which were very different from their 'Western' counterparts. In the Anglo-American context, the term 'profession' typically refers to high-status, highly paid and prestigious occupations which are characterized by complex scientific knowledge, requiring long training periods and formal qualifications.[17] Traditional 'liberal' professions such as medicine, law, accounting and engineering tend to be independent from the state. These professions are 'chartered' by the state, which means that they are represented by professional associations which are mandated to regulate the terms of entry, training and certification requirements; in return, professions 'promise' to ensure the quality of their members' work and pledge to work in the public interest. However, professions in the Anglo-American context have been widely criticized for breaking that promise and pursuing status and pay instead of the public good.[18] Moreover, professions in the West have also been criticized for continuous exclusion and discrimination of women who tend to be concentrated in 'feminized' lower-prestige and lower-income fields and specialities.[19] For example, the Soviet and 'Western' contexts differed dramatically in the number of professional women. Women constituted only 6 per cent of physicians in the US in 1950, and only 17 per cent in 1990.[20] In contrast, over 70 per cent of doctors in Soviet Russia were women in 1950, and 69 per cent in 1990.[21] These figures must, however, be seen in relation to the very different history and structure of professions in state socialism compared to the West.

Before 1917 in Russia and 1945 in Hungary, the development of professions in both countries largely resembled that of their Western counterparts. The contrast with the Western model was most radical in Russia. After the 1917 revolution, Russian professions were stripped of their institutional autonomy and independence as the state attempted to undermine the power of the intellectual class of bourgeois professionals.[22] Professionals were largely 'proletarized':[23] they became just another group of salaried employees in state-controlled organizations. In the case of Soviet medicine, existing professional associations, such as the Medical Council, were abolished by the Bolshevik government, which took control of professional regulation, education and entry requirements. Medical faculties became state-controlled vocational schools in the late 1930s and the number of doctors increased significantly to serve the new nationalized healthcare system. The medical profession's general development and day-to-day functioning were also determined by directives of the Ministry of Health.[24]

The Soviet legal profession had a somewhat similar fate. The early Bolshevik government dismantled the Bar Association, but partly restored it in the 1920s when regional colleges of advocates were formed (these could decide on admissions to the profession, but the Ministry of Justice and its local executive committees or *ispolkoms* still monitored their activities closely).[25] The number of lawyers, in contrast to doctors, decreased dramatically, since litigation was considered an attribute of capitalism and was expected to become redundant in a socialist state. Law was among the lowest-status, lowest-paid professions in the USSR.[26] Unlike doctors, however, Soviet lawyers managed to preserve some autonomy. For instance, solicitors remained one of the few self-supporting professions in the USSR: although their salaries were state-determined, they were derived entirely from client billings, through a fee structure determined by the Ministry of Justice.[27]

Developments in Hungarian professions were similar, but overall less radical than in Soviet Russia. The Hungarian Medical Chamber was dissolved immediately after World War II. General practitioners, who had been self-employed before the war, became 'district physicians' in the nationalized system of healthcare.[28] The number of doctors in Hungary increased, but to a smaller extent than in the USSR. Medical training remained within universities, and doctors' prestige did not drop as significantly as in Russia. There were also divisions within the profession: practitioners' status, pay levels and opportunities to boost pay through receiving informal gratuities from patients were all higher for city-based doctors than in rural areas.[29] Despite the dramatic restructuring of the profession, specialist training continued to be delivered in teaching hospitals, leaving opportunities for informal networks of professionals to survive. In law, the number of solicitors in Hungary decreased significantly after 1945 as it had in Russia, but the Bar Association remained at least formally active. It was radically reorganized in 1950: in-house lawyers were excluded from it altogether, while solicitors lost the right to maintain an independent private practice and were forced to work in semi-autonomous teams. Specialist training of lawyers was also redesigned: examination criteria were determined by the state, rather than the professional associations.[30]

In both countries, the deprofessionalization process under state socialism had a direct relationship to the changing gender composition in both law and medicine. Firstly, state control over higher education,[31] and professional regulation, made it possible to increase the number of professional women through ensuring their entry into higher education and subsequent mandatory work placements.[32] Secondly, in both societies, the restructuring of the system of professions led to a decrease in the prestige and remuneration of professionals. Communist ideology privileged working-class values and industrial labour, meaning that professions and intellectual labour were considered a 'non-productive' and, therefore, less socially valuable activity.[33] Both of these changes made it 'easier' for women to enter professional work.

The 'Woman Question'

The Communist struggle put the so-called 'woman question' firmly on the agenda of socialist states. Marx, Engels and the Bolshevik feminist Aleksandra Kollontai had all considered that, for class struggle to succeed, an essential prerequisite was to integrate both men and women by abolishing the oppression of one sex by another that existed in capitalist societies.[34] Both Soviet Russia and Hungary passed laws that established women's equality in political and legal matters and in marriage. Direct discrimination at work was also tackled. By the late 1970s, about 90 per cent of women in Soviet Russia were in education or working full time, and women comprised 51 per cent of the economically active population, while in Hungary 64 per cent of women were economically active in 1980 – a higher number than in most capitalist economies.[35] In both countries women also entered professions such as medicine and law, and represented significant percentages in the historically male-dominated areas.[36]

An essential element of the Communist pursuit of gender equality at work was to reduce gender inequality in education, and by the late 1970s men's advantage over women in higher education had disappeared in both Russia and Hungary.[37] Soviet ideology dictated that women should be emancipated, specifically that 'domestic enslavement' should be combated.[38] To 'free up' women for paid work, the socialist states strove to relocate some household duties into the public sphere: workplace canteens were established, and there was an 86 per cent increase in the number of childcare facilities, such as free nurseries and kindergartens, between 1961 and 1970 in Russia.[39] In Hungary the number of children enrolled in nurseries increased from approximately 7,000 in 1951 to more than 40,000 in 1970.[40] Policy measures were adopted in both countries to make it easier to balance work and motherhood: long, state-funded maternity leave, free childcare and other social benefits let women participate in paid work at about the same rate as men.[41]

Women's entry into the workplace was not just, however, driven by the state's ideological commitment; it was also a matter of economic necessity.[42] Human losses after World War II had resulted in great labour shortages, and to keep up with the rapid pace of industrialization the state needed female workers. The stakes of integrating women into the economy may have been slightly higher in Russia, given its agrarian economy and tremendous post-war demographic crisis. For the most part, work for women was not a choice – socialist ideology dictated that every able-bodied adult was obliged to be in regular and continuous employment. In addition, healthcare, pensions and most benefits families could get (such as access to childcare facilities and housing benefits) depended on employment status, making work a necessity.[43] Unemployment did not officially exist under state socialism, and the state's attitude towards those who were not in employment varied from tolerance towards housewives to prosecuting those who presented a 'danger to society' by willingly 'avoiding' work.[44]

Despite the inclusion of women in the workforce and their representation in many occupations, horizontal and vertical gender segregation persisted in paid work in both countries. Women were concentrated in more 'feminine' sectors such as education and services, while men were clustered in higher-paid and more prestigious industries such as construction and heavy industries.[45] In Soviet engineering, for instance, women's participation increased but never exceeded 46 per cent.[46] This segregation was seen by the general population as natural, since the dominant gender ideology rendered men the primary breadwinners.[47] Furthermore, despite some positive discrimination (quotas for women's participation), women in both countries remained under-represented among political elites and in managerial positions even in feminized industries.[48]

Finally, the gender division of unpaid work in the household saw little change: despite women's inclusion in paid work, housework and childcare continued to be regarded as women's duties. This resulted in the infamous 'double burden', which was exacerbated by poor infrastructure, shortages of food supplies, queues and long working hours.[49] This situation significantly impeded women's career progression in both countries. Women were also deemed to have a demographical duty to the state as mothers, and although the 'woman question' in Soviet Russia had been declared solved, it came back on to the agenda in the 1960s when the declining birth rate prompted discussions about the negative consequences of women's employment on their duty as mothers.[50] In Hungary, discussions about women's situation from the mid-1960s onwards also increasingly focused on demographic problems.[51] These developments clearly underscore the dual expectations that socialist states had of women.

In light of this, several studies have questioned whether women were actually liberated by state socialism. Mary Buckley suggests the process is better characterized as the mobilization rather than the liberation of women; others, meanwhile, contend that the ideal of gender equality was genuinely embraced, especially in the early periods of socialist societies.[52] Éva Fodor has argued that the simple opposition of either idealizing state socialist regimes or dismissing state socialist achievements in women's emancipation has been an unproductive framework for understanding these developments. Instead, Fodor characterizes women's position in the world of paid work and politics in late state socialism as 'limited inclusion'.[53] Although most women were in paid work, they were often seen as 'second-rate' employees; it was difficult for them to enter the high-prestige specialities and top managerial positions and they were significantly under-represented in the sphere of politics.[54] The concept of 'limited inclusion' highlights that masculine privilege in paid work was contested by the state socialist experiment and a new form of gender inequality emerged.

The Terms of Women's Inclusion in the Professions

Women's inclusion in professions in Russia and Hungary had several similarities. Both countries saw the widespread gendering of professions, with women expected to choose more 'feminine' specialities; the normalization of the 'double burden', meaning that women were expected to 'choose' careers and jobs which were more compatible with their role as mothers; and the greater acceptability of women working in lower-paid sectors because they were not seen as primary breadwinners. Vertical segregation was also widespread in both countries, as managerial positions were seen as more appropriate for men. Despite these similarities, however, the unique history of each country and the two states' differences in 'socialisms' created important divergences in the experiences of professional women.

In medicine, firstly, women's inclusion followed a similar pattern in both countries, but the degree of integration varied. Soviet medicine started to become female-dominated in the 1920s, and by the 1950s 70 per cent of doctors were women.[55] This 'female supremacy' was seen as an example of achieving equality between sexes in a socialist society.[56] There were a number of reasons why the number of women in Soviet medicine was so high. The first was linked to the expansion of medicine: in the late 1930s, when the Party decided to double the number of medical graduates, entry into medical education was subject to gender quotas and quotas for the 'proletariat' and people from rural backgrounds.[57] Secondly, medicine was seen as a more appropriate profession for women than, for instance, engineering because women were seen as naturally suited to caring, and seen as a 'safer' career for potential mothers than industrial work.[58] Thirdly, as discussed above, medicine was considered a non-productive and less 'valued' profession, reflected by physicians' low salaries (according to one study, a Soviet physician's salary was typically 20 per cent lower than a factory worker's).[59] Such devaluation made the profession more 'suitable' for women who were not considered primary breadwinners. All in all, women came to be a good 'fit' for this profession, while men were concentrated in more prestigious and higher-paid fields such as engineering or industrial production.[60] Even within medicine, women were clustered in particular specialities that were seen as 'more feminine', such as those related to women and children: in the 1970s, women comprised around 70 per cent of paediatricians, obstetricians and gynaecologists and other lower-status specialities, while only 30 per cent of surgeons were women, since their specialism was seen as more prestigious and more 'masculine'.[61]

In Hungary, only 15 per cent of doctors were women in 1952; however, their share had increased to a third by 1970 and to 47 per cent by 1990,[62] though these figures were still significantly lower than Russia's. There was also strong gender segmentation between medical specializations: by the end of the state socialist period, women had come to dominate less prestigious specializations such as paediatrics (73 per cent), ophthalmology (77 per cent) and dermatology (70 per cent), while they were almost completely absent from surgery (9 per cent) and obstetrics and gynaecology (8 per cent).[63] Interestingly, unlike in Russia, obstetrics and gynaecology has always been a male-dominated speciality in Hungary. The literature offers virtually no explanation for this curious difference, but it is probably related to the context of practising these specialities in Hungary. Only qualified gynaecologists and obstetricians were allowed to provide these services, including cervical cancer screening; given the widespread practice of informal gratuities and the fact that Hungary (unlike Russia) never completely abolished private practice,[64] this speciality must have been very lucrative and thus remained male-dominated.

Both countries also witnessed widespread vertical segregation within the medical profession. Managerial positions were seen as more appropriate for the 'stronger sex', and according to one study, men made up 50 per cent of 'all chief physicians and executives of medical institutions in 1969' in Russia even though only 15 per cent of medical professionals were men.[65] The patterns were similar in Hungary. Given these gendered patterns of segregation, researchers suggest that women's inclusion was limited.

In law, meanwhile, women's inclusion in both countries followed a similar but not identical pattern. Unlike in medicine, there was a drastic decline in the overall number of lawyers, both in Russia and Hungary.[66] Within this reduced profession, women constituted about 30 per cent of Soviet lawyers in 1949 and 21 per cent of lawyers in Hungary in 1973.[67] Law, like medicine, showed clear gendered patterns across specializations: women were concentrated in the least prestigious areas, such as civil law, and in the USSR they comprised 99 per cent of notaries.[68] These areas were considered more 'appropriate' for women because the regular and relatively short working hours made it easier to combine work with caring for the home and children. Moreover, civil law was considered 'clean' work, as opposed to 'dirty' criminal law which involved working with prisoners. Men, on the other hand, were concentrated in criminal or international law – the only specialities that retained higher status.[69] With a career in criminal and international law, men were also more likely to pursue political careers or enter the very prestigious sphere of diplomacy.[70] Similarly to medicine, although women constituted a high proportion of law graduates, not many women were found in top managerial positions.

Hungary, however, differed from Soviet Russia in that the reduction in the number of lawyers in Hungary was more dramatic. Many Hungarian lawyers of Jewish descent had perished in the Holocaust, while other lawyers who were unwilling to work in the new state-determined professional structures had to leave the profession: in 1960, 14 per cent of law graduates were working in manual occupations.[71] Although more women started to study law at university in socialist Hungary, the process of their integration was slow and they remained vastly under-represented: their share was only 4 per cent in 1960 which had increased to 21 per cent by 1980.[72] In the mid-1970s most women in the legal profession worked as in-house corporate lawyers or as judges, while they were almost completely absent from the ranks of solicitors (only 10 per cent of them were women in 1973),[73] and state prosecutors. The strict, almost militaristic organization of the prosecutor's office probably made it 'less suitable' for women, although in the second half of the state socialist period the number of women among public prosecutors did increase.[74] By 1990, approximately one-third of all law graduates were women,[75] and they outnumbered men among judges.[76] Despite the very slow and modest increase in the number of female lawyers, a discourse of public concern about the 'feminization' of the profession emerged in the 1980s when women first outnumbered men among first-year law students.[77] This suggests that the legal profession continued to be regarded as prestigious and feminization, which they felt was synonymous with devaluation, was seen as a threat. The discourse persisted after the end of state socialism.

Gender, Professions and the Post-Socialist Context

The end of the Cold War and the withdrawal of Soviet armed forces from the countries of the Eastern bloc was followed by the first multi-party elections, in 1990 for Hungary and 1991 for Russia. In 1991 the USSR itself was dissolved, causing dramatic political and economic changes for socialist societies. These included a shift from a state-controlled to a market economy, privatization and marketization, as well as mass unemployment and a fundamental change in social organization. The post-state socialist transformations had many gendered effects.[78] The state-led discourse of women's emancipation disappeared in both Russia and Hungary; in fact, the collapse of industries and mass unemployment gave rise to rhetoric suggesting that paid jobs should first be offered to men while women should return to what Gorbachev had called their 'purely womanly mission', that is, domesticity.[79] But, while women in both countries were significantly affected by unemployment and the insecurity of the transition,[80] neither country saw a drastic decline in the number of women in professional work.[81]

Post-socialism did, however, pose new challenges for working women. Firstly, public sector jobs remained low paid, while in the private sector pay was higher but so was insecurity. Secondly, gender discrimination increased in both countries, and although new 'gender equality' legislation was introduced in Hungary as part of the EU accession process, both old and new regulations were often disregarded by employers.[82] Thirdly, the socialist welfare system began to collapse. A significant drop in the number of affordable childcare places made it more difficult to balance paid work with family care, which was still deemed to be women's duty. Moreover, while extended maternity leave remained available in both Russia and Hungary, the value of maternity benefits declined, and long absence from the workplace was more detrimental to women's careers in the emerging capitalist labour markets than it had been under state socialism.[83]

In medicine, the most important changes for both Russian and Hungarian professionals were the new opportunities for private practice. This, however, led to vast inequalities of pay and working conditions between the private and public sector, with public sector pay becoming extremely low. Gender segregation patterns among doctors persisted in both countries,[84] and there was some evidence that in post-Soviet Russia women's access to more prestigious specialities and positions had deteriorated since the end of state socialism.[85] The medical profession's efforts to re-establish autonomy from the state remained weak, especially in post-Soviet Russia, and gender equality was not on the agenda of the re-emerged professional associations.[86]

Both countries' legal professions, on the other hand, did much better after the fall of the regime. Post-socialist markets became open to international business, creating demand for litigation and solicitors. Civil, commercial, economic and tax law (low-status and female-dominated specialities under state socialism) became revalued in the new market economies.[87] Although there were worries that women would be forced out of the profession as soon as the state withdrew its protection in the 1990s, this was not the case, and women continued to dominate those fields.[88] However, there was an influx of men into these specialities, so at the time of writing it remained to be seen how this would affect female lawyers in the longer term. The number of lawyers in Hungary increased rapidly, reflecting the needs of the market economy. This rapid growth facilitated women's entry into the profession, and by 2001 40 per cent of all law graduates were women, an increase from 33 per cent in 1990.[89] Yet although female lawyers were initially in a better position than men to take up the private sector's new jobs, by the 2010s there was some evidence that law was becoming 're-masculinized' because of interlinked processes of discrimination and women self-selecting into more 'secure' state employment.[90] The socialist legacy meant the Hungarian judiciary remained feminized, and although there were unofficial efforts to stop this trend, 68 per cent of Hungarian judges were women in 2013.[91]

Conclusion

In both Russia and Hungary, women's inclusion in the professions was shaped by the economic, political and ideological contexts that determined both the socialist gender regimes and the structural organization of professional work. A commitment to socialist ideology in both countries, bolstered by the labour shortage and economic necessity, created a strong agenda to include women in paid work, while deprofessionalization and the devaluation of the professions facilitated the channelling of women into these jobs. Moreover, since socialist gender ideology constructed women as workers *and* mothers, professional work was a good 'match' because it allowed women to balance the two roles.

However, despite similar trends in women's professional employment, the Hungarian and Russian situations were by no means identical, because of differences in the historical development of socialism in the two countries and because of the relationship between them. In both countries, the history of socialism was fragmented. This meant that policies on gender inclusion shifted from a genuine belief in gender equality in the early revolutionary years to the re-traditionalization of the gendered division of labour from the late 1960s in Hungary and after perestroika in the USSR. Moreover, gender equality policies were not simply 'adopted' from the USSR by Hungary; after the 1956 revolution gender equality policies were not implemented as zealously as in Soviet Russia. Although Hungarian leaders still followed the Soviet model, there was more negotiation and adaptation of the 'centralized' gender politics imposed by the USSR, partly motivated by popular resentment about the imposition of policies and ideologies. Specific historical circumstances also produced contextual differences in the pattern of women's inclusion in professional work in each country. For instance, since the Hungarian professions had preserved slightly more autonomy than their Soviet counterparts, professional communities could more successfully resist the state's pursuit of mandatory gender equality: this resulted in more traditional gender patterns persisting (as with law) and a stronger disavowal of the 'feminization' of professional work.

In conclusion, although Soviet Russia served as a model for gender policies for state socialist countries, the policies were not simply transferred to and fully emulated in other societies. Using gender as a category of analysis, the chapter has suggested that Russia and Hungary represent different varieties of state socialism: while there are significant similarities, the patterns of women's inclusion in professional work in these two countries are contextually conditioned, and thus divergent. The question remains how useful any comparison of this nature may be. This chapter suggests that, if one proceeds with caution and takes into account historical variations in state socialism between countries as well as changes within each country over time, then it is possible to tease out meaningful intersections, similarities and contrasts. Our analysis challenges the concept of the Soviet bloc as a unified entity as well as narratives about the transition to post-socialism as a simple story of improvement in the situation of women. Understanding contextual differences, then, becomes a starting point for unpacking the variety of gender regimes in different socialist and post-socialist societies. The next chapter further demonstrates the importance of this approach to analysis when exploring another contested topic related to the region's contemporary gender regimes: the intimate yet public politics of sexual citizenship, gender recognition and 'LGBT' rights.

Notes

1. The authors have made equal contributions to this chapter.
2. Gail W. Lapidus, *Women in Soviet Society: Equality, Development, and Social Change* (Berkeley: University of California Press, 1987), 153; János Fóti, Gabriella Kapitány, and Miklós Lakatos, 'A foglalkoztatottság alakulása 1980 és 1996 között', *Statisztikai Szemle* vol. 75, no. 7 (1997): 565–81. The lack of reliable and comparable official data means that direct comparison is not always possible, or is only possible for a certain date.
3. Barbara Einhorn, *Cinderella Goes to Market: Citizenship, Gender and Women's Movements in East Central Europe* (London: Verso, 1993).
4. Michael P. Sacks, *Women's Work in Soviet Russia: Continuity in the Midst of Change* (New York: Praeger, 1976), 74.
5. Raewyn Connell, *Gender and Power: Society, the Person and Sexual Politics* (Stanford: Stanford University Press, 1987).
6. Ben Fowkes, *Eastern Europe 1945–1969: From Stalinism to Stagnation* (Harlow: Pearson, 2000). The USSR ejected Yugoslavia from the bloc in 1948.
7. See also Simić, this volume.
8. Sarah Ashwin (ed.), *Gender, State and Society in Soviet and Post-Soviet Russia* (London: Routledge, 2000); Joanna Goven, 'Gender and Modernism in a Stalinist State', *Social Politics* vol. 9, no. 1 (2002): 3–28.
9. See Éva Fodor, *Working Difference: Women's Working Lives in Hungary and Austria, 1945–1995* (Durham, NC: Duke University Press, 2003).
10. Fowkes, *Eastern Europe*.
11. See Martin Malia, *Soviet Tragedy: a History of Socialism in Russia* (New York: The Free Press, 1994).
12. See Ashwin (ed.), *Gender, State and Society*; Linda Edmondson (ed.) *Women and Society in Russia and the Soviet Union* (Cambridge: Cambridge University Press, 2008).
13. Gil Eyal, Ivan Szelényi, and Eleanor Townsley, *Making Capitalism without Capitalists: the New Ruling Elites in Eastern Europe* (London: Verso, 1998). See also Takács, this volume.

14. Melinda Kalmár, *Ennivaló és hozomány: a kora Kádárizmus ideológiája* (Budapest: Magvető, 1998).
15. Radio Free Europe, 'Kadarism: Is It Here to Stay?' (HU OSA 300–8–3–3944), records of Radio Free Europe/Radio Liberty Research Institute (Publications Department: Background Reports; Open Society Archives at Central European University, Budapest), available at: catalog.osaarchivum.org/catalog/osa:9c3f6605-0745-4083-baa6-8bfab901bbec (accessed 20 June 2016).
16. Bennett Kovrig, 'Hungarian Socialism: the Deceptive Hybrid', *East European Politics and Societies* vol. 1, no. 1 (1986): 113–34.
17. Keith M. MacDonald, *The Sociology of the Professions* (London: Sage, 1995).
18. See Magali S. Larson, *The Rise of Professionalism* (Berkeley: University of California Press, 1977).
19. See Anne Witz, *Professions and Patriarchy* (London: Routledge, 1992); Celia Davies, 'The Sociology of Professions and the Profession on Gender', *Sociology* vol. 30, no. 4 (1996): 661–78.
20. Elianne Riska, *Medical Careers and Feminist Agendas: American, Scandinavian and Russian Women Physicians* (New York: Aldine de Gruyter, 2001), 38.
21. Riska, *Medical Careers*, 38.
22. Harley D. Balzer (ed.), *Russia's Missing Middle Class: the Professions in Russian History* (Armonk, NY: M. E. Sharpe, 1996).
23. Riska, *Medical Careers*.
24. Jeni Harden, 'Gender and Work in Soviet Russia: the Medical Profession' (PhD thesis, University of Strathclyde, 1997).
25. Eugene Huskey, *Russian Lawyers and the Soviet State: the Origins and Development of the Soviet Bar 1917–1939* (Princeton, NJ: Princeton University Press, 1986).
26. William M. Mandel, 'Soviet Women in the Work Force and Professions', *American Behavioural Scientist* vol. 15, no. 2 (1971): 255–80.
27. Huskey, *Russian Lawyers*.
28. Richard Weinerman, *Social Medicine in Eastern Europe: the Organization of Health Services and the Education of Medical Personnel in Czechoslovakia, Hungary and Poland* (Cambridge, MA: Harvard University Press, 1969).
29. See Weinerman, *Social Medicine* and Tibor Valuch, Magyarország társadalomtörténete a XX. század második felében (Budapest: Osiris, 2001), 162.
30. Andras Sajó, 'The Role of Lawyers in Social Change: Hungary', *Case Western Reserve Journal of International Law*, vol. 25 (1993): 137–46.
31. For instance, in Hungary women made up only 16 per cent of the population with completed higher education in 1949; this increased to 40 per cent in 1980 and 45 per cent in 1990: Hungarian Central Statistical Office (HCSO), *Magyarország népessége és gazdasága: múlt és jelen* (Budapest: HCSO, 1996).
32. An interesting characteristic of socialist higher education was 'class quotas' (e.g. enforced in Hungary between the late 1940s and the early 1960s) designed to limit the entry of students from professional and other non-manual backgrounds to diminish their advantages, albeit with limited success: Eric Hanley and Matthew McKeever, 'The Persistence of Educational Inequalities in State-Socialist Hungary: Trajectory-Maintenance versus Counterselection', *Sociology of Education* vol. 70, no. 1 (1997): 1–18.
33. Riska, *Medical Careers*.
34. Mary Buckley, *Women and Ideology in the Soviet Union* (Ann Arbor: University of Michigan Press, 1989).
35. Lapidus, *Women in Soviet Society*, 173; István Polónyi and János Tímár, 'A népesség, a gazdasági aktivitás és a nemzetközi migráció távlatai Magyarországon 1950–2050', *Közgazdasági Szemle* vol. 49 (2002): 960–71.

36. Mandel, 'Soviet Women'.
37. Theodore P. Gerber and Michael Hout, 'Educational Stratification in Russia during the Soviet Period', *American Journal of Sociology* vol. 101, no. 3 (1995): 611–60.
38. Buckley, *Women and Ideology*.
39. Mandel, 'Soviet Women', 256. On the earlier Soviet period see also Kaminer, this volume.
40. HCSO, *Kisgyermekek napközbeni ellátása* (Budapest: HCSO, 2012): 3.
41. Lynne Haney, *Inventing the Needy: Gender and the Politics of Welfare in Hungary* (Berkeley, CA: University of California Press, 2002); Theodore P. Gerber and Olga Mayorova, 'Dynamic Gender Differences in a Post-Socialist Labour Market: Russia, 1991–1997', *Social Forces* vol. 84, no. 4 (2006): 2047–75.
42. Buckley, *Women and Ideology*; Einhorn, *Cinderella*.
43. Teela Jyrkinen-Pakkasvirta, 'Women's Work and [the] Threat of Unemployment in St. Petersburg', in Anna Rotkirch and Elina Haavio-Mannila (eds), *Women's Voices in Russia Today* (Aldershot: Dartmouth, 1996), 3–32.
44. See, for instance, Ferenc Kőszeg, speech in Hungarian Parliament, *Parlamenti Napló*, 10 February 1992, available at: www.parlament.hu/naplo34/174/1740036.html (accessed 14 February 2015).
45. Buckley, *Women and Ideology*; Harden, 'Gender and Work'; Fodor, *Working Difference*.
46. Mandel, 'Soviet Women', 262.
47. Ashwin (ed.), *Gender, State and Society*.
48. Fodor, *Working Difference*.
49. Einhorn, *Cinderella*.
50. Susan Gal and Gail Kligman, *The Politics of Gender after Socialism: a Comparative-Historical Essay* (Princeton, NJ: Princeton University Press, 2000); Harden, 'Gender and Work'.
51. Haney, *Inventing the Needy*.
52. Buckley, *Women and Ideology*; Mandel, 'Soviet Women'. See also Simić, this volume.
53. Fodor, *Working Difference*.
54. Navarro, *Social Security and Medicine*; Einhorn, *Cinderella*; Fodor, *Working Difference*.
55. Riska, *Medical Careers*, 38.
56. Mandel, 'Soviet Women', 270.
57. Donald A. Barr and Rudi Schmid, 'Medical Education in the Former Soviet Union', *Academic Medicine*, vol. 71, no. 2 (1996): 141–5; Harden, 'Gender and Work'; see also Hanley and McKeever, 'The Persistence of Educational Inequalities'.
58. Harden, 'Gender and Work'.
59. Barr and Schmid, 'Medical Education', 141.
60. Vicente Navarro, *Social Security and Medicine in the USSR: a Marxist Critique* (Lexington, MA: Lexington Books, 1977).
61. Riska, *Medical Careers*, 81.
62. HCSO, *Statisztikai Évkönyv 1970* (Budapest: HCSO, 1971), 437; Népjóléti Minisztérium [Ministry of Social Welfare], *Évkönyv 1990* (Budapest: Ministry of Social Welfare, 1991), 120.
63. Népjóléti Minisztérium, *Évkönyv 1990*, 120.
64. Weinerman, *Social Medicine*.
65. Mandel, 'Soviet Women', 270.
66. Huskey, *Russian Lawyers*; Miklós Szabó, 'A jogászképzés társadalmi funkciójáról-húsz év múlva', *Jogtörténeti Szemle*, Special Issue (2005): 27–32.
67. Robert G. Storey, 'U.S.S.R. People's Courts and Women Lawyers', *Women Law Journal*, no. 48 (1962): 21–9, 21; Erika Kispeter, 'Working Mothers: Career,

Motherhood and Transition in the Lives of Women Lawyers in Hungary' (MA thesis, Central European University, Budapest, 2006), 14.
68. Phoebe W. Brown, 'Russian Women Lawyers in Post-Soviet Russia', *Georgia State University Law Review* vol. 12, no. 2 (1996): 381–430.
69. Brown, 'Russian Women Lawyers'.
70. Brown, 'Russian Women Lawyers'.
71. Péter T. Nagy, 'A diplomások és az általuk betöltött foglalkozások', in Viktor Karádi and Péter T. Nagy (eds), *Iskolázás, értelmiség és tudomány a 19–20. századi Magyarországon* (Budapest: Wesley János Lelkészképző Főiskola, 2012), 163.
72. Szabó, 'A jogászképzés társadalmi funkciójáról', 28.
73. Valuch, Magyarország társadalomtörténete, 164.
74. Andrea Tóti, 'Mobilitásvizsgálat a Komárom-Esztergom megyei jogászság körében', *Jogtörténeti Szemle* no. 4 (2000), available at: http://jesz.ajk.elte.hu/toti4.html (accessed 12 February 2015).
75. Szabó, 'A jogászképzés társadalmi funkciójáról-húsz év múlva', 28
76. Tóti, 'Mobilitásvizsgálat'.
77. Fodor, *Working Difference*, 148.
78. See, e.g., Ashwin (ed.), *Gender, State and Society;* Sarah Ashwin (ed.), *Adapting to Russia's New Labour Market* (London: Routledge, 2006); Einhorn, *Cinderella*; Gal and Kligman, *Politics of Gender*; Gillian Pascall and Anna Kwak, *Gender Regimes in Transition in Central and Eastern Europe* (Bristol: Policy Press, 2005); Nanette Funk and Magda Mueller (eds), *Gender Politics and Post-Communism: Reflections from Eastern Europe and the Former Soviet Union* (New York: Routledge, 1993).
79. Sarah Ashwin and Elaine Bowers, 'Do Russian Women Want to Work?', in Mary Buckley (ed.), *Post-Soviet Women: from the Baltic to Central Asia* (Cambridge: Cambridge University Press, 1997), 21–37; Joanna Goven, 'Gender Politics in Hungary: Autonomy and Antifeminism', in Funk and Mueller (eds). *Gender Politics.*
80. Einhorn, *Cinderella*; Ashwin (ed.), *Gender, State and Society*; Funk and Mueller (eds) *Gender Politics.*
81. Ashwin and Bowers, 'Do Russian Women Want to Work?'; Éva Fodor, 'Gender in Transition: Unemployment in Hungary, Poland and Slovakia', *East European Politics and Societies* vol. 11, no. 3 (1997): 757–83.
82. Christy Glass and Éva Fodor, 'Public Maternalism Goes to Market: Recruitment, Hiring and Promotion in Postsocialist Hungary', *Gender and Society* vol. 25, no. 1 (2011): 5–26; Irina Kozina and Elena Zhidkova, 'Sex Segregation and Discrimination in the New Russian Labour Market', in Ashwin (ed.), *Adapting*, 57–86.
83. Ashwin (ed.), *Gender, State and Society*; Ashwin (ed.), *Adapting*; Glass and Fodor, 'Public Maternalism'.
84. HCSO, 'Nők és férfiak Magyarországon 2006' (Budapest: HCSO, 2007), 46.
85. See Harden, 'Gender and Work'; Riska, *Medical Careers*; Jeni Harden, '"Mother Russia" at Work: Gender Divisions in the Medical Profession', *European Journal of Women's Studies* vol. 8, no. 2 (2001): 181–99.
86. Glass and Fodor, 'Public Maternalism'.
87. Brown, 'Russian Women Lawyers', Fodor, 'Gender in Transition'.
88. Brown, 'Russian Women Lawyers'.
89. Szabó, 'A jogászképzés társadalmi funkciójáról', 28.
90. Kispeter, 'Working Mothers'.
91. National Office for the Judiciary, 'Az Országos Bírósági Hivatal elnökének 2013. évi beszámolója', available at: birosag.hu/sites/default/files/allomanyok/obh/elnoki-beszamolok/1_napirend.pdf (accessed 12 February 2015).

14

Transnational 'LGBT' Politics after the Cold War and Implications for Gender History

Catherine Baker

Alongside the contention over reproductive politics and gender equality in the public sphere that characterized the gender politics of eastern Europe and the former USSR throughout the post-Cold War period, by the turn of the millennium a novel object of struggle had also emerged: the complex of political claims over sexuality, gender identity and citizens' relationship to the state that was often known, simplistically, as LGBT rights. These movements operated in a transnational space in the sense that their networks spanned national borders and they often looked to European and global, as well as national, institutions and publics for support. At the same time, each country presented comparable yet distinct contexts for LGBT activism, complicating the analytical work of drawing conclusions across the whole region. LGBT political struggles did not proceed at the same pace or in the same order in every country, and what appeared to be 'advances' might later be reversed amid increasing state homophobia/biphobia/transphobia. LGBT politics and activism were as complex to contextualize as the women's movements of the past or present with which gender historians have consistently been concerned. The deeper understanding of sexual diversity and gender non-conformity that their work made possible meanwhile presents historians of earlier periods with an interpretive problem in its own right: how should historians approach sexualities or gender non-conformity?

The collapse of state socialism in eastern Europe and the former USSR had contradictory consequences for people whose sexualities did not correspond to heteronormative models of exclusive male/female relationships and/or who understood their gender differently to the gender they had been assigned at birth. On one hand, the so-called 'retraditionalization'[1] or 'repatriarchalization'[2] of gender regimes after state socialism enabled religious institutions to influence state policy and subjected people to new levels of homophobic and transphobic rhetoric.[3] On the other hand, greater freedoms of association and expression enabled liberation and advocacy movements to campaign for visibility and rights. After widespread political struggles over 'Pride marches' and state-registered partnerships, it could even be suggested that 'homosexuality ha[d] trumped', or at least joined, 'reproductive rights' – such a 1990s touchstone – as symbols of what social conservatism opposed.[4] The politics of sexualities and gender variance had become central to understanding gender, nationalism and post-socialism. Moreover, these politics were transnational, linked to post-Cold War dynamics of European political institutions and social movements. Risks of generalization about space, time and modernity nevertheless complicated the task of contextualizing this historical moment of struggle.[5]

During the 1990s and 2000s, politicians who hailed their states' progress towards EU accession criteria as a 'return to Europe' implied that eastern European nations were rejoining, after Soviet and Communist repression, a spatially and ideologically defined community of values that was 'Europe'.[6] Accession, for states that sought it, was a pragmatic and symbolic goal. In this same period, EU concepts of 'fundamental rights' were gradually (and contestedly) being extended to incorporate aspects of lesbian, gay, bisexual and transgender (LGBT) equality, meaning that accession would involve some level of compliance with EU expectations about LGBT rights (which had not been features in the pre-Communist Europe supposedly being 'returned' to).[7] For better or worse, 'LGBT rights' became symbols of 'Europeanization' across central and eastern Europe.[8] This framework even extended into states that did not seek EU membership, such as Russia, through membership of the Council of Europe and its European Court of Human Rights (ECHR). Meanwhile, activist movements too built solidarities across national borders.[9]

This topic, the most recent in the volume, presents similar problems of temporality (can historians say there has been inexorable progress towards equality?) and spatial comparison (how far does evidence set 'eastern Europe and the former USSR' apart as a region, especially in comparison to 'the West'?) that other historians of gender and sexuality in this region face. Robert Kulpa and Joanna Mizielińska, in particular, contend it would be mistaken to expect LGBT activism, or even LGBT identities, to have developed in eastern Europe and the ex-USSR following the same chronological stages as the US movements which have become the benchmark for 'Western' models of LGBT activism; in post-socialist Poland, argues Mizielińska, 'everything happened almost simultaneously [...] instead of a slow adoption of categories, names and ideas'. '[P]ostcolonial discourses on sexuality', she suggested, were more useful than anglocentric frameworks for understanding LGBT politics in eastern Europe.[10]

Indeed, even in the field of European history, historians are cautious in making claims about 'common European cultures of sexuality': as Matt Cook and Jennifer Evans recognize, sexual and gender identities should always be seen as 'deeply contextual in terms of both space and time'.[11] The very terminology one might use to write about people's identities and behaviour in the past is shaped, however far historians strive to overcome this, by the analytical categories of any writer's present.[12] Comparatively discussing different places' and moments' sexual and gender politics inherently risks inappropriate generalization. Yet transnational factors and inequalities still shape specific contexts of sexual and gender politics,[13] as seen when considering how far the collapse of state socialism might have led to new understandings of sexual and gender identity – and how these might affect the study of gender non-conformity as well as sexuality in the past.

'Sexual Citizenship' after State Socialism

The topics of struggle in this chapter, including marriage equality, public protest and gender recognition, all pertained to the relationship between individuals and the state. They thus fell within wider transformations of 'citizenship' (the state/individual relationship) after state socialism.[14] This led some scholars to term such struggles contestations of 'sexual citizenship', implying it was a new form of late 20th-century political belonging in the West.[15] Taking 'citizenship' as an object of study requires attentiveness to its specific meanings in a given place and time,[16] but the idea can still help gender historians to see what was at stake at moments when the state's institutionalized heteronormativity and cisnormativity – that is, the presumptions that it was 'normal' for everyone to be heterosexual and to have the same gender identity they were assigned at birth – were being challenged.

One 1990s transformation in sexual citizenship, potentially linked in part to Council of Europe norms, was the decriminalization of sodomy in countries where this was still a criminal offence. Ukraine decriminalized it in 1991; Estonia and Latvia in 1992; Lithuania and Russia in 1993 (60 years after Stalin had reversed the Bolsheviks' legalization of sodomy in Russia);[17] Belarus and Serbia in 1994; Albania and Moldova in 1995; Macedonia and Romania in 1996; Bosnia-Herzegovina in 1998–2001 (as different post-war Bosnian state entities resolved their criminal codes); Kyrgyzstan, Kazakhstan and Tajikistan in 1998; Georgia and Azerbaijan in 2000; and Armenia in 2003; while as of 2015 sex between men remained illegal in Turkmenistan and Uzbekistan. The Council of Europe requirement for member states to have legalized same-sex activity probably influenced these timescales.[18]

Elsewhere, decriminalization had occurred before 1989, including in Hungary and Czechoslovakia (both 1962), Bulgaria and East Germany (1968),[19] and Slovenia, Croatia and Montenegro (which, as the Yugoslav state increasingly decentralized, all chose to decriminalize it in 1977).[20] Poland had decriminalized it in 1932.[21] This did not mean attitudes towards sexual 'minorities' were automatically more friendly in those states. Communism's 'silencing of public discourse' about homosexuality had ongoing social effects beyond the force of law;[22] laws legalizing sexual practices could still contain discriminatory provisions (such as unequal ages of consent) that stopped people leading their private lives on equal terms with straight and cisgender citizens, as Judit Takács has already demonstrated in this volume; and legislation did not insulate people from powerful social institutions such as the media or the Church.[23] Rather, the divergences show that legislative decisions were outcomes of national-level politics, where transnational socio-political developments were one factor but not all-powerful.[24] As with decriminalization, so too with civil partnerships, marriage equality and trans people's gender recognition.

Movements in most post-socialist states lobbied governments to introduce civil partnerships for couples the state regarded as the same gender (potentially an intermediate step before marriage equality). Slovenia and the Czech Republic introduced them in 2006, and Hungary in 2010.[25] Croatia's first centre-left government since independence from Yugoslavia, in power 2000–3, gave cohabiting same-gender partners inheritance rights equal to cohabiting male/female couples' in 2003; facing Church opposition, however, it excluded parental rights to win the parliamentary vote.[26] A later Croatian left-wing coalition introduced civil partnerships (the Life Partnerships Act) in 2014, though parental rights still depended on a legal workaround not full adoption rights. Meanwhile, in 2013, a Church-led campaign against civil partnerships, invoking the supposed defence of 'the family', had been able – shortly after Croatia had joined the EU, yet 'without much noise from Brussels'[27] – to amend the constitution through a referendum to define marriage as between a man and a woman, restricting future Croatian governments from upgrading civil partnerships to marriage. Slovenia's United Left party, meanwhile, proposed an equal marriage bill from opposition in 2015 after a previous left-liberal coalition had tried to extend the Family Code's civil partnership rights in 2012;[28] yet the 2012 and 2015 initiatives both failed after a 'Civil Initiative for the Family and Children's Rights' forced referendums to be held.

Partnership equality struggles in Croatia and Slovenia were not identical, but their similarities – the referendum as the major site of resistance to parliamentary moves towards equality – revealed how contingent legislative change could be; whether a law would pass depended more on parliamentary coalition politics and pro/anti-reform public campaigns than any direct influence from European institutions. This contingency challenged notions of inevitable step-by-step change (the idea that progress would automatically flow from decriminalization, through civil partnerships, to equal marriage).[29] The European Parliament might have exerted 'symbolic importance' in its 2006 resolution calling on EU members to eliminate sexual orientation-based discrimination throughout society, but had no force to undo Polish, Latvian and Lithuanian constitutional amendments that had explicitly defined marriage as between a man and a woman to obstruct future equal marriage campaigns.[30] Likewise, while the ECHR ruled against Russia's bans on Moscow Pride marches in 2010, they were not reversed.[31]

During the EU enlargement period, partnership rights and other LGBT-related laws became legislative symbols with which campaigners, evaluating governments against supposed common standards, could map policy benchmarks across countries. This 'mapping' was literal in the International Lesbian, Gay, Bisexual, Trans and Intersex Association (ILGA) 'Rainbow Map', which used ILGA's index of pro-LGBT and discriminatory legislation to depict an East/West axis dividing Europe. Rainbow Maps from 2012 onwards ended up coloured as 'green on the West (for more rights) and red in the East (for fewer), while Central Europe is yellow (in between)'.[32] Previous maps kept all countries the same light-pink colour but their icons (including legal scales and red prohibition signs) created a similar divide.[33]

However, legislative indexes gave very limited accounts of political contestations over sexual orientation and gender variance, as Rahul Rao's essay on 'the locations of homophobia' observes for global sexuality politics.[34] Different countries' civil unions contained varying sets of rights, and if these changed later an index would not pick them up. Anti-discrimination laws did not guarantee they would actually be implemented, nor that authorities would respect individuals who reported discrimination or violence.[35] The images of LGBT people's social status created when laws or, as in Kosovo after 2008, whole constitutions were drafted to correspond to international human rights standards could thus be unrealistic.[36] Beyond simply comparing laws and policies, scholars also needed to trace the impact of reforms in everyday and intimate domains.[37]

Gender historians, with their awareness of how social institutions are reshaped when meanings of gender change, might therefore ask whether civil partnerships (where these were introduced in the 2000s) signalled any extra transformations in the gendered institution of the family beyond the post-socialist transformations of the 1990s – or whether non-heteronormative parents still viewed fathers' and mothers' roles heteronormatively (which sociologists in the Czech Republic, for instance, could just about begin to ask).[38] Meanwhile, activist debates over how far to prioritize marriage equality as a goal – when it did not address other structural inequalities and still limited state recognition to 'the couple form' of relationships and parenting – echoed in scholarship.[39] Political struggles for 'sexual citizenship' were an emerging area of study in east European and post-Soviet gender history. Far less often discussed, yet equally important to understanding the politics of sexualities and gender identity, were the political demands of people whose genders did not match those they had been assigned at birth.

Transgender Rights as a Political Demand

Compared to information about sexual orientation-related laws, even basic comparative information relating to transgender people and the state was collated less frequently in scholarship (especially for countries not involved in EU accession).[40] Single-country academic studies about trans people's legal status were also rare, though research from the Czech Republic, Poland and Hungary suggested questions that could be asked about other countries,[41] against the background of transgender studies' emergence as an academic field in North America.[42] Activist groups and international human rights organizations were, by the mid-2010s, more likely (though not guaranteed) to recognize gender variance alongside sexual identities and practices as a distinct subject of interest. Their reports, and the articles trans activists published online, usually offered more detailed evidence about trans experiences and trans people's relationship with the state.

Official 'gender recognition' procedures for people to change the gender marker on identity documents and change their name to match their gender nearly always, as Anna Kłonkowska shows for Poland, took narrow, essentialized and medicalized views of who constituted a 'true transsexual'.[43] These restrictions in gender recognition (just as widespread in most other countries, with a few exceptions including Ireland and Argentina) excluded people who were not heterosexual; who expressed their gender in ways that did not match conservative social norms; whose gender was not male or female; who wanted to have a *lack* of gender recognized; or who did not intend to undergo (or could not afford) the surgery and/or hormone treatment usually required before the state would legally recognize a trans person's gender.[44] Moreover, gaps between law and practice for transgender rights were even wider than for sexuality-related laws.[45]

Thus, gender recognition might ostensibly be allowed but without any official criteria for demanding it; it might have been made contingent on 'full' gender reassignment surgery (genital surgery) without the state making this treatment available; a precondition for it might be sterilization and/or divorce, interfering with trans people's reproductive and partnership rights; or having gender dysphoria diagnosed might involve such invasive psychiatric treatment that trans people preferred to avoid it altogether. The Russian trans activist Yana Sitnikova, for instance, suggested that trans people in Russia should not push for a centralized gender recognition system (Russian regional civil registries set gender recognition criteria themselves, and these varied widely) in case they received one as coercive as Ukraine's, involving compulsory psychiatric detention.[46] Polish trans campaigners, meanwhile, sought parliamentary reforms that would codify gender recognition and state that medical treatment was not required. Anna Grodzka, former president of the campaign group Trans-Fuzja, became a Polish MP in 2011 and proposed a Gender Accordance Act in 2012 that appeared likely to pass until, in 2015, President Andrzej Duda vetoed it and the parliament did not make necessary preparations for a re-vote.[47] Again, each country's activists faced specific circumstances, but obstacles to gender recognition were similar across the region and, importantly, around the world.[48]

Early-2000s 'LGBT'-based research rarely mentioned gender recognition and trans healthcare; a decade later, these often (though not always) did appear in 'LGBT' rights reports. By then, trans organizations such as Poland's Trans-Fuzja had just started to emerge in many countries,[49] and access to online information about trans healthcare, rights and identities enabled trans people to recognize themselves and others as part of a social collectivity while being able to stay anonymous. If the Internet had a 'transformative' effect on US trans activism,[50] this also held somewhat for eastern Europe and the ex-USSR[51] – Trans-Fuzja's Wiktor Dynarski wrote that the 'transgender movement in Poland would have had no chances in coming into being if it was not for the Internet';[52] the British writer Juliet Jacques, author of *Trans*, wrote of her surprise, during a visit to Kyrgyzstan, at being asked by the Bishkek Feminist Collective for her views about an online controversy over transphobia in the UK press[53] – but material access to digital communications technologies still (as elsewhere) restricted who could benefit from this medium. Identity labels themselves could quickly spread. Simultaneously, challenges to cissexism and transphobia in activism and social theory began persuading some (though not all) researchers and organizations to design explicitly trans-inclusive work. International institutions played a subsidiary role. In 2007, the Yogyakarta Principles (launched at the UN Human Rights Council but not officially adopted by the UN) established standards for applying international human rights law to 'sexual orientation' and 'gender identity'. Some states revised anti-discrimination laws (however illusory their protection) to cover gender identity, but Yogyakarta had more effect on advocacy organizations, which appeared more likely afterwards to include gender recognition and trans healthcare in reports. European courts, whose rulings arguably helped 'construct a European norm on LGBTI rights' between 1981 and the present,[54] also made limited contributions related to trans equality.

The ECHR heard fewer cases on gender identity than sexual orientation and did not consider states obliged to offer gender recognition until 1992 (in a ruling against France).[55] Even then, and even after Yogyakarta had affirmed gender recognition should not depend on medical procedures or on divorce, it allowed states to insist on genital surgery before granting gender recognition.[56] In 2007, the ECHR heard its only trans-related case involving an eastern European state (L. v. Lithuania), ruling against Lithuania over a legal loophole where the 2001 Civil Code mentioned changing gender markers in principle but the Law on Gender Reassignment had never been adopted.[57] The few Lithuanians who had obtained gender recognition had had to fund surgery abroad and also bring Lithuanian court cases against the Civil Registry Office, all beyond most Lithuanian trans people's financial means. The law had still not been implemented in 2013, when two Lithuanian non-governmental organizations (NGOs) submitted evidence to the Council of Europe suggesting that the Church had urged the government to ban gender reassignment altogether.[58] This moment in the history of European LGBT jurisprudence was far less visible in academic literature than European institutions' pronouncements on Pride parades, which became a symbolic focal point for transnational LGBT politics in the region.

'Pride' and the Politics of Visibility

In the 2000s and 2010s, Pride marches – a campaigning model originating in North America – were a frequent subject of public contestation over LGBT rights and visibility in east European capitals and other cities. These annual marches were a 'temporary but also highly visible and politicized' activist intervention into urban space.[59] While 21st-century Western activists often critiqued their own cities' Prides as depoliticized, commodified and liable to co-option by the state, this critique was less applicable where parades were at greater risk of being banned by municipal authorities, being attacked by far-right groups during or after the march, being subjected to heavy police protection that isolated marchers from everyday city space, being forced on security grounds into marginal urban areas with little symbolic significance, or being cancelled because the state was ostensibly incapable of securing them against far-right threats.[60] They could still be called political protests in such circumstances, especially if held after being refused permission.[61] By drawing on the march as an established campaign model, organizers knowingly inserted their cities and nations into 'the core imaginary of a global "politics of pride"'.[62]

Yet this globalized imaginary still combined with more specific political contexts. Some activists renamed them 'tolerance', 'equality' or 'dignity' marches to adapt them to their judgements of what would be most politically effective.[63] Zagreb Pride organizers after 2009 started linking their marches directly to current political struggles in Croatia through their annual slogans. The 2009 slogan 'Zagreb Pride for an Open City – Join In' aligned Pride with ongoing 'Right to the City' protests against privatization of public space in Zagreb.[64] 2010's slogan stated provocatively 'Croatia Can Swallow It!', while 2011 (the tenth anniversary) reverted to a more general 'The Future is Ours'. The 2012 slogan 'We Have Family! The Thousand-Year Croatian Dream' both hailed the planned Life Partnerships Act and ironized characteristic slogans of the first Croatian president, Franjo Tuđman, who had often spoken of reinstating Croatian sovereignty after 1,000 years and enabled strong Church influence in politics – a heteronormative nationalism that 'estranged gay men and lesbians from the national corpus'.[65] The 2013 slogan 'This is a Country for Us All', challenging the anti-equal marriage campaign, argued for full LGBT inclusion in the nation. The slogan for 2014 (with the Life Partnerships Act about to be passed) transferred a Western progress narrative to name the march 'On the Right Side of History', while in 2015 (when the party Tuđman founded had won a presidential election and appeared to be reviving 1990s nationalist discourse while threatening media freedom) Pride again took a more radical position on national politics by declaring itself 'Louder and Braver: Anti-Fascism Without Compromise!'. Pride was a transnational format but also a container where more localized contestation could occur.[66]

Pride marches, like civil partnerships, became another indicator of freedom and LGBT 'equality' for international activists and the EU. Both marches and rainbow flags acquired symbolic associations with imagined 'European', Western or cosmopolitan values, as public arguments about Pride frequently revealed.[67] In 2010, for instance, the Serbian government supported Belgrade Pride after cancelling it on 'security' grounds in 2009 (as it would in 2011–13); organizers and Serbian politicians both 'unambiguously linked the Parade to the European integration of Serbia'.[68] In 2008 when Belgrade hosted the Eurovision Song Contest, an annual televised music competition with a large gay fandom, Serbian television executives had spoken similarly.[69] The symbolic association between LGBT equality and 'Europe'/'the West' could be made not only to write one's city or nation into that imagined geopolitical–ideological space,[70] but also (as in the discourses of many national Churches or socially conservative governments) to distance one's nation from such an idea of 'Europe' altogether.[71] These narratives circulated transnationally, and movements learned from each other; yet this did not mean different countries' and cities' municipal, national and transnational politics should be aggregated into a binary between a homophobic East and a tolerant, liberal West with the implication that eastern Europe needed to 'catch up'.[72] Pride's symbolic goal of visibility, meanwhile, was tactically significant for activists but was not necessarily desired by all LGBT people at all times, nor did it automatically have emancipatory potential.

These arguments have been made both about public space and about cultural production. Francesca Stella's research in post-Soviet Moscow, for instance, suggested that what she defined as 'queer space' was 'neither territorially concentrated nor immediately visible' to straight Muscovites, even when people met in the open air; non-activist gays and lesbians sought privacy more than visibility.[73] Cinema could depict sexually diverse and gender-variant characters without necessarily altering any oppressive social practices and structures:[74] most countries' post-socialist cinema repertoires, for instance, contained films about LGBT characters made by cisgender, straight directors who used LGBT themes as 'metaphor[s] to address other cultural concerns'.[75] (Similar observations could be made about patterns of LGBT representation in many other countries' films.[76]) Fewer films were made depicting LGBT experiences for their own sake, and these were less likely to be distributed in mainstream national media (indeed might be more widely seen at foreign film festivals than at home).[77] Gender-non-conforming stars in some countries' popular music markets, such as Azis in Bulgaria or Verka Serduchka in Ukraine, presented complex embodied personas that were not easily reducible to universal identity terms nor a binary of visibility and repression.

Scholars rethinking LGBT visibility and activism in the region also grew increasingly critical of geopolitical generalizations. Why, argued Joanna Mizielińska, should scholars assume eastern European LGBT movements' history would follow a linear narrative based on how US activism had unfolded, when late socialist and post-socialist political and economic conditions presented different contexts of material situations, citizenship and gender politics?[78] Even Moscow's Pride marches (annually banned by Moscow's mayor, annually re-attempted by organizers), Stella suggested, maybe appealed more to international campaigners than to LGBT Muscovites outside the organizing group.[79] Researchers of sexuality and gender variance also needed to avoid the assumption that anglophone terms such as 'LGBT' or 'queer', which could connote specific approaches to activism, would always have those connotations when adopted in other languages.[80]

Nevertheless, the politics of sexuality and gender identity in multiple countries exhibited similar dynamics of contestation: over ideologies of gender, sexuality and nation; over religious institutions' power in society; over use and control of public space; over the state's power to regulate intimate behaviour and stratify access to rights associated with officially recognized relationships; and over the politics of representation and visibility (in activism, popular culture and everyday social life). They unfolded in a transnational setting influenced, but not determined, by European institutions and international campaign groups, and by cross-border solidarities built up between movements across and beyond Europe.[81] These transnational contexts helped account for the many geopolitically driven narratives that – especially around the time of the 2004 EU accessions,[82] and again in the mid-2010s – linked attitudes to LGBT equality (or the state policies treated as benchmarks for this) to the associated nation's imagined degree of 'European' belonging. As during the Cold War, but with different practices as referents, these perceptions frequently led to imagining a values-based division between 'East' and 'West'. As such, they fuelled yet another round of 'symbolic geographies' that constructed western against eastern Europe, or Europe against the Balkans, based on hierarchies of modernity, rationality and 'civilization'.[83]

LGBT (Geo)Politics after the Cold War

Post-Cold War geopolitical narratives about LGBT equality or repression reshaped these earlier 'symbolic geographies' to place sexual equality and (sometimes) recognition of transgender identities among the core components of European national identities and the identity of 'Europe' itself.[84] A temporal element of this spatial hierarchy implied that the East was 'lagging behind', or needed to 'catch up with', the West on LGBT rights; why, for instance, did European Parliament resolutions condemn homophobia in eastern Europe only? Intervening against these narratives, Robert Kulpa and Joanna Mizielińska's 2011 volume *De-Centring Western Sexualities* challenged scholars to think beyond frameworks that cast eastern Europe as a periphery to a more advanced western European metropole.[85] They also sought to contextualize the region globally through synthesizing post-socialist and postcolonial perspectives. Noting that 'cultural attitudes and legal provisions for lesbian and gay people are becoming important factors in creating and maintaining modern divisions of "Us" [...] and "Them"', they compared the construction of western/eastern European spaces on the axis of sexual citizenship with the parallel separation of an imagined West from Islam and/or sub-Saharan Africa[86] – a racialized hierarchy that critical scholars of sexual politics such as Jasbir Puar (whose term 'homonationalism' often denotes such hierarchies) had already pointed out.[87]

Scholars working in this vein emphasized that ex-state socialist countries should not be viewed as inherently more homophobic, biphobic or transphobic than 'the West'.[88] Instead, homophobia, biphobia and transphobia needed to be *explained*, by (as Hadley Renkin suggested) situating post-socialist LGBT politics within wider politics of post-socialist belonging and power, and by accounting for people's 'actual, on-the-ground activities' not just their symbolic locations.[89] Such explanations would also need to recognize that movements against, as well as for, LGBT equality were transnationally shaped. A 'transnational mobilization of the religious right', for instance, connected resistance to LGBT rights in Poland, France, Russia and elsewhere, and movements' tactics and symbols were often exchanged.[90]

Public discourses in western Europe and North America nevertheless sharpened, rather than complicated, the imagined East/West divide around LGBT politics when state homophobia and transphobia intensified in mid-2010s Russia. Between 2006 and 2011 a few Russian *oblasts*' authorities (in Ryazan, Arkhangelsk and Kostroma) had legislated against what they called the promotion of homosexuality to minors.[91] A St Petersburg politician, Vitaly Milonov, first got a similar law adopted by his city Duma in 2012, then took the campaign to federal level. Russia's federal Duma criminalized 'propaganda of sodomy, lesbianism, bisexualism and transgenderism amongst minors' in June 2013.[92] The move gained extra international attention because Russia was soon to host the Sochi Winter Olympics in February 2014, at a time when activists regularly accused states of using such 'mega-events' to distract from human rights violations.[93] The 'anti-homopropaganda' law reversed freedoms that had opened up in Russia in the early 1990s,[94] emphasizing again that (as Valerie Sperling noted) 'movement away from homophobia [and biphobia, and transphobia] and sexism should not be assumed to be teleological'.[95] It caught up activists such as Yelena Klimova, founder of an online support group for LGBT teenagers, who was fined 50,000 roubles in July 2015,[96] and exacerbated the impunity that skinheads believed they enjoyed when committing homophobic/biphobic/transphobic attacks. Meanwhile, it expressed the wider gender politics of Putin's narrative of Russian national identity.

Putin's discourse that a strong Russian state was necessary to protect the nation's traditions, morals and children against a perceived moral threat from the West had been anticipated by city-level politicians such as Yuri Luzhkov, the mayor of Moscow who described his opposition to Pride marches in similar terms (his successor Sergei Sobianin issued a 100-year ban on Moscow Pride in 2012),[97] or Milonov, who called on Russian television to boycott Eurovision in 2014 when Austria's representative – the eventual winner – was a bearded drag queen, Conchita Wurst. It also echoed the conspiracy theories of the 1990s sexologist Dilya Enikeeva, who had presented homosexuality as alien to Russian culture and posited a secret gay plot within Russian media to use 'propaganda' to gain sexual access to minors.[98] Simultaneously, it sat among other policies that gendered Putin's state as a strong, masculine protector of the Russian ethno-cultural nation, including his warning that Russia would face demographic decline unless marriage and fertility increased; his own public image emphasizing physical strength and endurance; the imprisonment of members of the feminist punk art collective Pussy Riot after their 2012 protest in Moscow's Cathedral of Christ the Saviour; the repression of NGOs through the so-called 'foreign agents' law, affecting LGBT groups and others; and, following the 2014 Maidan revolution in Ukraine, Russia's annexation of Crimea and support for eastern Ukrainian Russian-speaking separatists.[99] Research suggested that LGBT people in Russia recognized the law's political motivations but, unsurprisingly, were still psychologically harmed by it.[100] The Russian legislation also created a model that conservatives in other countries, including Kazakhstan, Belarus, Lithuania and Moldova, could use in advocating similar bans.

The scholars whose work set the research agenda on post-Soviet sexualities had mostly conducted fieldwork before these developments, though some could acknowledge them in their books' conclusions.[101] Instead, the main academic debates on this topic concerned how to historicize and globally situate post-Soviet sexual identities at a time when freedom of sexual and gender expression had seemed to be improving. Laurie Essig, Brian James Baer and Francesca Stella, writing between 1999 and 2015, all interpreted these questions differently. Essig, seeking 'queerness in the public sphere', was surprised to find that sexuality had not flourished as 'a politically organizing identity', and ended up suggesting sexualities in Russia were inherently more fluid than US sexualities.[102] Baer considered Essig had overemphasized the public sphere's importance to sexual identity and that she tried too hard to fit her observations into Judith Butler's theory of gender performativity.[103] Stella, following Kułpa/ Mizielińska, aimed to avoid 'polarised essentialist notions of "western" and "Russian" sexualities'; she focused on lesbians' everyday strategies of disclosure and identity management, rather than looking specifically for public 'comings-out'.[104] Each scholar explained their interpretations with reference to new turns in queer and feminist theory, showing how evolving theoretical frameworks could help form new research questions. Another reconfiguration of possibilities for studying sexualities and gender variance, in the past as well as the present, appeared to emerge from the confluence of transgender activism and scholarship, though again with caveats over whether theoretical models based on one society's sexual/gender histories could be exported elsewhere.

Transgender Scholarship and Gender History

The vocabulary of 'transgender', 'transsexual' or 'trans' identities in eastern Europe and the ex-USSR, and the development of activism around them in the 2000s, was part of the globalization of these terms beyond North America, where they had originated. In the meantime, gay and lesbian groups adopting the Western 'LGBT' acronym as a label arguably popularized trans terminology before trans people in the same countries had even started using it.[105] Yet transgender *histories* do not commence with the declaration of transgender *identities*; earlier histories of gender variance can also be told. Indeed, some may appear (however fleetingly) from time to time in comparative gender history surveys, such as the 'sworn virgins' tradition in and around Albania and Montenegro (women who took on masculine identities and dress in place of a male heir),[106] or the life of Sándor Vay, a Hungarian youth whose case history became one of the first (though much-pathologized) descriptions of gender variance in late 19th-century European sexology.[107] This is not a matter of retrospectively projecting the label of 'transgender' to accommodate past individuals into present categories; rather, it is a matter of incorporating transgender-inclusive understandings of gender and embodiment, and trans scholars' perspectives, into historians' questions about non-normative sexualities and gender variance in the past.

In a 2006 anthology seeking to establish transgender studies as a field, Susan Stryker and Stephen Whittle (themselves both trans academics) suggested such perspectives could, and in their view should, broaden how cis scholars conceptualized gender.[108] Firstly, trans scholarship warned against extending ideas of the social construction of gender so far that they became detached from evidence about trans people's own embodied experiences.[109] Secondly, it argued that authority to produce knowledge about gender variance should not lie with clinicians who had pathologized it as a mental illness or ethnographers who had exoticized it when observed in non-Western cultures;[110] instead, as Dean Spade wrote, trans people should be 'subjects of knowledge rather than case studies', with what Talia Mae Bettcher termed 'first-person authority' over their own genders.[111] This reservation is particularly important when much historical evidence about gender variance derives from people's interactions with medical and psychiatric systems. Trans scholars emphasized, moreover, that knowledge about gender variance should be applied in fighting structures that marginalized trans people rather than just used for building social theory.[112] Just as significant for gender history, meanwhile, was trans scholars' aim to 'challenge the unifying potential of the category "woman"', an intervention that deserves considering in more depth.[113]

Evelyn Brooks Higginbotham, Joan Scott and gender historians following their lead have used lines of race, class and other categories to break down an 'essentialized common identity of women' – as Susan Gal and Gail Kligman, among other scholars, do in east European gender studies. Yet even then, gender historians may well think of (in Scott's words) 'the similarity of [women's] sexual organs' as binding the category together.[114] Enquiries about 'women' as a category more rarely extend to women who were born with *dis*similar organs to the cisgender norm but whom evidence suggests also experienced their gender as female; while lesbian histories have often represented 'cross-dressers' assigned a female gender at birth as lesbians, even when there is strong evidence they sought to live as men or described their gender in non-binary ways.[115] Seeking as full an account as possible of what Stryker termed 'the embodied experience of the speaking subject',[116] while avoiding singling out gender-non-conforming people as uniquely subject to the 'gendering processes' of their historical contexts,[117] gender historians could become better equipped than ever before to account for the complexity of gender variance and its relationships to sexuality. Historians of Soviet Russian gender and sexuality, for instance, have already shown how Soviet psychiatrists and sexologists linked homosexuality, 'hermaphroditism' and gender-variant self-presentation within Soviet concepts of gender.[118] Yet the most available literature on gender variance when they were writing was precisely the work that transgender scholars have critiqued as limited or even actively hostile,[119] and this restricted what questions they could ask.

When Lynne Attwood was writing on Soviet gender roles in 1990, for instance, the literature on 'transsexualism' she could refer to in her endocrinology chapter included work by the radical feminist Janice Raymond and the sexologist John Money.[120] Raymond's characterization of trans women as deviant men who posed threats to cis women (a belief which Attwood did not share) was already being rebutted by trans women, including Carol Riddell and Sandy Stone;[121] Money's view that intersex children's gender identity would shift depending on which form of genital surgery he conducted was similarly being challenged, by intersex activists including Cheryl Chase.[122] The shift of analytical lens in these critiques put the individual, not the psychiatrist, at the centre of determining gender – while providing just as scathing a critique of clinicians' attempts to maintain binary gender stereotypes through medicalizing gender non-conformity.[123] Joanne Meyerowitz's history of gender reassignment and transgender identities in the 1930s–80s USA would similarly try to centre the agency of the people who had sought healthcare and recognition, and to consider what language people in any given moment used to describe themselves.[124]

To what extent, however, is this aim possible when historians can only perceive an individual through records kept and made by clinicians and courts? Dan Healey's study of sexual and gender dissent in revolutionary Russia faced this problem when commenting on cases including that of Evgeniia Fedorovna M./Evgenii Fedorovich M., who, presenting as male, had joined the revolutionary Cheka, been able to obtain male identity documents, and married a woman. M. came to the authorities' attention after repeated drunk-and-disorderly arrests and was sent for psychiatric assessment. M.'s psychiatric report included extracts from an autobiographical account subtitled 'the Brief Confession of a Person of the Intermediate Sex, a Masculine Pseudo-Hermaphrodite'. M. did not express a wish for surgery, in contrast to another person Healey describes as 'the 23-year-old woman who in 1923 told Dr Izrael Gel'man, "I want to be a man. I impatiently await scientific discoveries of castration and grafting of male organs (glands)."'[125] Since most languages implicate historians in determining subjects' genders as they write, transgender scholarship poses an epistemological challenge here: where there is evidence of incongruence, variance or dissent, how do we know the gender of our historical subjects? At the very least, the bases of claims to know and write our subjects' genders need to be clear.

Recent studies have already started recognizing the absence of transgender perspectives in existing literature on gender in eastern Europe and the ex-USSR,[126] and for the present day one is more likely to read about violations of trans people's human rights than how they negotiate the structural conditions they face.[127] Future gender historians might seek to account for why people assigned female at birth seem more prominent in the contemporary history of gender non-conformity than people assigned male at birth when for most regions it is the reverse;[128] to broaden understandings of reproductive justice to include the procedures that many trans people seeking gender recognition had to confront; or, linking gender history with the history of medicine and psychiatry, to contextualize trans people's pursuit of recognition and therapy as in another setting Joanne Meyerowitz has done for the 20th-century USA.[129] Yet transgender scholarship and activism would urge historians also to recognize that 'visibility' for many trans or indeed non-heterosexual people is not an intrinsic goal; to design and apply their research in ways that fight the intersecting forms of discrimination and violence that gender-non-conforming people face; and to centre trans people as experts, inside and outside the academy, on their own lives.

Conclusion

Asking why the politics of sexuality and gender variance in eastern Europe and the ex-USSR became a transnational issue after the collapse of state socialism and the end of the Cold War requires an account of 'Europeanization' processes since the 1990s and of how 'LGBT politics' themselves became a geopoliticized symbol in international affairs. It also raises questions about how historians should understand identities and temporalities: for instance, if historians of sexuality in the West had linked the 'production' or 'invention' of homosexual identities to the social transformations of industrial capitalism and the place of medical knowledge in the late modern state's exercise of power,[130] would sexual orientation-based personal or political identities similarly be seen to emerge in post-socialist eastern Europe and to become bases for political 'liberation' movements there – or would the public disavowal of homosexuality under state socialism mean that the post-state socialist region would retain fundamentally different models of sexual and gender variance? If this was an open question in the early 1990s, the contours of an answer were becoming more apparent two decades later. Meanwhile, new understandings of sexual and gender non-conformity created further research agendas for studying sexuality and, especially, gender variance in the past. The emergence of new identities and theorizations of power through LGB, queer and trans movements was continuing to create new research questions and interpretive frameworks, in a dynamic that has shaped the history of gender and sexuality since its inception.

Yet these were predominantly interpretive and theoretical models from North America, and researchers from the region had to make their arguments intelligible to anglophone centres of knowledge production in order to be able to influence their wider discipline. As Kułpa and Mizielińska's anti-universalizing intervention in sexuality studies argued, North America and western Europe were inappropriate yardsticks for measuring the region's histories of sexual and gender non-conformity. The politics of translation perpetuated intellectual asymmetry, with works such as Krzysztof Tomasik's history of sexual minorities in state socialist Poland or Jelisaveta Blagojević and Olga Dimitrijević's edited volume on gay and lesbian history in Serbia still untranslated and inaccessible to gender historians who did not speak Polish or Serbian.[131] The challenge for scholars of these topics was how places and people that had contingently, and problematically, been aggregated as an analytical region could be integrated into a globalized history of sexual and gender politics – one that would, as Inderpal Grewal and Caren Kaplan argued, centre 'power structures, asymmetries, and inequalities' in explaining how people became political subjects and struggled for agency over their intimate, embodied lives.[132]

Kułpa and Mizielińska's objective of, as their book title read, *De-Centring Western Sexualities* echoed studies grounded in Africa, the Middle East and Asia that have also decentred the West as a model for global sexual politics, and that have criticized the binary lens of 'equality versus homophobia, backwardness versus progress', which Western activists, scholars and today even politicians project on to the globe. Rahul Rao, for instance, makes especially valuable observations for gender historians in tracing 'unmistakeable continuities' between contemporary LGBT politics and the 'prior debates over the Woman Question' in which early 20th-century imperial feminisms were implicated;[133] in eastern Europe or the ex-USSR, what kinds of continuities between post-socialist LGBT politics and previous political projects might historians trace?

Transnational LGBT politics after the Cold War demonstrated, like struggles over reproductive rights, that the fall of state socialism did not automatically bring about bodily autonomy and full intimate 'citizenship' for people marginalized under post-socialist gender regimes. Indeed, patriarchal and religious forms of nationalism replaced the public silence (and covert state surveillance) of sexual and gender 'minorities' under state socialism with public opposition and sometimes open violence. These struggles, which continued as this volume was being written, exemplified the role that notions of nation and modernity continued to have at the beginning of the 21st century in shaping gender regimes. A hundred years after Czech maternalists counselled mothers on preserving the health of the nation, British and Yugoslav lovers created new identities around novel forms of creative and gendered expression, or Communists inscribed new masculinities and femininities into the public culture of the early USSR, the course of gender history continued to be played out where ideologies of state and nation met people's most intimate lives, selves and desires.

Notes

1. Gail Kligman, 'The Politics of Reproduction in Ceauşescu's Romania: a Case Study in Political Culture', *East European Politics and Societies* vol. 6, no. 3 (1992): 400.
2. Mitja Velikonja, 'Lost in Transition: Nostalgia for Socialism in Post-Socialist Countries', *East European Politics and Societies* vol. 23, no. 4 (2009): 537. See also Zaharijević, this volume; Select Bibliography, this volume.
3. On post-socialist gender politics, see Susan Gal and Gail Kligman, *The Politics of Gender after Socialism: a Comparative-Historical Essay* (Princeton, NJ: Princeton University Press, 2000); Susan Gal and Gail Kligman (eds), *Reproducing Gender: Politics, Publics, and Everyday Life After Socialism* (Princeton, NJ: Princeton University Press, 2000); Barbara Einhorn, *Citizenship in an Enlarging Europe: from Dream to Awakening*, 2nd ed. (Basingstoke: Palgrave Macmillan, 2010).
4. Agnieszka Graff, 'We Are Not (All) Homophobes: a Report from Poland', *Feminist Studies* vol. 32, no. 2 (2006): 445.
5. See Robert Kulpa and Joanna Mizielińska (eds), *De-Centring Western Sexualities: Central and Eastern European Perspectives* (Farnham: Ashgate, 2011); compare Inderpal Grewal and Caren Kaplan, 'Theorizing Transnational Studies of Sexuality', *GLQ* vol. 7, no. 4 (2001): 663–79.
6. Milada Anna Vachudová and Tim Snyder, 'Are Transitions Transitory?: Two Types of Political Change in Eastern Europe since 1989', *East European Politics and Societies* vol. 11, no. 1 (1997): 1; Nicole Lindstrom, 'Between Europe and the Balkans: Mapping Slovenia and Croatia's "Return to Europe" in the 1990s', *Dialectical Anthropology* vol. 27, no. 3–4 (2003): 313–29; Ksenija Vidmar-Horvat and Gerard Delanty, 'Mitteleuropa and the European Heritage', *European Journal of Social Theory* vol. 11, no. 2 (2008): 209.
7. See Joke Swiebel, 'Lesbian, Gay, Bisexual and Transgender Human Rights: the Search for an International Strategy', *Contemporary Politics* vol. 15, no. 1 (2009): 19–35.
8. Philipp M. Ayoub and David Paternotte (eds), *LGBT Activism and the Making of Europe: a Rainbow Europe?* (Basingstoke: Palgrave Macmillan, 2014); Markus Thiel, 'Transversal and Particularistic Politics in the European Union's Antidiscrimination Policy: LGBT Politics under Neoliberalism', in Manuela Lavinas Picq and Markus Thiel (eds), *Sexualities in World Politics: How LGBTQ Claims Shape International Relations* (London: Routledge, 2015), 75–91. See also (published after this chapter was written) Bojan Bilić (ed.), *LGBT Activism and Europeanisation in the (Post-) Yugoslav Space: On the Rainbow Way to Europe* (London: Palgrave Macmillan, 2016); Bojan Bilić and Sanja Kajinić (eds), *Intersectionality and LGBT Activist Politics: Multiple Others in Serbia and Croatia* (London: Palgrave Macmillan, 2016).
9. Jon Binnie and Christian Klesse, 'The Politics of Age, Temporality and Intergenerationality in Transnational Lesbian, Gay, Bisexual, Transgender and Queer Activist Networks', *Sociology* vol. 47, no. 3 (2013): 580–95.
10. Joanna Mizielińska, 'Travelling Ideas, Travelling Times: on the Temporalities of LGBT and Queer Politics in Poland and the "West"', in Robert Kulpa and Joanna Mizielińska (eds), *De-Centring Western Sexualities: Central and Eastern European Perspectives* (Farnham: Ashgate, 2011), 92.
11. Matt Cook and Jennifer V. Evans, 'Introduction', in Matt Cook and Jennifer V. Evans (eds), *Queer Cities, Queer Cultures: Europe since 1945* (London: Bloomsbury Academic, 2014), 1.

12. Grewal and Kaplan, 'Theorizing Transnational Studies of Sexuality', 671.
13. See, e.g., Jon Binnie, *The Globalization of Sexuality* (London: Sage, 2004); Robert M. Buffington, Eithne Lubhéid and Donna J. Guy (eds), *A Global History of Sexuality: the Modern Era* (Chichester: Wiley, 2014).
14. Einhorn, *Citizenship in an Enlarging Europe*, 110–12.
15. Diane Richardson, 'Sexuality and Citizenship', *Sociology* vol. 32, no. 1 (1998), 83–100; Jeffrey Weeks, 'The Sexual Citizen', *Theory, Culture and Society* vol. 15, no. 3–4 (1998), 35–52; David Bell and Jon Binnie, *The Sexual Citizen: Queer Politics and Beyond* (Cambridge: Polity, 2000).
16. Kathleen Canning and Sonya O. Rose, 'Gender, Citizenship and Subjectivity: Some Historical and Theoretical Considerations', *Gender and History* vol. 13, no. 3 (2001), 427–43; Francesca Stella, *Lesbian Lives in Post-Soviet Russia: Post/Socialism and Gendered Sexualities* (Basingstoke: Palgrave Macmillan, 2015), 27.
17. Laurie Essig, *Queer in Russia: a Story of Sex, Self, and the Other* (Durham, NC: Duke University Press, 1999), 13–14; Dan Healey, *Homosexual Desire in Revolutionary Russia: the Regulation of Sexual and Gender Dissent* (Chicago, IL: University of Chicago Press, 2001), 183–9.
18. Achim Hildebrandt, 'Routes to Decriminalization: a Comparative Analysis of the Legalization of Same-Sex Sexual Acts', *Sexualities* vol. 17, no. 1–2 (2014): 240–5.
19. Sasha Roseneil, Isabel Crowhurst, Tone Hellesund, Ana Cristina Santos and Mariya Stoilova, 'Changing Landscapes of Heteronormativity: the Regulation and Normalization of Same-Sex Sexualities in Europe', *Social Politics* vol. 20, no. 2 (2013): 176.
20. Roman Kuhar, 'Ljubljana: the Tales from the Queer Margins of the City', in Matt Cook and Jennifer V. Evans (eds), *Queer Cities, Queer Cultures: Europe since 1945* (London: Bloomsbury Academic, 2014), 138.
21. Łukasz Szulc, 'Queer in Poland: Under Construction', in Lisa Downing and Robert Gillett (eds), *Queer in Europe* (Farnham: Ashgate, 2011), 160.
22. Brian James Baer, *Other Russias: Homosexuality and the Crisis of Post-Soviet Identity* (Basingstoke: Palgrave Macmillan, 2009), 43. See also Nárcisz Fejes and Andrea P. Balogh (eds), *Queer Visibility in Post-Socialist Cultures* (Bristol: Intellect, 2013).
23. Roseneil et al., 'Changing Landscapes', 176; Hildebrandt, 'Routes', 232; Dean Vuletić, 'Out of the Homeland: the Croatian Right and Gay Rights', *Southeastern Europe* vol. 37 (2013): 40–1.
24. See Takács, this volume.
25. Kelly Kolmann, 'Deploying Europe: the Creation of Discursive Imperatives for Same-Sex Unions', in Ayoub and Paternotte (eds), *LGBT Activism*, 98. The Slovenian partnership law was passed in 2005 and implemented in 2006.
26. Katja Kahlina, 'Local Histories, European LGBT Designs: Sexual Citizenship, Nationalism, and "Europeanisation" in Post-Yugoslav Croatia and Serbia', *Women's Studies International Forum* vol. 49 (2015): 76.
27. Jelena Subotić, 'Out of Eastern Europe: Legacies of Violence and the Challenge of Multiple Transitions', *East European Politics and Societies* vol. 29, no. 2 (2015): 413.
28. Roman Kuhar and Alenka Švab, 'The Only Gay in the Village? Everyday Life of Gays and Lesbians in Rural Slovenia', *Journal of Homosexuality* vol. 61, no. 8 (2014): 1096–7.
29. Adam Bodnar and Anna Śledzińska-Simon, 'Between Recognition and Homophobia: Same-Sex Couples in Eastern Europe', in Daniele Gallo, Luca Paladini and Pietro Pustorino (eds), *Same-Sex Couples Before National, Supranational and International Jurisdictions* (Berlin: Springer, 2014), 211–47.
30. Mark Walters, 'Sexual Orientation Discrimination in the European Union: the Framework Directive and the Continuing Influence of the European Parliament',

International Journal of Discrimination and the Law vol. 8, no. 4 (2007): 280–1. See also Nicole Butterfield, 'Sexual Rights as a Tool for Mapping Europe: Discourses of Human Rights and European Identity in Activists' Struggles in Croatia', in Fejes and Balogh (eds), *Queer Visibility*, 13–33.

31. Francesca Stella, 'Queer Space, Pride, and Shame in Moscow', *Slavic Review* vol. 72, no. 3 (2013), 478.

32. Kevin Moss, 'Split Europe: Homonationalism and Homophobia in Croatia', in Ayoub and Paternotte (eds), *LGBT Activism in Europe*, 215.

33. The first ILGA Rainbow Map, in 2009, covered laws about 'lesbian, gay and bisexual people' only (not trans or intersex): 'Rainbow Europe: Legal Situation for Lesbian, Gay and Bisexual People in Europe', ILGA Europe, July 2009, available at: www.ilga-europe.org/sites/default/files/Attachments/europe_map_a_2009.jpg (accessed 27 July 2015). In 2012 the 'Rainbow Index' was, importantly, extended to cover trans and intersex matters, with separate sexual orientation-related and gender identity-related subheadings in most sections: 'ILGA-Europe Rainbow Index, May 2012', ILGA Europe, May 2012, available at: www.ilga-europe.org/sites/default/files/Attachments/ilga-europe_rainbow_index_side_b.pdf (accessed 27 July 2015).

34. Rahul Rao, 'The Locations of Homophobia', *London Review of International Law* vol. 2, no. 2 (2014): 169–71.

35. Jelisaveta Blagojević, 'Between Walls: Provincialisms, Human Rights, Sexualities and Serbian Public Discourses on EU Integration', in Kulpa and Mizielińska (eds), *De-Centring Western Sexualities*, 30; Roseneil et al., 'Changing Landscapes', 181.

36. Agathe Fauchier, 'Kosovo: What Does the Future Hold for LGBT People?', *Forced Migration Review* vol. 42 (2013): 36.

37. See Joan Wallach Scott, *Gender and the Politics of History* (New York: Columbia University Press, 1988), 43–6.

38. Compare Kateřina Nedbálková, 'Rendering Gender in Lesbian Families: a Czech Case', in Kulpa and Mizielińska (eds), *De-Centring Western Sexualities*, 131–48; Simona Fojtová, 'Czech Lesbian Activism: Gay and Lesbian Parental Rights as a Challenge to Patriarchal Marriage', *Journal of Lesbian Studies* vol. 15, no. 3 (2011): 356–83.

39. Roseneil et al., 'Changing Landscapes', 187–8.

40. For the post-2007 EU, see, e.g., Stephen Whittle, Lewis Turner, Ryan Combs and Stephenne Rhodes, *Transgender EuroStudy: Legal Survey and Focus on the Transgender Experience of Health Care* (Brussels: ILGA-Europe and Berlin: Transgender Europe, 2008), 22–3, available at: tgeu.org/wp-content/uploads/2009/11/transgender_web.pdf (accessed 30 July 2015); Cristina Castagnoli, 'Transgender Persons' Rights in the EU Member States', European Parliament Directorate General for Internal Policies, Policy Department C: Citizens' Rights and Constitutional Affairs (PE 425.621), June 2010, 13–28, available at: www.lgbt-ep.eu/wp-content/uploads/2010/07/NOTE-20100601-PE425.621-Transgender-Persons-Rights-in-the-EU-Member-States.pdf (accessed 30 July 2015); European Union Agency for Fundamental Rights, *Being Trans in the European Union: Comparative Analysis of EU LGBT Survey Data* (Luxembourg: Publications Office of the European Union, 2014), available at: fra.europa.eu/sites/default/files/fra-2014-being-trans-eu-comparative_en.pdf (accessed 13 October 2015).

41. Bence Solymár and Judit Takács, 'Wrong Bodies and Real Selves: Transsexual People in the Hungarian Social and Health Care System', in Roman Kuhar and Judit Takács (eds), *Beyond the Pink Curtain: Everyday Life of LGBT People in Eastern Europe* (Ljubljana: Mirovni institut, 2007), 141–68; Barbara Havelková, 'The Legal Status

of Transsexual and Transgender Persons in the Czech Republic', in Jens M. Scherpe (ed.), *The Legal Status of Transsexual and Transgender Persons* (Antwerp: Intersentia, 2015), 125–46; Anna M. Kłonkowska, 'Making Transgender Count in Poland: Disciplined Individuals and Circumscribed Populations', *TSQ: Transgender Studies Quarterly* vol. 2, no. 1 (2015): 123–35.

42. See, e.g., Susan Stryker and Stephen Whittle (eds), *The Transgender Studies Reader* (London: Routledge, 2006); Julia Serano, *Whipping Girl: a Transsexual Woman on Sexism and the Scapegoating of Femininity* (Berkeley, CA: Seal Press, 2007); Susan Stryker, *Transgender History* (Berkeley, CA: Seal Press, 2008); Sally Hines and Tam Sanger (eds), *Transgender Identities: Towards a Social Analysis of Gender Diversity* (London: Routledge, 2010).

43. Kłonkowska, 'Making Transgender Count', 126.

44. See Talia Mae Bettcher, 'Trapped in the Wrong Theory: Rethinking Trans Oppression and Resistance', *Signs* vol. 39, no. 2 (2014): 401–3.

45. E.g. Havelková, 'Legal Status', 125–6.

46. Yana Sitnikova, 'Transgender Activism in Russia', *Freedom Without Wings*, 28 January 2014, available at: www.freedomrequireswings.com/2014/01/report-transgender-activism-in-russia.html (accessed 30 July 2015). See also Nadzeya Husakouskaya, 'The Sex Change Commission in Ukraine', *openDemocracy*, 22 October 2014, available at: www.opendemocracy.net/od-russia/nadzeya-husakous-kaya/sex-change-commission-in-ukraine (accessed 30 July 2015). In Kazakhstan, similarly, a nominally granted 'right to sex change' in 2009 actually added 'increasingly coercive and humiliating procedures': Kyle Knight, *'That's When I Realized I Was Nobody': a Climate of Fear for LGBT People in Kazakhstan* (New York: Human Rights Watch, 2015), 15–16, available at: www.hrw.org/sites/default/files/report_pdf/kazakhstan07154_up.pdf (accessed 30 July 2015).

47. Trans-Fuzja, 'Presidential Veto Upheld: Polish Parliament Did Not Vote on the Gender Accordance Act', *Trans-Fuzja*, 9 October 2015, available at: transfuzja.org/en/artykuly/press_releases/presidential_veto_upheld_polish_parliament_did_not_vote_on_the_gender.htm (accessed 13 October 2015). Grodzka lost her seat in the November 2015 elections.

48. Whittle et al., *Transgender EuroStudy*.

49. Joanna Mizielińska and Robert Kulpa, '"Contemporary Peripheries": Queer Studies, Circulation of Knowledge and East/West Divide', in Kulpa and Mizielińska (eds), *De-Centring Western Sexualities*, 14.

50. Eve Shapiro, '"Trans"cending Barriers: Transgender Organizing on the Internet', *Journal of Gay and Lesbian Social Services* vol. 16, no. 3–4 (2003): 166.

51. See Solymár and Takács, 'Wrong Bodies, Real Selves', 149; Phillip M. Ayoub and Olga Brzezińska, 'Caught in a Web?: the Internet and Deterritorialization of LGBT Activism', in David Paternotte and Manon Tremblay (eds), *The Ashgate Research Companion to Lesbian and Gay Activism* (Farnham: Ashgate, 2015), 229–30.

52. Wiktor Dynarski, 'The History of Transgender Activism in Poland' (2009), available at: http://learningtrans.files.wordpress.com/2011/03/the-history-of-transgender-activism-in-poland-wiktor-dynarski-04-2009.pdf (accessed 20 October 2015). Alicja Kowalska, 'Polish Queer Lesbianism: Sexual Identity Without a Lesbian Community', *Journal of Lesbian Studies* vol. 15, no. 3 (2011): 324–36, argues the Internet similarly catalysed lesbian identity in Poland.

53. Juliet Jacques, *Trans: a Memoir* (London: Verso, 2015), 298–9.

54. Anna van der Vleuten, 'Transnational LGBTI Activism and the European Courts: Constructing the Idea of Europe', in Ayoub and Paternotte (eds), *LGBT Activism*, 120.

55. Van der Vleuten, 'Transnational LGBTI Activism', 124.
56. Damian A. Gonzalez-Salzberg, 'The Accepted Transsexual and the Absent Transgender: a Queer Reading of the Regulation of Sex/Gender by the European Court of Human Rights', *American University International Law Review* vol. 29, no. 4 (2014): 817; Amets Suess, Karine Espiniera and Pau Crego Walters, 'Depathologization', *TSQ: Transgender Studies Quarterly* vol. 1, no. 1–2 (2015): 74.
57. Gonzalez-Salzberg, 'The Accepted Transsexual', 817–18.
58. Vladimir Simonko (Lithuanian Gay League) to Genevieve Mayer, 10 December 2013, Committee of Ministers Archive, DH–DD(2014)120E, 24 January 2014, available at: wcd.coe.int/com.instranet.InstraServlet?command=com.instranet.CmdBlobGet&InstranetImage=2441923&SecMode=1&DocId=2099950&Usage=2 (accessed 29 July 2015).
59. Stella, 'Queer Space', 461.
60. Joanna Mizielińska, 'Travelling Ideas', 86; Stella, 'Queer Space', 469; Graff, 'We Are Not (All) Homophobes', 439; Hadley Z. Renkin, 'Homophobia and Queer Belonging in Hungary', *Focaal* vol. 83 (2009): 21; Kuhar, 'Ljubljana', 146; Darja Davydova, 'Baltic Pride 2010: Articulating Sexual Difference and Heteronormative Nationalism in Contemporary Lithuania', *Sextures* vol. 2, no. 2 (2012): 35, 41; Vuletić, 'Out of the Homeland', 51–2; Moss, 'Split Europe'; Kahlina, 'Local Histories'; Marek Mikuš, '"State Pride": Politics of LGBT Rights and Democratisation in "European Serbia"', *East European Politics and Societies* vol. 25, no. 4 (2011), 834–51; Sanja Kajinić, '"Battle for Sarajevo" as "Metropolis": Closure of the First Queer Sarajevo Festival according to Liberal Press', *Anthropology of East Europe Review* vol. 28, no. 1 (2010): 62–82.
61. Kuhar, 'Ljubljana', 147; Graff, 'We Are Not (All) Homophobes', 440–1; Stella, 'Queer Space', 469; Anna Gruszczynska, '"I Was Mad About It All, About the Ban": Emotional Spaces of Solidarity in the Poznan March of Equality', *Emotion, Space and Society* vol. 2, no. 1 (2009): 44–51. Compare Francesca Romana Ammaturo, 'Spaces of Pride: A Visual Ethnography of Gay Pride Parades in Italy and the United Kingdom', *Social Movement Studies* vol. 15, no. 1 (2016): 19–40.
62. Hadley Z. Renkin, 'Perverse Frictions: Pride, Dignity, and the Budapest LGBT March', *Ethnos* vol. 80, no. 3 (2015): 415.
63. Joanna Mizielińska, 'Travelling Ideas, Travelling Times: on the Temporalities of LGBT and Queer Politics in Poland and the "West"', in Kulpa and Mizielińska (eds), *De-Centring Western Sexualities*, 90; Hadley Z. Renkin, 'Perverse Frictions: Pride, Dignity, and the Budapest LGBT March', *Ethnos* vol. 80, no. 3 (2015): 409–32.
64. Bojan Bilić and Paul Stubbs, 'Unsettling "the Urban" in Post-Yugoslav Activisms: Right to the City and Pride Parades in Serbia and Croatia', in Kerstin Jacobsson (ed.), *Urban Movements and Grassroots Activism in Central and Eastern Europe* (Farnham: Ashgate, 2015), 119–38.
65. Vuletić, 'Out of the Homeland', 38.
66. Binnie and Klesse, 'Politics of Age', 583; Renkin, 'Perverse Frictions', 415.
67. Kahlina, 'Local Histories', 75.
68. Marek Mikuš, '"State Pride": Politics of LGBT Rights and Democratisation in "European Serbia"', *East European Politics and Societies* vol. 25, no. 4 (2011): 834–51.
69. Marijana Mitrović, '"New Face of Serbia" at the Eurovision Song Contest: International Media Spectacle and National Identity', *European Review of History* vol. 17, no. 2 (2010): 171–85.
70. Blagojević, 'Between Walls'; Kahlina, 'Local Histories', 77; Stella, 'Queer Space', 469.

71. See, e.g., Graff, 'We Are Not (All) Homophobes', 447; Stella, 'Queer Space', 471–5; Richard Mole, 'Nationality and Sexuality: Homophobic Discourse and the "National Threat" in Contemporary Latvia', *Nations and Nationalism* vol. 17, no. 3 (2011): 540–60; Srdjan Sremac and R. Ruard Ganzevoort (eds), *Religious and Sexual Nationalism in Central and Eastern Europe: Gods, Gays, and Governments* (Leiden: Brill, 2015).

72. Kahlina, 'Local Histories', 75.

73. Stella, 'Queer Space', 469, 479–80. See also Gordon Waitt, 'Sexual Citizenship in Latvia: Geographies of the Latvian Closet', *Social and Cultural Geography* vol. 6, no. 2 (2005): 174–5; Cai Wilkinson and Anna Kirey, 'What's in a Name?: the Personal and Political Meanings of "LGBT" for Non-Heterosexual and Transgender Youth in Kyrgyzstan', *Central Asian Survey* vol. 29, no. 4 (2010): 487–8; Čarna Brković, 'The Quest for Legitimacy: Discussing Language and Sexuality in Montenegro', in Tanja Petrović (ed.), *Mirroring Europe: Ideas of Europe and Europeanization in Balkan Societies* (Leiden: Brill, 2014), 163–85.

74. Nárcisz Fejes and Andrea P. Balogh, 'Introduction: Post-Socialist Politics of Queer In/Visibility', in Fejes and Balogh (eds), *Queer Visibility*, 3.

75. Kevin Moss, 'Straight Eye for the Queer Guy: Gay Male Visibility in Post-Soviet Russian Films', in Fejes and Balogh (eds), *Queer Visibility*, 199; Kevin Moss and Mima Simić, 'Post-Communist Lavender Menace: Lesbians in Mainstream East European Film', *Journal of Lesbian Studies* vol. 15, no. 3 (2011): 271–83; Brian James Baer, 'Body or Soul: Representing Lesbians in Post-Soviet Russian Culture', *Journal of Lesbian Studies* vol. 15, no. 3 (2011): 284–98.

76. See, e.g., Helen Hok-Sze Leung, 'Unsung Heroes: Reading Transgender Subjectivities in Hong Kong Action Cinema', in Stryker and Whittle (eds), *The Transgender Studies Reader*, 686.

77. Anikó Imre, 'Global Popular Media and the Local Limits of Queering', in Fejes and Balogh, *Queer Visibility*, 232–9.

78. Mizielińska, 'Travelling Ideas', 92. See also Kahlina, 'Local Histories'; See also Andrea P. Balogh, 'Kinging in Hungarian Lesbian Culture', *Journal of Lesbian Studies* vol. 15, no. 3 (2011): 299–310; Marina Yusupova, 'Pussy Riot: a Feminist Band Lost in History and Translation', *Nationalities Papers* vol. 42, no. 4 (2014): 604–10.

79. Stella, 'Queer Space', 476–7.

80. Mizielińska, 'Travelling Ideas', 97. See also Łukasz Szulc, 'From Queer to Gay to Queer.pl: The Names we Dare to Speak in Poland', *Lambda Nordica* vol. 4 (2012): 65–98.

81. See, e.g., Binnie and Klesse, 'Politics of Age'.

82. The Czech Republic, Cyprus, Estonia, Hungary, Latvia, Lithuania, Malta, Poland, Slovenia and Slovakia joined the EU in 2004. Romania and Bulgaria joined in 2007, and Croatia in 2013.

83. See, e.g., Milica Bakić-Hayden and Robert M. Hayden, 'Orientalist Variations on the Theme "Balkans": Symbolic Geography in Recent Yugoslav Cultural Politics', *Slavic Review* vol. 51, no. 1 (1992): 1–15; Larry Wolff, *Inventing Eastern Europe: the Map of Civilization on the Mind of the Enlightenment* (Stanford, CA: Stanford University Press, 1994); Maria Todorova, *Imagining the Balkans* (Oxford: Oxford University Press, 1997).

84. See Éric Fassin, 'National Identities and Transnational Intimacies: Sexual Democracy and the Politics of Immigration in Europe', *Public Culture* vol. 22, no. 3 (2010); Fatima El-Tayeb, *European Others: Queering Ethnicity in Postcolonial Europe* (Minneapolis: University of Minnesota Press, 2011).

85. Mizielińska and Kulpa, '"Contemporary Peripheries"', 11–26.

86. Mizielińska and Kulpa, '"Contemporary Peripheries"', 20.
87. Jasbir K. Puar, *Terrorist Assemblages: Homonationalism in Queer Times* (Durham, NC: Duke University Press, 2007). See also, e.g., El-Tayeb, *European Others*.
88. See also Rao, 'The Locations of Homophobia'.
89. Renkin, 'Homophobia', 27.
90. Agnieszka Graff, 'Report from the Gender Trenches: War Against "Genderism" in Poland', *European Journal of Women's Studies* vol. 21, no. 4 (2014): 434. See also Michele Rivkin-Fish and Cassandra Hartblay, 'When Global LGBTQ Advocacy Became Entangled with New Cold War Sentiment: a Call for Examining Russian Queer Experience', *Brown Journal of World Affairs* vol. 21, no. 1 (2014): 95–109; Srđan Sremac and R. Ruard Ganzevoort (eds), *Religious and Sexual Nationalisms in Central and Eastern Europe: Gods, Gays and Governments* (Leiden: Brill, 2015).
91. Cai Wilkinson, 'Putting "Traditional Values" Into Practice: The Rise and Contestation of Anti-Homopropaganda Laws in Russia', *Journal of Human Rights* vol. 13, no. 3 (2014): 365–6.
92. Wilkinson, 'Putting "Traditional Values" Into Practice', 366.
93. Rivkin-Fish and Hartblay, 'Global LGBT Advocacy', 96–7.
94. See Essig, *Queer in Russia*; Baer, *Other Russias*.
95. Valerie Sperling, *Sex, Politics and Putin: Political Legitimacy in Russia* (Oxford: Oxford University Press, 2015), 308.
96. RFE/RL, 'Russian Gay Teen Support Group's Founder Fined', *Radio Free Europe/Radio Liberty*, 29 July 2015, available at: http://www.rferl.org/content/russia-gay-teen-online-support-group-fined/27157423.html (accessed 29 July 2015).
97. Stella, 'Queer Space', 471–2; Stephen Amico, *Roll Over, Tchaikovsky! Russian Popular Music and Post-Soviet Homosexuality* (Urbana: University of Illinois Press, 2014), 202–3; Emil Persson, 'Banning "Homosexual Propaganda": Belonging and Visibility in Contemporary Russian Media', *Sexuality and Culture* vol. 19, no. 3 (2015): 256–74.
98. Brian James Baer, 'Now You See It: Gay (In)Visibility and the Performance of Post-Soviet Identity', in Fejes and Balogh (eds), *Queer Visibility*, 41.
99. Anna Rotkirch, Anna Temkina and Elena Zdravomyslova, 'Who Helps the Degraded Housewife?: Comments on Vladimir Putin's Demographic Speech', *European Journal of Women's Studies* vol. 14, no. 4 (2007): 349–57; Stella, 'Queer Space', 479; Rivkin-Fish and Hartblay, 'Global LGBTQ Advocacy'; Sperling, *Sex, Politics and Putin*; *Nationalities Papers* vol. 42, no. 4 (2014, special issue on Pussy Riot).
100. Irina V. Soboleva and Yaroslav A. Bakhmetjev, 'Political Awareness and Self-Blame in the Explanatory Narratives of LGBT People Amid the Anti-LGBT Campaign in Russia', *Sexuality and Culture* vol. 19, no. 2 (2015): 293.
101. E.g. Amico, *Roll Over*; Stella, *Lesbian Lives*.
102. Essig, *Queer in Russia*, xiii, 56.
103. Baer, *Other Russias*, 31–4.
104. Stella, *Lesbian Lives*, 2, 46, 105–9.
105. Mizielińska and Kulpa, '"Contemporary Peripheries"', 14.
106. Antonia Young, *Women Who Become Men: Albanian Sworn Virgins* (Oxford: Berg, 2000); Aleksandra Djajić-Horváth, 'Of Female Chastity and Male Arms: the Balkan "Man-Woman" in the Age of the World Picture', *Journal of the History of Sexuality* vol. 20, no. 2 (2011): 358–81.
107. Anna Borgos, 'Sándor/Sarolta Vay, a Gender Bender in Fin-de-Siècle Hungary', in Steven Tötöy de Zepetnek and Louise O. Vasvári (eds), *Comparative Hungarian Cultural Studies* (West Lafayette, IN: Purdue University Press, 2011), 220–31;

Richard von Krafft-Ebing, 'Selections from *Psychopathia Sexualis with Special Reference to Contrary Sexual Instinct: a Medico-Legal Study*', in Stryker and Whittle (eds), *The Transgender Studies Reader*, 21–7.

108. Stephen Whittle, 'Foreword', in Stryker and Whittle (eds), *The Transgender Studies Reader*, xi–xvi; Susan Stryker, '(De)Subjugated Knowledges: an Introduction to Transgender Studies', in Stryker and Whittle (eds), *The Transgender Studies Reader*, 1–17. As an overview, see also Sally Hines, 'Introduction', in Sally Hines and Tam Sanger (eds), *Transgender Identities: Towards a Social Analysis of Gender Diversity* (London: Routledge, 2010), 1–22.

109. Viviane Namaste, 'Undoing Theory: the "Transgender Question" and the Epistemic Violence of Anglo-American Feminist Theory', *Hypatia* vol. 24, no. 3 (2009): 11–32.

110. Suess et al., 'Depathologization'; Evan B. Towle and Lynn M. Morgan, 'Romancing the Transgender Native: Rethinking the Use of the "Third Gender" Concept', *GLQ* vol. 8, no. 4 (2002): 469–97.

111. Dean Spade, 'Mutilating Gender', in Stryker and Whittle (eds), *The Transgender Studies Reader*, 317; Talia Mae Bettcher, 'Trans Identities and First-Person Authority', in Laurie J. Shrage (ed.), *'You've Changed': Sex Reassignment and Personal Identity* (Oxford: Oxford University Press, 2009), 98–120.

112. Namaste, 'Undoing Theory'.

113. Stryker, *Transgender History*, 7.

114. Joan Wallach Scott, 'Introduction', in Joan Wallach Scott (ed.), *Feminism and History* (Oxford: Oxford University Press, 1996), 4–5; Gal and Kligman, *Politics of Gender*, 106. Hines, 'Introduction', 12, makes a similar point about social theory.

115. Nan Alamilla Boyd, 'Bodies in Motion: Lesbian and Transsexual Histories', in Stryker and Whittle (eds), *The Transgender Studies Reader*, 422–5; Judith Halberstam, *In a Queer Time and Place: Transgender Bodies, Subcultural Lives* (New York: New York University Press, 2005), 47–75.

116. Stryker, '(De)Subjugated Knowledges', 12.

117. Toby Beauchamp and Benjamin D'Harlingue, 'Beyond Additions and Exceptions: The Category of Transgender and New Pedagogical Approaches for Women's Studies', *Feminist Formations* vol. 24, no. 2 (2012): 47.

118. Including the contested question of whether, as Masha Gessen suggested, Soviet psychiatrists had attempted to force cisgender lesbians into gender reassignment: Essig, *Queer in Russia*, 36–46; Stella, *Lesbian Lives*, 47.

119. See Sandy Stone, 'The *Empire* Strikes Back: a Posttranssexual Manifesto', in Stryker and Whittle (eds), *The Transgender Studies Reader*, 223.

120. Lynne Attwood, *The New Soviet Man and Woman: Sex-Role Socialization in the USSR* (Bloomington: Indiana University Press, 1990), 100–1.

121. Carol Riddell, 'Divided Sisterhood: a Critical Review of Janice Raymond's *The Transsexual Empire*', in Stryker and Whittle (eds), *The Transgender Studies Reader*, 144–58 (originally 1980); Stone, 'The *Empire* Strikes Back' (first academically published 1991). See also Stryker, *Transgender History*, 105–11.

122. Cheryl Chase, 'Hermaphrodites with Attitude: Mapping the Emergence of Intersex Political Activism', *GLQ* vol. 4, no. 2 (1998): 189–211.

123. Stryker, *Transgender History*, 94.

124. Joanne Meyerowitz, *How Sex Changed: a History of Transsexuality in the United States* (Cambridge, MA: Harvard University Press, 2002).

125. Healey, *Homosexual Desire*, 62–3, 69–72.

126. Stella, *Lesbian Lives*, 164.

127. Wilkinson and Kirey, 'What's in a Name?', 485.

128. David Valentine, *Imagining Transgender: an Ethnography of a Category* (Durham, NC: Duke University Press, 2007), 163.

129. Meyerowitz, *How Sex Changed*.

130. John D'Emilio, 'Capitalism and Gay Identity', in Ann Snitow, Christine Stansell and Sharan Thompson (eds), *Powers of Desire: the Politics of Sexuality* (New York: Monthly Review Press, 1983), 100–13; Michel Foucault, *The History of Sexuality*, trans. Robert Hurley (London: Penguin, 1990–2, 2 vols).

131. Krzysztof Tomasik, *Gejerel: mniejszości seksualne u PRL-u* (Warsaw: Wydawnictwo Krytyki Politycznei, 2012); Jelisaveta Blagojević and Olga Dimitrijević (eds), *Među nama: neispričane priče gej i lezbejskih života* (Belgrade: Heartefact, 2014). See Dimitrijević, this volume; Łukasz Szulc, 'Book Review: Krzysztof Tomasik, *Gejerel: mniejszości seksualne u PRL-u*', *Sexualities* vol. 18, no. 8 (2015): 1018–19.

132. Grewal and Kaplan, 'Theorizing Transnational Studies of Sexuality', 671.

133. Rahul Rao, 'Queer Questions', *International Feminist Journal of Politics* vol. 16, no. 2 (2014): 203.

Select Bibliography

Allcock, John B., and Antonia Young (eds). *Black Lambs and Grey Falcons: Women Travelling in the Balkans* (Oxford: Berghahn, 2000).

Ashwin, Sarah (ed.). *Gender, State and Society in Soviet and Post-Soviet Russia* (London: Routledge, 2000).

Aspasia: the International Yearbook of Central, Eastern and Southeastern Women's and Gender History. Published annually since 2007.

Attwood, Lynne. *Creating the New Soviet Woman: Women's Magazines as Engineers of Female Identity, 1922–53* (Basingstoke: Palgrave Macmillan, 1999).

Attwood, Lynne. *The New Soviet Man and Woman: Sex Role Socialisation in the USSR* (London: Macmillan, 1990).

Baer, Brian James. *Other Russias: Homosexuality and the Crisis of Post-Soviet Identity* (Basingstoke: Palgrave Macmillan, 2009).

Baer, Elizabeth R., and Myrna Goldenberg (eds). *Experience and Expression: Women, the Nazis, and the Holocaust* (Detroit, MI: Wayne State University Press, 2003).

Batinić, Jelena. *Women and Yugoslav Partisans: a History of World War II Resistance* (Cambridge: Cambridge University Press, 2015).

Bernstein, Frances Lee. *The Dictatorship of Sex: Lifestyle Advice for the Soviet Masses* (DeKalb: Northern Illinois University Press, 2007).

Bilić, Bojan (ed.). *LGBT Activism and Europeanisation in the (Post-)Yugoslav Space: On the Rainbow Way to Europe* (London: Palgrave Macmillan, 2016).

Bilić, Bojan, and Sanja Kajinić (eds). *Intersectionality and LGBT Activist Politics: Multiple Others in Serbia and Croatia* (London: Palgrave Macmillan, 2016).

Blagojević, Jelisaveta, Katerina Kolozova and Svetlana Slapšak (eds). *Gender and Identity: Theories From And/Or On Southeastern Europe* (Belgrade: Women's Studies and Gender Research Center, 2006).

Borenstein, Eliot. *Men without Women: Masculinity and Revolution in Russian Fiction, 1917–1929* (Durham, NC: Duke University Press, 2001).

Buckley, Mary. *Women and Ideology in the Soviet Union* (Ann Arbor: University of Michigan Press, 1989).

Bucher, Greta. *Women, the Bureaucracy, and Daily Life in Postwar Moscow, 1945–1953* (New York: Columbia University Press, 2006).

Bucur, Maria. 'An Archipelago of Stories: Gender History in Eastern Europe', *American Historical Review* vol. 113, no. 5 (2008): 1375–89.

Bucur, Maria. *Eugenics and Modernization in Interwar Romania* (Pittsburgh, PA: University of Pittsburgh Press, 2002).

Bucur, Maria. *Heroes and Victims: Remembering War in Twentieth-Century Romania* (Bloomington: Indiana University Press, 2009).

Chatterjee, Choi. *Celebrating Women: Gender, Festival Culture, and Bolshevik Ideology, 1910–1939* (Pittsburgh, PA: University of Pittsburgh Press, 2002).

Clements, Barbara Evans. *Bolshevik Women* (Cambridge: Cambridge University Press, 1997).

Clements, Barbara Evans, Rebecca Friedman and Dan Healey (eds). *Russian Masculinities in History and Culture* (Basingstoke: Palgrave Macmillan, 2002).

Daskalova, Krassimira (ed.). 'The Birth of a Field: Women's and Gender Studies in Central, Eastern and Southeastern Europe', *Aspasia* no. 4 (2010): 155–205 and no. 5 (2011): 128–203.

Daskalova, Krassimira (ed.). 'Clio on the Margins: Women's and Gender History in Central, Eastern and Southeastern Europe', *Aspasia* no. 6 (2012): 125–85 and no. 7 (2013): 132–213.

Daskalova, Krassimira, and Susan Zimmermann. 'Women's and Gender History'. In Irina Livezeanu and Arpad von Klimo (eds), *The Routledge History of East Central Europe since 1700* (London: Routledge, in press).

De Haan, Francisca, Krassimira Daskalova and Anna Loutfi (eds). *A Biographical Dictionary of Women's Movements and Feminisms: Central, Eastern, and South Eastern Europe, 19th and 20th Centuries* (Budapest: CEU Press, 2006).

Downing, Lisa, and Robert Gillett (eds). *Queer in Europe* (Farnham: Ashgate, 2011).

Edmonson, Linda (ed.). *Gender in Russian History and Culture* (Basingstoke: Palgrave, 2001).

Edmondson, Linda (ed.). *Women and Society in Russia and the Soviet Union* (Cambridge: Cambridge University Press, 2008).

Einhorn, Barbara. *Cinderella Goes to Market: Citizenship, Gender, and Women's Movements in East Central Europe* (London: Verso, 1993).

Einhorn, Barbara. *Citizenship in an Enlarging Europe: from Dream to Awakening*, 2nd ed. (Basingstoke: Palgrave Macmillan, 2010).

Engel, Barbara (ed.). *A Revolution of Their Own: Voices of Women in Soviet History* (Boulder, CO: Westview Press, 1998).

Engel, Barbara. 'Russia and the Soviet Union', in Bonnie G. Smith (ed.), *Women's History in Global Perspective*, vol. 3 (Urbana: University of Illinois Press, 2005), 145–79.

Engel, Barbara. *Women in Russia, 1700–2000* (Cambridge: Cambridge University Press, 2004).

Ewing, E. Thomas. *Separate Schools: Gender, Policy, and Practice in Postwar Soviet Education* (DeKalb: Northern Illinois University Press, 2010).

Feinberg, Melissa. *Elusive Equality: Gender, Citizenship and the Limits of Democracy in Czechoslovakia, 1918–1950* (Pittsburgh, PA: University of Pittsburgh Press, 2006).

Fejes, Nárcisz, and Andrea P. Balogh (eds). *Queer Visibility in Post-Socialist Cultures* (Bristol: Intellect, 2013).

Fidelis, Małgorzata. *Women, Communism, and Industrialization in Postwar Poland* (Cambridge: Cambridge University Press, 2010).

Fidelis, Małgorzata, Renata Jambrešić Kirin, Jill Massino and Libora Oates-Indruchová. 'Gendering the Cold War in the Region', *Aspasia* no. 8 (2014): 162–90.

Field, Deborah A. *Private Life and Communist Morality in Khrushchev's Russia* (New York: Peter Lang, 2007).

Fodor, Éva. *Working Difference: Women's Working Lives in Hungary and Austria, 1945–1995* (Durham, NC: Duke University Press, 2003).

Funk, Nanette, and Magda Mueller (eds). *Gender Politics and Post-Communism: Reflections from Eastern Europe and the Former Soviet Union* (London: Routledge, 1993).

Gal, Susan, and Gail Kligman. *The Politics of Gender after Socialism* (Princeton, NJ: Princeton University Press, 2000).

Gal, Susan, and Gail Kligman (eds). *Reproducing Gender: Politics, Publics, and Everyday Life after Socialism* (Princeton, NJ: Princeton University Press, 1999).

Ghodsee, Kristen. *The Left Hand of History: World War II and the Unfulfilled Promise of Communism in Eastern Europe* (Durham, NC: Duke University Press, 2015).

Goldman, Wendy Z. *Women at the Gates: Gender and Industry in Stalin's Russia* (Cambridge: Cambridge University Press, 2002).

Goldman, Wendy Z. *Women, the State and Revolution: Soviet Family Policy and Social Life, 1917–1936* (Cambridge: Cambridge University Press, 1993).

Haney, Lynne. *Inventing the Needy: Gender and the Politics of Welfare in Hungary* (Berkeley: University of California Press, 2002).

Hassenstab, Christine, and Sabrina P. Ramet (eds). *Gender (In)Equality and Gender Politics in Southeastern Europe: a Question of Justice* (London: Palgrave Macmillan, 2015).

Hawkesworth, Celia (ed.). *A History of Central European Women's Writing* (Basingstoke: Palgrave, 2001).

Haynes, John. *New Soviet Man: Gender and Masculinity in Stalinist Soviet Cinema* (Manchester: Manchester University Press, 2003).

Healey, Dan. *Homosexual Desire in Revolutionary Russia: the Regulation of Sexual and Gender Dissent* (Chicago, IL: University of Chicago Press, 2001).

Ilic, Melanie. *Life Stories of Soviet Women: the Interwar Generation* (London: Routledge, 2013).

Ilic, Melanie (ed.). *Women in the Stalin Era* (Basingstoke: Palgrave Macmillan, 2001).

Ilic, Melanie, Susan E. Reid and Lynne Attwood (eds). *Women in the Khrushchev Era* (Basingstoke: Palgrave Macmillan, 2004).

Jancar-Webster, Barbara. *Women and Revolution in Yugoslavia, 1941–1945* (Denver, CO: Arden, 1990).

Johnson, Janet Elise, and Jean C. Robinson (eds). *Living Gender after Communism* (Bloomington: Indiana University Press, 2007).

Jolluck, Katherine R. *Exile and Identity: Polish Women in the Soviet Union During World War II* (Pittsburgh, PA: University of Pittsburgh Press, 2002).

Jovanović, Miroslav, and Slobodan Naumović (eds). *Gender Relations in South Eastern Europe: Historical Perspectives on Womanhood and Manhood in 19th and 20th Century* (Münster: Lit Verlag, 2004).

Kaganovsky, Lilya. *How the Soviet Man Was Unmade: Cultural Fantasy and Male Subjectivity under Stalin* (Pittsburgh, PA: University of Pittsburgh Press, 2008).

Kaminer, Jenny. *Women with a Thirst for Destruction: The Bad Mother in Russian Culture* (Evanston, IL: Northwestern University Press, 2014).

Kelly, Catriona. *A History of Russian Women's Writing, 1820–1992* (New York: Oxford University Press, 1994).

Kligman, Gail. *The Politics of Duplicity: Controlling Reproduction in Ceausescu's Romania* (Berkeley: University of California Press, 1998).

Koenker, Diane P. 'Men against Women on the Shop Floor in Early Soviet Russia: Gender and Class in the Socialist Workplace', *American Historical Review* vol. 100, no. 5 (1995), 1438–64.

Krylova, Anna. *Soviet Women in Combat: a History of Violence on the Eastern Front* (Cambridge: Cambridge University Press, 2010).

Kulpa, Robert, and Joanna Mizielińska (eds). *De-Centring Western Sexualities: Central and East European Perspectives* (Farnham: Ashgate, 2011).

Lapidus, Gail W. *Women in Soviet Society: Equality, Development, and Social Change* (Berkeley: University of California Press, 1978).

Long, Kristi. *We All Fought for Freedom: Women in Poland's Solidarity Movement* (Boulder, CO: Westview Press, 1996).

Lukić, Jasmina, Joanna Regulska and Darja Zaviršek (eds). *Women and Citizenship in Central and Eastern Europe* (Aldershot: Ashgate, 2006).

Markwick, Roger D., and Euridice C. Cardona. *Soviet Women on the Frontline in the Second World War* (Basingstoke: Palgrave Macmillan, 2012).

Naiman, Eric. *Sex in Public: the Incarnation of Early Soviet Ideology* (Princeton, NJ: Princeton University Press, 1997).

Northop, Douglas. *Veiled Empire: Gender and Power in Stalinist Central Asia* (Ithaca, NY: Cornell University Press, 2004).

Ofer, Dalia, and Lenore J. Weitzman (eds). *Women in the Holocaust* (New Haven, CT: Yale University Press, 1998).

Penn, Shana. *Solidarity's Secret: the Women Who Defeated Communism in Poland* (Ann Arbor: University of Michigan Press, 2005).

Penn, Shana, and Jill Massino (eds). *Gender Politics and Everyday Life in State Socialist Eastern and Central Europe* (Basingstoke: Palgrave Macmillan, 2009).

Pennington, Reina, and John Erickson. *Wings, Women, and War: Soviet Airwomen in World War II Combat* (Lawrence: University Press of Kansas, 2001).

Pető, Andrea. 'Writing Women's History in Eastern Europe: Towards a "Terra Cognita"?', *Journal of Women's History* vol. 16, no. 4 (2004): 173–81.

Ramet, Sabrina P. (ed.). *Gender Politics in the Western Balkans: Women and Society in Yugoslavia and the Yugoslav Successor States* (University Park: Pennsylvania State University Press, 1999).

Röger, Maren, and Ruth Leiserowitz (eds). *Women and Men at War: A Gender Perspective on World War II and its Aftermath in Central and Eastern Europe* (Osnabrück: fibre, 2012).

Shulman, Elena. *Stalinism on the Frontier of Empire: Women and State Formation in the Soviet Far East* (Cambridge: Cambridge University Press, 2012).

Sperling, Valerie. *Sex, Politics and Putin: Political Legitimacy in Russia* (Oxford: Oxford University Press, 2015).

Starks, Tricia. *The Body Soviet: Propaganda, Hygiene, and the Revolutionary State* (Madison, WI: University of Wisconsin Press, 2008).

Stella, Francesca. *Lesbian Lives in Post-Soviet Russia: Post/Socialism and Gendered Sexualities* (Basingstoke: Palgrave Macmillan, 2015).

Stoff, Laurie S. *They Fought for the Motherland: Russia's Women Soldiers in World War I and the Revolution* (Lawrence: University Press of Kansas, 2006).

Tlostanova, Madina. *Gender Epistemologies and Eurasian Borderlands* (Basingstoke: Palgrave Macmillan, 2010).

Verdery, Katherine. 'From Parent-State to Family Patriarchs: Gender and Nation in Contemporary Eastern Europe', *East European Politics and Societies* vol. 8, no. 2 (1994): 225–55.

Wingfield, Nancy M., and Maria Bucur (eds). *Gender and War in Twentieth-Century Eastern Europe* (Bloomington: Indiana University Press, 2006).

Wood, Elizabeth A. *The Baba and the Comrade: Gender and Politics in Revolutionary Russia* (Bloomington: Indiana University Press, 1997).

Zahra, Tara. *Kidnapped Souls: National Indifference and the Battle for Children in the Bohemian Lands, 1900–1948* (Ithaca, NY: Cornell University Press, 2008).

Žarkov, Dubravka. *The Body of War: Media, Ethnicity, and Gender in the Break-Up of Yugoslavia* (Durham, NC: Duke University Press, 2007).

Zirin, Mary, Irina Livezeanu, Christine D. Worobec and June Pachuta Farris (eds). *Women and Gender in Central and Eastern Europe, Russia, and Eurasia: a Comprehensive Bibliography*, 2 vols (London: Routledge, 2007).

Index

Printed in Great Britain
by Amazon

62099199R00160